THIS ROUGH MAGIC

THIS ROUGH MAGIC

The Making of an Artistic Director

a memoir by
RICHARD MONETTE

as told to David Prosser

First edition, second impression.

Published in Canada by the Stratford Shakespearean Festival of Canada.
www.stratfordshakespearefestival.com

Library and Archives Canada Cataloguing in Publication

Monette, Richard, 1944-2008
This rough magic : the making of an artistic director : a memoir / by Richard Monette ; as told to David Prosser.

Includes index.
ISBN 978-0-9730509-1-2

1. Monette, Richard, 1944-2008. 2. Theatrical producers and directors—Canada—Biography. 3. Actors—Canada—Biography. I. Prosser, David John, 1953- II. Stratford Festival of Canada III. Title.

PN2308.M65A3 2007 792.02'33092 C2007-902774-1

Typeset in Giovanni by Erin Wilson Graphic Design, Goderich.

Printed and bound in Canada.

The Stratford Shakespearean Festival of Canada
P.O. Box 520, Stratford, Ontario, Canada N5A 6V2

2 3 4 5 11 10 09

This book is dedicated, in deepest love and gratitude, to M. Joan Chalmers, C.C., O.Ont. Joan has always been a tremendous friend and ally not only of the Stratford Festival of Canada but also of me personally throughout my tenure as artistic director. Without her generous financial support, it would not have been possible for the Festival to publish these memoirs.

CONTENTS

FOREWORD

by William Hutt

I was in my early 40s. He was 19. And I had just seen his Hamlet. It wasn't a great Hamlet, perhaps not even a memorable one. But it had one outstanding and unique feature: the pride of possession. It was *his* Hamlet. There was no arrogance in this pride of ownership. Rather, it was like the pride of the Olympic sprinter who, instead of mourning the failure to win a medal, celebrates the victory of reaching in the final heat his all-time personal best. The Hamlet was spoken with clarity and sound rhythms in a strong, commanding voice with a clear, sharp-edged stage presence. Two things were abundantly evident: the boy had talent and future—and his name was Richard Monette.

A few years later, the entire acting ensemble of the Stratford Festival was assembled on the challenging main stage of the Festival Theatre in a meet-and-greet session for the 1965 season. My chores that year included appearances in *Henry IV, Part 1*, *Julius Caesar* and Chekhov's *The Cherry Orchard*. As I was contemplating the tasks ahead, I became suddenly aware of the young Monette standing across the stage from me, appearing to be in a state of both awe and anticipation. I had not seen him since his Hamlet, but I was struck by how appropriate, how apt, it was that at that moment he should be standing on that stage. It was as if he had been fleeing from one blind alley to another until benign Fate with prophetic wisdom landed him in exactly the right place and at the right time. A place where he could hone his many skills, where he could both challenge and be challenged; a place of many mansions ready to be inhabited and many doors waiting to be opened. I walked across the space between us, shook his hand and said, "Welcome home."

I am past my mid-80s now. He has said goodbye to 60. And I have just returned from the ritual of Christmas Eve at Richard Monette's. What is always dazzling about the evening is the lavish presentation. It is a celebration. A celebration that is full, complete, unstinting, dedicated and all but overwhelming in its generosity of spirit. Filling the corner is a massive tree, alive with strings of coloured lights, tiny figurines and glittering bulbs. Mounded under the tree is a pile of brilliantly packaged gifts, spreading halfway across the room. Side tables are laden with bowls of nuts, bite-sized nibbles and open boxes of candies. And candles everywhere. At the dinner table are knives, forks and spoons to meet every need, spread out beside rich damask napkins; a personal gift at each place, plus a jokey headdress of some sort pertinent to the Santa Claus legend; and wine glasses that sing when you tap them with your fingernail—one for each wine assigned to each of the four courses.

The extravagance with which he marks the Christmas season has, I know, much to do with counterbalancing the haunting memories of deprivation and chaos in his childhood. But despite being by nature a confirmed, endearing celebrant, and in sharp contrast to hosting this richly charged event, Richard is noticeably without affectation, without pretension, approaching the point of being without ego. Only when his work is attacked does it seem to rise and become engaged. But even at that the suspicion lingers that it isn't the ego that is wounded but rather a deep aching disappointment that his efforts have been misunderstood. Still, whichever it is, the disappointment is real and the hurt bewildering.

Richard directs neither for the cynic, the critic nor the high-flying intelligentsia. He directs, without prejudice, for the groundlings, the common man who enters the theatre with his disbelief left behind in the parking lot. His productions are not bland conceptual blueprints. They are celebrations. Celebrations as full, dedicated and generous as those Christmas Eve rituals. Celebrations of language and of the spoken word; of different worlds, eras and cultures; of the author's bright palette of human passions, eccentricities, frailties and endless capacity for betrayal. They are, as well, a salute to Richard's deep, abiding and at times indulgent love of actors. They surge with a humanity and a level of accessibility and grasp that brings people to the theatre and theatre to the people.

Having once invoked the pride of ownership and made the "home" entirely his own, he opened the doors to thousands upon thousands of guests, invited them in and, with his "rough magic," has taken them places they cannot go themselves, and kept them safe.

PREFACE: THE VENTRICLE OF MEMORY

Love's Labour's Lost, Act IV, scene 2

When I was about three years old, my mother dressed me up as an Arab sheik. The occasion was some sort of costume contest, perhaps at a Halloween party or—since we lived in Montreal—for Mardi Gras. She draped me in a white sheet, adorned me with necklaces from her jewellery case and made me up with her lipstick. I won that contest, and I have a vivid memory of my mother proudly holding me aloft, as everyone around me shouted with joy. I have often wondered if that moment of experiencing love from perfect strangers was what later made me want to be an actor.

I have also wondered if the vertigo from which I suffered in adult life might have its roots in another early childhood memory. My mother was taking me to visit my grandmother once, when our taxi hit a dip in the road beneath one of Montreal's many overpasses. Its door flew open, and I started to tumble out. My mother caught my hand just in time and hauled me back in, but I can still recall my feet, in their little boots, momentarily hitting the pavement as it sped by.

These incidents were real—my mother confirmed them—but I am conscious nonetheless that memory plays strange tricks. It has a way of heightening reality, compressing events and making them more dramatic, just as Shakespeare did in his history plays. Actress and director Martha Henry has told me that when she first visited the Stratford Festival of Canada, as a young woman, she was taken backstage at the Festival Theatre. She came away with a clear memory of white carpets and chandeliers. Later, when she got her first acting job at the Festival, she was bewildered to find that its backstage area had never featured any such impractical luxuries.

Designer Susan Benson put it another way. In 1993, when the Festival was reviving Brian Macdonald's legendary production of *The Mikado*, she said to me, "I'll have to make the colours far more vivid this time, because in people's memories things are much brighter than they actually were."

My recall is no more trustworthy than anyone else's. I may have performed involuntary dramaturgy on my recollections, unconsciously reshaping a scene here, tightening up a line of dialogue there. Others may remember the same events differently. Still, even the most unreliable memories, like dreams, are distillations of some essential truth. Who I am, as an artist and as a human being, has been shaped by what I *remember*, consciously or subconsciously, accurately or otherwise; and any self-portrait done from memory, however disingenuous or clumsily executed others may judge it to be, inevitably reveals something about its subject.

This book is *not*, by the way, the story of my 14-year tenure as the Stratford Festival's artistic director. It is the story—more interesting, in my view—of how I *arrived* at that position: how the shy, lonely, French- and Italian-speaking child of non-artistic parents came to be a Shakespearean actor and director and, ultimately, the head of North America's largest classical theatre company.

So if, in Hamlet's words, you would pluck out the heart of my mystery, read on.

CHAPTER ONE

Such Strange Mysteries

King Henry VIII, Act I, scene 3

My French-Canadian great-grandfather, Israël Carrière, could cure eczema by the touch of his hand. Not only was he the seventh son of a seventh son, he also had a pronounced bump on his forehead, the legacy of falling down a well in his youth. So it was only to be expected that he would have some kind of special power.

French-Canadians used to be particularly prone to eczema, which had been widespread among *les filles du roi* ("the king's daughters"), the first female settlers sent to Quebec by Louis XIV of France, and so there was great demand for Israël's healing touch. With his finger, he would reach into his mouth and touch the underside of his tongue, where the tissue formed a kind of cross. Then he would touch the sufferer with the same finger, and the eczema would disappear.

Israël had no idea how he came to have this gift, and he did not want it known. He didn't want his farm turning into some latter-day Lourdes. Once, when he was out working in the fields, a neighbour whose baby had eczema came to the house looking for him. My great-grandmother, Elisabeth, told the neighbour where to find him, for which he was furious with her. But he cured the baby nonetheless.

That, at least, was the story I learned as a child, and it did not occur to me to doubt that it was true. On some level, I still believe it, even though I am not remotely superstitious. I know this is a contradiction. But Israël's daughter, my grandmother, told me about his magical powers, and she would not have lied.

In the late spring of 1992, I accepted an offer to become the eighth artistic director of the Stratford Festival of Canada. I told no one the news until June 13, two days before it was to be announced at a press conference in Toronto. Then I telephoned my brother, Mark, in Los Angeles, where he works in the television industry.

On June 15, the day of the announcement, Mark showed up at the hotel where I was staying. I greeted him in amazement: "What are you *doing* here?"

"Well, Richard," he replied, "this doesn't happen every day. None of our grandparents could read or write. And now here you are, head of one of the largest English-speaking classical theatre companies in the world."

He had a point. On the face of it, nothing in my relatively unsophisticated parentage—French-Canadian on my father's side, Italian on my mother's—had made it likely that I would attain such a position, to say nothing of remaining in it for 14 seasons, longer than any other artistic director in the Festival's history. Even my becoming a Shakespearean actor in the first place seemed an improbably long shot. No one else in my family had the remotest interest in theatre or any of the arts, with the sole exception of my uncle Gentile, who taught architecture at McGill University and was an accomplished painter.

On the other hand, the family lore and experiences that I had absorbed as a child included elements of the dramatic, the eccentric and the downright fantastical, of which the story of my great-grandfather curing eczema was only one example. So perhaps I was not so unprepared for my chosen career. Classical theatre isn't altogether literal or easily explicable, and neither was the world in which I grew up.

My great-grandparents
Elisabeth Meunier and Israël Carrière

I was very fond of great-grandfather Israël, who was born in 1877 and lived till 1956, 12 years after my birth in 1944. He was a man of jolly temperament, who constantly smoked a pipe. I loved the smell of it. Sitting on his knee, I would listen to the radio with him—particularly to a drama series called *Les Belles Histoires des Pays d'en Haut*. Everyone in Quebec listened to it, and it later became an even more popular TV series.

Israël and Elisabeth's daughter, Eva, my paternal grandmother, was born in 1899. Her husband, five years her senior, was Alfred Monette, whose family had been in Quebec since 1683. Alfred and Eva had two children: a daughter, Lorraine (who would later cause her family great consternation by marrying a Protestant), and, in 1919, a son, Maurice Raphael Monette, who was my father.

Grandmother Eva told me that, just before Israël died, he raised his hand up in the air, keeping his arm straight, then lowered it again. "You know what he was saying?" she asked me. "He was saying what an honest life he'd led." I'm not sure how my grandmother arrived at this interpretation, but obviously she knew her father well and knew that he was a good person. On his deathbed, Israël gave me his watch. To my great regret, it is one of the few possessions in my life that I have lost.

Grandfather Alfred Monette was tall, full of compassion and a handsome man in his time. Like Eva, he had grown up on a farm but was later employed as the janitor in the same apartment building where I lived with my parents, on rue Durocher in the Atwater area of Montreal. I used to spend time with him while he worked. I thought he was a wonderful man. Eva, unlike my grandmother on the Italian side, was not a very good cook. She seldom rose above meat and potatoes, always bland and overdone. But whenever we would get together for meals, Alfred would say the same brief grace: "Thank God, and the cook." And then, looking at the food spread out before him, he would invariably say: "Look at all the colours. There *must* be a God."

Our apartment on rue Durocher

When I was little, Eva would tell the story of going to visit some friends who had a television set and finding them sitting in front of it, all dressed up in their best clothes with their hats and their purses. When she asked the reason for this unwonted formality, her friends indicated the figures on the screen and replied, "If we can see them, they can see us." Recalling this now is an uncomfortable reminder that when I was growing up TV was still relatively exotic, and there were no such things as computers, DVDs, cell phones or CDs, never mind MP3 players. (It makes me feel even more of an antique to think of the things I *did* grow up with, such as record players, mimeograph machines and deliveries by the iceman.) At some point, Alfred and Eva must have acquired a TV of their own, for I have a memory of watching the Queen's coronation on it in 1953. But I think Alfred took a skeptical view of the new-fangled technology and its content. He never believed, for example, in the moon landing; he was convinced it was a hoax.

My brother Mark wasn't entirely correct in saying that none of our grandparents could read or write. Alone among them, Eva did know the alphabet and could write things down phonetically. This difference between her and her husband gave rise to an incident when I was 13 years old that remains one of my most painful memories.

Alfred and Eva were taking me across the country by train to visit their daughter, my aunt Lorraine, in Vancouver. On the first evening of the trip, Alfred had to sign for the dinner bill. Being unable to write his name, he marked it with an X. My grandmother, thinking I was asleep in the upper berth of our compartment, then began to attack him for being illiterate. Why this should suddenly become an issue for her I don't know; it seems inconceivable that she had only just learned of it after several decades of marriage. Perhaps it was because it had now been revealed to a third party, the man who brought the bill. Anyway, she ranted at him in French: "If I had known you were so ignorant, I never would have married you." I know she didn't mean to be cruel, but her words must have broken Alfred's heart. My eyes filled with tears as I listened from my bunk bed, yet I was too ashamed to reveal that I had been witness to my beloved grandfather's humiliation. So I held still, feigning sleep, and cried in silence.

Decades later, in my 2002 production of the musical *My Fair Lady*, actress Cynthia Dale was playing Eliza Doolittle, the Cockney flower girl who seeks to raise herself from the gutter by learning the speech and manners of the privileged classes. Eliza has a quick wit and a sharp tongue, but early on in rehearsals, I felt that Cynthia was making her too pert. So I told her: "I know this is a musical, but poverty is really unattractive. I know, because I come from a poor family." I spoke about the pain of ignorance, about how poverty makes you brutish, and how it changes your face, like the peasants in Van Gogh's *The Potato Eaters*, a painting that had fascinated me when I saw it years before at an exhibition in Montreal. And I told her the story of that long-ago train ride with my French-Canadian grandparents.

From then on, Cynthia rooted her character's feistiness in a sense of how high the stakes would really be for someone in that position. I shall never forget the moment in that production when Eliza, realizing she has been educated out of her class, asks: "What's to become of me? What's to become of me?" Cynthia played it with such conviction that it became—as it should be—the crux of the piece.

Throughout my career, I have used the memories of my early life, particularly the painful ones, to articulate the roles I have played and the productions I have directed.

The Italian side of my family was just as colourful as the French; indeed, it featured a certain amount of mental instability.

My maternal grandfather was born in the small town of Palena in the province of Chieti, part of that region of central Italy that used to be called the Abruzzi (comprising what its former Bourbon rulers called "Closer Abruzzo" and "Farther Abruzzo") but is now referred to only in the singular as the Abruzzo. Palena lies at one end of a mountain range known as the Majella, an ancient Etruscan word that can mean "breast" or "honey" and that also refers to Maja, a Roman goddess of springtime, fertility and, according to some sources, illusion.

My grandfather was a foundling, discovered on a church doorstep by a local policeman, who called him Antonio—presumably after the patron saint of Palena—and gave him the surname Tondino. In Italian, the word *tondo* refers to a circular painting or bas-relief, and *tondino*, its diminutive, means a small ceramic dish. It was an appropriate choice: terracotta *tondi* by the Renaissance sculptor Luca della Robbia adorn the walls of the Foundlings' Hospital in Florence. Or perhaps the policeman chose the name because a baby, too, might be described as a small round object.

According to family legend, Antonio was the son of a count, though what this claim was based on no one knew. He lived in an orphanage till he was 18, then became a bricklayer and married my maternal grandmother, Lucia Liberatore. Lucia came from a well-off family, who disapproved of the match. They may have been prescient, since Antonio later became a chronic alcoholic.

While still in Italy, Antonio and Lucia had the first of their nine children, a girl they called Giuseppina. Then Antonio decided to come to the New World to make his fortune, leaving his wife and daughter behind until he was ready to send for them. After he'd been gone for a while, however, Lucia took matters into her own hands: she set out on a donkey, with the infant Giuseppina in her arms, and trekked down the Majella to Naples, where she took passage for New York. On arrival, she found that Antonio had gone to Canada.

Eventually, the couple were reunited and settled in Quebec, where their second child, Anna, was born in 1912. A further seven children followed: Carmen, Paul, Florentina (my mother), P'tit Jean (so called because he was small), Rudolph, Gentile and Peter. During the Second World War, the family felt that Anna's name was too Italian for comfort, and so they changed it to Alice. Some of her siblings' names were anglicized as well: Giuseppina became Josephine, P'tit Jean became Johnny, Gentile became Gerry, and my mother, Florentina, became Florence. Lucia was left to care for all nine children—to say nothing of 13 boarders—when Antonio passed out drunk in a snowdrift and died at the age of 45.

My favourite photograph of myself, aged three

I never knew Antonio, whose fatal misadventure occurred before I was born. I do, however, have vivid memories of grandmother Lucia, who lived to an advanced old age. Though she always had a very upright posture (a legacy of carrying things on her head, as poor people did in Palena), by the time I knew her she had no teeth and an incredibly wrinkled face. I am always reminded of her by Maria's line in *Twelfth Night*: "He does smile his face into more lines than is in the new map, with the augmentation of the Indies."

She had one of those Godfather voices that sound as if the speaker is perpetually on the verge of tears. I would say to her, "How are you, Grandmother?" and she would reply, "*Va bene, va bene*"—"I'm well, I'm well"—in what sounded like a wail of misery. To alleviate her asthma, she would inhale the fumes from a herbal medicine that she burned in a little metal can. Every morning of her life, she would eat a hard-boiled egg, drink a Coca-Cola and inhale what I later came to realize smelled exactly like marijuana.

When I was little, Lucia would try to amuse me by reciting a rhyme in Italian about a cat that was married to a mouse. One day, the cat was chasing the mouse, which ran into a huge vat of spaghetti sauce. The cat then ate the sauce, with the mouse in it, and said: "*Como bono marita!*—What a delicious husband!—*Tipiti-tipiti-ta!*" Whether the rhyme was traditional or of my grandmother's own composition I never found out, but the fact of her reciting it to me would always horrify me, because I knew what had happened to her daughter Carmen, the only one of her nine children who did not survive infancy. Giuseppina, a.k.a. Josephine, the eldest sister, had been carrying baby Carmen in one arm while tending to a huge pot of spaghetti sauce on the stove. As she leaned over to stir it, she accidentally lost her hold on the baby, who fell into the bubbling sauce and was scalded to death.

As a sensitive child of five or six, I couldn't imagine how my grandmother could find it in her to recite to me this appallingly close-to-home rhyme of the cat and the mouse. It was not until later that I began to understand how recasting life's tragedies into some form of storytelling, even just a nursery rhyme, could be a way of dealing with the unthinkable.

This incident, by the way, contributed to the complexity of the Tondino siblings' names. The next child to be born after Carmen's death was the first son, my uncle Paul, whose birth the family celebrated by cooking 21 chickens. But Paul wasn't actually his name: he was originally called Carmen (which in Italian can be either a male or a female name) in memory of his late sister. As he grew up, though, this new Carmen didn't much care for the ambiguity of his name (or, indeed, for the story that lay behind it), so he renamed himself Paul. As for Josephine, she married a man called Guido, who had a wooden foot. But she had a weak heart, and it was rumoured in the family that she could never have sex with him. Still, he adored her and stayed with her all his life. When she died, he burned every photograph he had.

Perhaps the most enigmatic of the family stories concerned a friend of my grandmother's called Therese, who, as a joke, would give me little pieces of coal to eat. As my grandmother had done, Therese had come from Italy to join her husband in North America. But she had apparently arrived by some supernatural mode of transport, for both my grandmother and my mother insisted that Therese had been brought to America by a "flaming lion."

To this day, I have no idea what they meant by that. But at the time, I had no trouble accepting it. As a Catholic child, I came from a tradition of belief that included such mysteries as transubstantiation and the virgin birth. To my young mind, here was simply another aspect of the magical way the world worked: a flaming lion—whatever that might be—had met my grandmother's friend Therese in Naples and carried her across the ocean. The story had a darker

My parents, Maurice Monette and Florence Tondino, on their wedding day

element, too. Therese's husband in America had supposedly killed a man who had accused him of impotence, and that was why she had come across: to help him flee to Canada.

In her later years, Lucia began to lose her mind. When I was about 11 or 12, she said to me, "I will give you five dollars if you tell me I'm not crazy." Lying through my teeth, I said, "Grandmother, I don't want the five dollars. You're not crazy." But by then she was. She would see witches flying on their brooms through the windows of her apartment block. "*La strega!*" she would scream. "*La strega!*"—"The witch!"

I don't know the circumstances of my parents' first meeting or the details of their courtship. But everyone said that Florence Tondino was very beautiful as a young woman, and that my father was desperately in love with her. She had dark, dark eyes (mine are green, from my father), and a typically Italian complexion. Eva, my French-Canadian grandmother, used to call her *la noire*: "the dark one," an epithet that carried more than a hint of disdain for her ethnicity. (I suppose if Eva had known any Shakespeare, she could have called her the Dark Lady of the Monettes.) My mother also had a reputation as a tomboy, being the first woman in the family circle ever to play on a softball team. She was tough-minded and of a fiery temperament.

My brother, Mark, was born in 1951, when I was seven years old. By then, our father had lost the slimness of his youth.

Though my father had become quite fat when I knew him, photographs of him as a young man show him as slim and very handsome. He grew up not in Quebec but in Vankleek Hill (renowned, apparently, as the gingerbread capital of Ontario). But when I was a child, I understood that he came from a place called "Vant-le-Kill," because that was how my family pronounced it. It was not until I was an adult, driving one day past the sign for Vankleek Hill on the highway, that I suddenly realized, "Oh, my God: *that*'s what it is."

Maurice Monette and Florence Tondino were married in Montreal on May 19, 1941, in Notre Dame de la Défense, an Italian church noted for its frescoes by Guido Nincheri ("Montreal's Michelangelo")—including one depicting Mussolini on horseback, riding among the saints. I was born at the Royal Victoria Hospital three years later, on June 19, 1944, almost exactly two weeks after D-Day.

My parents were very fond of the movie *Casablanca*, in which Humphrey Bogart's character is named Rick Blaine. So taken were they with the way that his co-star, Ingrid Bergman, pronounced this name—"Reeck, Reeck"—that they named me Richard. Sometimes they would call me that, and sometimes Rick; when I was a teenager, I myself favoured the latter form. (Who wouldn't want a little bit of Bogie's glamour?) Once, in 1970, I happened to meet Ingrid Bergman backstage at a West End theatre. We were both waiting to congratulate Zoe Caldwell on her performance in Terence Rattigan's play *Bequest to the Nation*. I was itching to tell Bergman, whom I remember as being

Dissimilar siblings: Mark has a long face and a Roman nose, like our mother. I inherited the rounder features of our father.

staggeringly tall, that I owed my name to the way she said "Reeck" in *Casablanca*. But I didn't quite have the nerve.

I remained an only child until September 20, 1951, when, at the age of seven, I was joined by my only sibling, my brother Mark. I adored this new arrival from the moment he was brought home. I had been a lonely child, and now I had a companion with whom I could play piggyback and whose feet I could tickle. Emotionally, Mark was a sort of innocent in my life, and I felt very protective of him. He had become a tantrum-throwing little beast by the time he turned eight, but he subsequently grew into a wonderfully stable, good-natured adult who is not only my brother but also my dearest friend.

My mother was a woman of vivid imagination, with a great sense of humour and a flair for the theatrical. If I lingered too long in my bed when I was a little boy, she would come into my bedroom with my toy rifle and point it at me, saying, "I'm going to shoot you." She had a curious habit of showing both her upper and lower teeth when she smiled. This may have been because a full set of teeth was a comparative rarity in French Canada at that time: people would have them pulled out, because they couldn't afford to have them fixed. So perhaps my mother's strange grimacing smile was a little show of vanity on her part. She was also a shrewd observer of character, with a knack for accents and mimicry, and she wasn't afraid to make a deliberate scene when that would serve her purposes. It is clear to me, looking back, that I am indebted to her both for my acting talent and my own touches of artistic temperament.

With my doll Pom-Pom: a symbol of lost innocence

She was interesting, original and funny, and I loved her deeply. But, though there was no malice in her intent, it was she who first inflicted on me the kind of pain that changes the way you look at the world.

I had a doll called Pom-Pom. I don't remember who gave it to me, but I loved it and took it everywhere with me. When I turned six, though, and had to go to school, my mother decided that it was time for me to put aside childish things. So she took me, with Pom-Pom, to a hatch in the wall of our first-floor apartment. This hatch opened onto a chute, which led to the incinerator in the basement. I knew this, because I had been down there with grandfather Alfred, hanging out with him as he performed his janitorial duties. My mother opened the hatch of the chute.

"You have to grow up now," she said. "You're going to school." And she told me to throw in my doll.

Though I fully realized that Pom-Pom would burn and be gone forever, I made a conscious decision to comply. I *did* want to grow up. So, as if in a dream, I dropped my doll into the chute. Later, after my mother had gone, I raced down to the basement to look in the incinerator, hoping that perhaps, by some miracle, Pom-Pom might have survived. But all I found were embers.

I knew, even at the time, that my mother was doing this for my own good. And I am sure that, for all her imagination, she had no idea of the effect it would have on me. It was a turning point in my life: the moment when my childhood innocence went up in flames. Years later, when I first saw the movie *Citizen Kane*, I gasped in recognition at the end, having had in Pom-Pom my own version of Rosebud. (I gasped again, more recently, when I saw a film called *Period of Adjustment*, based on a play by Tennessee Williams, in which a doll is thrown on a fire.)

Throughout my directing career, I have paid a small tribute to the child I once was and to the innocence I lost that day. In almost every production I have directed, I have included, placed discreetly somewhere on the stage, a little doll.

My father, a businessman, did not share my mother's imaginative qualities. There was a forced cheeriness in his manner: he was one of those men who laugh a lot but have absolutely no sense of humour. My own laugh, I now realize with some discomfort, sounds exactly like his. On the whole, the Monettes were a more down-to-earth breed than the Tondinos. It might be argued that they supplied the other essential quality in a theatre artist: practicality. Theatre cannot be created by imagination alone: you have to be hard-headed enough to ensure that the curtain will go up on a certain date at a certain time. But despite his practicality, my father's career was a checkered one.

After high school, he took accounting courses at McGill University and the University of Toronto, then worked for a Montreal dry-cleaning and laundry company, rising to become executive vice-president of one of its affiliates. There was an irony in this: my father was frankly anti-Semitic, yet the company he worked for was Jewish-owned. I could never comprehend this prejudice of his, and I remember my glee at his discomfiture on one occasion when someone assumed that he himself was a Jew.

One happy result of his employment in the laundry trade was that I always had crisp, clean white shirts when I was growing up. My mother, who had excellent taste, ensured that the rest of my wardrobe was as smart as the family finances would allow. I retained the habit of dressing neatly throughout high school and university, and this, combined with the fact that I was well-spoken, led people to believe that I came from a wealthy family. In 1967, though, my father quit his job and worked first for a fuel oil company, then as a building manager for high-rise offices. Then, in 1974, he became a shareholder in a golf club. That venture proved short-lived, and he began to drink even more heavily than he had before. From that point on, his career went into a downward spiral.

He was never a particularly good parent. He did not, for instance, think of teaching me to drive or of engaging me in other typical father-son activities. But he did do one thing for me for which I shall always be grateful: he sent me to Loyola High School, a great institution at which, as I am fond of saying, I was educated beyond my intelligence. This was at a time when anglophone culture was still in the ascendancy in Montreal. Quebec's language laws had not yet been enacted, and to be French was, in the eyes of the English social élite, to be a second-class citizen. My father was not only embarrassed by the fact that he was French-Canadian, he was also convinced that francophones would never get ahead in business in Montreal—and at the time, he was probably right. So he wanted me to be educated in English.

The Church, of course, had other ideas. I had a French surname; therefore I should go to a French school. So my father wrote to Cardinal Léger, saying—and I had this from his own lips—"If you don't allow my son to go to this Irish Jesuit private school, I am going to take my wife, myself and my *sixteen* children out of the Church." This strategic exaggeration worked, and my father got his way. If he hadn't, my future would have been very different indeed.

I cannot say enough in praise of Loyola High School or of the post-secondary institution I went on to attend, Loyola College (which later merged with Sir George Williams University to become Concordia University). The teachers in both places were wonderful, and they took a deep interest in me. In my first year there, I took history from Laurier LaPierre, later a senator and well-known author and broadcaster. He was a brilliant teacher, who loved his subject. At our first class, he came in wearing his academic gown and with a stack of books under his chin. He put the books down on the desk, took out his pipe (those were very different days back then) and said: "Gentlemen,"—for Loyola was an all-boys' school—"history was made in the bedroom. Good afternoon." Then he picked up his books and left. With that stunningly effective introduction, he ensured our rapt attention for the remainder of the course. I have used similar guerrilla tactics from time to time in my own career.

Even though I didn't play sports, I was quite popular with my fellow students and enjoyed a certain public profile. I had already, in grade school, discovered the thrill of performing, scoring big hits in two successive St. Patrick's Day concerts. (In one, I was part of a group that sang and acted out the Irish song "Clancy Lowered the Boom," in which I appeared as Clancy's fiancée, Cathy O'Grady, wearing a wedding dress borrowed from one of my aunts.) Continuing in this vein at Loyola, I played Mark Antony in an abridged version of *Julius Caesar* and memorized a whole section of *Paradise Lost* for a public-speaking competition. Indeed, this was how I managed to pay for my high school education: by winning awards for debating and public speaking.

Dressed as Cathy O'Grady for a grade school concert

Recently, I met a Festival patron who had been at Loyola with me. He told me that on one occasion, our English teacher had me read aloud John Keats's "Ode to a Nightingale." The entire class, he said, went silent during my reading, and at the end the teacher was in tears. The patron said it was a memorable moment in his life, and he had followed my career ever since. Alas, I have no recollection of that incident at all.

My Jesuit teachers were very interested in all of this: they saw that I had a gift, and they were extremely supportive of it. I, in turn, was like a sponge: a new world had opened up to me, and I was avidly interested in everything it had to offer. In the course of my high school and college education, for example, I read every single extant piece of ancient Greek drama.

Meanwhile, Greek drama was what life at home was beginning to resemble. I was 13 when my parents' marriage started to seriously disintegrate, though in retrospect I think the problems began from

Our parents' marriage was already in trouble by the time this photo was taken, some time in the late 1950s.

the moment they exchanged vows. My father began to spend less and less time at home—no longer the apartment on Durocher but one on Walkley Avenue in Notre-Dame-de-Grâce, to which we had moved when I was six, not long after the Pom-Pom incident—and my mother began to drink, something I'd never seen her do before. She'd been a fastidious housekeeper, but gradually our home became a mess, with beer bottles strewn everywhere. She insisted on coming to Mark's first communion, even though we weren't at all sure she'd be fit to do so—and was so drunk that she fell down, much to everyone's embarrassment. She also began to take pills. And, as her mother had done before her, she began to lose her sanity.

She had always had a startling ability to step outside the boundaries of normal behaviour when it suited her. My aunt Alice recalled going with her to see the film *Gigi* when it first came out in 1958. Seeing the long line-up, my mother announced: "Alice, we're not standing here waiting for all these people. I'm going to get us in." Upon which, she pushed her way to the head of the line, shouting, "Let me through! I'm crazy! I'm crazy! Let me through!" It worked: the box office people gave her two tickets just to get rid of her.

One night when my father came home late, she said to me: "Richard, don't let this upset you: I just want to scare your father." She then opened the kitchen cupboard and began throwing every available plate at him as he walked through the door. Then she produced a long carving knife and struck the blade of it on the edge of the table so that it vibrated—"Doi-oi-oinggg!"—like a knife in a cartoon. "Maurice," she warned him ominously: "tonight, you don't wake up." I don't know how well she succeeded in frightening my father, but she certainly frightened me.

But those outbursts had been conscious and deliberate. The moment when I realized my mother was crossing the line between temperament and insanity came when I was 17, studying for my first-year university exams. To give myself a break, I had gone to see the film *Days of Wine and Roses*—a splendid movie, as I recall, but perhaps not the best choice in escapist entertainment, since it dealt with alcoholism, and my mother was by then far down that same road. When I came home, she got out of bed, and we spent some time chatting till she suddenly said, quite calmly, "Richard. There's a mouse stealing your slipper." She didn't shriek; her eyes didn't roll back in her head. She was just making an observation, the way you might say, "My, it's warm in here." There was, of course, no mouse. I sat up with her for the rest of the night, till the light of dawn. She was under the impression that there were nurses in the room, just as my grandmother had seen witches. "They've come to take me away," she said. "But I'm not going."

Again, years later, I made use of this long night's journey into day in one of my productions. In 1996, I directed *King Lear*, a play that resonates with anyone who has had difficulty with a parent. In Act IV, Lear enters, mad, crowned with weeds and flowers, and says, "Look, look, a mouse!" In discussing this moment with

William Hutt, who was playing the title role, I recalled that long-ago night with my mother. "When people start hallucinating," I said, "sometimes they're quite, quite lucid. They don't always rave." After that, Bill played the moment with great lucidity, which made it all the more haunting.

The catastrophe that was my parents' marriage reached its peak the night my father tried to strangle my mother with a telephone cord. This took place in their bedroom, the once-pristine walls of which had become soiled with menstrual blood and feces. In a disturbingly Oedipal moment, I found myself holding my mother, who was wearing only a shift, in my arms and ordering my father to leave the house. As soon as he did so, I let go. My mother immediately ran outside, still in her shift—this was in the middle of a Montreal winter—and got down on her hands and knees in front of my father's car. My brother Mark, who was then still just a little boy, was with me, watching this lurid melodrama unfold in the glare of the car headlights. I remember saying to him, as our father revved the car with our mother in the snow in front of it: "Don't worry, I'll take care of you. I don't think he'll do anything. He's too much of a coward"—though I did not, by any means, feel assured of this. Strangely, although this scene is forever seared into my mind, I can't remember how it resolved itself. At any rate, vehicular homicide did not take place that night.

In her lucid moments, my mother would realize she was in need of help. At one point, she had submitted herself to electro-convulsive therapy as part of a notorious series of CIA-sponsored experiments that were conducted at McGill University in the 1950s and early '60s. I remember her saying to me, "You know, Richard, it really *hurts*." Later, she decided she wanted to be institutionalized and became quite ingenious in her efforts to achieve this. On one occasion, we went to a local emergency room, where we found four or five people ahead of us. My mother immediately applied the same technique she had used in the *Gigi* line-up. "Pay no attention to this," she said to me, and the next thing I knew she was on the floor, rolling and screaming like Linda Blair in *The Exorcist*. Again, she was admitted right away.

In the winter of 1963, when I was 19, I put my academic studies on hold and went to Toronto, where I had been offered my first professional stage role. In my absence, my mother went off to stay with grandmother Lucia and sent Mark first to my other grandparents,

Alfred and Eva, on Fort Street, and later to live with my aunt Alice. My father held on to the Walkley Avenue apartment for some time after that, though he hardly ever stayed there anymore. While she was staying at Lucia's, my mother again decided that she wanted to be taken into care. So she packed a suitcase, put on her hat and telephoned the police to announce that she was going to a nearby intersection to throw herself in front of a car. The police came and told her to go back inside. When they'd gone, she telephoned them again. They came again, and again told her to go inside. The third time she phoned them, instead of taking her to a mental hospital as she had hoped, they arrested her for what was then the crime of attempted suicide.

I knew nothing of this till Mark, then 12 years old, came to Toronto on his own to visit me for Christmas. I went to meet him off the train, and as we walked through Union Station, I asked him—not without some trepidation, for our Christmases at home had always been very tense and unhappy—"How's Mother?"

"Oh," he replied. "Mother's in jail." And there she remained for three months.

My first professional headshot, at the age of 19

She did eventually succeed in getting herself admitted to St. Jean de Dieu, an old-style insane asylum where, by a bizarre coincidence, my grandmother Lucia's brother, Pietro Liberatore, had died of syphilis. I went to visit her there, and having negotiated corridors filled with wild-eyed inmates tearing off their clothes and generally behaving like something out of the film *Suddenly Last Summer*, I found her calmly sitting up in bed, knitting. She greeted me cheerfully—"H*ello*, Richard!"—as if nothing were amiss.

"How are you?" I asked.

"I'm fine," she replied. "I like it here. And I want to thank you for visiting me every night." (This was disconcerting, since it was my first visit.) "But," she went on, "you always sit at the end of the bed, and you're very fat"—which I wasn't, at the time—"and you're wearing a wedding dress." I could only assume she was remembering my high school triumph in "Clancy Lowered the Boom."

"Mother," I said (for I was then struggling with rather more than the usual adolescent uncertainties, of which more later), "is it any wonder that I have problems?"

I was lucky to have had good times with my mother when she was well. Mark was less fortunate: being seven years younger, he saw none of the things that once made our mother exciting and interesting. He saw only the slide down. For that reason, I think I was angrier on his behalf than on my own.

I reached a turning point with my mother the day I found she had taken an overdose of pills. I phoned my aunt Alice, who came and took her to the hospital, while I looked after Mark. Later, I too went to the hospital, where I found my mother in a coma. "If you'd gotten her here five minutes later," said the doctor, "she would have died." Alice and I waited by her bedside until she regained consciousness, and then I began to scream obscenities at her: "You selfish c___! How *dare* you do this to your children and to your sister? Have you no care for anyone?"

My aunt, I am sure, was deeply shocked to hear me use such language. But there was a deep rage within me: while I felt sorry for my mother and was greatly relieved that she was still alive, I could not accept her attempt to abandon us, her children. As a child, I'd always sided with our mother, while Mark tended to sympathize with our father. Mark felt deeply betrayed when our father, after years of protracted absences, finally left home for good. This overdose incident, on the other hand, made me begin to reassess my feelings about our mother. I began to realize that this hard-done-by woman had made her own contribution to the disintegration of her marriage, her family and herself, and had now become a professional sick person who would forever crave attention. I never stopped loving her, though, and I was deeply distraught when she died in 1972.

Though he kept his sanity, my father's decline was no less calamitous than my mother's. He associated for a time with a woman who ran a brothel staffed by very young girls. After I left home, I had almost no communication with him—with one startling exception.

When I was 33, he rang me up out of the blue and invited me to join him at an orgy. It was perhaps the most shocking proposal I have ever heard. "Father," I said, "I respectfully decline."

The last straw for Mark's relationship with our father came in the 1970s, when Mark married a wonderful American woman named Christine Bridge and decided to move with her to Los Angeles. He made an appointment to meet our father to say goodbye—but our father did not show up.

Estranged from both his sons, Maurice Monette ended up living on welfare and died, in 1983, at the age of 63.

The family stories I grew up with—great-grandfather Israël's miraculous curative powers, grandmother Lucia's story of Therese and the flaming lion, and her nursery rhyme with its grotesque real-life parallel—all added up to a kind of personal mythology for me. Such tales were not only of a piece with the saints and miracles of the Catholic religion that I believed in as a child but also evoked memories of Old Country superstition: the kind of thing referred to in Molière's *Don Juan*, when Sganarelle talks of *loups-garous* and the *Moine-Bourru*: werewolves and the Bogeyman. In addition, the scenes I witnessed at first hand in my family seemed to point to a certain inherent instability in the universe as I knew it: I had seen for myself how things could start out well enough and then go terribly wrong.

This is why I have always found it easy to respond in an immediate way to classical mythology. The stories of Oedipus marrying his own mother, of Atreus serving Thyestes the flesh of his children at a banquet, of Clytemnestra butchering her husband in his bath, never struck me as emotionally overblown or alien to real-life experience. They represent extreme cases, to be sure, heavily laden with metaphor, but they were never beyond my ability to accept. In my work in the theatre, I have always been comfortable with stories that depart from the purely literal and rational, because such departures were familiar to me from an early age.

In 1997, Mark and I went to seek out our roots in Palena. Together with Mark's new partner, Judy (Christine having died of an aneurysm at the tragically early age of 45), we visited the church where our Italian grandparents, Antonio Tondino and Lucia Liberatore, had been married—the same church, presumably, on whose steps Antonio had been found as a baby.

We sought out an ancient priest, who told us that the church had been bombed by the Allies during the Second World War and then rebuilt. "It's ugly now," he said. He told us that when the original church was destroyed, only two of the saints' statues that it contained had survived. They were the statues of Saint Antony and Saint Lucia.

I told the priest that Antonio and Lucia were the names of our grandparents—that in all likelihood they had been named after those saints. What an amazing coincidence, I remarked, that those should be the two statues to have remained intact.

The priest agreed. He said it was a miracle.

Tracing our Italian roots: in 1997, Mark and I visited our maternal grandparents' home town of Palena.

CHAPTER TWO

O, What Learning Is!

Romeo and Juliet, Act III, scene 3

"The only great theatre you see is when you are young."

That remark, or something very like it, was made by the legendary Tyrone Guthrie, first artistic director of the Stratford Festival. I cannot recall where I first came upon it; I think it was in the published text of a lecture that he gave somewhere. In any case, it has always seemed to me to embody a great truth, and I have quoted it many times during my own tenure.

Guthrie did not mean it literally; otherwise, adult theatregoing would have little point. But it is true that those of us who go to the theatre, and those of us who work in it, do so in the hope—sometimes fulfilled, sometimes not—of recapturing that sense of transcendent magic we once experienced as children in a darkened auditorium, rapt at the wonder of it all.

Tyrone Guthrie, Stratford's first artistic director

I must have been about 12 or 13 when I saw my first play: a romantic comedy called *Jenny Kissed Me*, by Jean Kerr. I was taken to it by a friend from high school who bore the memorable name of Ed Sullivan and to whom I owe my discovery of how truly magical live theatre could be. I have no reason to suppose that the production, an amateur one, was in any way distinguished, but there was one thing in it that took my breath away. The plot concerned a plain Jane who becomes beautiful when she falls in love, and it was at the moment of her transformation, which the actress achieved by the time-honoured method of taking off her glasses and shaking out her hair, that I fell in love with the theatre.

I'd experienced only one thing like it before: when I was taken to the cinema to see a re-release of *The Wizard of Oz*. When Dorothy arrived in Oz and the screen changed from black-and-white to Technicolor, I was so astounded that I felt my heart had stopped. I simply couldn't believe—couldn't even quite understand—what I'd just seen. That transformation in *Jenny Kissed Me* was, for me, just such a moment of pure magic. (Another film that made a deep impression on me as a child was Walt Disney's *Cinderella*, which I was taken to see one summer while I was staying at the farm where grandparents Alfred and Eva used to live. When we came home, I went out to their barn and talked to the mice. I couldn't understand why they wouldn't talk back or sing to me, like the mice in the movie.)

After that first encounter with live drama, I started going to as many plays as I could, though in Montreal at that time English-speaking theatre was almost entirely amateur or, at best, semi-professional. Still, Ed and I went to university productions, to the Mountain Playhouse, to His Majesty's Theatre (now torn down), to La Poudrière, where we saw *Death of a Salesman*, and to the Montreal Repertory Theatre, where I recall seeing Leo Ciceri play Macbeth. My tastes formed quickly: I remember a production of *The Merchant of Venice* that even at my young age I found so ludicrously bad that Ed and I hooted and shrieked in our back-row seats.

Standards were much higher at the French-speaking Théâtre du Nouveau Monde, which mounted professional productions of classics by Corneille and Racine, and where I first saw such actors as Jean Gascon and Jean-Louis Roux. Yet I felt curiously removed from performances there. I found them dauntingly aristocratic in style, partly because they were given in standard Parisian French, which I had never learned; my French was the working-class Quebec dialect known as *joual*. I felt much more in tune with the more populist theatre of Gratien Gélinas, whose *Bousille et les justes* I saw when it was first produced by La Comédie-Canadienne.

In February 1959, when I was 14 and my parents' marriage was already breaking down, my father drove Ed and me to New York, where we saw three Broadway musicals: *Bells Are Ringing*, with Judy Holliday; *The Most Happy Fella*, the cast of which included the nine-year-old Bernadette Peters; and the original production of *My Fair Lady*, with Edward Mulhare (who by then had taken over from Rex Harrison) as Professor Higgins. Ed and I then saved up for a second excursion later that same year: my first trip to the Stratford Festival of Canada.

We saw both productions presented at the Festival Theatre that season: *As You Like It*, with Irene Worth as Rosalind, Kate Reid as Celia, Douglas Campbell as Touchstone and William Hutt as

Jaques; and *Othello,* with Douglas Rain as Iago, Frances Hyland as Desdemona and Douglas Campbell again (with his own flaming red hair) in the title role. Star-studded casts, both of them, and glorious production values: for those reasons alone, Stratford would have impressed me. But it was the Festival Theatre itself, with designer Tanya Moiseiwitsch's revolutionary thrust stage at its heart, that stunned me most of all. I had never seen such a remarkable theatre in my life. As we waited for each performance to begin, I was unable to fix my eyes on any one thing. My astonished gaze roamed wildly around the space like that of a child in the world's biggest candy store. I was mesmerized, from start to finish.

Tanya Moiseiwitsch's revolutionary thrust stage

The effect on me was even more profound than I realized at the time, as became apparent when I returned the next year, 1960, to see *King John, A Midsummer Night's Dream* and *Romeo and Juliet.* I don't remember at which of those productions this happened, but as I was being ushered down the aisle to my seat, I instinctively genuflected toward the stage: bent down on one knee, as Catholics did at the sacrament of the Eucharist. It was a deeply unconscious, visceral response: a transference of emotion from a religious setting to a secular one. Catching myself halfway down, I thought: "This is really embarrassing. Am I losing my mind?"

In retrospect, this must indeed have been an early sign of a change that was to come upon me in a year or so. But it wasn't my mind I was going to lose; it was my faith.

One summer when I was still in high school, my uncle Peter, one of that multitude of Tondino siblings, gave me a job in the kitchenware factory that he managed. My job was to count up the nuts, bolts and other widgets used in the manufacturing process. I had absolutely no aptitude for this and spent most of my time at my desk writing poetry. (I was quite the *littérateur* in those days: at school I even edited a magazine of poems and short stories.) At the end of the summer, my uncle said to me, "Richard, I don't think you're cut out for this work. According to your figures, this company is bankrupt. And I know we're not."

That was the first and last "real" job I ever had, and from it I learned that I could never work at something that didn't engage my imagination. But what *was* I going to do? I didn't much care for the sight of blood, so I couldn't be a doctor. Despite my prowess at public speaking, I didn't *want* to be a lawyer. Like many Catholic boys, I had briefly considered the priesthood, but the social life that went with that career seemed to leave a lot to be desired. It was fortunate, then, that I discovered an interest in the theatre. Of course, there remained the question of whether the theatre would be interested in *me*.

One of my teachers at Loyola High School, Father Peter Larisey, helped me on my way by recommending me to St. Michael's College in Winooski, Vermont. Affiliated with Catholic University in Washington, D.C., the college had its own theatre, St. Michael's Playhouse, which mounted five or six productions each summer, using professional actors. For a fee of $200, students could enrol in an apprenticeship program there, taking classes and gaining basic hands-on experience in the practicalities of theatre work. One week you might be building sets or running lights; the next, running sound or cleaning out the latrines. In addition, you got to play small roles on stage alongside the "real" actors. I worked there twice: in the summer of 1961, between high school and college, when I was 17, and again the following year.

The actors there at the time included a couple of future celebrities, including a very young, very thin Jon Voight. He looked quite different then: almost albino, with an extremely pale complexion and white-blond hair. I didn't recognize him at all when *Midnight Cowboy* came out in 1969. Susan Anspach, who later starred in the films *Montenegro* and *Five Easy Pieces*, was also in the company, as was Jackie Gleason's daughter, Linda, whom I remember coming back from a trip to New York once and teaching us all how to dance the Twist. We tried it out in a local bar, to the bewilderment of the regular patrons. It was my first taste of what life in the professional theatre might actually be like, the main difference being that, because of

St. Michael's religious connection, the whole company would gather together in prayer before every performance—not a bad idea, since each show got only one week of rehearsal.

My first stage appearance there was in a play called *Say, Darling*. I had a brief scene at the beginning with the leading man, my sole purpose being to establish his character's name and the fact that the scene took place in an airport. I don't recall the exact dialogue now, but—with apologies to the authors—it was supposed to go something like this:

Me: "Hi, Jack."

Him: "Hi, Charlie."

Me: "Where ya goin'?"

Him: "To Frisco." And so on.

On opening night, I delivered my first line as usual: "Hi, Jack." But instead of replying, "Hi, Charlie," the leading man said, "Hi, Harry."

Now, if I had been an experienced actor, I would have taken this trivial slip of the tongue in my stride. But I was not an experienced actor. With all the misplaced intensity of the beginner, I was determined to preserve my character's integrity at all costs. So I replied, "My name's not Harry."

The leading man stopped dead in his tracks. "What? Oh. . . ." He glared at me, icily. "No-o-o-o-o. No, no . . . of course not. Your name . . . is . . . *Charlie*. Hi, Charlie." We then continued as scripted till my exit. As soon as he came offstage, thinking I had deliberately tried to throw him, my scene partner came up to me in a fury: "Don't you *ever* do that to me again!" From that I learned my first important lesson about the theatre: if the audience ain't gonna notice it's broke, don't try to fix it.

Among the acquaintances I made at Winooski were two women in their mid-20s. I went with them once to New York, where we stayed with a female friend of theirs. This friend, 26 years old and a devout Catholic, was trapped in an unhappy marriage, yet her religion told her that divorce was unthinkable. The pain of the situation was destroying her: she was in therapy and she had developed ulcers from the stress. I could well understand, from my own experience, what she was going through. I had urged my mother many times to divorce my father, but she could never bring herself to take a step so radically at odds with the teachings of the Church. Curiously, it was this stranger's plight that finally triggered my loss of faith.

Any religion, I thought, after talking to her, that inflicted this kind of pain was not something I wanted to be a part of. From that time on, except for funerals, I never went to church again.

This left an enormous gap in my life. During that summer that I had worked for my uncle Peter, I had gone to mass every lunchtime, searching for answers to my questions about the meaning of my life. Why, for instance, should my parents' marriage have been so miserable, while other couples could enjoy a long and happy relationship? There did not appear to be any particular reason. Was the pain of life, then, quite pointless; its pleasures a matter of blind luck? With my faith gone, I still needed something to help me

Jon Voight is the young man on the couch in this scene from a play called *Golden Fleecing* at St. Michael's Playhouse in 1961. I'm at the far left, in the uniform; the others are Jim Christy, Dana Haskell, Carol Emshoff, David Little and Tom Baker.

answer those questions. Fortunately, there are two principal ways of finding meaning in the randomness of life. One is religion, which offers us the idea that things are "meant" to be the way they are, as ordained by some higher power. The other, in which we create our own meaning by shaping and ordering the raw material of life into something that has structure and beauty, is art.

My uncle Gentile Tondino, the painter, once told me, "You *have* to paint nature, because nature doesn't know itself." In other words, we need art for the same reason we need religion: to help us know and understand ourselves and the world we live in, and to find meaning in what otherwise would seem arbitrary. It is no accident that theatre—Western theatre, anyway—has its roots in religious rites: the ancient Greek festivals of Dionysus. In a theatre, as in a place of worship, we hear certain prescribed words spoken, we witness certain actions performed. Through those words, those actions, we relate the passages of our lives—birth, marriage and death—to those of other human beings and become part of a larger community, both present and past. By elevating ordinary human experience into the timeless universalities of tragedy and comedy, we find consolation for our sorrows, affirmation of our joys.

So it was no huge leap for me to transfer my faith from the altar to the stage: to exchange the religious, Catholic answer to life's mysteries for the humanistic but still spiritual one offered by the theatre. The theatre was already becoming my family, replacing the one that was disintegrating at home and giving me the social companionship I craved. Now it would also become my church. And to me the theatre had one compelling advantage over most organized religions: it did no one any harm. As I believe the director Trevor Nunn once said in an interview, if you do a bad production of *Macbeth*, it's unfortunate. But nobody gets killed.

I did have some lingering qualms about the implications of having to play evil or morally obnoxious people. I was comforted, however, by something I read in the *Summa Theologica* of Thomas Aquinas. Or so I recall: as with the Guthrie quote, I have since searched for it in vain, so perhaps it was not in the *Summa* after all but in some commentary on it. In any case, it was a passage to the effect that artists inhabit a separate moral universe—not that they are exempt from morality in their real lives, just that they serve a special purpose: using their imaginations to explore good and evil in order to gain a better understanding of both.

Ever since reading that, wherever it was, I have thought of artists as being like doves sent out from the Ark: unless we go out to explore, we cannot know where to find land.

In my final year of high school, I won a public-speaking competition sponsored by the Rotary Club of Montreal. My prize was a gold medal and a scholarship of $400, which enabled me, in September 1961, to enrol in Loyola College. There I embarked on an honours BA, majoring in English, while also seeking to gain as much acting experience as I could. That November I appeared in a college production of John Steinbeck's *Of Mice and Men* and was praised by the *Montreal Star*'s critic, Jacob Siskind: "Richard Monette began his performance as Candy in a very low key and I was completely unprepared for the venom and the magnetism of his outburst in the final act. Here we saw a man who had begun to dream again find his castles in the air shattered by forces he could not control. Monette made Candy a truly tragic figure, and his performance in that scene is one I will remember."

The following February, the Canadian Intervarsity Drama League, a group founded to promote the dramatic arts in Canadian colleges and universities, held its annual festival at Montreal's McGill University. The all-girls' school Marianopolis College needed someone to play the one male role in their entry, Patricia Joudry's *The Song of Louise in the Morning*, so the director, John Juliani, imported me from Loyola. Adjudicator Guy Beaulne disliked the play ("a long, over-written melodrama") but praised my performance in it, calling me "brilliant" and "intelligent" and giving me the award for best actor.

As Fumblededum in
An Unemployed Jester is Nobody's Fool in 1963

The next year, 1963, the festival was held at Hart House in Toronto, and I again took part. It was attended by practically everybody on the Toronto theatre scene—mostly, people said, because there was a free meal. I played the leading role in a play called *An Unemployed Jester Is Nobody's Fool*, which had been written by a friend and fellow Loyola student, James Hassinger. The adjudicator was David Gardner, who had chaired the founding committee of the National Theatre School in Montreal and was now producing and directing television drama.

He not only gave me another best-actor award but later the same year offered me a leading role in an experimental TV play by Len Peterson, *With My Head Tucked Underneath My Arm,* that he was producing for the CBC. So I made my professional debut not on stage but on the small screen, a medium in which I had no previous experience. As a bonus, I formed a lasting friendship with David and his wife, Dorothy.

All this was enormously encouraging. I had already realized, though, that it was in classical theatre that I wanted to make my mark—and that I would therefore have to do something about my voice. I spoke English with a peculiar accent, a blend of French and Italian, and at the time this was hardly an asset for an aspiring Shakespearean. So in my first year of college, I had gone for help to a woman who would become my first mentor and would remain an inspiration to me all my life: Eleanor Stuart.

Dorothy and David Gardner

Miss Stuart—even now it's hard for me to think of her as "Eleanor," perhaps because she always called me "Mr. Monette," even though I was all of 17 when I first met her—was an actress and teacher whose students had included John Colicos and Christopher Plummer. A severe-looking Scot who always wore black, she had impeccably made-up eyes and a wide slash of a mouth that she accentuated with bright red lipstick. She'd been in the Stratford Festival's inaugural company in 1953, playing the Duchess of York in *Richard III* and the Countess of Rossillion in *All's Well That Ends Well,* and had stayed on for a few more seasons, playing, among other roles, Jocasta in *Oedipus Rex* in 1954 and 1955. To my regret, I saw her act only once: in 1961, her last season at the Festival, when she played the strong-willed matriarch Volumnia in *Coriolanus,* opposite Paul Scofield. When I met her, I realized how well her imposing appearance and forceful personality had suited her to that role.

She was now teaching at the National Theatre School and also maintained a roster of private students to whom she gave lessons in the upper-storey apartment on Mountain Street where she lived with her mother.

"Mr. Monette," she asked me at our first meeting, "why have you come to me?"

I replied, "Because I would like to be as great an actor as Laurence Olivier or John Gielgud."

There was a brief pause. "Mr. Monette, we have a *great* deal of work to do."

Eleanor Stuart as Volumnia in the Stratford Festival's 1961 production of *Coriolanus*

In the truest sense, Eleanor Stuart taught me to read. I had never understood the full value of words, certainly not in a dramatic context, until I studied with her. She was old-school in her thinking, but that was exactly what I needed and wanted. "The theatre requires a Spartan discipline," she once said to me. "If you don't have it, don't attempt to go into it." I knew that I couldn't learn the craft of acting just by performing; I had to be taught. And Miss Stuart had both a gift and a vocation for teaching.

We worked mostly on Shakespearean and Greek plays, for which she had a remarkable empathy. Jacob Siskind had written to Michael Langham, then artistic director of the Stratford Festival, praising my performance in *Of Mice and Men*, and as a result, I was offered an audition for the Festival's 1963 season. Miss Stuart worked intensively with me on my audition piece, Romeo's final speech in Juliet's tomb, determined that I should not content myself with a generalized gloss of meaning but should understand the implication of every word. She had on her desk the multi-volume *Oxford English*

Dictionary, and she made me look up every word in the speech. We once spent an entire 45-minute session on a single sentence:

O here
Will I set up my everlasting rest
And shake the yoke of inauspicious stars
From this world-wearied flesh.

"Mr. Monette, what does *yoke* mean?"

"It's something on an ox."

She sent me to the dictionary. "So in this sense, what does it mean?"

"Well, it's something heavy around his neck: his fate."

"Yes. Say the word like that."

The Montreal Star praised my performance as Candy (centre) in *Of Mice and Men* at Loyola College in 1961. The other student actors in this shot are Patrick Kenniff (left) and Sean Kelly.

I tried this line this way and that, never to her satisfaction, until I thought I would go mad. Then I said it once more and suddenly thought: "That's it! I've got it." In the same moment I also thought: "If she tells me that's *not* it, then I don't know *what* she's talking about."

But, by George, I *had* got it. "Very good, Mr. Monette. Next week we shall move on to the next sentence."

Despite my labours on the yoke of inauspicious stars, I didn't get into the Stratford Festival company that time round. (I still have the rejection letter, which I framed and mounted on the wall above the toilet in my house. It found a companion piece, 30 years later, in the letter confirming my appointment as artistic director. Both letters were written by the same man: John Hayes, the Festival's producer.)

One of the most striking things about Miss Stuart was her respect for living things. One day, a fly was buzzing around us as we worked. I rolled up a newspaper and was about to swat it when she stopped me sharply: "No, no, Mr. Monette! You must never kill anything living." She opened the window, and we spent some considerable time trying to shoo the fly out without harming it. "There's a line in *King Lear* about flies," she remarked pointedly: "As flies to wanton boys are we to the gods, / They kill us for their sport."

On another occasion, I brought her a rose. She thanked me profusely, but then she said, "You must never bring me a rose again. They die so quickly."

She was even protective of inanimate objects, particularly books. Once, while we were studying a Shakespeare play, I cracked the spine of my Signet paperback edition so that it would lie flat. She was appalled. "Mr. Monette, would you like it if I did that to *your* spine?"

Eleanor Stuart was something of an eccentric, but she had an extraordinary humility and a true dedication to the theatre. Theatre is a celebration of life, and she revered theatre as she revered life. I, in turn, admired her as much for her values as for her craft. She was not a rich woman; in fact, I think she was extremely poor. But she would never accept payment from a student if she thought that student couldn't afford it. Morally, as well as artistically, she was one of the greatest role models in my life. To this day, when I contemplate some new step, I often ask myself, "Would Miss Stuart approve of this?"

While I was at Loyola College, I also acted with a group called The Paupers, which performed in the McGill University students' union during the summer holidays. There I made two life-long friends. One was the actor David Francis, who went on to appear in several Stratford Festival seasons, and the other was a young art student who would become an Academy Award-winning filmmaker: Aviva Slesin.

Aviva—the name means "spring"—was born in the Shauliai ghetto in Nazi-occupied Lithuania in 1943. Her uncle arranged for her to be smuggled out of the ghetto in a suitcase, to be adopted under a false identity by a non-Jewish family. Three days later, the uncle and the rest of the family were deported to the Stutthof concentration camp in Poland. Aviva was only one of many such "hidden children" whose story she later told in her film *Secret Lives*. Reunited with her mother after the war, she went to live in New York, then in Montreal, where she studied art at McGill for two years before dropping out.

She then returned to New York, where she lived in Greenwich Village and attended Parsons School of Design. She started her career as a film editor (her credits included *The Rutles*, Eric Idle's send-up of the Beatles), then became a documentary filmmaker in her own right. In 1987, she won an Oscar for *The Ten Year Lunch: The Wit and Legend of the Algonquin Round Table*.

The early years of our friendship encompassed such milestones of the American civil rights movement as Martin Luther King's "I have a dream" speech, the March on Washington and the bombing of the 16th Street Baptist Church in Birmingham, Alabama. Aviva was very well informed about these and other current events, while I was profoundly naïve. The only black person I'd ever encountered was a tall, distinguished-looking Parisian who hung out in a Montreal coffee house wearing a beret, and it came as a shock to me to learn about American racial segregation. My friendship with Aviva helped open my eyes.

My friend Aviva Slesin, with whom I acted at college, became an Academy Award-winning filmmaker.

In the years after Aviva left McGill, I visited her in New York whenever I could. Ours was not a romantic relationship but a journey of self-discovery: a time of filling up the well. We were young, we were passionate about the arts, and we were stimulated by the vast cultural resources of the Big Apple. We went to art galleries and museums, to the theatre and to art-film houses to see films by Ingmar Bergman and Federico Fellini. Then we would sit up talking till five in the morning.

I saw many Broadway musicals: I was intrigued by their staging, their structure, how they got their laughs. Comedy is a fascinating combination of skill and inspiration: how do you get a thousand people in a theatre to instantly agree that something is funny? If there is a "science" of humour, it must rival quantum physics in its seeming irrationality. Ann Curtis, a designer with whom I have worked many times, told me that she once did a production of *Me and My Girl* in which the leading lady wore green grapes in her hair during one of the numbers, which always got a laugh. Then that actress left the show and was replaced by another performer, who happened to be black. Ann made a new set of grapes for her, but this time she made them red, thinking they would look better with the actress's colouring. From that point on, the number didn't get a single laugh. Ann changed the grapes back to green, and back came the laughs.

Likewise, in 1989, when I directed a one-act adaptation of *The Comedy of Errors* as part of a double bill with a similarly truncated *Titus Andronicus*, I'd devised some business involving cabbages being thrown around on stage. "It has to be cabbages," I said. "We can't use lettuce, because lettuce goes 'squish' when it hits something, whereas cabbages go 'crunch.' " Strange but true: cabbages are funny and lettuce is not. I am sure it was largely from my early experience of musicals that I unconsciously absorbed those kinds of arcane insights.

On one of my New York trips, in 1962, I went to see the musical *I Can Get It for You Wholesale* and was greatly impressed by the woman who played Miss Marmelstein, the secretary. This actress, who looked to me to be in her 50s, had two scenes: in the first act, she was kissed by her boss and made a comic exit with her knees knocking together from excitement. Then, halfway through the second act, she re-entered, still with knocking knees. I thought the actress was brilliant at what she did, but I also guessed she'd been playing that same sort of part all her life. I told Aviva I didn't want to be that kind of actor: someone who finds they can do a certain "type" and goes on recycling it for 30 or 40 years.

As I learned later, the actress I'd seen play Miss Marmelstein was actually the 20-year-old Barbra Streisand, making her Broadway debut. It was that brief performance in *I Can Get It for You Wholesale* that made her a star, and two years later, on another trip to New York, I saw her again as the headliner in *Funny Girl*, in the first week of its opening.

Still, I'd been right about one thing: I didn't want to be someone who shirked challenges. A year later, when I was 19 years old, that resolve was put to the test when I was invited by the Crest Theatre in Toronto to play my first professional stage role: a little thing called Hamlet, Prince of Denmark.

Eleanor Stuart once said to me, "Mr. Monette, it takes 20 years to make an actor," and of course she was right. So when I announced, after barely two years of studying with her, that I was going off to Toronto to play Hamlet, she gave me a look that could confound a Sphinx. She did not, however, attempt to dissuade me. Instead, she worked on the play with me for the next two months as I prepared to plunge in at this deepest of all possible ends.

In 1963, the Crest Theatre was practically the only professional company in Toronto. It had been founded a decade earlier by Donald and Murray Davis, and their sister, Barbara Chilcott. I have never understood why these remarkable theatrical pioneers, a trio of such striking looks that people said they were descended from gypsies, have never received the recognition or the thanks they deserve. They presented serious work, without public subsidy; they provided professional opportunities for Canadian artists; and, by forming connections with such internationally recognized figures as J. B. Priestley (who wrote the play *The Glass Cage* especially for them), they gave Canadian theatre reason to be taken seriously abroad. Quite apart from the fact that I personally owe Donald, Murray and Barbara a great debt of gratitude, they did extraordinary service to their country, and I hope that history will eventually give them their due.

The 400th anniversary of Shakespeare's birth was coming up in 1964, and many theatres in North America were preparing to celebrate it with productions of his plays. The Crest had planned to produce *Hamlet* with Bruno Gerussi in the title role and John Hirsch as director; however, Bruno had dropped out and John had followed suit. Marigold Charlesworth and Jean Roberts, who were then running the Central Library Theatre in Toronto, agreed to step in as co-directors. But they still lacked someone to play the Prince.

At that time, November 1963, I was still attempting to keep up with my studies at Loyola College, where I had just entered my third year, while at the same time pursuing what was now my budding television career. I had just finished another CBC television play called *First Love,* during which, appropriately enough, I lost my virginity to a lovely older woman from England, who also introduced me to fine chocolate and Scotch whisky, and told me all about this wonderful new pop group called the Beatles. I pined for her for about a year and a half after she left town. It was some time after *First Love* finished shooting that I went to the Central Library Theatre to see *The Fantasticks*, which Jean and Marigold had directed. I ran into them there, and they suggested I come and audition for their *Hamlet*. (Word must have gotten around that I'd been good in my TV roles.) I accepted gladly, thinking this was a great opportunity to finally get a crack at something Shakespearean—perhaps even Horatio or Laertes.

My audition was on November 22, a Friday. When it was over, Jean, Marigold and Murray gathered round me. "What would you say," asked Murray, "if we offered you the title role?"

I was astounded. I believe the first words out of my mouth were "But I'm in college"—to which they could have responded (but didn't), "Well, so is Hamlet."

My objection was by no means a trivial one. Getting an education was very important to me, not just because of what I'd overheard on that train ride with my grandparents but because I genuinely hungered for knowledge. To take on a role as huge as Hamlet wasn't something I could fit in between classes. I would have to put my academic studies on hold.

"Can I think about it?"

"Yes. Call us tomorrow."

I walked out of the theatre, found the nearest café and sat down with a cup of coffee, completely stunned. To make my professional stage debut as Hamlet: wasn't that what the ancient Greeks called *hubris*? I needed advice, and the only people I knew in Toronto were David and Dorothy Gardner. I sat there for about an hour, trying to summon up the gumption to call them. Eventually, I came out of my daze and resolved to go find a phone. As I did so, I suddenly became aware that a radio was on, and there was a great commotion among the other patrons. Through the hubbub I heard an announcer saying, ". . . and it has been confirmed that President Kennedy is dead."

Everyone in that coffee shop but me had been listening to the radio, shocked by the news of Kennedy's assassination in Dallas that very same day. Such is the self-absorption of the actor that even when I got through to David Gardner on the phone, I could think only of my own dilemma. "Have you heard what's happened?" he said, after I identified myself. "Yes, yes," I said impatiently. "But I've been offered Hamlet. What should I do?"

In fact, the choice was clear. Most actors go through their careers without ever having the chance to play Hamlet: an offer like the one I had just received might never come again. Besides, Murray, Marigold and Jean seemed to have confidence in me, so why not? Accordingly, I secured a one-year leave of absence from the ever-supportive Loyola College and broke the news to my mother that I was leaving home to play Hamlet.

"Oh," she said. "Is that a good role?"

"Alas, poor Yorick": my professional stage debut as a teenage Hamlet at Toronto's Crest Theatre in 1964

The Crest paid me $80 a week, for which I was also required to participate in an initiative of Barbara Chilcott's devising: a school touring program called the Hour Company. Such outreach programs are common nowadays, but back then the Crest's was the only one there was. We would start at 10 a.m., setting up our platforms at the first of the two or three schools we'd visit that day, perform an hour's worth of excerpts from various plays at each school, then pack up, go back to the theatre and present *Hamlet* in the evening. It made for a long day.

The rehearsal period for *Hamlet* was spread over quite a long time, about a month and a half, but because the Crest played in repertory, many of the cast had other commitments. So our total rehearsal time amounted to only 10 six-hour days, forcing us to go at it like bulls in a china shop. My fellow cast members included Bill Brydon as Claudius, Barbara Bryne as the Player Queen, Jackie Burroughs as Ophelia, Barbara Chilcott as Gertrude, Robert Christie as Polonius and Neil Dainard as Laertes. Horatio, Hamlet's friend and fellow student at Wittenberg University, was played by Ken James, a pugilist as well as an actor, and a man considerably older than me, even though we were supposed to be peers. One day, he turned to Marigold and asked, in his throaty boxer's voice: "Hey, Marigold. How come I'm still at school with this guy? Am I a dummy?"

Our directors formed a sort of good-cop, bad-cop team: Jean was motherly and life-affirming, while Marigold was the tough one. "You know, Richard," Marigold said to me, with deceptive suavity, late in the rehearsal period, "we open in a week."

"Yes?"

"So when are you going to start to act?"

I was pole-axed. I had thought I was bringing a lot of emotion to the part: I was shedding real tears in the rehearsals. But, as I would learn, it's not what *you* feel as an actor that counts; it's what you can make an audience feel. And it's very hard to judge how you're coming across, especially in a tragedy, where you don't have laughter to give you feedback. You may *think* you're pulling out all the stops, but from the audience's point of view you may be having no effect at all.

I was concerned, too, about my Ophelia, Jackie Burroughs, who I couldn't help noticing had started to cry at every rehearsal. I was quite intimidated by her—I had seen her act several times before, and compared to her I was a nobody—but eventually I summoned up the courage to ask, "Are you crying because of something I'm doing?"

"No," she replied, "I'm crying because I'm so terrible in this play."

Of course, I assured her that she was just fine. What I didn't know at the time was that Jackie *always* cried as an opening night loomed. About 25 years later, we worked together again on a radio play. We were called to the studio, and I said, "Jackie, do you have an urge to cry? If so, I think you should do it now and not during the take."

"Yes," she replied, as brightly as if I'd suggested a nice cup of tea, "I think I will." She went to the washroom, had a good cry, came back and did the take.

Hamlet opened at 8:30 on the night of Tuesday, January 14, 1964. The top ticket price was $3, with an additional $2.25 for the black-tie reception afterward at the Park Plaza Hotel. My performance was hampered somewhat by my Elizabethan costume, which I did not receive until opening night. I had a belt with a scabbard made of felt, and my dagger, which was top-heavy, kept falling out of it and clattering onto the floor during my soliloquies. I also managed to stick the point of it into my hand during one particularly impassioned moment. But I got through the performance—which, given my inexperience at the time and the fact that I started to run out of voice by about the end of Act I, was something of an achievement in itself. As Samuel Johnson famously remarked about dogs walking on their hind legs, "It is not done well; but you are surprised to find it done at all."

The next morning, the Toronto *Telegram* carried a review by Ronald Evans under the ominous headline "Hamlet—A Tragedy." The first paragraph read, in its entirety: "Stop reading right here . . . if you happen to be Richard Monnette." I wondered if, by giving my surname that extra *n* throughout his review, he was offering me an alibi for posterity ("No, that wasn't me who did that Hamlet; it was another actor with an almost identical name"), but alas, they corrected the spelling for the paper's second edition.

What followed was bad, even when it was good ("handsome in a fleshy fashion"), though Evans was even-handed enough not to "dump all the blame for this dull disaster on young Mr. Monnette." Jean and Marigold came in for their share of scorn, as did most of my fellow actors. So did the set ("a revolving tangle of steel tubes and planks") and the electronic background music: "Half the time it sounds as if the 9:14 freight from Hornepayne is coming thundering out of the wings; the rest of the time you'd swear a herd of ferrets were trapped in the heating system." No marks for talent-spotting there: the music for our *Hamlet* was written by the then 24-year-old Robert Aitken, now one of Canada's most distinguished flautists, conductors and composers.

But the *Telegram* review was graciousness itself compared to that of

Nathan Cohen in the *Star*: "It is inconceivable that I shall ever see a more lamentable exposition . . . misbegotten on every possible level . . . deplorably cast and performed . . . Mr. Monette is valueless." This essentially set the tone for my future relationship with the critics.

Understandably, I turned up for the next night's performance in a state of some despair. Although I hadn't been solely blamed for the production's shortcomings, I was still the leading player. I went in not knowing how I was going to face the rest of the company that night, never mind get through the remaining three months of the run. But as I walked into the dressing room, Bill Brydon, whose performance as Claudius had also been savaged by the critics ("perversely disguised as some Persian rug merchant in murky makeup . . . a stalking, monotonal effigy"), defused the situation for me.

"Jesus," he said, as soon as I opened the door, "if I'd known you were going to be so bad, I never would have accepted this part." We all laughed and started to relax.

"To a nunnery, go": with Jackie Burroughs as Ophelia

The kindest of the reviewers was Herbert Whittaker of *The Globe and Mail*, who always took the endearing route of simply not mentioning anything he didn't like. Acknowledging my lack, "perhaps inevitable in a young actor," of wit, irony and compassion, he went on to say, "This student Prince has moments that will undoubtedly establish strong identification from the school audiences at which the production is so wisely aiming." This turned out to be prescient: despite its evisceration in the press, the Crest Theatre *Hamlet* played to about 50,000 people, most of them students, who received it with great enthusiasm. Thirty years later, when I began my tenure as artistic director at Stratford, I received letters from people saying it was still the best *Hamlet* they'd ever seen—thus validating that elusive quotation from Tyrone Guthrie.

Herbie Whittaker, by the way, told me later that a rumour had gone around at the time that I was Barbara Chilcott's illegitimate son. "That's nonsense," I retorted. "I'm the illegitimate son of Murray Davis." This, I need hardly add, was an equally preposterous idea.

Not all student audiences were uniformly impressed, mind you. At one performance, as I finished my first soliloquy, there came sailing out from the front row, to land with a plop on the stage, a single rubber galosh. And there was one occasion when I wondered—not for the last time in my career—if the nature of dramatic illusion is always as clearly understood by the public as actors assume it is. Jackie Burroughs had introduced me to a friend of hers, Ben Solway, who quickly became one of my own dearest friends and remains so to this day. (It was he who took me to my first expensive restaurant, where he taught me how to crack the shell of a lobster, which I'd never eaten before, and discouraged me from mopping my plate with a hunk of bread.) Ben was in the public-relations business, and one of his clients was the Baycrest Centre for Geriatric Care, incorporating the Jewish Home for the Aged. The Crest Theatre had donated 10 complimentary tickets for *Hamlet* to the home, and Ben had asked me if I would meet with those who'd be attending, eight residents and two volunteers, after the performance. The residents who came were effusive in their compliments, but I was nonplussed when one of them, an 84-year-old woman, came up to me and said, "Listen: when you get back to Denmark, I've got a brother there. Give him my regards."

Ben Solway, another life-long friend

Ben found this tale hilarious and would tell it over and over again. On one occasion, when he told it to a group of Baycrest donors, one of his listeners commented: "What a stupid lady. Didn't she know Denmark's a big country?"

Thanks to Shakespeare's quatercentenary, Toronto enjoyed a double dose of melancholy Danes that year. In February, while our *Hamlet* was still running, another production of the same play opened at the O'Keefe Centre with a somewhat better known Richard in the title role: Richard Burton. Directed by John Gielgud, the production was a pre-Broadway tryout. In his review, Nathan Cohen called it "an unmitigated disaster," so at least I was in good company.

Needless to say, it was the talk of the town, particularly since Burton was accompanied in Toronto by Elizabeth Taylor, with whom he had begun a much-publicized affair during the filming of *Cleopatra* and whom he would marry in my home town of Montreal on March 15, the month after his *Hamlet* opened. They were the most famous couple in the world and, as I had the privilege of discovering for myself, charming beyond belief.

Ben Solway had a pair of tickets for Burton's *Hamlet*, and he invited me to go with him. Burton, whom I'd only ever seen on film before, was wonderful in the role, but I did notice—because, of course, I knew the text by heart—that he made one slip. There's a passage in the soliloquy "O, what a rogue and peasant slave am I" that goes:

> Am I a coward?
> Who calls me villain, breaks my pate across,
> Plucks off my beard and blows it in my face,
> Tweaks me by the nose, gives me the lie i' th' throat
> As deep as to the lungs? Who does me this?

But what Burton actually said at the performance Ben and I attended was, "Who tweaks me by the nose and blows it in my face?" Then, realizing what he'd done, he spoke about 10 lines of something incomprehensible—I swear it was Welsh—while struggling to suppress his laughter. (David Francis, who saw my *Hamlet*, tells me that I made a *faux pas* of my own, in the scene where the players re-enact the murder of Hamlet's father to catch the conscience of the guilty Claudius. At one point in that scene, Hamlet comments, "Wormwood, wormwood." At the performance David saw, I apparently called out, "Woodworm, woodworm.")

Ben had proposed that I send a note backstage, explaining who I was and asking if I could meet Burton after the performance. An usher came to us at the intermission with the message that, indeed, he would be happy to receive a fellow Hamlet. So both Ben and I went backstage ("It's my goddamn ticket," said Ben: "I'm going with you") and met the star in his dressing room. We were received with impeccable hospitality.

"Do you drink?" Burton asked me.

"I wouldn't mind a drink, Mr. Burton," I replied.

"Good," he said. "All actors should drink." He poured me a large scotch. "Have you cut the soliloquies?"

"No," I said, "only one at the end, for time."

"Good. My friend Alan Badel is going to play Hamlet, and they're cutting all the soliloquies. I told him: you *can't*, you *can't*. It's *plot*, it's *plot*."

My awe at meeting Richard Burton was exceeded only by my awe at meeting the icon of feminine glamour who was also present in his dressing room: his wife-to-be, Elizabeth Taylor. She was then at the height of her beauty: a diminutive, fragile-looking woman with huge violet eyes. When she extended her tiny, delicate hand, I took it gingerly, as if I were handling a priceless piece of porcelain. I was rewarded with a crushing grip that would have made Charles Atlas yelp.

Burton was very generous to me. "I'd like to come and see your show," he said, with every appearance of sincerity: "I'm sure I can pick up some pointers from you. But every time Elizabeth and I go out, we're mobbed." Our brief conversation came to a close when a message arrived that the then premier of Ontario, John Robarts, wanted to meet the famous couple. Burton was all set to go, but Taylor tried to decline. Burton insisted that she go with him, whereupon she turned to me and sighed: "You know, I never do anything right. They ask me not to come to the play because it'll be distracting. Then they want me to show my face after all because they say it'll sell tickets."

I sent Burton and Taylor a pair of tickets for our production. They didn't come, of course, but Burton immediately took the trouble to write me an extremely gracious note, thanking me for the tickets and expressing his regrets that he hadn't been able to use them.

"I wanted and was planning to come so very much," he wrote. "It is, as I said in the dressing room, always good to see how some one else does a role one is playing."

He explained that he hadn't been able to attend the performance because he'd had a rehearsal, and added, "I hope that sending the tickets did not prevent you from having a completely full house!"

CHAPTER THREE

Wise Saws and Modern Instances

As You Like It, Act II, scene 7

After the Crest Theatre *Hamlet* closed at the end of March 1964, I was offered a summer season at the Loeb Drama Center in Massachusetts, a 550-seat theatre that had been founded four years earlier by the arts and sciences faculty at Harvard University. My roles were Berowne in *Love's Labour's Lost*, the Gardener and Mowbray in *Richard II* and the Third Gentleman in *The Winter's Tale*. It was Marigold Charlesworth and Jean Roberts, I believe, who had recommended me to the Loeb, a gesture of faith that I am sorry to say I rewarded with a juvenile prank.

The Third Gentleman's role in *The Winter's Tale* consists of a couple of speeches in Act V, outlining events that have happened offstage, to which I was convinced no one in the audience ever really listened. So I made a bet with someone else in the company that I could insert an invented line containing a reference to *The Tempest*—"If this be not true, I'll drown my book"—and no one would be any the wiser. Of course, I had failed to take into account the fact that this was Harvard. One night, the audience included the eminent Shakespearean scholar Arthur Colby Sprague, who immediately wrote—and posted on the bulletin board—a letter castigating the Loeb for allowing an actor to be so cavalier with Shakespeare's language. Another valuable lesson: there's always *somebody* who's listening and who notices when you don't deliver the proper goods.

On my return from Massachusetts, I resumed my studies at Loyola College but was again distracted by acting opportunities, one of them a role in a National Film Board docudrama about prisons, directed by Peter Pearson. It was filmed during two weeks over Christmas in a prison in Montreal, where we, the actors, rubbed shoulders with the real inmates. We were each put into our own individual cells to change into our convicts' garb and weren't summoned for what seemed like an hour, which may have been the director's way of getting us into the right frame of mind. If so, it worked. I thought they'd forgotten about me.

It certainly wasn't your average movie shoot. Once, when we were eating in the cafeteria during a break, an inmate pointed to the cook and said to me, "You see him? He used to be a doctor. He's in here because he killed his wife's baby, which he knew was by another man. He delivered the baby himself, and then he killed it by smashing it on the wall." I instantly lost my appetite.

Another of the inmates hanged himself while we were there, the news of which disturbed me greatly.

Having failed in 1963 to get into the Stratford Festival company, I had auditioned a second time the following year. Again, I had been rejected. Now, in the early spring of 1965, I had my third audition with Michael Langham. Third time lucky, I thought. The audition, however, did not go terribly well. As I stepped up onto the platform in the rehearsal hall to do my piece, I thought I heard Michael say something, so I replied, "I beg your pardon?" which drew from him a very blank look. I realized later that what I had heard was a squeaky floorboard. Then, halfway through my piece, I forgot the words. (In later years, whenever that happened to an actor auditioning for me, I'd say, "Don't worry. I dried in a Festival audition too.")

Michael Langham:
"The theatre is a fickle mistress"

When I was finished, Michael said to me, "Are you sure you want to do this? You know, the theatre is a fickle mistress."

"Oh, yes," I assured him, airily, "I know." Back then, of course, I knew no such thing, though in time I would come to regard Michael's remark as one of the great pillars of theatrical wisdom. He then told me, on the spot, that I would get an offer.

At the back of the Festival Theatre at the time were some bushes, behind which was a garden terraced with rock, sloping down to the grasslands below. As I left the building after my audition, in a fit of exuberance I leaped over the bushes, not quite realizing what was on the other side. I was wearing white jeans, so naturally I fell and slid all the way to the bottom. Fortunately, I didn't hurt myself, but I never got the grass stains out of those jeans.

I have always suspected that William Hutt, who had attended the opening night of my *Hamlet* in Toronto, had spoken to Michael Langham about me, though Bill has no recollection of doing so.

At any rate, on the first day of rehearsals for that 1965 season, when the company was gathered on the stage of the Festival Theatre for the traditional meet-and-greet, Bill came up to me and spoke the words to which he alludes in his foreword to this book: "Welcome home, Richard."

At the time, I didn't know quite why Bill said that or what he intended it to mean. After all, he couldn't have known about the disintegration of my actual home or about my quasi-religious experience on my second visit to Stratford six years earlier. All I knew was that it was one of the most encouraging remarks that had ever been made to me as an artist. And its significance to me has deepened immeasurably over time.

Here are two more pieces of theatrical wisdom that I have always treasured. One, which seems to contradict Michael Langham's remark about the theatre being a fickle mistress, was offered to me by actor Leo Ciceri during my first Stratford season. "Lovers come and go," he said, "but the theatre remains constant." There is, I have come to realize, truth in both Michael's and Leo's observations. My other favourite aphorism came from actor Len Doncheff, with whom I appeared in a production of Frank Wedekind's *Spring Awakening* in 1985 at CentreStage in Toronto. I was in the dressing room whining about something when Len rebuked me with these words: "Richard, the theatre takes what it needs, not what you have to offer it."

That would have been a good motto for my first season at Stratford. Having already got the longest role in Shakespeare under my belt, I felt I had plenty of the most eloquent music to offer the Festival. What the Festival needed from me in 1965, though, were a wordless presence as Lord Harcourt (whose few lines had been cut) in *Henry IV*, Parts 1 and 2, directed by Stuart Burge, and a single line of dialogue as Dardanius in *Julius Caesar*, directed by Douglas Campbell. I was also to understudy William Needles as Yepihodov in Chekhov's *The Cherry Orchard*.

As I remember it, my one line in *Julius Caesar* was "What, I, my lord? No, not for all the world." It comes toward the end of the play when Brutus asks Dardanius and another minor character, Clitus, to help him end his life. For years, I have been certain that those were the first words I spoke on a Stratford stage. But recently I made the fatal mistake of checking the text of *Julius Caesar*, wherein I found that "What, I, my lord?" is said not by Dardanius but by Clitus, played in our production by an actor called Henry Hovenkamp. Perhaps the characters' lines were reassigned, though the prompt script in the Festival Archives gives no indication that this was so. I can offer no explanation for this anomaly. White carpets and chandeliers, anyone?

Two aspects of that *Julius Caesar* stand out clearly in my mind. One was a long crowd scene in which we had to generate mutinous "rhubarb" noises: "Pluck down images!" "Smash statues!" "Death

My first Stratford Festival season: as Dardanius (far left, foreground) in *Julius Caesar*, 1965, with Henry Hovencamp as Clitus, William Hutt as Brutus, Roland Hewgill as Volumnius and Edward Rudney as Strato

to tyrants!" or whatever else we could think of to say. One of our number, Eric Christmas (a wonderful comedian, now deceased), would run around shouting, "Rip paper! Rip paper!"

The other thing that impressed me was the way that William Hutt, as Brutus, dared to use his own Canadian voice. At the time, the accepted pronunciation for North American actors doing Shakespeare was the so-called mid-Atlantic accent, which offered clarity of diction without evoking any identifiable geographical region. This was what I had learned under Eleanor Stuart, and it did have its advantages: it didn't distract the listener by drawing attention to itself. But it was also disempowering. Speaking with that accent, you were, quite literally, neither here nor there: it divested you of personality. I was startled to hear Bill, who could do anything he chose to with his voice, sounding on stage like what he was: Canadian. I had the feeling that it was a very political decision on his part.

When Robin Phillips became the Festival's artistic director in 1975, he insisted that actors use their own native accents—Canadian, British or whatever—when playing Shakespeare, and that is still the usual practice today. Exceptions are sometimes made, though, when a director wants to locate a Shakespeare play in some particular milieu, such as 20th-century "Noo Yawk." A favourite story around the Festival concerns the late Michael Mawson, a staunch Canadian, who was playing Ægeon in *The Comedy of Errors* in 1994. It was an aggressively contemporary production, dressed in Armani-style suits, and the director, Richard Rose (also Canadian), was trying to get Michael to use the American pronunciation of the word *duke*.

"Don't say 'dyook,' Michael," urged Richard. "Say 'dook.'"

"I can't say 'dook,'" replied Michael. "It would make me pook."

One of the ways I learned about acting Shakespeare was by listening to spoken-word records. I had recordings of, among others, Laurence Olivier as Hamlet and Henry V, of Charles Laughton and Orson Welles, and of John Gielgud doing the "seven ages of man" speech from *As You Like It*, and I would make careful note of every nuance of phrasing, intonation and emphasis. I had plenty of backstage time on my hands during performances of *Julius Caesar* and the two parts of *Henry IV*, and since I was already in the habit of listening, I didn't while it away by reading or doing crossword puzzles, as more experienced actors might; instead, I listened to every performance on the Tannoy in my dressing room.

Shakespeare's verse has a great pulse and rhythm, and here was an unparalleled opportunity for me to study how Canada's finest actors—Douglas Campbell, Peter Donat, William Hutt, Frances Hyland, Douglas Rain, Kate Reid, Tony van Bridge and many others—spoke that verse. It was like listening in on a master class every night. Douglas Rain, for instance, gave a brilliant performance as Prince Hal, and when I came to play the role myself some years later, I remembered every single line reading he gave. I made my own choices, of course, but they were informed by my memories of what he had done.

I also took part in two in-house workshops that summer, to prove to the Festival that I could in fact act. One was a new Canadian play that had not hitherto been performed: John Herbert's *Fortune and Men's Eyes*, the subject matter of which—society's inhumane attitude toward homosexuality, which was still a criminal offence at the time, and the appalling conditions that existed within Canada's prison system—I considered to be of great importance, particularly after my experience on the NFB penitentiary film that past winter. The other workshop, directed by William Hutt, was of Arthur Miller's *Incident at Vichy*. One of the characters in that play is an actor, a Jew, who has books in his library that are on the Nazis' list of prohibited titles. When the Germans enter Paris, he gathers all those books together, wraps them up carefully and hides them in sewers all over the city. When he returns home from doing this, however, he realizes that he has left his name written in every single one.

Bill asked us why we thought the character allowed this to happen. We offered various reasons, none of them entirely convincing. Finally, Bill offered a reason of his own: "Perhaps it's because every actor secretly wants to reveal himself: to expose his inner self." I remember thinking at the time that this was probably true of me.

That winter found me again juggling my professional engagements and my much-interrupted studies—not at Loyola College now but at York University, to which I had transferred because I wanted to be in Toronto, where the work was. Among other things, I was invited back to the Crest Theatre to play Simon Bliss in Noël Coward's *Hay Fever*, with Susan Clark—who went on to win an Emmy Award for her portrayal of Olympic gold medallist Babe Didrikson Zaharias in the 1975 TV movie *Babe*—as my sister, Sorel. Mary Savidge played Judith Bliss, and the production (described by Nathan Cohen as a "conspiracy to erase what remains of poor Mr. Coward's reputation") was directed by her husband, Joseph Shaw, who has been one of my dearest friends ever since.

I was startled by how Joseph and Mary used to shriek at each other in rehearsal: it was my first real experience of theatrical temperament. But then perhaps they didn't realize they were doing it. Once, after a run-through, Joseph asked me, "Richard, why are you screaming?" I had no idea I'd been doing so: another example of the gulf between what you *think* you're doing and what the audience perceives.

I had a sharp lesson of quite a different sort one afternoon when I went to a friend's house and had two martinis at around three o'clock, quite forgetting that I had a performance to do at five o'clock that afternoon and another at eight. I don't know if I was actually drunk or just terrified that I might be drunk, but I was in a complete panic. Though I got through the show all right, I vowed from that day on never again to drink before a performance—a vow that I managed to keep with, I think, only one exception, and that was under circumstances of considerable stress. (Those circumstances are described in Chapter Five.)

As Sebastian in *Twelfth Night* (Stratford Festival, 1966), with Martha Henry as Viola

The next season at Stratford, 1966, David William was directing *Twelfth Night* with Martha Henry as Viola, and he needed someone to play Sebastian, Viola's twin brother. He took me for a walk on the soccer field behind the theatre, near where I'd had my inadvertent triumphal slide, and asked me, "Do you know who Carl Jung is?" When I said I did, he proceeded to discuss Jung's ideas about twins and about finding your other half. Fortunately, I'd read enough Jung to know what he was talking about, and I got the role.

Martha and I would do our makeup together, trying to make ourselves look as much like each other as possible. She'd try to give herself a cleft in her chin, like mine, and I would try to widen my eyes, like hers. The first time we did this was for a publicity photo shoot, and when we emerged from the dressing room and went out on the stage, we received a round of applause from our fellow actors. The photos from that shoot show us both with moles on our foreheads. There's a point in the play where Viola says, "My father had a mole upon his brow," and Sebastian replies, "And so had mine," so we thought our characters might each have inherited this trait. We thought better of it later and dispensed with the moles.

We seemed to do a good job of being each other's alter egos: every time we reached that magical moment near the end of the play when the two are finally reunited, the audience audibly gasped. Again, though, I seemed blithely unaware of my actions in that scene, which required me to occupy centre stage without speaking, just listening to the other characters. I thought that was exactly what I was doing, until Eric Donkin, who was playing Antonio, said to me, "Do you realize you're mouthing everybody else's words?"

Roberta Maxwell: a long-enduring friendship

The part of Olivia was played by Roberta Maxwell, a splendid actress with whom I formed an extremely close friendship that endured for many years and generated many letters between us. (In 1994, the first season of my tenure as artistic director, she played Sganarelle's Wife and Lisette in *Husbands and Cuckolds*, a double bill of two comedies by Molière, and I have always regretted that I did not manage to find other roles for her in subsequent seasons.)

One day early on in our friendship, Roberta and I were walking along one of Stratford's residential streets when we inadvertently obstructed the progress of a child on a bicycle. He couldn't have been more than five or six years old, but he decided to let us have a piece of his mind by screaming at us the worst insult he could think of: "You . . . you . . . *actors!*" It was my first experience of the peculiar mindset that still exists among a few Stratford residents who seem never to have forgiven the Festival for coming along in 1953 and preventing the city from disappearing off the map after the death of the railway industry that had previously driven its economy.

Another example of hostility toward the theatrical profession occurred in my third season at Stratford when I was walking past a downtown pharmacy with two other male members of the company. Some teenage youths were hanging about outside, and, as we passed them, they offered us a greeting of a sort traditionally accorded to any man who dares to become involved in the arts: "Hey, fags!" Unfortunately for these louts, one of our number had some training as a pugilist, and in one smooth movement he turned and single-handedly levelled all three of them to the ground. I was agog. I'd never seen anything like it before, nor have I since, and I regarded our avenging angel with awe and admiration from that moment on.

The 1966 season also included a version of *Henry VI*, directed by John Hirsch and designed by Desmond Heeley. We used a script that had been prepared for the Royal Shakespeare Company by John Barton, who had edited down Shakespeare's original trilogy into one play. (Among ourselves, we called it "Henry VI, Parts One-and-a-Half.") I had several non-speaking roles in the production, including a fiend from hell, one of several conjured up by the "witch" Joan of Arc. My fellow fiends and I, wearing headpieces with eyeballs sticking out on springs, would come on from the "voms," the two tunnels that open onto the stage from under the seating in the Festival Theatre auditorium. *Vom* is short for *vomitorium*, a Latin word that Tanya Moiseiwitsch, the designer of the stage, disliked intensely, perhaps because it conjured up visions of ancient Romans sticking feathers down the backs of their throats to make themselves throw up. However, this common belief that a vomitorium was a place where decadent banqueters made room in their stomachs for more gourmandizing is mistaken. In ancient Rome, the word meant what it means now: a passageway from which large numbers of people can disgorge themselves into an open space.

Anyway, the fiends' headpieces were preset for us in the voms, ready for us to put on just before we entered. At one performance, I went to my place only to find that my headpiece was missing. This was a problem: I couldn't go out on stage just looking like an ordinary soldier. There was, however, a bucket of stage blood there, waiting to be used for a later battle scene. In a moment of inspiration, I grabbed the bucket and emptied its entire contents over my head. At least I would look like *something* hellish. Martha Henry, who was playing Joan, looked at me *very* strangely: I hope she doesn't still think it was a prank.

Meanwhile, Michael Langham was revisiting his legendary *Henry V* of 10 years earlier, in which francophone actors from Montreal's Théâtre du Nouveau Monde had played the members of the French court. With the Vietnam War now at its height, the 1966 production was darker and more cynical than its 1956 predecessor, in which Christopher Plummer had played the victor of Agincourt in full romantic-heroic mode. This time around, Douglas Rain was in the title role, and again Michael had enlisted Québécois actors—Jacques Galipeau, Jean Gascon, Gaëtan Labrèche, Diana Leblanc, Guy L'Ecuyer, Denise Pelletier, Jean-Louis Roux and Marcel Sabourin—to make up the French court. Those actors, many of whom I had seen perform at TNM in my teens, had a wonderful sense of style and *joie de vivre*: I remember vividly the elaborate picnics, with delicious pâtés and champagne, that they enjoyed on their days off.

Desmond Heeley's sketch of the fiends in *Henry VI*

Michael had asked me if I could do a French accent. I'd said I could and was cast as Montjoy, the French herald. (I've been told that people still remember with delight my pronunciation of Montjoy's first line: "You know me by my *habite*.")

Montjoy has three scenes in which he arrives with messages that are important to the plot and in which he has to maintain an air of haughty superiority toward the English king—in this case, Douglas Rain, an actor of whom I, at the age of 21, was quite simply terrified. To complicate matters, I had to come on with a standard—a flag on a long pole—and I had no idea how to handle such an unwieldy prop. I had to go for help to William Hutt, who gave me private lessons in standard-bearing in his living room.

As Douglas and I rehearsed these scenes, something odd began to happen. We had been blocked—"blocking" being theatrical parlance for the positioning of actors on stage—with Douglas standing centre stage and me at the mouth of one of the two voms. But each time we rehearsed, Douglas would place himself a little closer to the mouth of the vom opposite mine. In order to keep him in sight and maintain the onstage relationship between us, I was forced to emerge further and further from my vom. This went on at every rehearsal until I found myself playing the scene practically centre stage.

This was not only disconcerting but puzzling: why would a senior actor yield centre stage to a relative newcomer? Eventually, I realized that Douglas wanted to see if I could hold the stage. He was teaching me that when two people are playing a scene, regardless of where they have been placed by the director, each of them has to be good enough to merit a central position.

As Montjoy in *Henry V* at Stratford in 1966

He had another example in store for me. In performance, my second scene always won me a round of applause as I exited, after which there was a bit of business in which Douglas threw a purse of gold to someone. On one particular occasion, he threw the purse early, before I had quite left, which distracted the audience enough to prevent them from applauding. Afterwards, Douglas said to me, "You didn't get your round tonight."

"No, Mr. Rain," I replied with remarkable frankness, given my terror of him, "because you didn't give it to me."

Douglas looked at me inscrutably, then winked, and thereafter he always waited till I had gone before he threw the purse. By replying as I did, I had shown that I understood that it takes both people in a scene to get a round of applause. I remember him saying something, too, during that production that further illustrated the point that creating a moment in the theatre—or, indeed, a role—is a collaborative effort. "*I* don't play the king," he said. "Everyone *around* me plays the king."

The advice that would have the profoundest effect on me in my future as an artist, however, came from Michael Langham. Clearly at one point in rehearsal I was being a little too theatrical, for Michael came over to me and said, very simply, "Richard, acting is *being*." This remark, connecting itself in my mind with Bill Hutt's observation the previous season about actors wanting to reveal themselves, sparked a flash of insight. Up to that point, I had always thought of a role as something you *put on*, like a putty nose or a wig or a false moustache. In fact, a role is something you find within yourself: not a putting on but a drawing out, as Miss Jean Brodie would say. Though it took me another 10 years to learn how to fully put this into practice, Michael's remark became the fourth and most fundamental pillar of wisdom that has guided me throughout my career in the theatre.

On the closing night of *Henry V*, Michael came backstage, accompanied by an extremely tall man whom he did not introduce. I have no way of corroborating this, but I believe it was Tyrone Guthrie. I wish I'd had the courage to ask, for if it was Guthrie, then that was the only time I have ever been in his presence. Then, to my bewilderment, Michael started to give us notes on our performances. I said: "Michael, we've closed. Why are you giving us notes?" He replied, casually, "Oh, you never know when you might play this again." He must already have been aware that a taping of the production for CTV television was being planned for the following year. It was shot in a studio in, of all places, the Toronto suburb of Agincourt.

At the end of the season, on Michael Langham's advice, I returned to Montreal, transferred back to Loyola and, resisting for the time being the temptation to seek out any more acting work, at last completed my BA. I was then invited back to Stratford for a third season in 1967, Canada's centennial year.

That season, Alan Bates was playing the title role in *Richard III*, directed by John Hirsch. A Hungarian-born Holocaust survivor, John was a brilliant director, but he had his own quirky ways of communicating with actors. In *Richard III*, I played one of a flurry of messengers who come on in Act IV, scene 4, bringing the king news of various defections and insurrections. My lines were informational to the point of absurdity: something in the nature of "Sussex has gone to Essex, and Essex has gone to Wessex, and saucy Worcester is dead." I exaggerate, but still. . . . In rehearsals for this, John stopped me and said, "Richard, Richard, vot are you doing?"

I said, "Well, what would you like me to do, Mr. Hirsch?" (I called everyone "Mister" in those days, not just people I was afraid of.)

He replied, "I vould like you to sound like you're a public microphone."

So the next time we did it, I tried my best to sound like someone making an announcement over a loudspeaker. Again he stopped me. "Richard, Richard, vot are you doing?"

John Hirsch: brilliant but quirky

"Well, Mr. Hirsch, last time you asked me to do it like a public microphone."

"A public microphone? No, no; I vant you to be naturalistic."

So the next time, I tried to make this most unnatural of speeches sound like ordinary conversation. John stopped me again. "Richard, Richard, vot are you doing?"

"Well, Mr. Hirsch, first you asked me to do it like a public microphone; then you asked me to do it naturalistically, so I'm doing it naturalistically. I'm confused: what *do* you want?"

"Vot do I *vant*? I vant you to sound like a *naturalistic public microphone*."

John had also directed that *Cherry Orchard* in 1965, in which I'd understudied Bill Needles. I'm not fond of Chekhov, but that production and a *Three Sisters* that John directed in 1976 are still two of the best productions of any play that I've ever seen. Kate Reid, who played Madame Ranevskaya, was simply wonderful. But I remember a dress rehearsal in which she was having some difficulty with her props. She had three things to handle at the same time, as I recall: a purse and a piece of paper and a handkerchief. John, watching from the auditorium, was wearing track pants, his usual mode of dress. As Kate fumbled with her purse, John suddenly yelled out: "Look at her! Look at her! This expensive actress cannot use props! Look at her!" And then he grabbed hold of the waistband of his track pants and pulled it right over his head. It was something he did when he was overwrought. He was such a colourful character. And brilliant.

Kate was one of those great actresses who have a visceral quality to them. She once said to me something about playing Shakespeare that put me in mind of my travails with Eleanor Stuart over the yoke of inauspicious stars: "If you get one line right a night, you're doing well."

In John's production of *Richard III*, Lady Anne was played by Zoe Caldwell. She and Alan Bates were superb in their main scene together: absolutely electric. But at one early performance, Zoe turned to me as she was waiting to go on stage and said, "I've lost what I had in this scene, haven't I?" And I, not knowing if I was doing the right thing, but feeling instinctively that she wanted a truthful answer, gave it to her: "Yes."

It was true: the scene was no longer as powerful as it had been in rehearsal. But what astounded me was that an actress of her stature would ask me, a relative beginner in the business, so direct a question. It was an extraordinary gesture of respect toward a fellow artist of infinitely lesser experience, and I hoped that the honesty of my answer was equally respectful of her as someone who was clearly more interested in her art than in her ego. In any case, she regained every particle of the electricity that the scene had formerly had.

I had two other roles that season: Peter Simple in David William's production of *The Merry Wives of Windsor* and Eros in Michael Langham's production of *Antony and Cleopatra*. Roberta played Ann Page in *Merry Wives* (which, as it turned out, would be the last production we'd act in together). During rehearsals for it, Leon Pownall, who was playing Bardolph, became a father and named his son Peter. The character I was playing is, as his name suggests, a simple, open person, an innocent, and so I kept in my mind an image of the most innocent person I knew of at the time: Leon's newborn baby. When Leon complimented me on my performance, I replied, "Well, I based Peter Simple on your son." I didn't mean that the way it must have sounded, but Leon took great offence and was very angry with me for a while. Nearly 40 years later, in 2006, I told Peter this story at his father's memorial service. He was amazed.

Christopher Plummer and Zoe Caldwell played the title roles in *Antony and Cleopatra*, and I will never forget something that Zoe did in the final scene. She'd applied henna to her hands, and this caused her to hold them away from her body, open, as if in supplication. I thought it was a fantastic choice: a simple technical thing that gave this immensely regal character just the right touch of vulnerability—not just to her enemies in the play but to the audience as well.

Zoe Caldwell as the titular queen of Egypt in Stratford's 1967 *Antony and Cleopatra*

Rehearsals for the production had to start without Chris, who was off in Greece shooting the film *Oedipus the King*, and so his understudy, Max Helpmann, stood in for him as we worked out the blocking. Near the end of the play, Antony asks Eros to kill him. (Assisted-suicide requests seemed to be becoming the hallmark of my participation in the Roman plays.) Rather than stab Antony, however, Eros falls on the sword himself. Self-stabbing is always a tricky thing to pull off convincingly on stage, and I had a bright idea about how to do it. I would go up to Antony and point the blade of the sword at his heart, while holding on to his shoulder with my other hand. Then I would suddenly clasp our bodies together. As I did so, I would reverse the direction of the sword, so that when we fell apart again, it would be revealed that my character had in fact impaled himself. If I could do this adroitly enough, there would be some ambiguity (for the audience and possibly also for Antony himself) about which of us had actually been stabbed. It would be like that movie cliché where two people struggle for a gun, a shot goes off, and then there's a moment's pause until one of them realizes he's the one who's been shot and sinks to the floor.

I tried this out with Max, and Michael Langham approved it. Then Chris arrived back from his movie shoot. Christopher Plummer was one of my idols: I had seen him act several times at Stratford before, and to be on stage with him was somewhat intimidating, to say the least. When we came to rehearse the stabbing scene with him, I looked over inquiringly at Michael. He gave no reaction, so I assumed he had explained to our leading man what I intended to do. So I went up to Chris, put my arm round his shoulder, clasped him to me in an embrace of death, then started to fall backwards. Taken completely by surprise, Chris caught me before I hit the floor, looked up at Michael and said, "What the f___ is going on here?"

As Eros (right), about to do the decent thing by Christopher Plummer's Antony

Michael, who had a mischievous streak in him, said, "Richard, you explain this to Chris."

"No, Mr. Langham," I said, "I think you'd better explain this to Mr. Plummer." And I promptly left the rehearsal hall. The next day, Chris came up to me in the Greenroom, the Festival Theatre's dining area, and said, "That was a very good idea you had." So we kept it in.

In 1996, Chris returned to Stratford after a long absence to perform in *Barrymore* at the Avon Theatre. As an opening-night gift, I gave him a photograph that was taken of that scene during the run of *Antony and Cleopatra*, on which I had inscribed the words "Portrait of a young artist and future artistic director dying in the arms of a star."

Another memorable example of the mischievousness of Michael Langham arose during the scene of "Egyptian bacchanals" on board Pompey's galley, which Michael wanted played as an out-and-out orgy. So among other things, he asked me and Al Kozlik, who was playing Decretas, to kiss and simulate sex.

Al and I didn't know each other terribly well. "Al, do you *mind* doing this?" I asked.

"No-o-o," he replied, cautiously but gamely. So we went to't.

"You know," I said to him as we cavorted, "the audience isn't going to listen to one word of this scene. I bet you this business will be cut." And sure enough, after we'd done it twice in rehearsal, Michael said, in a note session, "Al, Richard: from here on, conduct your personal lives at home."

In those first three Festival seasons, I worked with directors of the very first rank: Stuart Burge, Douglas Campbell, John Hirsch, Michael Langham and David William. I studied their work, their very different approaches and techniques, and from all of them I learned something that would be invaluable to me in my later career as a director. But it was from Michael in particular that I learned how to use the Festival Theatre's thrust stage.

Michael once said, "If Shakespeare were alive today, he'd be writing movie scripts." What he meant was that a Shakespeare play, with its constant changes of scene, is like a screenplay. It's constantly ahead of you, one scene overlapping into the next, which is precisely why Tyrone Guthrie wanted that innovative stage in the first place. Consequently, when Michael blocked a play, he'd always be moving it forward. As one scene would end, say, at the mouth of the vom, another would already be beginning up on the balcony. He was like a choreographer: he always kept people moving. As a result, his productions had an enormous energy and thrust, both in terms of their narrative and in terms of how the verse was spoken. He was a master, and I stole from him everything that I could.

There remained another factor that would have an enormous influence on my work, even though I thought I had turned my back on it: the Catholic Church. It has, for instance, been pointed out to me that in my productions I have presented priests and other churchmen as figures of great power and influence (for good or evil), even when this is not called for in the text. For example, in my 1996 production of *King Lear*, Geordie Johnson, who was playing the hypocritical villain Edmund, was costumed as a priest. By making this choice, I wasn't trying to denigrate the priesthood. To someone of my background, priestly garb is an automatic signifier of trustworthiness, and so the device was simply my instinctive answer to the question of why everyone else in the play so readily accepts Edmund's lies. Of course, the patrons who wrote in to complain didn't quite see it that way.

No doubt my lapsed Catholicism also reveals itself in elements of visual splendour in my productions. The Catholic Church knows how to lay on the pageantry, and so do I. At the same time, the sort of "Technicolor moments" that I experienced at *The Wizard of Oz* and *Jenny Kissed Me,* and that I have often tried to achieve in my own productions, don't necessarily involve spectacle. What the French call a *coup de théâtre* needn't be a falling chandelier or a helicopter descending *ex machina.* It can be as simple as a gesture or an unexpected stage movement. I shall never forget Susan Wright, playing Paulina in David William's 1986 production of *The Winter's Tale,* throwing herself on the ground to deliver one of her speeches: an utterly simple but extraordinarily effective physical articulation of the scene. Never one to balk at stealing a good idea, I had Seana McKenna do the same thing in 2004 as Katherine of Aragon in *King Henry VIII.* Again, the effect was riveting.

Toward the end of the 1967 season, Michael Langham's last as artistic director, I received an offer for the following year, in which Jean Gascon would share the artistic leadership with John Hirsch. Michael said to me, "The new people who are coming in after me really think highly of your work," and indeed my offer was a good one: Valère in *Tartuffe* and Demetrius in *A Midsummer Night's Dream.* But the playbill also included *Romeo and Juliet,* and in the company at the time were a number of younger actors—among them Neil Dainard, Briain Petchey, Leon Pownall, Kenneth Welsh and, well, me—whom I considered eminently qualified to play Romeo. Instead, it had been decided to bring in someone from New York—not a star, but an unknown 23-year-old who had never, as far as I knew, done any Shakespeare at all.

As it happened, I had seen the actor in question perform in Tennessee Williams's *The Rose Tattoo,* and I had to admit that he was extremely good-looking, to the point of being beautiful. But to bring in a nonentity from outside who had no other obvious qualifications for the role felt wrong to me, both personally and politically. I believed that such an institution as Stratford should, for the sake of its own continuity and indeed for the sake of the country, try to cultivate its own younger actors and help them rise to the challenges of the great roles. Otherwise, there could be no real future there for people like me. I felt so strongly about this that I turned my offer down.

The "nonentity" engaged to play Romeo was in fact the young Christopher Walken, a fine actor who subsequently became a huge film star, so bringing him in was rather more far-sighted than I had given the Festival credit for. But my decision to leave, in which I remained adamant even when Jean Gascon himself phoned and urged me to reconsider, was still the right one for me. There was a world elsewhere, and I had other lessons to learn.

Late one night that October, when the season had just ended, I stole into the darkened Festival Theatre. My contract was not yet over, because the Festival was taking two of the season's productions, *Antony and Cleopatra* and *The Government Inspector*, on tour to Expo 67 in Montreal. (I was in the former, and Roberta was in the latter, so our farewells to each other would be postponed for a little while longer.) But I wasn't coming back to Stratford, and I had no idea if I would ever again perform in that wonderful space. Maybe the theatre was a fickle mistress, but in this case it was I who was walking out the door, after having tried so hard to get in.

I went up on the stage and reached out my hand to touch the fabled central pillar of the on-stage balcony: the spot that Guthrie and his designer, Tanya Moiseiwitsch, had decreed should be the absolute centre of the building. It was a deeply spiritual gesture: a kind of homage to something larger and more enduring than myself—a sacrament I was performing in a temple from which I might well have just permanently banished myself by turning down a perfectly good offer.

After some time, I suddenly became aware that I was not alone. Someone else was on the stage with me. Peering at the newcomer, I realized that it was Roberta, obeying the same impulse that had brought me to that centre pillar.

We stood there together in the dark, saying goodbye.

CHAPTER FOUR

With Speed to England

Hamlet, Act III, scene 1

The spring of the previous year, 1966, had seen the demise of two of Canada's pioneering theatrical ventures: the Crest Theatre and the Canadian Players. The latter had been created in 1954 by Tom Patterson, founder of the Stratford Festival, and Douglas Campbell, and for the next decade it had presented touring productions of the classics across Canada and, on occasion, in the United States. In 1965 the company had modified its focus, continuing to tour but also establishing a home base in Toronto's Central Library Theatre, with Marigold Charlesworth as its artistic director and Jean Roberts as its administrator. Unfortunately, that season's perhaps overly ambitious program had resulted in a substantial deficit. Meanwhile, the Crest Theatre had had its funding withdrawn by the Canada Council. Both the Crest and the Canadian Players thus found themselves in serious financial straits at the same time. Their respective boards tried to save the situation by forming a merged entity, the Crest Canadian Players Foundation, but this last-ditch effort was unable to prevent the two companies from passing into history.

From the wreckage emerged a new company with a new mandate, Theatre Toronto. It was the brainchild of William Graham, president of the Crest Canadian Players Foundation, who declared in an interview with the Toronto *Telegram* that if he never saw the plays of Strindberg, Shaw and Shakespeare again, it would be too soon. "Canadian theatre has lived so completely in the past for so long," he said, "it has completely lost touch with anyone under the age of 60." Theatre Toronto, he promised, would be "a completely contemporary theatre, bringing to Toronto new plays that have attracted serious critical attention."

To achieve this, the new company went shopping for an artistic director with an international reputation. They wanted Peter Ustinov, but in the end they settled for someone who wasn't as universally known but whose star was fast rising in England and elsewhere. He had the same agent as Ustinov, and his name was Clifford Williams.

The inaugural 12-week season that Clifford put together, to be presented early in 1968, would consist of four plays in repertory, beginning, daringly enough, with the world première of a new Canadian drama: *The Drummer Boy*, an English translation of *Joli tambour* by Jean Basile. Auditions were held in the fall of 1967, around the time I was deciding not to return to Stratford. I'd heard that they wanted to find someone "off the street" to play the title role in *The Drummer Boy*, that of a 19-year-old boy accused of raping an 11-year-old girl. At the same time, the role was a substantial one, while the formality and period setting of the play, which was loosely based on events that occurred in New France in the 1750s, called for actors with classical skills. I auditioned for Clifford and got the part, thus becoming part of a company that included, among others, Bernard Behrens, John Colicos, Colin Fox, Amelia Hall, Barbara Hamilton and my friend and mentor from the Crest's *Hay Fever*, Joseph Shaw.

I would come to have great respect for Clifford Williams, who would play a significant role in my artistic life over the next couple of years. Born in 1926 in Cardiff, Wales, where his father was a plumber, he'd started out as a ballet dancer, something you'd never have guessed from his short, stocky build. As he told it, he'd thought in his teens that ballet would be a good way to meet girls, and so he'd auditioned for a small company called the Anglo-Russian Ballet. He'd got in, he said, because there was a wartime shortage of men strong enough to lift ballerinas. Later, he'd served in the army, then devoted himself to the theatre, acting at the Royal Shakespeare Company and with Joan Littlewood's Theatre Workshop, directing at the Arts Theatre in London and forming the first professional mime company in Britain.

Joseph Shaw in the title role of *Julius Caesar* at the Stratford Festival in 1965

In the early 1960s, he'd obtained a staff position with the RSC and almost immediately scored a huge hit with a production of *The Comedy of Errors*, whereupon he'd been promoted to the post of associate director. He would go on to direct dozens of other productions at the RSC in the decades to come, while also working in commercial theatre around the world. He had patiently built his career brick by brick, through many years of hard work and perseverance, and was one of the most balanced and imperturbable directors I have ever known.

One of the things that excited people about Theatre Toronto was that it wasn't going to be a shoestring operation. A lot of money had been raised—it was rumoured at the time that Clifford's salary would be in the neighbourhood of $40,000, which in 1968 was an astronomical sum—and the performances were going to take place in Toronto's flagship venue, the recently renovated Royal Alexandra Theatre. Till then, the Royal Alex had been exclusively a road house, home to touring productions and big stars from abroad, many of whom I'd seen perform there. It was, and is, a beautiful theatre, steeped in glamour, and I was thrilled to think that I would actually be performing on its stage.

As Denis Quévillon, the title character in Theatre Toronto's *The Drummer Boy* in 1968

I was also impressed by the generosity, boldness and community spirit shown by the theatre's owner, Ed Mirvish. To agree to house a new home-grown company, making its debut not with a proven New York or London hit but with a new Canadian play, in an era when the phrase "Canadian play" was practically a synonym for "commercial disaster," was an act of great courage and great faith, and Ed deserves full credit for it.

The Drummer Boy opened on January 17, 1968. At first, it didn't seem as if the new venture was going to get off to an auspicious start: the first actor to speak walked on stage, dried stone dead and walked right off again. However, we quickly recovered and went on to enjoy something of a triumph. Excitingly staged by Clifford, the play was almost guaranteed to provoke controversy: as if the subject of child rape weren't shocking enough, there was a graphic prison scene in which my character was beaten and subjected to an attempted forcible sodomization by the other inmates. Still, the critics responded favourably, for the most part. Herbie Whittaker called the show "dark, powerful and ambiguous," though Nathan Cohen, of course, dismissed it as "a sputtering jumble" and "a quivering botch."

Audiences, the only critics who count, received us enthusiastically, though I do remember that on opening night one resounding "Boo!" rang out from the auditorium. I was surprised, and a little disappointed, to be told later that it had come from the playwright John Herbert, whose *Fortune and Men's Eyes* I had workshopped at Stratford. I never did find out what it was, particularly, that he had objected to.

Though I played the title role, the star of *The Drummer Boy* was John Colicos, who played a Jesuit priest. A brilliant actor who took his work very seriously, John nonetheless had a chronic problem with the giggles in one particular scene that he shared with me. They occurred during a speech in which he had to describe my character's crime in words so ludicrously arcane that they sounded like gibberish. Despite the grimness of its subject (or perhaps because of it), John found the language of this speech utterly hilarious, and he always had the greatest difficulty getting through it without breaking up. On one occasion, he resorted to smashing his hand down hard on the table, hoping that the pain would sober him up; the shock of it, however, just made him laugh all the more. One night the problem became so acute that he actually had to walk off stage in the middle of the scene.

John later became a well-known face on television, particularly in science fiction. Among countless other roles, he played Count Baltar in the original *Battlestar Galactica* series and was the first actor to portray a Klingon in the original series of *Star Trek*.

The second production to open in our repertory was Jules Feiffer's satirical comedy *Little Murders*, in which I played Kenny. Directed by Peggy Ashcroft's son, Nick Hutchinson (who later started the Caravan Farm Theatre in Vancouver and became a director of the National Theatre School), it wasn't as well received as *The Drummer Boy*, though I personally was gratified to be told by Feiffer himself that I was the best Kenny he'd ever seen.

What earned Theatre Toronto its place in theatrical history, however, was that season's third production: the North American première of *Soldiers* by the German playwright Rolf Hochhuth.

On the other side of the Atlantic, *Soldiers* had become a public scandal long before it even reached the stage. It was, you might say, a *cause célèbre* championed by an *enfant terrible*, the *enfant* in question being one of the most controversial figures of British theatre in the 1960s, Kenneth Tynan.

A graduate of Magdalen College, Oxford, where his flamboyance of dress and manner had rivalled that of Oscar Wilde three-quarters of a century earlier, Tynan had risen to prominence in the mid-1950s, as the brilliant theatre critic for the London *Observer*. Then, in 1963, he'd traded in his newspaper job for that of dramaturge when Laurence Olivier, artistic director of Britain's newly established National Theatre, had hired him as his literary manager. But Tynan's was a name familiar even to people who'd never been near a theatre in their lives: besides being a vocal advocate for sexual freedom and a defender of pornography, he'd achieved nationwide notoriety when, on a late-night talk show on November 13, 1965, he'd become the first person to use the f-word on British television.

Kenneth Tynan, critic and controversialist

When Tynan first saw a draft of *Soldiers* in 1966, he'd immediately embraced it as just the kind of fiercely controversial material he wanted the National to present. Not only did Hochhuth's play question the morality of the Allied bombing of German cities during the Second World War, it also put forth the startling claim that Winston Churchill—who had died in 1965, almost universally revered as his country's wartime saviour—had orchestrated the death, in a 1943 plane crash, of the Polish general Wladyslaw Sikorski.

Hochhuth claimed that proof of this allegation was held in secret vaults in Switzerland, though no such evidence was ever produced.

Tynan had succeeded in persuading Olivier of the play's importance, but both were overruled by the National's board, which unanimously and publicly rejected *Soldiers* as "unsuitable for production." (The board's chairman, Oliver Lyttelton, who'd been created Viscount Chandos in 1954, had been opposed from the beginning to being associated with "so grotesque and grievous a libel.") Tynan, who had obtained the English-language performance rights, then sought to produce the play himself, only to run afoul of the archaic censorship laws that at that time still had a stranglehold on British theatre. Under legislation dating back to 1737, every new play had to be submitted to the Lord Chamberlain's Office for vetting before it could be performed. The Lord Chamberlain had the power to demand changes or deletions in the script, or to forbid its production entirely, and he could do so not only on the predictable grounds of bad language or indecency but also in cases where a living person was depicted in an unfavourable light. Aside from its allegation about Churchill, by then safely dead, *Soldiers* painted an unflattering portrait of the still-living Sir Arthur "Bomber" Harris, head of Bomber Command during the war, and that, as far as the British establishment was concerned, put it beyond the pale.

Denied the necessary licence to produce *Soldiers* in Britain, Tynan readily gave his consent when Clifford Williams, who in 1963 had directed Hochhuth's *The Representative* (also known as *The Deputy*) at the RSC, expressed an interest in mounting it in Canada. In its original German, *Soldiers* had already premièred in Berlin in October 1967, but this would be its first production in English.

Soldiers opened in Toronto on February 28 to intense public interest. *The New York Times* sent its critic, who gave it a laudatory review. I personally didn't much like the play, even though I was in it; I found it turgid. But the houses were full, and the press was saying that it was one of the most important plays of the decade. For me, by far the most memorable thing about it was John Colicos's astounding performance as Churchill. I'd seen John play the semi-human Caliban in *The Tempest* at Stratford in 1962 and had heard of his tremendous success a decade earlier at London's Old Vic when he played the "fourscore and upward" King Lear at the preposterously young age of 23 (thereby easily topping my teenage Hamlet), but I was quite unprepared for his complete transformation in this role. He had Churchill down to a T; in fact he seemed to *be* Churchill. It was a sensational reincarnation of an iconic figure.

So far, the Theatre Toronto season had more or less lived up to its billing: some productions had turned out better than others, but the plays being presented were at least worthy of attention. I did not consider that to be true of our fourth and final offering of 1968, *A Festival of Carol's* by John Hearn. Billed as "the comedy with an apostrophe 's'," this too was a new Canadian play getting its first public airing, and it was bizarre beyond belief. I played a character called Detective Gentle, in a gold lamé Liberace suit, a female wig and a tiara with a sheriff's badge attached. At least I didn't have to wear a chest wig, as John Colicos did. Meanwhile, Barbara Hamilton portrayed a transvestite poet, and . . . oh, never mind. Enough said.

John Colicos: an amazing transformation

Although I hated the play, I had nothing but admiration for its director, Richard Digby Day. Like Clifford, Richard had been born in Cardiff, but unlike Clifford (who'd had no formal theatre training), he'd studied acting at the Royal Academy of Dramatic Art before becoming the first person to train there as a director. He was now artistic director of the New Shakespeare Company, which performed in the Open Air Theatre in London's Regent's Park. (David William, a co-founder of the company in 1962, had served as its first director of production.) Richard had first come to Canada in 1965, to direct *Twelfth Night* in Victoria, B.C., and had returned several times since. Now, in addition to his Regent's Park job back home, he was Clifford's second-in-command at Theatre Toronto.

At first meeting, Richard struck me as being like one of those caricature Englishmen out of a P. G. Wodehouse novel who say, "What, what?" all the time. I soon found him to be extremely knowledgeable, highly opinionated and acutely perceptive, and I would come to owe him, too, a great debt of gratitude.

One of my fondest memories from that first Theatre Toronto season is of the warm friendship I formed, despite the considerable disparity in our ages, with Amelia Hall. In 1953, as Lady Anne in *Richard III*, Amelia had been the first actress to speak on the Stratford Festival stage, and I had already met her during my own first seasons at Stratford, when, among other roles, she played Mistress Quickly in *Henry V*. It wasn't until we were in the Theatre Toronto company together, though, that we really got to know each other.

Amelia Hall: a friendship fondly remembered

Our friendship lasted till her death in 1984. The last time I saw her, in fact, was the night before she died, when I took her to a production of *Toad of Toad Hall* in Toronto. We went out to dinner beforehand, and I pressed her to have a martini. "Oh, do you think I should?" she asked, to which I replied, with unconscious prescience, "Oh, go on, Millie: you only live once." So she had the martini. After the play, when we were coming back on the subway, she said her tooth was hurting her, which someone told me later can be a sign of an impending heart attack. The next day she died.

Soldiers had engaged the interest of a New York producer, Herman Shumlin, who agreed to undertake a transfer of our production in the spring. Although I had only a small part, appearing in a prologue to the play proper, I was one of the five or six members of the original

Canadian cast chosen to go with *Soldiers* to New York. (The others included John Colicos, of course, Colin Fox and Joseph Shaw.) I was told that the play was going to be rewritten and that my part would consequently be expanded. It wasn't; in fact, I ended up with fewer lines than I'd had in Toronto. But still, I was greatly excited at the prospect of my Broadway debut.

We opened on May 1, 1968, at the Billy Rose Theatre, where Colin and I shared a dressing room on the very top floor. Kenneth Tynan came to see the show, and I remember feeling very flattered when Clifford brought him all the way up the stairs to meet us. I was a great admirer of Tynan, whose reviews I'd read when I was at school and university. I thought he was the best drama critic

As Dorland's Son in Theatre Toronto's production of *Soldiers* at the Royal Alexandra Theatre in 1968

of that or any era, with the possible exception of Bernard Shaw. He wrote fabulously well, and it was from his criticism that I gained my understanding of the British theatre of the 1950s. I was too much in awe of him to say all this at the time, but a couple of years later, when our paths once again entwined, I did try to convey to him what an enormous influence he'd had on my life: how profoundly his writing had affected this unsophisticated young French-Italian-Canadian growing up in Montreal. As I might have expected, this meant nothing to him, and he just looked at me curiously.

In the end, our show did not do as well in New York as we had hoped. (How many times in the annals of Canadian theatre have *those* words been uttered?) *Soldiers* closed on May 18, barely two and a half weeks after it had opened. Still, it had been an entirely worthwhile experience: not only had I been able to spend time with my friends Aviva and Roberta, who was now also in New York, but my name had now appeared, if not in lights, at least on a poster at the entrance to a Broadway theatre. Well, sort of. When I went to take a closer look at the sign outside the Billy Rose, it took me a moment to find my name. Oh, wait, there it was: "Richard Nanette."

Earlier in the year, I had applied for a Canada Council grant to go and see theatre in England, and with perfect timing it came through the week after *Soldiers* closed in New York. So I packed my bags, got on a plane and arrived in London, where the only person I knew was David Francis, my friend from the Paupers theatre group in Montreal. He had gone to London to attend drama school and was now acting there occasionally, supplementing his income by working as a freelance correspondent for the CBC.

It is an odd quirk of mine that I have always had difficulty with change, in the monetary sense. When I receive coins, I seem to have no idea of what they are worth, nor can I figure out how to sort them into whatever amounts might be required. As can be imagined, this handicap became infinitely more challenging when I was presented with my first handful of pre-decimalization British change: an incomprehensible jumble of half-crowns, florins, shillings, sixpences, thrupp'ny bits, ha'pennies and probably farthings as well. I was in a strange country with no clear idea of what to do next, and I couldn't even figure out the money. I got as far as what was then the BOAC terminal at Victoria Station, and then, randomly stuffing coins into a pay phone, I called David and threw myself on his mercy. He immediately took the Underground to Victoria to collect me, and most generously provided me with a place to stay until I had found my feet.

This was the first time I had been outside North America, and I found it immensely exciting. I had taken my degree in English literature, and suddenly here I was in the city in which so much of that literature had its roots. I remember being surprised at how short all the buildings seemed to be: in my naïvety, I had expected the architecture of London to look like that of New York. I immediately set about visiting Eastcheap and all the other places that were mentioned in the classics I had appeared in. I went to museums and art galleries, and I went to as many plays as I could.

This included, of course, productions by the Royal Shakespeare Company, which, at the time, impressed me greatly. I thought the RSC actors were far more at ease with Shakespearean verse than ours: somehow they made it sound more colloquial, less bombastic. Nowadays, I take quite a different view: the quality of verse-speaking at the Stratford Festival seems to me to be far ahead of that at our English counterpart. I'm not sure if the change is in me or in the respective organizations: perhaps a bit of both.

I also took the opportunity to see work by my erstwhile Theatre Toronto employers, Clifford Williams and Richard Digby Day. At the Open Air Theatre in Regent's Park I caught Richard's productions of *The Merry Wives of Windsor* and *The Two Gentlemen of Verona*, while at the Old Vic I was fortunate enough to see one of the groundbreaking productions for which Clifford is most remembered: his all-male *As You Like It*. It was incredibly beautiful, and made such an impression on me that I went to see it twice more.

No less unforgettable, though for quite different reasons, was *Paradise Now*, which I saw at the Round House, a venue favoured by the avant-garde. *Paradise Now* was a creation by The Living Theatre, the American experimental company formed in 1947 by Julian Beck and Judith Malina that was now working primarily in Europe. As the audience entered the theatre, they were confronted by an actor lying on the stage, while a miked voice counted slowly backwards from 100. This went on for about 20 minutes, long past the show's advertised starting time. At last, the voice reached the end of its countdown. "Three . . . two . . . one," it intoned. "Ladies and gentlemen, once again this actor has failed to levitate." The result was pandemonium, as patrons angrily left the auditorium amid groans, boos and cries of "Rubbish!"

I had arrived in England at a heady time. The "Swinging Sixties" were at their height: the sexual revolution ushered in by the introduction of the contraceptive pill to Britain in 1961 had reached a milestone in 1967 with the legalization of homosexual acts in private between consenting adults. British society was undergoing massive change, and one example of that was the liberalization, at long last, of the British theatre. A Labour government, under Prime Minister Harold Wilson, had been in power since 1964, ending nearly a decade and a half of Conservative rule, and in the year of my arrival, 1968, the British Parliament passed the Theatres Act, abolishing the Lord Chamberlain's role as a censor of the theatre. This was a historic change, and one in which the controversy surrounding *Soldiers* had played no small part.

The new legislation did not formally take effect until September 26 that year, but theatre companies were already throwing out the old taboos. For the Royal Shakespeare Company that June, Clifford directed a production of Christopher Marlowe's *Doctor Faustus*, in which an actress named Maggie Wright played Helen of Troy in the nude—something that would have been impossible just a year earlier. (At least, it would have been impossible for her to *do* anything in the role: a quaint loophole in the previous law had allowed you to be nude on stage as long as you didn't actually move, which had enabled such burlesque establishments as London's celebrated Windmill Theatre to present artistically posed nude tableaux.) And sometime later that summer, rehearsals began for the British production of the rock musical *Hair*, in which, for one brief and discreetly lit moment, the entire cast would emerge naked from under a giant sheet. *Hair* opened, rather cheekily, on September 27, the day after the new Theatres Act became law. I was at that opening, and at the end, along with other members of the audience, I got up on stage and danced.

One beneficiary of the new Theatres Act, at least for a while, was *Soldiers*, which Kenneth Tynan was now at last able to present in Britain. Tynan asked Clifford to remount his Toronto and New York production, and John Colicos was asked to reprise his role as Churchill. The play opened in London on December 12, 1968, to extremely positive reviews. Less than a month later, however, lawsuits for libel were launched against Hochhuth, Tynan, his co-producer Michael White and various others connected with the production. The suits came not, as might have been expected, from "Bomber" Harris or relatives of Winston Churchill, but from, of all people, the pilot who had flown the plane in which Sikorski had died. The show closed in March the following year, and the whole affair left a very nasty taste in many mouths.

On my return to Canada in the fall, thanks to a recommendation by David Gardner, I at last got my chance to play Romeo (or at least a piece of him), in a TV collage of scenes from the play for the Ontario Educational Communications Authority, better known today as TVOntario. The program was directed by Kurt Reis, who'd directed the Crest's Hour Company presentations during my *Hamlet*; my Juliet was Diana Leblanc, who'd been in the *Henry V* cast with me at Stratford and with whom I now formed a much closer friendship. Then, having been promised another season's work by Clifford and Richard, I returned to Theatre Toronto.

We opened our second season at the Royal Alex on January 9, 1969, with Christopher Marlowe's *Edward II*: a notoriously difficult play in which the king is dispatched at the end in a most unpleasant way with a red-hot poker. It was not one of Clifford's triumphs, despite the presence of William Hutt in the title role. Ralph Hicklin of the *Telegram* called it a "miserable" production, "under-directed, under-rehearsed and cursed with the most malignant costumes and sets I have seen in a fairish time." He had a point about the costumes: they'd been made out of a kind of vinyl material called, I believe, Aqua Queen, which was (and perhaps still is) used for the linings of shower curtains. I have no reason to suppose that this fabric was anything less than exemplary when it came to keeping splashes off your bathroom floor, but as material to be worn on stage it left something to be desired. For one thing, it was too stiff for our purposes, as we discovered on opening night in a scene in which the king knelt down to pray. As Bill Hutt sank to his knees, he disappeared from view inside his robes, which remained standing like a tent.

My own appearance in the piece, as the king's young son, Prince Edward, carrying his dead father's head, was mercifully brief, so I was surprised when, for some reason, I received considerable critical praise for it. In 2005, when I directed the play myself at the Stratford Festival's Studio Theatre, I told Harry Thomas, the 15-year-old actor playing the Prince, "Don't worry about a thing. I've played this role, and apparently I was brilliant. So just do everything I tell you, and you'll be marvellous."

Edward II was the last production that Clifford directed for Theatre Toronto. Both of the next two, George Bernard Shaw's *In Good King Charles's Golden Days* (in which I played the painter Godfrey

Knellar, whom, judging by his self-portrait in the National Portrait Gallery in England, I rather resembled) and Carlo Goldoni's *The Servant of Two Masters* (with Heath Lamberts as Truffaldino), were directed by Richard Digby Day. Richard had a special affinity and flair for Shavian comedy, and *In Good King Charles's Golden Days* was hailed by Herbie Whittaker in *The Globe and Mail* as "the best over-all production of anything the company has done." *Servant,* in which I played Silvio opposite Diana Leblanc's Clarice, fared less well: with exquisitely diplomatic faint praise, Herbie said that the production gave "enough promise that this Venetian classic will be a very amusing show."

The only slight headache with *In Good King Charles's Golden Days,* for those of us performing in it, was that Richard had insisted that we pronounce *all* the consonants in the word *government.* There would be no getting away with "guv'mint." This proved too much for our unattuned Canadian tongues, particularly since Richard also insisted that we deliver the dialogue at a million miles an hour. "When you finish this play," he said, "you should all be exhausted. If you're not, you're not working hard enough." So we'd race through our lines at breakneck speed, then, every time we came to *that* word, shudder to a halt as we painstakingly articulated the syllables "Gov. Ern. Ment," before picking up the pace again. Since the word *government* occurs about every second line in the play, this was a challenge, to say the least. But we had wonderful costumes, not made out of shower curtains.

As Godfrey Knellar in Theatre Toronto's *In Good King Charles's Golden Days,* 1969

After that, however, Theatre Toronto began to fall apart. *The Servant of Two Masters* had actually replaced a scheduled production of Günter Grass's *The Plebeians Rehearse the Uprising,* and suddenly Clifford and the company's designer, the brilliant Ralph Koltai, were no longer around, leaving matters wholly in Richard's hands. There was one more production, *The Killing of Sister George*, directed by Tim Bond, but thereafter Theatre Toronto, like the Crest and the Canadian Players before it, disappeared from the scene for good, leaving behind it a deficit in the neighbourhood of $80,000. And this time there seemed to be nothing else emerging in Toronto to fill the void.

Before he returned to the United Kingdom, Richard Digby Day invited me to join his New Shakespeare Company for their summer season that year in Regent's Park. He offered me two roles: Lorenzo in *The Merchant of Venice* and Panthino in a revival of his *Two Gentlemen of Verona*, which I'd seen during my visit to London the year before. I remember sitting with Joseph Shaw on the stairs at the Royal Alex, sometime shortly before our last performance there, and asking him what he thought I should do. Should I accept this invitation and go to England?

Richard Digby Day: a debt of gratitude

"Yes," Joseph replied firmly. "Go." It would be good for me to get out of the country, he said. I didn't seem happy here, so I should go and do something about it while I was still young. Being in another culture would stimulate me, and besides, there were more opportunities for an actor in England at that time than there were in Canada. It occurred to me that perhaps I could become a big success there—perhaps even a star. This was the only time in my life when such an idea seriously attracted me. I hadn't thought of stardom before (and I've never wanted it since), but now I found myself thinking that if I applied myself in Britain there was a chance I might actually become a household name.

It wasn't an easy choice. It had been hard enough leaving home at 19 to go to Toronto. I'd felt a heavy burden of responsibility toward my mother and, especially, toward my brother, Mark, who was still only 12 when I left and for whom I'd been coming home from school every day to make lunch. I'd felt that I was abandoning them to their fate, even though I'd returned often to Montreal to visit in the years since. At the same time, I'd known that I *had* to go, for my own self-preservation. I couldn't cope with things at home anymore: it was too painful. And had I stayed, my parents might well have dragged me down with them. Besides, with my father increasingly absent and my mother withdrawing into her own world of addiction and psychosis, it hadn't entirely felt as if I was running away from home; in a sense, home had already run away from me. And so I had made my choice.

Now, at the age of 24, I was faced with an even more wrenching version of that choice. If I did go to England, it wouldn't be as a summer visitor this time. I would go with every intention of staying for an indefinite period. I would be saying farewell, perhaps for good, to my family and the country I had grown up in. Again, however, it was quite clear to me that I needed to go.

Before joining Richard's company, I gave myself a holiday: six weeks driving across Spain (chosen because it was cheap, and I had very little money) with a friend and fellow actor, Briain Petchey, with whom I'd worked both at Stratford and in the second Theatre Toronto season. It was my first time on the European continent, and I felt I was in a different world. We then spent all of one night in Paris, where I just had time to see Notre Dame Cathedral before leaving the next day for London and the start of rehearsals for *The Merchant of Venice*.

A curious phenomenon afflicted me during those rehearsals: whatever I did, I could never seem to arrive for them on time. I'm still not quite sure why this was so, though many explanations have been offered. Some people say that chronic lateness is a form of passive aggression; others that it is a sign of some deep and abiding fear. Whatever the reason, lateness had never been a problem for me at Stratford or in Toronto; in London, however, I was late, sometimes by as much as 20 minutes, for every single rehearsal.

Matters reached a head one day when a run-through was scheduled. This was a very important rehearsal: the producer was going to be there, along with the entire management of the company. Unfortunately, there was also going to be a labour strike on the London Underground, my usual means of transport. To get to the rehearsal hall from where I lived, I would have to go by bus. I had been given directions, but it was a complex journey, involving several transfers. So I set my alarm clock for about 6:30 in the morning—allowing myself a good three hours' travel time—and asked the people I was sharing my lodgings with to wake me if I failed to emerge. Just to be on the safe side, I asked some others in the company to telephone me as well.

I got up on time. But, through some inexplicable combination of dawdling, indecision and plain old getting lost, I still managed to arrive a full half-hour late. Richard was, quite rightly, incensed. "If you hadn't come 3,000 miles to play this role," he screamed at me in front of the entire company, "I would fire you." Reduced to tears, I could do nothing but apologize and keep on reiterating that I couldn't understand how the trip could possibly have taken me three and a half hours. "It's a kind of sickness," I whimpered. "I think for some reason I'm afraid to come here." There may have been something in that: certainly in the years since, I've noticed that when I am late for something, it's usually because some part of me wants to avoid it. But why it should have affected me so dramatically at that time remains a mystery.

As Panthino (left) in *The Two Gentlemen of Verona* in Regent's Park in the summer of 1969

On possible explanation occurs: deep down, I may have felt like an interloper, both in the company and in the country. Like so many Canadian actors at the time, I found it hard to shake off the notion, eagerly fostered by so many theatre critics (and confirmed, as I then thought, by my own visits to the RSC), that English actors were inherently better at Shakespeare than we were. And since I'd come with the intention of staying in England—indeed, in the hopes of becoming a star—I felt I had to assume an English accent. To play Shakespeare in England I'd have to blend in, otherwise people would ask themselves, "Where has he come from?" Emotionally, this made me feel like an outsider trying to get in, wanting to belong. And artistically, it reinforced my bad habit of thinking of acting as something you "put on," except that in this case it was an accent I was putting on, not a false nose.

Of course, if you already feel like an outsider, you can always rely on someone to help you feel it even more. On one occasion I was putting on my makeup in the communal dressing room at Regent's Park, with about 35 other actors, when one of them, a middle-aged man, said to me in tones loud enough for everyone else to hear, "How do you feel about taking a job from an English actor?"

Looking back on that remark, I feel it clarified for me my opinions about "cultural nationalism," opinions that I still hold to this day. Although it was true that I had turned down my Stratford Festival offer because Christopher Walken was being brought in to play Romeo, I hadn't sought to make Walken feel uncomfortable. I believed then, and I believe now, that art is not best served by labour laws. The person who gets a role should be the person the director wants, regardless of other concerns. At the time, though, I didn't articulate any of this to my interlocutor. As dead silence fell and 35 pairs of ears pricked up for my response, I simply retorted: "I feel fine about it. In my country, all the British actors are taking *our* jobs. That's why I'm here." Which was true enough: even though the immediate catalyst for my departure had been an American actor, not a British one, there were still, at that time, plenty of English accents to be heard on Canadian stages.

Open-air theatre is a true test of an actor's powers—or rather, of his or her capacity for dogged persistence in the face of impossible odds. You rehearse indoors in a hall, then you go outside to perform what you have rehearsed in an environment where subtlety and nuance are out of the question. No wonder that Tyrone Guthrie had rejected out of hand the idea of an open-air stage for the fledgling Stratford Festival. "Mother Nature," he'd remarked back in 1952, "has a way of missing her cues."

In Regent's Park, it wasn't just the weather and the indigenous fauna we had to contend with. The hour at which our performances began, seven o'clock, also happened to be feeding time at the nearby zoo, so we had to shout over the roaring of lions and the trumpeting of elephants. And, of course, there was another source of distraction undreamed of in Shakespeare's day: the regular passage overhead of jet airliners. More than once, as Lorenzo in *The Merchant of Venice*, I would look up at the sky and say to my Jessica, played by Alison Fiske, "Look how the floor of heaven / Is thick inlaid with patens of bright gold," only to have a Boeing 727 roar by. Experienced Regent's Park actors would memorize the flight schedules and pace their delivery accordingly, trying to ensure that the thunder of planes would coincide with someone else's scene, not theirs.

During this time, as a working actor in London, I was living a life of not-so-genteel poverty. I would buy a dozen scones and a pound of butter and live on that for a week. And since there seemed to be no refrigerators in England, the butter quickly became rancid. At some point, I made contact with another Canadian, Barbara Hamilton, who'd been in the Theatre Toronto company with me and who was now appearing in the original London production of *Anne of Green Gables*, and on one occasion when I was completely broke, I asked to borrow a pound from her. She gave me five, on which I was able to live for a month. Later, when we were both back in Canada, I bought her a bottle of her favourite perfume and wrapped it in a five-pound note.

Still, even though I wasn't making much money, and stardom still seemed a little way off, I'd been fortunate compared to many in my profession. Since making my debut at the Crest, I'd more or less gone straight from one job to another, and this luck seemed to be holding in England, too. No sooner, for example, did the Regent's Park season end in the fall of 1969 than I was hired to play, of all things, Montjoy in a production of *Henry V* being presented by the Lyric Hammersmith Company for two weeks at the Theatre Royal in the resort town of Bath. (Michael Langham had been right: you never know when you'll find yourself reprising a role.) The director, Michael Meacham, was a friend of David William's, and David had recommended me. Whatever objections might be made about British directors coming over to Canada, it was certainly working in my favour now: I was being well looked after by the British imports I'd worked with in Stratford and Toronto.

There were disappointments, of course: at one point while I was in London I auditioned for Agatha Christie's *The Mousetrap* (billed at the time as being in its "17th inexorable year") but didn't get in because, as I'd predicted, I didn't sound English enough. I had the same response when I auditioned for the National Theatre. By and large, though, my career never seriously languished. I wasn't having to pound the streets of London, and that was in large part thanks to my growing network of connections.

It can seem such a small world when you work in the theatre: everybody seems to know everybody else, and that network means that you run into people in the most unlikely places. In the Regent's Park *Merchant of Venice*, for instance, Nerissa had been played by Barbara Bryne, who'd also been in the Crest Theatre *Hamlet* with me. She had then appeared in *Henry VI*, *Twelfth Night* and *Richard III* with me at Stratford, and then in *In Good King Charles's Golden Days* and *The Servant of Two Masters* at Theatre Toronto. She would return to Stratford in seasons to come, including the early years of my tenure as artistic director. In the *Henry V* company in Bath, I first met another two actors who would later come to the Festival: Ian White, who was playing the Constable of France, and Bernard Hopkins, playing Bardolph and the Duke of Orleans. Bernie in particular befriended me, and showed me around Bath, a city that, even after Spain and Paris, seemed to me as exotic as the moon.

With Bernard Hopkins (right) in Bath during *Henry V*

King Henry himself, by the way, was played in that production by James Fox, who'd starred in the film comedies *Those Magnificent Men and Their Flying Machines* and *Thoroughly Modern Millie*, while the Chorus was played by a future James Bond, Timothy Dalton.

That year, in addition to heading up the Regent's Park company, Richard Digby Day became artistic director of the English-speaking division of the Welsh Theatre Company, a touring company of which Clifford Williams was board chairman. Showing remarkable faith in me despite my demonstrated propensity for tardiness, Richard invited me, after *Henry V* ended its two-week run early in October 1969, to join his new company on a six-month tour.

We presented several productions in repertory all over Wales, including Cardiff, Swansea and such towns as Neath, Cross Hands, Aberystwyth and Mold. Even though the mountains there reminded me of Canada, I felt even more of an outsider in Wales than I had in London, partly because this was a time when support for Plaid Cymru, the Welsh nationalist party, was particularly strong. I remember going into pubs in some communities where, the moment they heard us speaking in English, the locals would switch to Welsh.

Clifford Williams: balanced and imperturbable

As a Canadian, of course, I was reminded of the linguistic and cultural divisions in my native province, where the increasingly violent activities of the separatist group Front de libération du Québec would culminate that same October in the kidnapping and murder of provincial labour minister Pierre Laporte. Like that dressing-room comment in Regent's Park, the Welsh pub patrons' pointed behaviour was an example of how pride in national identity can cut both ways: on the one hand it grounds people in a place and a culture; on the other, it can lead to a depressingly tribal form of exclusion.

One cold, windy day late in the tour, I was flipping through a copy of *Plays and Players* magazine when a familiar name sprang out at me. Clifford Williams, fresh from a West End hit with Anthony Shaffer's mystery-thriller *Sleuth*, was going to direct the London production of *Oh! Calcutta!*

Like most people in Britain at the time, I knew *Oh! Calcutta!* only by its scandalous reputation. Described by its deviser, the ever-controversial Kenneth Tynan, as "a revue of elegant erotica for the thinking voyeur," it was a collection of sketches about sex by such eminent authors as Samuel Beckett, Jules Feiffer, John Lennon, Edna O'Brien, Joe Orton, Sam Shepard, Tennessee Williams and Tynan himself, interspersed with musical numbers and dance. The material was explicit, and much of it was performed in the nude.

The show's title, and the iconic image used on the posters and the program cover, came from a painting by the French surrealist Clovis Trouille that shows a reclining woman, seen from the rear, draped only in a long silk veil that neatly frames her naked bottom. On closer inspection, the buttocks thus delineated appear to be exactly the same shape as the head of a penis. Beneath this visual pun is inscribed a linguistic one: "Oh! Calcutta! Calcutta!" As an English phrase, this is meaningless. When spoken aloud, however, it sounds like an exclamation in French: "*Oh! Quel cul t'as! Quel cul t'as!*," which could be translated, politely, as "Oh! What a lovely ass you have!"

Still smarting from the vitriol that had come his way over *Soldiers*, Tynan had chosen to produce *Oh! Calcutta!* in New York rather than England. When it had opened off-Broadway, at the appropriately named Eden Theatre, on June 17, 1969, the reviews had been savage: Clive Barnes of *The New York Times* had called it "the kind of show to give pornography a dirty name." Nonetheless, it had become a huge hit, with a second production opening in Los Angeles, and now Tynan was planning a London production for the summer of 1970 with Clifford as director.

A nude revue didn't seem to me to be Clifford's kind of thing at all. At Theatre Toronto, when we'd been doing *Edward II*, a play rampant with illicit lust, he'd asked me if I thought there was any sex in it. "Ye-e-s," I'd said cautiously, wondering if it was a trick question, "there is." But he'd seemed genuinely not to know, and indeed we never dealt with the issue in our production. Anyway, highly amused by the thought of Clifford trying to give stage directions to a bevy of bare bosoms and bums, I sat down and, as a joke, wrote him a breezy letter asking him if, in casting his erotic revue, he might have any need for a young English-speaking French-Italian-Canadian with a Jesuit education.

Our tour of Wales culminated in March 1970 in the coastal town of Swansea, where we delivered an entire compendium of Western drama in a single day. Beginning at 10 o'clock in the morning and going through till 11 at night, I played the Devil in Bernard Shaw's *Don Juan in Hell*, the Boy in W. B. Yeats's *Purgatory*, Solange in Jean Genet's *The Maids* and, I believe, Tegeus-Chromis in Christopher Fry's *A Phoenix Too Frequent*. (Or it may have been Fabrizio in Carlo Goldoni's *Mistress of the Inn*, which was also one of my roles on that tour.) I also played, with an atrocious Welsh accent, a tiny part in Dylan Thomas's *Return Journey*, in which Thomas describes coming home to Swansea, his home town, after its bombing in the war.

As the Devil in the Welsh Theatre Company's 1969-70 tour of *Don Juan in Hell*

Swansea was a surprise to me. I had expected something very quaint and old, but because it had been rebuilt after the bombing, everything was modern and new. Still, I found a beautiful spot there called Caswell Bay, where I stood and looked out over the sea and at the countryside around me. This vista seemed to me to contain the essence of everything that Thomas had described so eloquently in his poetry. The photo of me on the cover of this book was taken somewhere in Wales: it may even have been in Caswell Bay.

With the tour over, Richard then invited me back to Regent's Park for the summer, offering me a role I had always wanted to play: that of Puck in *A Midsummer Night's Dream*. For once in my career, I suddenly found myself torn between two equally attractive offers, because at the same time I had also auditioned for, and—thanks perhaps to my now almost perfect English accent—been accepted by, the Royal Shakespeare Company. The man who auditioned me, David Jones, told me that of all the people they'd seen that time round I was the only one with charm. (He, too, would subsequently turn up at the Stratford Festival, where he directed *Twelfth Night* in 1975 and *All's Well That Ends Well* in 1977, but he didn't remember me.) They were offering me only a tiny part at the RSC, a walk-on in *The Winter's Tale*, whereas Puck was a major role, but still: a foot in the door at Britain's leading classical company was not an opportunity to be taken lightly. Most of my friends, in fact, were advising me to forget Puck and take the RSC.

I decided to phone Clifford Williams and ask his advice. The solution he ended up proposing was not at all one that I expected. In the course of our telephone conversation, Clifford casually mentioned that he was having casting difficulties with *Oh! Calcutta!* One of the Americans who had been supposed to transfer over to the London cast had opted out. I laughed and said, "Well, I could always come and audition." Clifford laughed and said, "Why not?" I laughed and said, "All right, I will." He laughed and said: "We're having auditions tomorrow. Come." We both laughed and hung up. The next day, fortified by a double scotch, I went to the Piccadilly Theatre in Soho, where the auditions were being held.

A queue of applicants had already formed at the stage door when I arrived. All but two were female: actresses, models, showgirls, housewives and the sort of young woman whose employment is to be permanently unemployed. A mixed bag, but they had one thing in common: all of them were stunning. As we waited, the women adjusted their makeup, fiddled with their hair and inspected their nails. I caught snatches of their conversation:

"I hear they're only looking for beautiful people. I don't stand a chance."

"I wouldn't do it even if I had the chance, but I thought the experience of auditioning would be good for me."

"Even if I did get it, I couldn't do it. I'm in a show already."

"I've heard it's really bad."

"My agent told me not to come."

"I only came to meet Clifford Williams."

"I wonder if they're going to ask us to strip."

The stage manager appeared and told us, much to our relief, that we would not be required at this stage to remove any clothing. One by one, the women went in and came out again, each of them afterwards declaring that Clifford was "really very nice," as if they had been expecting some slavering creep.

When my turn came, I strode in, feeling poised and beaming with confidence. Clifford said I looked pale and told me to relax. I asked him if he thought I was right for the job. He said yes. Were there any good acting parts in the show, I asked? Some, he said. Would the, er, exposure help my career? "No." Would it hinder it? "No." Was the money good? "Yes." Should I do it? "Yes." Why? "Since you've now been in—what is it?—22 Shakespeare productions, a change would be good for you."

I asked him to give me the weekend to think it over and left the room without even having done an audition.

I spent that weekend telephoning everyone I could think of: in London, in Toronto, in Montreal, in New York. (It occurred to me after a while that I would *have* to take the job just to pay my phone bill.) On learning the reason for my call, the reaction of my London friends was invariably silence, followed by a sharp intake of breath and a hesitant "Well. . . ." My friends in North America, all of whom had known me for years and all of whom had already seen the New York production of *Oh! Calcutta!*, took a different tack: in each case, their initial reaction was to dissolve into helpless laughter. Then, when told that I was serious, they would sober up and say that they couldn't *quite* imagine me in that show—though, er, um, of course, I should go ahead and do it if I *really* wanted to.

I wasn't altogether sure how to take that: just what was so funny about the idea of me appearing nude on stage? I went to my bedroom, undressed and examined myself critically in front of the mirror. Maybe I wasn't Apollo, but I certainly wasn't Quasimodo either. When I sucked in my stomach, I could be really quite attractive, from certain angles, in subdued lighting. Sort of like a virile Porky Pig. Anyway, I realized that this was no longer simply a question of weighing one acting job over another: perversity and vanity were now also at work within me, along with the growing realization that whatever choice I made now would have immense and unknowable implications for my whole future career.

I called one more friend, an actor named Larry Aubrey, who'd been my understudy in *Twelfth Night* at Stratford and who was now also in England, and invited him to go for a long walk in the fresh air. Three hours and much discussion later, I had drawn up in my mind a persuasive list of reasons in favour of doing *Oh! Calcutta!*

In the first place, a show devised by Kenneth Tynan and directed by Clifford Williams had to have *some* merits. The contributing authors, too, were all highly regarded. If the show was, as many

As Solange (left) in *The Maids* (Welsh Theatre Company, 1969-70), with Hugh Ross as Clair

claimed, nothing more than pornography, at least it was prestige pornography. In any case, it was bound to get a lot of attention, and despite what Clifford had said, an individual actor might be able to make an impact.

Besides, the New York production probably wasn't as bad as the critics had made out—and anyway, Clifford had said that the London version would be quite different. He himself had spent many weeks deliberating before he'd accepted the job, finally agreeing to do it only if changes were made to the script to take into account the different sensibilities of English audiences, and only if he got the best actors available.

It would also be a chance to be in on something new in the theatre. Nudity and eroticism had never before been explored so extensively on the "legitimate" stage; they might turn out to be just as valid subjects for the theatre as they were for painting, sculpture and film. And it would be a chance for me personally to try things I hadn't done on stage before. Never mind nudity: a revue also involved singing and dancing. Last, but by no means least, it would be an adventure: a precedent-setting test of the new Theatres Act. This could be exciting.

It also didn't hurt, given my penniless state, that they were offering a lot of money.

By the end of the weekend, I had asked everybody, including the postman, what I should do. Then, first thing Monday morning, I went to the office of *Oh! Calcutta!*'s producer, Michael White, and agreed to do it. Two days later, I signed the contract, insisting on only nine months rather than the full year they pressed me for.

I decided to fly back to Montreal, on borrowed money, for a brief holiday before rehearsals began. Before I left, my agent called to congratulate me, with no discernible sarcasm, on being the first person to sign for the show. He also relayed to me a message from Michael White that under no circumstances was I to see the American production. Since the London version was going to be so different, Michael did not want me to be influenced by what was on stage in New York. I swore that I would not go near it.

It had occurred to me that I had been hired "sight unseen," as it were, for I still hadn't had to do a nude audition—or, indeed, any kind of audition. So I made one last phone call to Clifford before going off on my holiday. I asked him if there was anything else he needed to tell me before rehearsals started.

"No," said Clifford, "nothing."

"Well, Clifford, I have something to tell you."

"What's that?"

"You've just hired the smallest 'Dick' in show business."

After a brief visit with my family in Montreal—"Well, at least you've got your BA to fall back on," sighed my mother when I told her my news—I went off to New York, where I managed to resist seeing *Oh! Calcutta!* for a full 32 hours. Then a female friend—strangely,

I cannot now remember who it was; it may have been Roberta—appeared with tickets and dragged me to the Eden Theatre, where we sat in the back row. When the music started, I grabbed my friend's hand and held it firmly. The cast appeared, shed the robes they wore and stood revealed in a stark white light. So far, so good. This much I had expected. But then the sketches began.

I was quite unprepared for their content, which was far more explicit than I had imagined. As the evening unfolded, my grip on my friend's hand became tighter and tighter. My eyes became narrower and narrower. By the end of the first half, they were locked into a permanent squint, and all circulation in my friend's arm had ceased. I wanted desperately to leave; she was determined that we should stay. So for the second half, we settled on a compromise: we relinquished our seats and stood at the back, near the emergency exit.

The second half began with two dance numbers, both of which were quite beautiful. I began to think there might be some redeeming quality to this exercise after all. Then came more sketches, and again I felt as if I were being pinned to the back wall by fire hoses pouring out streams of pointless filth. "The dancing is beautiful," I kept telling myself, like a Christian martyr praying at the stake. "The dancing is beautiful. The dancing is. . . ."

To be fair, people around me seemed to be having a marvellous time. All I could think of, however, was the fact that I'd just signed up to do some version of what I was seeing on stage. Every time an actor stripped off, or spoke those shocking lines, I experienced the moment along with him, or her. At last I thought I truly understood what Aristotle meant by catharsis: that blend of pity and terror you feel when watching a tragedy unfold. Michael White had been right: seeing the New York production had been a very bad idea. I simply hadn't been prepared for what I had just seen, far less for what I would have to *do*.

We emerged afterwards into what felt like the crystal-clear air of 12th Street. Finally retrieving her hand, my friend posed what had to be the question of the year: "You gave up the Royal Shakespeare Company to do *this*?"

It was a good question, and the real answer to it lay beyond my carefully considered list of good reasons to accept the offer.

That list had not included the most compelling reason of all: my painful, almost pathological shyness.

To anyone who knows me now, the idea of my being shy may seem absurd. It is quite common, of course, for actors, who earn their livings by making public displays of themselves, to be diffident and withdrawn in private. Indeed, it is possible that shy people are drawn to acting precisely because it enables them to behave, under the assumed identity of a stage role, with an abandon that they could not normally contemplate in their own lives. My own case, though, was even more paradoxical. Even in private life, people found me outgoing and gregarious. I could talk to people in social situations with the same ease and verve I had brought to my debating class at school. Yet deep inside me there was a strange kind of reserve, even fear. When I first joined the Stratford Festival company, I wouldn't shower after a performance with the other actors; I would wait for everyone else to be finished. Far more oddly, I didn't feel comfortable crossing the street at city intersections where people might be watching me. I would go several blocks out of my way to find a less crowded place to cross.

I cannot explain this bizarre phobia or reconcile it with the image my friends had of me as the life and soul of any party. I knew only that there was a chronic disconnection between what I felt and the sociable persona that I presented to the world. And I knew, from the direction I had received in my career up to this point ("Acting is being"), that people could sense this disconnection in my work on stage. My shyness made it difficult for me to just *be*, and that difficulty was impeding me as an actor. It was to overcome that shyness once and for all that I decided to go into *Oh! Calcutta!*

It was the most terrifying decision of my career. Strangely enough, though, I was never once late for rehearsals.

CHAPTER FIVE

Poor Naked Wretches

King Lear, Act III, scene 4

The cast of *Oh! Calcutta!* met for the first time on the morning of Monday, June 1, 1970, at the Donmar Warehouse in Covent Garden. Built in the 1870s as a vat room and hops warehouse for a local brewery, the Donmar had been converted into a rehearsal studio in 1961 by theatre impresario Donald Albery. (Later, in 1977, it would be operated as a full-fledged theatre by the RSC.) There would be 10 of us: five women and five men. At the moment, however, we were only eight: two of the men, Americans who were coming to us from the New York production, were scheduled to arrive within a couple of days.

After the usual introductions, Clifford launched into a 90-minute discussion of our legal position. Although the office of theatrical censor had been abolished by the Theatres Act of 1968, this did not mean that we were free of risk. In some ways, our position was even more precarious. Under the old legislation, once a licence to perform had been granted, a production could go ahead without fear of legal challenge; now, however, any member of the public who objected to a show that was already up and running could file a complaint with the police on the grounds that it would "tend to corrupt and deprave persons who are likely, having regard to all relevant circumstances, to attend it." If such a complaint were made about *Oh! Calcutta!*, the police would investigate and submit their evidence to the attorney-general, who would then decide, in consultation with the director of public prosecutions, whether to lay charges. (Later, when we were doing run-throughs of the show, our producers consulted the barrister, playwright and novelist John Mortimer, who told us that the chances of this happening were quite high.)

In my dressing room during *Oh! Calcutta!*

There were some curious wrinkles in the law. Charges could be laid against Clifford, as director of the show, and Michael White, as its producer, but not against Tynan, who had merely devised it.

As for the actors on stage, we would be all right as long as we strictly followed the instructions of our director; however, the least bit of improvisation on our part could get us arrested. We were thus instructed to keep very quiet about the fact that two major numbers in our show were to be almost entirely improvised. Most absurdly of all, even if we couldn't be prosecuted for *giving* a performance, we could be for *rehearsing* it, on a charge akin to "disturbing the peace." For this reason, Clifford told us, the Donmar's doors would be kept locked while we were inside.

He asked us to observe two points of policy. The first concerned the wildly speculating press, who were panting for any scraps of inside information. Already that morning, strange men (reporters, police or just thinking voyeurs?) had been seen lurking outside. Clifford and Michael wanted to keep the details of the show secret for as long as possible, so they asked us not to speak to any member of the press before clearing it first with our publicity manager. We were also asked not to reveal which authors had written which scripts. Tynan did not want to risk invading the privacy of any of the contributors, since it would naturally be assumed—and, for all we knew, it might well be the case—that the sexual fantasies described in their scripts were their own. Tynan also wanted the show to be judged as a whole, rather than dissected into its parts; furthermore, he wanted the audience to be presented with "a fascinating guessing game."

Clifford then concluded the morning's announcements with the news that the London Theatre Managers' Association, which controlled most West End venues, was boycotting *Oh! Calcutta!* and that consequently, for the moment at least, we had nowhere to perform. With that, we adjourned for lunch.

We ate at a round table, making small talk and eyeing one another up over the cannelloni. I had expected that my fellow cast members would be scruffy-looking hippies, yippies or yahoos. After all, what sorts of people—apart from me, of course, with my impeccable artistic motives—would want to be in a show like this? Rejects from *Hair*, perhaps? In fact, I was surrounded by a group of seemingly well brought up middle-class boys and girls, all as well scrubbed, neatly coiffed and smartly dressed as I.

My attention was first drawn to the funny little girl in the plain, round-rimmed glasses. This was Margo Sappington, a 22-year-old Texan who had already performed in and choreographed the New York and Los Angeles productions of *Oh! Calcutta!* and who would be doing the same for us. Seated beside her husband, Tom Andrasano, who would be assisting her but not performing in the show, she seemed as devoid of glamour as it was possible for a dancer to be. Her face bore no trace of makeup, she wore her hair in bunches, and her clothes appeared to be chosen for one reason only: working comfort. On stage, however, as we were to discover, she became a complete knockout. Nature had given her a perfect body, dance had given it firmness, and youth gave it everything else. She had technique, speed, precision and, most important of all, feeling, and when she began to dance, the world was hers.

In striking contrast, seated between Clifford Williams and Michael White, and spending most of the meal reading their palms, was an exotic-looking young black woman named Brenda Arnau. As tall and well-groomed as a *Vogue* supermodel, she was a cabaret singer who'd never acted before. American-born, with a spectacular body and a voice to go with it, she'd been performing in Europe for the past couple of years and had appeared on British television. She would provide *Oh! Calcutta!* with one of its highlights when, leaning on an oak pedestal and wearing nothing but a necklace and a pearl-encrusted hat, she sang an arrangement of "To His Black Mistress," a 17th-century poem by John Cotgrave.

Meanwhile, a Rubenesque, blue-eyed blonde named Linda Marlowe was having a boisterous conversation with a man who looked for all the world like a stereotypical Latin lover. Sultry-looking and whisky-voiced, Linda led you at first glance to expect the personality of Lauren Bacall: sophisticated, dark and just a little dangerous. The reality was closer to Lucille Ball: bounce and constant good humour, living life at the top of her voice and on the edge of a nervous breakdown.

The "Latin-lover" type she was talking to, Noel Tovey, was in fact an Australian of aboriginal and African-Creole heritage. Thirty-five years old, with a wife and a daughter, he'd spent the past 10 years in England, where he'd established a career in classical dance. (Besides Margo, he was the only trained dancer in our company.) Good-looking and over six feet tall, he soon revealed a keen intelligence and a ready wit. (Much later, when we came to perform the show, there would usually be an audible gasp from the audience upon his first disrobing. "Don't worry, madam," he'd invariably quip. "It won't bite.")

I was wrong, too, about the other man at the table, whom I'd taken for one of the backers on account of the suit and tie he wore; as any Briton off the street would have known, he was in fact Anthony Booth, an actor who had already achieved nationwide fame for his role as the "randy Scouse git": Alf Garnett's indolent and impertinent son-in-law in the controversial and hugely successful BBC sitcom *Till*

The cast of *Oh! Calcutta!* prepare to shed their robes in the opening number.

Death Us Do Part (later remade on American TV as *All in the Family*). Anthony—or Tony, as he was usually called—was Liverpool Irish, with all the convivial spirit and gift of the gab that such a background might imply. He had a daughter, Cherie, 15 years old at the time, from the first of what would be his four marriages; it was only recently that I learned that she had grown up to become Cherie Blair, a successful lawyer and the wife of former British prime minister Tony Blair.

That left the two other women in the company. One of them, Pamela Farbrother, had a remarkable face: a broad, full mouth, high cheekbones and large, limpid eyes, half hidden by a wide-brimmed hat, giving her an air of mystery and haunted beauty. In repose, she gave the odd impression that the top and bottom halves of her body had never been properly introduced; in motion, however, she was all harmony, grace and expressiveness.

The other, sitting directly across from me, was a beautiful and beatific-looking girl who looked no more than 17. She was in fact 22, but she was still the youngest woman in the cast. (At 25, I was the youngest man.) She seemed a stereotype of the innocent English actress fresh from drama school: shy, serious about her work and absolutely silent. When she did speak, though, you could detect immediately the hallmarks of a well-trained voice: powerful, with a sexy modulation. Her body was young and slightly boyish; her long brown hair framed a virginal, oval face. I found it impossible to imagine that mouth giving voice to the foul language I had heard in the New York production. The name of this vision—whom I later discovered I must have already seen on stage, holding a fan in the background in John Barton's celebrated RSC production of *Troilus and Cressida*—was Domini Blythe. She captured my heart immediately and has kept a part of it ever since.

Domini Blythe: a vision of innocent beauty

After the cannelloni, we actors who would have to reveal our fleshly imperfections to crowds of strangers every night skipped dessert, contenting ourselves with sipping our coffee while the management team munched their way through gâteaux and creamy pastries. Back in the rehearsal hall, we were to complete this day of orientation with some advanced Martha Graham exercises in modern dance. We'd been telephoned the night before and told to wear something loose, so I'd brought the loosest thing I owned: my bathing suit. I felt no end of a fool when I saw the leotards and tights sported by the others in the cast: was I the *only* non-dancer here?

It was a great relief when Tony Booth stumbled out of the dressing room wearing *his* bathing suit.

Class was dismissed at five o'clock, but two of us were kept behind: Pam Farbrother and I. We were the only two members of the company who had not yet done a nude audition. To some extent, since we'd already been cast, this was a mere formality, just something to go through so we'd all feel we were starting off on an equal footing. Yet it was also a crucial test. Margo had learned from the two previous productions that, when it came to the crunch, some people just couldn't go through with the stripping. It would be better to find that out now rather than later. The nude audition was also a check for physical deformities or peculiarities. One young woman who had auditioned in New York had been considered perfect for the job until she stripped and revealed two well-shaped but asymmetrical breasts. It had been felt that the show had enough novelty without them. Misogynistic as that may sound, the hard fact remains that the theatre is one of very few areas of employment where people can legitimately be accepted or rejected on the basis of their appearance.

The rehearsal hall was cleared of everyone except Clifford, Margo, Tom and Clifford's assistant, Nick Renton. Pam went in first; then, when she was done, I followed. Strangely, I felt none of the nervousness that accompanies an ordinary audition. I had got the job already, and I had no physical peculiarities that I knew of. I just wanted to get this rite of initiation over with so we could proceed.

Margo set up an improvisation for me: the same one that everyone in the cast had had to do. "You've just written a book," she said. "You hear unexpectedly that a publisher has accepted it. You drive out to the country. You find yourself walking in the woods. It is sunny and hot. You come across a pool of water. You take off your clothes and get into the water. You compose a letter to a friend. You get out of the water and put your clothes back on."

The aim of improvisation is to make you more spontaneous as an actor: to be in the moment and just *do*, without thinking too precisely on the event. However, I hadn't done much improvisation, and I didn't much like it. It made me feel self-conscious and, as a result, contrived: quite the opposite of the intended effect. Nonetheless, I did as instructed, and at the end—refreshed, perhaps, by my imaginary swim—I felt clean and confident. When I put my clothes back on again, Margo and Tom gave me a small round of applause and told me I had done well. Clifford came over to me and muttered in my ear: "I noticed that when you put your clothes back on, you put your socks on first. Neat little bastard, aren't you?"

Afterwards, I went out for a drink with Pam, who was beginning to have reservations about the whole thing. She'd heard poor reports of the New York production and doubted that ours would ever actually get on the stage. Even if the law didn't shut us down, she predicted, the critics would. I gave her a brief and judiciously expurgated account of what I'd seen in New York. It didn't help: by the time I was finished, she looked utterly miserable.

That night, by chance, I came across a quotation from Stravinsky: "Most artists are sincere, and most art is bad." Comforted a little by the thought that, whatever the outcome of our efforts might be, we were at least sincere in our intentions, I slept soundly.

It may be true that deep down all actors are exhibitionists—just as all spectators are voyeurs—but anyone who says they can appear for the first time naked on stage in front of 900 people and not be nervous or embarrassed is either a liar, an idiot or very peculiar. One way for an actor to handle nudity on stage is to think of the naked body as just another costume. "It's not really *my* flesh; it's the character's." But this approach—really just another way of throwing up a protective barrier—was not what was wanted in *Oh! Calcutta!* We were to think of ourselves as people first and performers second. It was to be *us* up there; we couldn't hide behind our characters. We were to be naked in our minds as well as in our bodies. To enable us to achieve this, we were put through a rehearsal process unlike anything I'd encountered before: a process I can only describe as group therapy.

The director of the New York production, Jacques Levy, had been a clinical psychologist before coming to work in the theatre. He'd devised a program of "sensitivity exercises" to help his actors be uninhibitedly naked with each other, as a prelude to being the same way with an audience. Pornography treats people as objects: it demands an aesthetic, emotional and moral detachment from those involved. But actors, as opposed to strippers or porn stars, aren't those kinds of people. And so the exercises that Levy had devised and that Margo now began to lead us through concentrated on building us into a loving, trusting group. Whatever we would be required to do on stage—and at times it would humiliate us or dehumanize us or make us look ridiculous—we would still have that group feeling to remind us that we were people, not things.

The exercises began mildly enough. One of the first was called Sound and Movement. We were divided up into two groups of four (the two American men still not having arrived) and sent to opposite sides of the room. A member of one group would make an abstract movement, accompanied by an abstract sound, and take it across the room to someone in the other group. That person would then have to make a sound and movement of their own in reply and take it in turn across the room to someone from the first group, and so on. The idea was to reveal to us our own personal mannerisms, so that we would learn to get beyond them and, eventually, to develop a kind of non-verbal vocabulary that we could use in the show.

Movement exercises in my "dance gear"

Those mannerisms became immediately obvious. Noel always ended up like an Indian limping around a campfire. Pam would make baby noises and waddle like a duck. Brenda, from the first day of rehearsal to the last, would execute a sophisticated pelvic grind. Tony invariably turned into a bear and growled. Linda would suck in her tummy, stick out her bum and shake her head like a hot spaniel. Domini would emit high-pitched squeaks and rush around the room like a water sprite, while I, she later told me, usually cut my way through the air with sharp, angular thrusts, "like a refugee from Kabuki."

Another exercise had a more sinister name: Submission. One person, designated the "victim," would stand in the centre of the room. The rest of us were told to go up to the victim, one at a time, and do to him or her whatever we wanted. The victim had to accept whatever was done and respond accordingly. The object of this was to make us less afraid of looking ridiculous and to encourage us to trust the other members of the group: since everyone would have a turn as victim, it was unlikely that anyone would do anything too invasive. Still, this exercise definitely became sexier as people became acclimatized and curiosity took over. A curious thing happened, though, the second time we did it. Linda Marlowe was the victim, and when it came my turn to do something to her, I decided to do something that would just be "me": something I might do in real life to someone I liked. So I went up to her and kissed her gently on the lips—not in an aggressively sexual way, but sweetly and innocently. This made everyone else in the room extremely uncomfortable. A most ingenious paradox: somehow it was more acceptable to take unaccustomed liberties with each other's bodies than it was to just be ourselves.

That, too, may be why the last exercise of the day, Eye Contact, was also the most difficult. In this exercise, we sat in a circle, held hands and locked eyes with each member of the group in turn. It had been easy enough to fake the other exercises: in each of them we had been required to *do* something, and it was always possible to perform an action without being in any way committed to it. But Eye Contact required us not to *do* but just to *be*. The eyes really are the windows of the soul, and it's almost impossible to meet someone's gaze for a long time without feeling self-conscious. Some of us made funny faces. Others hid behind glazed eyes.

The exercises would conclude with a Truth Session, in which we'd sit around and discuss the day's experiences. People were remarkably candid: Brenda, for instance, said she hadn't liked being touched. I admitted that I'd faked it in some of the exercises. Some of us confessed to being uneasy about the whole thing. How could we trust someone we didn't even know? Margo had an answer to that: "Because we're all beautiful people, aren't we?" To which Clifford quickly replied, "Oh, I don't know about that." There was truth in both statements. Margo's position was perhaps the necessary one to take: to start with suspicion would have been fatal to our enterprise. But Clifford's caution was more realistic. In any case, the question of trust was in everyone's minds, because we were all worried about the

Big Moment that must surely be imminent: when were they going to ask us to take off our clothes?

We had already, in fact, had to do so during that first day's exercises, in order to change into robes like the ones we would eventually wear in the show's opening number. But we had done so, modestly, in the washrooms. We hadn't been asked—yet—to discard the robes.

On the third day of rehearsal, we began as usual with the dance exercises in the morning. Then it was off to the pub for lunch, then back to the rehearsal hall, where we changed into our robes. The afternoon began with another round of Sound and Movement, which even at this early stage was beginning to feel tedious. We each in turn ran across the room, making our predictable sounds accompanied by our predictable movements. Margo then asked two of us to do the exercise together—then three, then four, till all of us were in the middle of the room, leaping about like kangaroos and screaming like banshees.

Then, out of the corner of my eye, I saw Margo throw off her robe. Noel followed suit. Suddenly, the rest of us were tearing off our robes, still jumping about and shouting. Only Brenda hesitated, but Noel and Margo managed, in a friendly way, to help her out of her robe. Suddenly, everyone stopped. All I could hear was our own heavy breathing. It had finally happened. I caught a glimpse of the stage management team: never had I seen faces so transfixed. Before we had time to consider our state, Tom told us to lie down where we were and close our eyes, which we did for about five minutes. I could not, however, relax. Adrenaline seemed to be flooding through my body, and I could barely breathe. I assumed we were all thinking the same thing: what happens now?

Tom went from person to person, grasping an arm here, a leg there, and adjusting each limb so that it touched some part of the body of the nearest other person. Eventually, we were all connected like a human daisy chain, lying on the ground, gasping for air. We lay together like that for a few minutes, till Margo asked us to get up and form a tight circle. We huddled close together, naked body to naked body, our eyes fixed on our own toes. There was some giggling and some awkward conversation, mostly about our toes, which we wiggled. Margo then asked each of us to stand and turn around slowly, one at a time, while the others watched. Then we put on our robes and broke for coffee.

I was dying for something stronger, but at least I was breathing again. We sat around in our robes, while Clifford and the stage management pretended to be absorbed in their paperwork. Margo had brought in some fruit, and we sat there munching oranges and grapes, acting nonchalant as hell but not making much conversation. Noel leaned over to me and said, "Well, I'm glad *that's* over." Hardly the sentiment of the liberated people we'd all thought we were.

Margo called us back to work. She asked me to take off my robe and lie down on top of it, face down. Then she instructed the group to kneel around me and massage my naked body. Seven pairs of hands probed every square inch of my flesh. Someone remarked that I was a bit tense. Oh, really? Not wanting to be pegged as the uptight one of the group, I made a superhuman effort to relax. After a few minutes of this, Margo asked me to turn over.

I felt as helpless and as vulnerable as a patient on an operating table. Tentatively opening my eyes, I saw six faces gaping down at me while Margo rummaged in her bag. She pulled out a bottle of baby oil, which she poured all over me. Then she and my other fellow cast members continued their massage, their hands slithering over my body. The exercise concluded with them all blowing air over me from between their pursed lips. I did my best to remain blasé, but it was a losing battle. Eventually, this ordeal was over. I was left lying on my robe in a shaft of sunlight streaming in through the skylight as the attention moved on to the next person. When he was done, the group left him, and I got up to join in on the next. By the time we had finished the eighth and last person, we were exhausted.

The day's work over, we were asked again to discuss how we felt, though most of us, still digesting the experience, had little to say. Amid some mumbles of "Great" and "I enjoyed it," Brenda's was again the lone dissenting voice: she did not care, she said, for anyone but a professional masseur handling her in that way. The discussion over, we started to get dressed, there in the rehearsal hall. After all we'd been through, it seemed pointless to go to the washrooms to put *on* our clothes. But suddenly Margo said: "Look, this isn't a nudist colony. We have to keep nudity as something special." It was a point we had all overlooked: attempting to liberate ourselves from our inhibitions about our bodies did not mean we should become casual about them.

Before we left, Margo advised us not to discuss our work in the rehearsal room with our friends or lovers. They wouldn't understand, she said. One of those who ignored Margo's advice was Linda Marlowe, who had married for the second time just a week before we went into rehearsal. She went home and told her new husband about the day's proceedings, and the result, predictably, was a row. The same thing happened to Tony Booth; both of them vowed not to make the same mistake again.

The next day, Margo introduced us to a pleasant young man named Michael Childers, who had been the photographer on the New York production and who would be taking photos of us during that afternoon's session. These, she assured us, were to be used only for the photo montage in the opening number. Even though this was years before the Internet, we were understandably dubious. Who knew what could happen if those pictures somehow fell into the wrong hands? However, we were trusting enough to acquiesce, not quite realizing that the session ahead of us was going to take our explorations a significant stage further.

Not so much rehearsal as group therapy

The doors were locked, as usual. After we'd warmed up with a session of Sound and Movement, Margo and Tom gathered us, in our robes, to the centre of the room. We were told to shut our eyes and wander about until we bumped into someone. Then we had to disrobe whoever it was and explore their naked body with our hands until we could identify him or her. Once we had discovered the person's identity, we were to help him or her into their robe and repeat the process with another partner. This exercise was named, appropriately enough, Group Grope.

It was not quite clear to me what was expected of us in this. Since breasts and hair were dead giveaways, Margo had told us to concentrate on arms, legs and waists; other than that, she had set no limitations on what we were to do. So just how far, we wondered, were we supposed to go? What if our explorations became too intimate, and someone got upset? None of us wanted to take advantage of an unwilling partner, and none of us particularly wanted to risk being repudiated. Even more embarrassing—particularly for the men—was the possibility of sexual arousal. What if *that* happened? Noel had already asked about that potential problem before rehearsals started. "Problem?" Margo had replied, somewhat unhelpfully. "What problem? Erections are beautiful." For most of us, though, the sexual implications of our exercises did pose a problem. After three days of this, we were neither emotionally involved with each other, nor could we call ourselves perfect strangers. Besides, our relationship was professional, not personal. This was a job. These were co-workers, not friends or lovers. We were in a rehearsal room, not a palace of sensual delight. It was a very odd situation.

In the end, we put these considerations out of our minds and got on with it, only to find that our responses were, for the most part, asexual. The presence of Mr. Childers and the constant "Click, click, click" of his camera had a lot to do with that. I suspect my own preoccupations were not untypical. "Is he pointing that thing at me? Is he getting my best profile? Is my mother going to see this picture in a magazine somewhere?" These were hardly thoughts conducive to carnality.

In fact, some of those pictures did subsequently find their way into the newspapers, though nobody seemed able to explain how. Lawsuits were prepared, and an out-of-court settlement was finally arrived at. Nonetheless, the breach of trust, whoever was responsible for it, was intensely distressing for all of us.

From this point on, the exercises became more intimate, and our level of comfort with them grew. The fifth day brought nude dance improvisations. In my first attempt at this, I was partnered with Noel, then Tom joined in to make it a trio. Perhaps Noel and I were trying to compensate in a macho sort of way for the delicacy of the situation—three naked men grappling with each other—but our "dance" quickly degenerated into a kind of wrestling match. Then Margo asked me to partner her. I was doing my usual Kabuki refugee when suddenly—I don't know how she did it—Margo was off her feet and in the air. Next thing I knew, I was holding her above my head. I felt supremely confident: I knew that if I lost my balance, she would compensate for it; if I dropped her, she would land without hurting herself. With this assurance, my physical strength seemed to have doubled. My balance was perfect. My daring was sublime. Four days ago, I'd been an awkward kangaroo; now I was ready for the Royal Ballet. Brief and no doubt illusory as this moment of power was, it was a turning point for me. Never before had my body responded that way. What I gained that day, and never lost, was confidence in my own body, naked or not.

On the sixth day of rehearsal, we finally got to read a preliminary script.

After five days of intensive conditioning, the group had started to come together. We talked candidly to each other about our pasts, our sex lives, our fears, joys and ambitions. We laughed and cried and showed our frustrations. We made an effort to understand and tolerate one another. The obvious differences—age, nationality, colour, creed, education—were the simplest to cope with, while the more subtle disparities of personality, temperament and aspiration were not so easily surmounted. But the exercises had helped us to make allowances for each other's idiosyncrasies, to the point where we had come to behave like a community who had lived together for years. With that came a surprising tenderness and care for each other. If someone one day looked a little pale, for instance, he was given all the attention due a dying father.

Given all this refinement of our sensibilities, we now felt ourselves ready to approach a script of the most delicate and sophisticated wit (Coward, perhaps?), a nuanced, insightful and profoundly felt examination of the human comedy (Chekhov, maybe?) that would allow our wonderful spiritual selves to breathe. And what were we faced with? Crap. One hundred and twenty-three pages of unmitigated crap. Or so it seemed to our dismayed eyes. And this material, Clifford told us, was the result of a thorough winnowing process: almost as much again had already been discarded. So this was the crème de la crème, the pick of the porn. There was one consolation: additional sketches were to arrive shortly.

We began to read. Like any group of actors at a first read-through, we laughed at the jokes. But our laughter was forced. We tried to cover up the repugnance we felt, the men by attacking the words with hearty locker-room vulgarity, the women by being ultra-sophisticated and demure. But still there were one or two audible winces. We did our best. We were, after all, stuck with it. But one thing became apparent to us: the first time you say a four-letter word it's daring; the second time it isn't. The third time, it might be funny, but by the time the 10th one comes along, it no longer has any meaning or point at all.

The reading came to an end. Noel broke the silence: "It's as if they'd all dipped their pens in shit."

Domini and I in *Oh! Calcutta!*

The next day, Sunday, was a day of rest, thank God. On the Monday, it was confirmed to us that no West End theatre would be available for our show. The London Theatre Managers' Association was still determined to keep the disreputable *Oh! Calcutta!* off its stages. In the meantime, we had an agreement with a non-West End theatre, the Round House on Chalk Farm Road in the borough of Camden, where we would open on July 27 after 10 days of previews. Margo had seen the Round House and found it "acceptable." Clifford had earlier called it a "last resort"—a turn of phrase that in my ears sounded like an unfortunate echo of "last resting place." But Clifford had a gift for making the best of a bad job, and he now seemed full of enthusiasm for the place. Our lease there would extend only until September 11, but it was hoped that after that preliminary engagement, once the fuss had died down, we would at last be able to move into the West End.

In fact, the Round House—a former railway shed—was one of the most exciting theatre buildings in London. The man largely responsible for its transformation was the playwright Arnold Wesker, who'd intended it to be a sort of arts laboratory where projects that were uncommercial, unfashionable or lacking major financial backing might find a home. Peter Brook's experimental reworking of *The Tempest*, which had made an indelible impression on me, had been staged there, as had Tony Richardson's sensational production of *Hamlet* with Nicol Williamson in the title role. And it was there, on my first visit to England, that I'd seen *Paradise Now*, that outrageous Living Theatre piece with the non-levitating actor. But that avant-garde track record was precisely the reason why the Round House was not entirely suitable for our purposes. However novel and shocking *Oh! Calcutta!* might be, it would also be slick, resolutely commercial and aimed straight at the hearts of the middle class and the middle-aged—not at all the kind of thing with which the Round House was normally associated. Our venue's reputation as the home of artistic experiment might thus create expectations to which our show could not live up.

There were also technical incompatibilities. Our designer, Abd'Elkader Farrah (known professionally only by his last name), had made tentative sketches with a conventional proscenium-arch stage in mind. The Round House had a thrust stage with the audience on three sides, and so he had to make major revisions. There was nowhere above the stage to fly scenery, so everything would have to be wheeled on and off. Our permanent set, with its huge louvred and mirrored doors, would have to be made to completely different specifications, and a lot of money would have to be spent on improving the theatre's notorious acoustics. On top of all that, extra production costs would be entailed in a transfer to the West End—if we ever got that far.

But the main thing was that we had a venue. Now all we had to do was create a show to put in it. Having had our first read-through, we naturally expected that we would now begin "putting the show on its feet": blocking the sketches and choreographing dance routines. We were bewildered and disappointed to learn that we would be spending most of our second week on more exercises.

Matters came to a head on the hot, sunny afternoon of Tuesday, June 9. Margo had started us off on another Group Grope—an exercise that had been repeated so often that we were on intimate terms with every hair, muscle and mole among us. We were no longer exploring; we were covering old ground. The stillness of the afternoon was suddenly broken by a yell of frustration: "I've had enough of this!" It was Noel, standing in the middle of the room like a naked Cassandra, prophesying doom. There was no point, he proclaimed angrily, in doing these exercises at this stage of rehearsals. Nothing had been choreographed and, apart from one reading, we hadn't touched the text. Valuable time was being wasted—to say nothing of the fact that in the exercises he always ended up with Brenda, and Brenda didn't like to be touched. These exercises, he concluded, were useless.

A deafening pause ensued. Then Noel picked up his robe, swept to the phone and asked his agent to have him released from the show. The rest of us broke for lunch.

Noel's outburst had expressed what most of us were feeling. That day, Tony told me that he, too, had been on the verge of walking out; instead, he had decided to cope with his frustration by treating the exercises as a kind of joke. Many of the rest of us also felt we had done as much preparation for the nudity as we needed. This was, after all, supposed to be a rehearsal for a show, not a voyage of self-analysis.

I suspected that Margo had intentionally used endless repetition to push us past not only the point of novelty but also past any sense of easy familiarity, in order to achieve real self-awareness and real communication, and bring to the surface things we might not even admit to ourselves. This final breakthrough could be painful and upsetting, and some people just didn't want to make it. We all knew, for instance, that Brenda was reticent; she said so herself. But Noel had managed to develop a certain rapport with her, and so Margo always paired him with Brenda in an attempt to draw her out. But Brenda had remained unresponsive, and the result, instead of liberating her, had been to make Noel crack.

Noel and I went out to eat that evening. He poured out his concerns to me and in the end decided not to hand in his notice after all. Our little community would remain intact.

The next day brought new exercises. The novelty of what we had been doing had long since faded, and so had our interest. Our explorations had become generalized and perfunctory. Our fingers were no longer like nerve endings stimulated by strange contours; our hands wandered aimlessly over familiar territory. "Don't *pat*!" Margo scolded us. "Really *touch*." It had become necessary to regenerate our original spontaneity.

Margo gathered us together in a clump, our naked bodies not touching but leaving the smallest space between us that a person could conceivably pass through. Domini was chosen to go first. She had to move through the spaces between us without touching any part of anyone else with any part of her. The rest of us were to remain silent and still. If she did happen to brush against someone, that person was to say, "Touch."

Slowly Domini moved into the group, contorting herself into seemingly impossible positions to avoid touching us. She slithered through our legs, snaked over our feet, arched herself around our elbows. It demanded acute control of every muscle in her body. Each of us, in turn, followed suit. In the heat of the June afternoon, sweat poured down our bodies. Our muscles bulged with the strain; our brows furrowed with concentration. The narrow gaps that were so difficult to squeeze through became gulfs in the mind. For the person moving, the motionless bodies of the others seemed removed, inanimate, abstract. As I took my turn, squirming, wriggling and straining to keep from touching, I felt alone in my body and my mind. If anyone said "Touch," the word sounded like a sudden detonation.

After three-quarters of an hour of this, our simultaneous proximity and remoteness seemed agonizingly irreconcilable, the tension stretched to snapping point, the electricity between our bodies almost tangible. Suddenly Margo told us we could touch one another again. In an instant, the group collapsed as one. We fell together in a heap, touching as much of each other with as much of ourselves as we could. It was a sea of skin: arms, legs, fingers interlacing and enveloping. We lay together inert, the tension of enforced separation released in a flood of coming together. It was a moment of pure exhilaration.

In my mind, I compared the exercise with being in a museum, confronting a Henry Moore sculpture with a sign under it saying, "Do not touch." You would attempt to satisfy yourself by inspecting the sculpture as closely as possible, from every angle; but were you completely alone, you would sit on it, lie on it, slide over it, crawl through it, feel its texture and temperature and shape. In this exercise, we had felt that same way about each other: prohibition had rekindled our desire to touch. It also re-established a certain respect for each other's bodies. The liberties we took with someone in the rehearsal hall were not something that person *had* to submit to; he or she *permitted* them. Further, we were made aware of the shapes that a body can carve out of the air as well as the solid forms it assumes, and of the electricity that can be generated between two bodies in proximity.

Next, Margo played a record, and we moved about the room to the music. When it stopped, so did we. Then, in the silence, one of us would say a single word, anything that came to mind. Someone else would then do the same, and so on. The words could not overlap: if two people spoke at once, both had to stop speaking, and a third person would supply a word. This game of verbal Give and Take taught us to respect each other's contributions and be sensitive to their slightest impulses. After several attempts, we reached a point where we instinctively knew when to speak and hardly ever overlapped.

All of this, though we didn't know it at the time, would form a basis for the show's improvised finale, which would be entitled "Coming Together, Going Together." So the exercises hadn't been quite as irrelevant to the rehearsal process as Noel had feared. Still, it came as something of a relief when, at the end of the afternoon, Clifford announced that the next day, Thursday, we would actually begin staging the sketches.

In fact, the most memorable events of that Thursday were my singing audition with our musical advisor, John Dankworth (an experience too painful to discuss), and the long-overdue arrival of the first of our absent Americans. I had dragged myself away into a corner to die after my abortive attempt to favour Mr. Dankworth with a couple of verses of "Birth of the Blues," only to discover that the said corner was already occupied by a sleeping lump. The lump opened its eyes and then its mouth, which introduced the rest of it as Bill Macy.

Not to be confused with the younger film actor William H. Macy, Bill, then 48 years old, was a former cab driver from New York. He had worked twice before in England: in *America Hurrah* at the

Royal Court and as Caliban in Peter Brook's version of *The Tempest* that I'd seen at the Round House. As Caliban, Bill had no elaborate costume; Brook had told him, he said to me later, "I want to see the monster in *you*." A vulgar, warm-hearted, brave, difficult, funny man, Bill always said what was on his mind, whether you were interested or not. He used to say to me, "Richard, I've got my bullshit detector working all the time." He could tell when I wasn't really present, when I was just *acting*. He later achieved TV fame as Walter Findlay, the husband of Bea Arthur's character in the 1970s sitcom *Maude*.

Having been in the New York production of *Oh! Calcutta!*, Bill had already gone through the conditioning process. Still, his arrival entailed a further postponement of getting to grips with the text, as we spent another two days repeating our exercises to absorb him into our group. In our Truth Session that Friday, he remarked that the women in our company were less inhibited than the ones in New York. That same day, however, an incident occurred that destroyed our air of self-congratulation and brought home the fact that the old taboos were still very much with us.

With Domini in the *Oh! Calcutta!* sketch "Was It Good for You Too?" by Dan Greenburg

The Donmar had a huge skylight and a number of windows near the ceiling that looked out over the surrounding rooftops. These were great assets, letting in plenty of daylight and affording us, in the heat of high summer, a welcome supply of fresh air. They did much to counteract the claustrophobia that could be induced by our exercises. On this occasion, we were doing another Group Grope, with our eyes trustingly shut, when three workmen found their way, by accident or design, to the roof outside one of our windows. From that vantage point, they regarded our blind meanderings with fascinated amusement. I don't recall who first noticed these unwelcome spectators, but in an instant we all looked up to see the three smirking down at us. The moment they were spotted, they vanished, leaving only their leers imprinted on our retinas like the grins of three Cheshire Cats.

The women in our group were acutely upset. Margo tried to reassure us that the spectators' laughter had been induced by nervousness, which might have been true. The important thing, however, was that our privacy had again been invaded and our trust violated. The incident forced us to realize that, while we had largely overcome our embarrassment among ourselves, we weren't yet ready for voyeurs, thinking or otherwise. The ease we had established with each other was functional but artificial. Our little community operated in a vacuum: we could not expect the code of chivalry that operated within it to apply in the outside world. That thought gave rise to feelings as old as Genesis: we were naked and we were afraid.

On Saturday, June 13, a day shy of two weeks after our group had first met, we bade farewell to the Donmar. On Monday we would be in the Round House, and Clifford had promised us that this time we really would begin work on the text. The first phase was finally over, and our first preview was still a month away: a reasonable enough time in which to whip up our sexual soufflé.

To the scripts we had seen at that first read-through had been added several more, including one about a ventriloquist making love. We now had more material than we could use, so Clifford, Kenneth Tynan (who made his first appearance during this third week of rehearsals, watched one of the scenes and slipped away without introducing himself) and we, the actors, made choices according to various criteria: length, quality of writing or just personal preference. If two scripts seemed too similar in subject or style, one would be discarded. We winnowed the material down to 18 sketches to be rehearsed, of which 14 would actually end up in the show. Out went the lovemaking ventriloquist: too many technical problems. Out, too, went a 30-minute monologue by a lesbian: everyone's favourite, but just too long to use. And out went a sketch about four octogenarians having an orgy. Too many props—trusses, colostomy bags, false teeth and walking sticks—to say nothing of our embarrassment at its tastelessness.

Among the sketches that made the final cut was "The Empress's New Clothes," written by Tynan himself. Essentially a fashion show of women's underwear from Victorian times to the present, it featured costumes designed by the eminent pop artist Allan Jones, who was perhaps best known for his "forniphiliac" furniture designs: chairs and tables constructed out of mannequins in the female form. One of the drawings he had come up with for the sketch was an image of a high-heeled lace-up shoe, which evoked in me a powerful memory from when I was six years old.

My father had disappeared one night, and my mother was in a grim mood. "I'm going out, Richard," she said, as she put her foot up on a chair in order to lace up a shoe very similar to the one in the sketch. "I've got to find your father." She then sent me to stay for the night with my grandparents, Alfred and Eva. It was one of the first indications I had in my young life that all was not well in my parents' marriage, and it was astonishing to me how strongly the sight of that shoe design brought it all flooding back. Jones gave each of the actors who appeared in "The Empress's New Clothes" one of his original designs as a keepsake, and that particular sketch went to Domini. Long after the show was over, when she was clearing out some clutter, she unwittingly tossed it into a wastepaper basket. I retrieved it and had it framed for her, and she has it still.

This design sketch by Allan Jones evoked a vivid memory from my childhood.

Though our script was more or less in place, our problems were by no means over. The Round House stage was currently set for another play, which meant that the only place we could rehearse was the broad gallery that circled the inside of the theatre. For our purposes, however, this proved wholly inadequate. For one thing, it was as dark as the Black Hole of, well, Calcutta. For another, the floor was made of rough wooden planking: every few minutes, rehearsal would stop while we removed splinters from our bare feet. Even more problematic, it was open to view: anyone who happened to be passing through could see us cavorting in the nude—and for some reason there always seemed to be an inordinate number of people with business to attend to inside the theatre while we were rehearsing. The last straw came when we looked over the gallery rail and spotted a man with a camera on a tripod. A few of us rushed down the stairs, shouting abuse, grabbed the camera and took out the film. The man was so taken aback that he couldn't speak. The next day, we found out that he had been hired to photograph the theatre for a seating plan.

Clearly, the gallery was no place to rehearse. But finding an alternative proved to be more trouble than Joseph had finding the manger. Days were wasted as we were shunted from one venue to another. We rehearsed in union halls, army barracks, church halls, even a pub—and every time our landlords discovered who we were and what we were doing, they threw us out. Despite locked doors, papered windows and a sign that coyly announced us as "Somerford Productions," they always found us out. One proprietor not only asked us to leave but requested that the rent owed him be sent to Oxfam instead. Apparently he didn't want to soil his hands with our dirty money, but it would be all right for the starving poor. And so we became what actors have traditionally been called since the passing of the Poor Law in 1572: rogues and vagabonds. At the end of each day, the stage manager would tell us where we would be going next, and would issue us with little maps to get us there. Rehearsals never started on time, because someone always got lost on the way. (Much to my surprise, it never happened to me.)

Through it all, we remained loyal and hopeful. We rewrote, edited, reorganized, invented and generally pummelled some semblance of life into the scripts. The ones that had been used in New York already had a shape and were relatively easy to deal with. But organizing the new material was like wrestling with a nest of vipers.

June 18, the day before my birthday (26 years since I first came naked into this world!), was marked by two significant events: a British general election and the arrival, at last, of our remaining American, George Welbes.

My first impression was that George could have been a millionaire gigolo. Again, I was wrong. He had attended six universities before going into the theatre, but what he really wanted to do, he said, was work in a circus. Though not a trained dancer, he had such grace and strength that Margo had picked him in New York to partner her in the nude *pas de deux* "One on One." She'd sent him off to a few dance classes, and together they'd created the number that stole the show. In the event, I hardly got to know George. He left us to return to the States three days after we opened, so he was with us for only six weeks in all. He did, however, leave us with plenty of tips about the sketches and how they had grown out of rehearsals, and some expert advice on how to handle managements and audiences.

As for the general election, it resulted in the surprise overthrow of the Labour government by the Conservatives. This was not good news for us. Normally, an election would not affect the production of a musical revue, but it was under the Labour government that the Lord Chamberlain's power to censor the theatre had been abolished, and the Conservatives were known to be unhappy with this relaxation of control. Our position would be all the more tenuous under an unsympathetic government.

There was a subtler problem too. As we worked on the sketches and the idea of an actual opening night began to loom ever larger in our consciousnesses, a change began to come over us. In our sensitivity exercises, we'd developed the qualities of co-operation and non-competitiveness to a high degree. Now, however, our old instincts as professional performers began to reassert themselves. Territory rather than trust started to become our imperative. Each of us had the same motive: to come out of this looking better than everyone else on stage. We jockeyed for the best parts and fought to hold on to them, knowing that further cuts were to come. Ironically, the tensions this caused were exacerbated by the very sensitivity training we'd all undergone. For the past three weeks we'd been encouraged to speak our minds: to bring our antagonisms and criticisms out into the open. We'd overcome our inhibitions and learned to be frank. Now that our actors' egos had kicked in again, the result was an emotional free-for-all of petty jealousy and backbiting.

Our little community began to disintegrate in a withering crossfire of mutual criticism. Some members of the group again started grumbling about all the precious time that Margo had made us put into the preparatory exercises instead of working on the actual choreography. And why hadn't Clifford taken a firmer hand and put a stop to it? Others voiced the suspicion that Clifford was somehow working against Margo. Some became hostile to the show and to their fellow actors; others started treating the whole thing as a boring joke. As distrust and discontent grew among our ranks, Linda, Domini and I found ourselves being drawn more closely together. Not wanting to be forced into taking sides, we tried to balance our loyalties to both Margo and Clifford, taking, we hoped, the best from each of them.

With Domini in the show's wittiest sketch: "Until She Screams," written by Joe Orton

As for Bill and George, they too were at odds with Clifford. Their sensibilities were in tune with the New York production, which had been more subversive and more offensive than Clifford wanted the English one to be. Clifford wanted our show to be a romp, carried off with expertise, warmth and good humour; the New York show, however, was less a romp than a rape, and it was in that direction that Bill and George were urging it. Slowly but effectively, they began to impose themselves on the production, slipping back in lines that had been cut, insisting on naturalism where Clifford asked for clarity, on being themselves when Clifford asked for characterization.

The end result was a show that fell between two stools. Whatever concept Clifford had of *Oh! Calcutta!* was effectively destroyed, yet the Americans' vision of it was never fully realized either. We ended up with something daring enough to be interesting, yet professional enough to be safe. We set the audience on the brink but never pushed them over. We lobbed hand grenades at them that never exploded. No one was going to be seriously affected by seeing this show. It was, in short, the perfect recipe for a smash hit.

The first run-through, held after four weeks of working together, was a disaster. Run-throughs are possibly the only thing worse than auditions. You're never ready, and you have to show your absolute best, because if you don't look good, you could be fired. In this case, given the time and effort that had already been invested in us, it was more likely that the sketches that didn't seem to be working would be cut. But nobody wanted it to be *their* sketch that got cut.

Because the sketches had been rehearsed separately, this would be our first time performing them in front of each other. If there's one thing that makes actors nervous, it's performing in front of other actors. In Tony's words, "If you're good, they hate you and think they could do better. If you're bad, they hate you and think, 'I always knew it.' " To make matters worse, some of us still didn't know all our lines, and three of the four dance numbers hadn't even been choreographed yet.

Our audience—Clifford, Tynan, Michael White, musical advisor John Dankworth, musical director Mike Allen, lighting designer Richard Pilbrow, set designer Farrah, costume designer Freda Jackson (yes, there *were* costumes), the wig master, the assistant stage managers (I'd never seen so many) and whichever of the cast weren't performing the particular sketch in progress—sat at one end of the room. We performed at the other.

Our audience sat stony-faced throughout. Clifford lost his temper for the first and last time. Tynan's skull-like features became ever more sunken. Michael White looked as if he'd just heard the stock market had crashed. Only during the last sketch, "Until She Screams," a parody by Joe Orton of a typical English country-house comedy performed by Domini, Pamela, Linda, Noel and me, was there any laughter. This came as a surprise to us: although it certainly had the wittiest lines of any sketch in the show, "Until She Screams" had been the hardest one to rehearse, and we'd been sure it would be cut.

The run-through ended in silence. No notes were given. The big guns rolled out quietly, without a word to us, leaving us strewn about like corpses. Dismissed with our worst expectations fulfilled, we raced to the pub.

The next day brought further anxieties. Brenda had picked up the wrong script by mistake and found, when she got home, that she had Kenneth Tynan's copy, with all his notes on the run-through.

Naturally, she'd read them and, equally naturally, shared with the rest of us what she'd found. Tynan, we learned, was disappointed in two members of the cast. (I wasn't one of them, nor was Domini; on the contrary, Tynan was particularly pleased with us.) Sketches were going to be cut and others drastically revamped. The telltale script was discreetly put back where Brenda had picked it up, and we waited for the slashing to begin.

In the event, no one was let go, though the two actors who now knew that Tynan didn't think much of them were, understandably, unhappy and considerably less confident. Two sketches and one dance number were dropped; otherwise there were no major changes. Just deepening fear.

Before we knew it, we had one week to go to the first preview, to be held on July 14 (Bastille Day!). The moment of truth was almost at hand. The sets were under construction, the costumes were almost finished, and in one afternoon Margo choreographed the remaining two dance numbers. Clifford's encouragements went into overdrive. Advance ticket sales were enormous: every day, it seemed, the newspapers carried articles about the show, along with pictures and many editorial cartoons, and people were snapping up tickets for the previews in the certainty that the law would close us down.

The most serious problems facing us now were technical. Because of the inadequacies of the space backstage, our scene changes were taking longer than *The Ring of the Nibelung* performed underwater. Also, there was no orchestra pit, so our band had to be stuffed into a corner of the balcony, making communication between them and the actors on stage impossible. This didn't enhance the confidence of the non-singers among us.

On the morning of the first of our 10 previews, we were herded into the men's dressing room, where Kenneth Tynan told us that he had asked Michael White to postpone the first preview till the following day. Michael had refused, he said, but if we, the actors, stuck together on this issue, he might be persuaded to change his mind. Shortly thereafter, Michael himself arrived, and a tense discussion ensued. Tynan argued, with passion, that a preview of the show in its present state would do more harm than good. A couple of the actors pointed out that we were the ones who'd be suffering humiliation out there because of technical problems that had nothing to do with us. Michael remained unmoved. Bill Macy offered to give up his salary to cover part of the financial loss that a postponement would entail; a few others followed suit.

Michael agreed that the show was in poor condition but insisted that the backers did not want to lose their money on this first preview, especially since costs had already exceeded the budget because of our difficulty in finding a venue. And postponement would be unfair to people who'd queued for hours to get tickets specifically for that evening. Given the demand, it might not be possible to give them tickets for another night. Finally, there was always the sobering possibility that there might not *be* another night. The die was therefore cast.

This cartoon in the *Birmingham Evening Mail* was one of many that appeared in the British press in 1970.

We went dejectedly to the auditorium to rehearse the scene changes one more time. By mid-afternoon, we were exhausted. Tynan sent for his doctor, who gave us all a shot of Vitamin B12. Clifford gave us some final notes on stage and told us to try to relax during the performance. This was only the first of 10 previews, he said; there was still time. His good humour fooled no one. Directors, like football coaches, give the same pep talk before possible successes and possible disasters alike. Then suddenly, in an unpremeditated moment of *esprit de corps*, the entire company jumped on Clifford and pulled down his trousers. He was wearing cerise underwear. Cheerfully, he surrendered to this assault and jumped up and down, laughing with the rest of us, as the stagehands looked on in bewilderment. Dismissed until our call for that night's performance, we grabbed sandwiches and drinks at the theatre bar.

By curtain time, the combination of Vitamin B12, adrenaline and liquor had begun to take effect. We were by no means drunk, but we were certainly on a high. Places were called. We huddled together behind the louvred doors of the set. The enemy was out there, waiting.

The music began, the louvres opened, and out we went like Christians to the hungry lions to perform the opening routine, "Taking off the Robe." The purpose of this number was to introduce the audience to the nudity right off the bat: to amuse and titillate them, and shock them slightly, but also to put them at their ease. It said to them, essentially: "You don't have to wait all night for a furtive glimpse. Here it is, folks: everything you've paid to see in the first five minutes." But would it work?

We each stood in a different box of light as we began a sequence of stripper moves, each of us exposing a different part of his or her anatomy, manoeuvring our robes like matadors executing the *veronica*. Silence from the audience. Then came the big moment. One by one, we stripped off our robes and flung them on the floor, whereupon every light on the stage was turned up to an intense white glare. Despite all our preparation, I found my chest tightening with fear. Very deliberately, however, I said to myself: "My name is Richard Monette, and I am standing here naked in this white light. I am not hiding behind a character; this is *me*." There came a small gasp from the audience, followed by a burst of applause, then a cheer. They had accepted us.

Our relief was short-lived: the real test, the sketches, still lay ahead. The audience reacted politely to the first one, "Delicious Indignities," about the erotic travails of a young Victorian woman (Linda) who seeks shelter from a sudden downpour in the lodgings of a bachelor friend (Tony). Brenda's song, "To His Black Mistress," was received enthusiastically; then came the first of the sketches I appeared in, "Will Answer All Sincere Replies." Concerning a conventional young couple (Domini and me) who hook up with an older pair of swingers (Bill and Margo), it contained not only the first really crude language of the evening but also the first simulated orgasm (mine) that most people in the audience had ever likely seen on stage.

I girded my loins, so to speak. If they were going to throw tomatoes tonight, now was going to be the time. But the sketch began well: they were laughing! Not uproariously, but actually laughing. As the sketch progressed, the laughter increased. My simulated orgasm won a round of applause, as did the surreal noises Bill emitted during a scene depicting oral sex. We were stunned: this was the sketch we'd all hated the most in rehearsal. When we came off afterwards, Bill said to me: "We go out there and do this pile of shit, and they laugh their heads off. That *must* be good acting." We began to relax and enjoy ourselves.

The second act began with a nude group dance number, "Much Too Soon." ("Okay, girls," said Margo before we went on, "fluff up your bushes.") It was immediately followed by Margo and George's nude *pas de deux*, "One on One," which proved as much of a show-stopper as it had been in New York and is still the one thing about *Oh! Calcutta!* that most people remember. On we marched, without faltering, till we came to the finale, "Coming Together, Going Together," in which, as in our Give and Take exercises, we took turns spontaneously throwing out lines to represent the kinds of thoughts that might be going through our audience's minds. Because of the legal niceties of our position, we had been instructed to say, if questioned, that all of these lines had been scripted. We kept a meticulous record of them as they were invented, so that we could put them in a master script and claim that the actors had simply selected from them at each performance. Some of the more printable examples:

"Boy, they must have needed a job to get into a show like this."

"I think it's filthy, disgusting and embarrassing–but after all, George, that's why we came."

"If Mother asks you what you thought of the show, darling, just say you were bored."

"Next time, you choose the restaurant and I'll choose the show."

"Are you sure it was Kenneth Tynan who said there are no small parts, just small actors?"

"I've seen better knockers on doors."

"Oh, my God, that's my daughter up there."

"Oh, my God, that's my *father* up there."

"I wonder which sketch John Lennon wrote?"

"It'll never replace pantomime."

"I told you she wasn't a natural blonde."

"Why do they call it *Oh! Calcutta!*?"

"Because they couldn't call it *Oh! Bangkok!*"

"Who wrote this piece of shit anyway?"

Curtain call. The audience roared its approval. After the intensity of seven weeks of group therapy and rehearsal, after all the backbiting among the cast members, after the crisis over the technical problems, we had done it, and we were a success. Tension released from us in a rush; most of us were in tears, or close to them.

That first preview had all the excitement and release of birth. Never again did our show generate quite such electric vibrations. As with all theatre, much of the chemistry was contributed by the audience, who knew that night that they were part of something special, something unprecedented. It was the actors who mustered all the courage and talent to do it, but it was the audience who finally brought the show together and gave us the strength to keep it going for the rest of the run.

The next milestone was our official opening, on the night of July 27, 1970, to an audience full of critics and celebrities ranging from Sir John Gielgud to the pop singer Lulu. That audience proved to be deadly, and so, accordingly, was our performance—as, of course, were most of the reviews. The party afterwards, given by Robert Stigwood, one of the backers, was far more exciting. I was greeted at the door by a cop. Just inside I was introduced to a stuffed camel, and my entrance into a room filled with a couple of hundred strangers was heralded by Bill Macy's dulcet scream from the far side of the room: "Hey, Monette! Come here, you big faggot!"

It was some enchanted evening, and one of the biggest drunks of my life. It was like one of those great binges from the Golden Age of Hollywood, full of stars and liquor and food and fights and people being pushed into swimming pools in full evening dress. One of the people I met there was Trevor Nunn, then artistic director of the Royal Shakespeare Company. I said to him, "I'm so pleased to meet you, Mr. Nunn. Can you believe I turned down an offer from the RSC to do this piece of shit?"

I had overcome my shyness all right.

CHAPTER SIX

The Readiness Is All

Hamlet, Act V, scene 2

Even with all those famous writers as contributors, and despite what I believe was the complete sincerity of Kenneth Tynan, *Oh! Calcutta!* did not, in my opinion, have any real artistic merit—with the possible exception of "One on One," the truly beautiful *pas de deux* danced by George and Margo. (Although, as one commentator remarked, the aesthetic problem with nude ballet is that when the torsos come to a standstill, everything else keeps moving.) Otherwise, the show seldom rose above the level of a burlesque.

It did, however, make an important contribution to the sea-change in social attitudes taking place at the time, both in the theatre and outside of it. Only 63 years earlier, a mere verbal allusion in J. M. Synge's *The Playboy of the Western World* to "a drift of chosen females, standing in their shifts" had provoked a riot at the play's opening. Now audiences were confronted with real live females (and males too) *not* standing in their shifts, or in anything else. In that sense, our shiftlessness helped to promote freer and franker discussions of human sexuality than had been possible on British stages before.

We did have our much-anticipated brush with the law. One of our first previews had been attended by a notorious right-wing activist of the time, the Dowager Lady Birdwood. This redoubtable critic of the "permissive society" (how quaint *that* phrase now seems) was, curiously enough, Canadian by birth and an actress by training. Born Joan Pollock Graham in Winnipeg in 1913, she'd come to England with her family as a child and later studied at the Royal Academy of Dramatic Art. Because there was already a well-known British actress called Joan Graham, she'd changed her Christian name to Jane, becoming Lady Birdwood when she married Lord Christopher Birdwood in 1954.

She'd gone to *Oh! Calcutta!* with a Conservative member of the Greater London Council, Frank Smith, and his wife, Ida, and after the performance they'd all marched straight down to Kentish Town police station to lodge an official complaint. We were intrigued to learn, from a report in *The Sunday Times*, that in addition to her more predictable objections ("grossly obscene and erotic"; "no justification in any art form"; "produced by persons who are morally corrupt"), Lady Birdwood had denounced *Oh! Calcutta!* as "a communist plot." This took us all aback: while it was no secret that Kenneth Tynan had socialist tendencies, *Oh! Calcutta!* was nothing if not a capitalistic enterprise. There was plenty of pink in our show, but very little red.

The night after this complaint was reported in the press, Noel won cheers and applause for one of his improvised lines in the finale: "I think Lady Birdwood was right." Some time after that, two police officers arrived.

First, they asked to photograph the stage manager's script, which contained all the changes of text made in rehearsals, plus records of all the actors' movements. We showed them a carefully prepared one, guarding our own individual working scripts like FBI documents. Any deviation from the letter of the law in the way our roles and actions were described in the script, even if it would make absolutely no difference to what an audience would see on stage, could have dire consequences. John Mortimer, who'd sat in on some of our later run-throughs before we opened, had told us, for example, that it was very important that we be able to say we were always portraying characters, never just being ourselves. So for the dance numbers, we all had to be assigned in the script such names as "Follower Number One." Then the officers interviewed Clifford, beginning in a warm, chatty manner and gradually becoming more chilly and professional. Finally, they watched a performance, pads and pencils in hand. They took turns: one would describe what was happening on stage, while the other wrote it down; then they would change over. Maybe they thought it wasn't fair for one of them to have all the fun while the other did all the work. Their distasteful duty done, they made their report to the director of public prosecutions, Sir Norman Skelhorn, and we all waited for the axe to fall.

It never did. Though we didn't know it at the time (nor did anyone, for many years afterwards), the attorney-general at the time, Sir Peter Rawlinson, dispatched his own team of arbiters—including two school headmistresses, a law professor and a vicar—to see the show, and they reported back more or less in our favour, one of them suggesting that *Oh! Calcutta!* would be more likely to bore than to corrupt. As a result, Sir Peter decided, in consultation with Sir Norman, that convincing a jury of the show's obscenity would be a lost cause, and let the matter drop.

Lady Birdwood did not give up so easily. Several months later, she somehow obtained copies of the script and distributed them to members of Parliament; but by then her cause was well and truly lost. We were an entrenched phenomenon: the hit of the decade. Sir Peter's decision had opened the doors of the West End to us, and on September 30, 1970, we moved into the Royalty Theatre (now named the Peacock) on Portugal Street. The acoustics and sightlines there were better, and the auditorium, done up in red plush like a high-class brothel, was far more comfortable. But somehow it wasn't as much fun as our old railway shed.

In part, this was because by then we were no longer a *cause célèbre* so much as a tourist attraction. *Oh! Calcutta!* had quickly become the sort of show to which businessmen took their clients: one captain of industry told us he'd seen it seven times. Coach-loads from the provinces were the rule rather than the exception, and weekend excursion flights brought theatre parties from as far away as Madrid. Despite the rewards of being in a West End hit, I was glad I'd insisted on signing up for only nine months instead of the year-long contract that had been demanded. For me, *Oh! Calcutta!* was something that happened in the rehearsal hall, not in the theatre. I didn't, and don't, regret a moment of it—I had, after all, helped to make theatrical history—but after nine months, I had nothing more to learn from the experience, and I was more than ready to move on.

Oh! Calcutta! ran at the Royalty until 1974, when it transferred to the Duchess Theatre on Catherine Street. It continued there for another six years, finally closing in 1980 after more than 2,300 performances. This decade-long run reportedly earned Tynan about £250,000: a substantial enough sum at the time but only a fraction of what the show's backers must have taken in. In the short time I knew him, I grew to like Tynan a lot. Despite what many people thought, he wasn't in the least pretentious, and I felt immensely privileged to be in the company of so genuinely brilliant a man. In return, he seemed to genuinely appreciate my work. I also owed him one of my more intriguing might-have-been moments: at a party at his home (where he showed Domini and me his bedroom, which we were intrigued to notice was furnished with a mirror above the bed), the film star Ava Gardner tried to pick me up. Flattering as this was, I didn't take her up on it: for one thing, she was considerably older than I, and besides, I didn't feel it would be proper to abandon Domini.

As Algernon Moncrieff in *The Importance of Being Earnest* (1975), with Nicholas Pennell as John Worthing. Photo by Robert C. Ragsdale

As Sparger in *Kennedy's Children* (1975), with Brenda Donohue as Carla. Photo by Robert C. Ragsdale

As Romeo in *Romeo and Juliet* (1977). Photo by Robert C. Ragsdale

As Parolles in *All's Well That Ends Well* (1977), with Martha Henry as Helena. Photo by Robert C. Ragsdale

In the title role of *Hamlet* in 1976. Photo by Robert C. Ragsdale

As Sandy Tyrell in *Hay Fever* (1977), with Maggie Smith as Judith Bliss. Photo by Robert C. Ragsdale

As Andrei Vukhov in *Judgement* (1978). Photo by Robert C. Ragsdale

As Berowne in *Love's Labour's Lost* (1979), with Domini Blythe as Rosaline. Photo by Robert C. Ragsdale

As Prince Hal in *Henry IV* (1979). Photo by Zoe Dominic

As Edmund in *King Lear* (1979-80). Photo by Robert C. Ragsdale

As Prinz Carpenter in *Foxfire* (1980), with Jessica Tandy as Annie Nations.
Photo by Robert C. Ragsdale

As King Henry in *Henry V* (1980).
Photo by Robert C. Ragsdale

As Harry Thunder in *Wild Oats* (1981), with Keene Curtis (right) as Sir George Thunder.
Photo by Robert C. Ragsdale

As Sparkish in *The Country Wife* (1983), with Rosemary Dunsmore as Alithea.
Photo by Robert C. Ragsdale

As Benedick in *Much Ado About Nothing* (1987), with Tandy Cronyn as Beatrice.
Photo by Michael Cooper

As Domenico Soriano in *Filumena* (1997).
Photo by Cylla von Tiedemann

Douglas Campbell as William Blake in my production of *Blake* (1983). Photo by Robert C. Ragsdale

From left: Keith Dinicol as Dromio of Syracuse, Goldie Semple as Adriana, Geordie Johnson as Antipholus of Syracuse and Lucy Peacock as Luciana in *The Comedy of Errors* (1989).
Photo by Michael Cooper

Colm Feore as Benedick and Goldie Semple as Beatrice in my production of *Much Ado About Nothing* (1991). Photo by Tom Skudra

Stephen Ouimette as Moulineaux in *A Fitting Confusion*, which I directed in 1996. Photo by Cylla von Tiedemann

Megan Follows as Juliet and Antoni Cimolino as Romeo in *Romeo and Juliet* (1992). Photo by David Cooper

Janet Wright in the title role of *Shirley Valentine* (1992). Photo by Elisabeth Feryn

Leon Pownall as Mark Antony and Goldie Semple as Cleopatra in *Antony and Cleopatra* (1993). Photo by Cylla von Tiedemann

William Hutt in the title role of *King Lear* (1996). Photo by Cylla von Tiedemann

Martha Henry (left) as Regina and Diana Leblanc as Birdie in *The Little Foxes,* which I directed in 1996. Photo by Cylla von Tiedemann

Tom McCamus as King Arthur in *Camelot* (1997). Photo by Cylla von Tiedemann

In 1976, Tynan moved to California, where he died four years later, at the age of 53, of pulmonary emphysema. Roberta Maxwell once told me of meeting him in the latter part of his life, when he had resumed smoking after a 10-year abstinence. When she asked him why he would do such a thing, knowing that he had emphysema, he replied: "I have not written a word in 10 years. And I would rather live for a short period of time and write."

As for Lady Birdwood, she went on to have her own run-ins with the law, including two convictions in the 1990s for distributing anti-Semitic literature. She died in 2000 at the age of 87.

Despite all those Group Grope exercises, there was remarkably little hanky-panky between cast members of *Oh! Calcutta!* To my knowledge, only two romantic relationships formed among us during the entire time I was in the show. One was between Domini Blythe and George Welbes. The other, after George had left to go back to America, was between Domini and me.

With Domini at the opening night of *The Dirtiest Show in Town*

We'd connected instantly, from the moment we met. In one of those group exercises, I'd told Domini that I loved the way she moved her legs, quite unaware that she particularly hated what she called those "skinny and shapeless" limbs. My compliment had really touched her: had given her permission to appreciate herself, as she later put it. But still we were nothing more than friends, until her relationship with George ended with his departure. I was living in a house in Finsbury Park with Larry Aubrey and two other people at the time, and my room was on the ground floor. One night when I was asleep, the window opened, and in climbed Domini. Thus began my love affair with the only woman whom I have ever seriously wanted to marry.

It was, at its passionate height, a relationship that I can best describe as stormy. At times, it resembled the second act of Noël Coward's comedy *Private Lives*, in which Elyot and Amanda end up kicking, biting, scratching and breaking gramophone records over each other's heads. Indeed, I am ashamed to admit that Domini holds the distinction of being the only person I have ever slapped. I can only explain that I did so without thinking, as a shocked and automatic response to the fact that she'd just thrown a wooden coat hanger at me.

In New York in the 1970s, after *Oh! Calcutta!*

I was insanely jealous, especially since it seemed to me that everyone in London—and beyond—was madly in love with her. Once, after she'd come back from making a movie in Egypt, I accidentally found a love letter written to her by her Egyptian co-star. When I confronted her with it, she responded with the startling news that this erstwhile paramour was coming to London to visit, that he would be staying with us, and that she didn't want to see him.

I ended up showing my rival around London, taking him to art galleries and the theatre in order to steer him out of Domini's way, all the time thinking to myself, "I must be insane." But I was so in love with her that I'd do anything to keep her.

Eventually, the romantic phase of our relationship ended, and we both turned to new partners. But for some four years we enjoyed what still lives in my memory as one of the world's great love affairs, and in all the decades since we have continued to enjoy one of the world's great friendships.

Clifford Williams had been right in predicting that *Oh! Calcutta!* would neither help nor hinder my career, at least not directly. There was one brief moment, though, when a glimpse of the yellow brick road flickered in front of me as a result of my involvement with the show. I had been invited by a casting agent to meet Bob Fosse, who was looking for someone to play the role of Cliff in his forthcoming film of the Kander and Ebb musical *Cabaret.* When Fosse asked the agent how she knew me, she said, "I saw Richard in his last West End success."

"What was that?" Fosse asked.

"Well, I don't know if I should say this, but I saw him in *Oh! Calcutta!*"

To this Fosse responded, much to my surprise, "That's one of the best shows I've seen in two decades." Fosse was very gracious to me in that interview, but it was clear to both of us that I was in no way suited for the role, which eventually went to Michael York.

No, my destiny in 1971 lay not in Hollywood but back in Regent's Park, where the New Shakespeare Company was celebrating its 10th season with two productions: *Romeo and Juliet* and a revival of the previous season's *A Midsummer Night's Dream,* which had become a big hit. Richard Digby Day offered me Tybalt in *Romeo* and also Puck in the *Dream,* the same part I had wanted before but had turned down to do *Oh! Calcutta!*

Seldom in life do you get the chance to retrace your steps and go down a path not chosen, but instead of immediately accepting the gift of Puck with abject gratitude, I set about trying to improve the other component of my offer. Tybalt is a terrific part but only about 65 lines long, and I thought I deserved more. Since I was no longer quite the same shy young novice who had called everybody at Stratford "Mister," I decided to push to get what I wanted. Hugh Ross, a very fine actor with whom I'd already worked, both in Regent's Park and in Wales, and who'd become a good friend, had already been hired to play Romeo, so I set about angling for the next best thing: Mercutio.

I mounted a determined campaign, sending a flurry of telegrams to Richard and to the New Shakespeare Company's producer, David Conville, to the effect that I was, in Mercutio's words, "more than prince of cats." Finally, to get me off their backs, they did agree to let me read for the part, and I believe they were indeed going to offer it to me. But then, at the very last minute, along came an extraordinarily talented young actor named Gregory Floy, who gave a wonderful audition and got the part. So I ended up with Tybalt after all. (At least it was a bigger part than Balthasar, played in our production by the then 23-year-old Anthony Andrews, who 10 years later would find fame on both sides of the Atlantic as Sebastian Flyte in the TV miniseries *Brideshead Revisited*.)

In fact, my 1971 season at Regent's Park was by no means devoid of challenge, for Puck turned out to be a harder role than I'd anticipated. As an actor, you have to find your character's "arc": you have to figure out what kind of human being he is and what his journey consists of. If your character ends up changed at the end of the play from what he was at the beginning, you have to try to figure out the steps along the way and connect the dots into something that seems to have shape and coherence. But Puck seemed to me to defy this process: he seemed to be different in every one of his scenes, and I couldn't understand why.

Eventually it dawned on me that one of the key things about Puck is that he's *not* human but a "shrewd and knavish sprite." As he himself tells us in his first scene, he's a mischievous shape-shifter who can assume any form he wants, animal, vegetable or mineral:

> I jest to Oberon, and make him smile
> When I a fat and bean-fed horse beguile,
> Neighing in likeness of a filly foal:
> And sometime lurk I in a gossip's bowl,
> In very likeness of a roasted crab;
> And, when she drinks, against her lips I bob
> And on her wither'd dewlap pour the ale.
> The wisest aunt, telling the saddest tale,
> Sometime for three-foot stool mistaketh me. . . .

So I decided not to worry about the continuity of the role, because clearly there wasn't meant to be any. I ended up playing Puck as what he is: quicksilver personified.

This quality of discontinuity in Shakespeare isn't limited, by the way, to the character of Puck: it occurs in various forms throughout the canon. This is something that critics seem consistently unable to grasp: the fact that judiciously deployed discontinuity of character, of style, of tone, is one of the hallmarks of Shakespeare's genius. One of the most obvious examples is his use of low comedy in high-flown contexts. With few exceptions, the critics turned up their noses at my decision, in my 2006 production of *Henry IV, Part 1*, to explore the comedy inherent in the scenes with Hotspur (played by Adam O'Byrne), whose heroism and nobility of deportment are held up by the king as a reproach to his own disreputable son, Prince Hal (played by David Snelgrove). But humour at Hotspur's expense is also there in the lines, if you care to look for it, and it took no forcing or straining to bring it out. This extraordinary ability of Shakespeare's to integrate the sublime and the ridiculous is, to me, one of the things that make his plays so insightful into human nature.

My return to Regent's Park in 1971: as Puck in *A Midsummer Night's Dream*

As Puck, I had another challenge to contend with: my costume, or rather lack of it. I was playing the character as a North American Indian, and my costume—designed by a fellow Canadian, Mark Negin, who had started his career as a propmaker at the Stratford Festival in 1955 and had gone on to design for the Canadian Players and Theatre Toronto before coming to Britain—consisted of the skimpiest loincloth imaginable. When it was delivered to me, it came in a box approximately the size of an audiotape cassette. You might think that after *Oh! Calcutta!*, this wouldn't give me a moment's pause, but it wasn't my modesty I was concerned about. This was open-air theatre, after all, and we were in Britain. Heigh-ho, the wind and the rain.

Despite these challenges, I seem to have acquitted myself well. Domini thought I was an "absolutely superb" Puck, though as Tybalt she thought me a little too light on my feet. She said to me once, "I feel I could knock your Tybalt over with my finger."

Our season in Regent's Park ended in mid-August, and in the winter we were going to take the two productions, with some changes of cast, on tour through the north of England. First, though, as a favour to Linda Marlowe, one of my erstwhile cast-mates from *Oh! Calcutta!*, I made what I usually refer to as my soft-porn film.

Linda Marlowe: martial arts and machine guns

It wasn't really that at all, though it did contain some scenes of a semi-erotic nature. Titled *Big Zapper* and directed by another expatriate Canadian, Lindsay Shonteff (there seemed to be a lot of us about in Britain in the early 1970s), it was an ultra-low-grade action-movie spoof, based on a British comic strip of the time. Linda played a private detective called Harriet Zapper, whose male sidekick and lover—parodying those James Bond girls with such ludicrously suggestive monikers as Honey Ryder and Pussy Galore—was named Rock Hard. Linda wanted Mr. Hard to be played by someone she knew and was comfortable with, so she asked for me.

My role consisted mostly of making out with the Zapper or waiting for her in the back of her convertible while she—dressed for combat in high heels, hats and skirts slit to the thigh—punched, kicked, shot and karate-chopped an endless parade of thugs and villains. I still have among my papers two pages torn from some movie magazine of the time, containing an advertorial feature on the film. Bearing neither title nor date, they feature a brief column of leeringly sexist copy surrounded by lurid photos of Linda dispatching her unsavoury foes or wielding assorted bits of weaponry. In one particularly immodest pose, she is seen sitting on the ground, legs splayed, as she aims a heavy machine gun mounted on a tripod. Really, the things we actors do for our art. . . .

The first scene we shot was one in which we were in bed together. I remember the director of photography saying, "What are we going to do about that big red spot in the middle of his nose?" Another scene of intimacy between us was shot outdoors in a public park: I think it may have been Hampstead Heath. We hadn't bothered applying for permission to shoot there—the film had no budget to speak of, and certainly no money to waste on bureaucracy—so while the cameras rolled, half the film crew were stationed in the bushes as lookouts, to warn us of approaching policemen or passers-by.

Big Zapper was released in 1973, and frankly, I expected it to disappear without a trace. I was bemused, on my return to Canada, to find it playing at the old Imperial 6 (now the Canon Theatre) on Yonge Street in Toronto. It even generated a sequel, *The Swordsman*, in which I did not participate, and I understand that it remains a cult favourite among connoisseurs of cinematic bathos.

Domini had remained with *Oh! Calcutta!* after I had left, so we were separated from each other during October and November, while I went on the northern England tour with the New Shakespeare Company. It was an uncomfortable business. The theatres we played in were mostly older buildings that didn't have much in the way of heating. Few of them had showers, and those that did were pretty short on hot water. So, since my role as Puck required me to be covered from head to foot in body makeup, I'd either have to boil endless kettles of water after each performance of the *Dream* or just put on my clothes over the makeup and go home to wash. So much for the glamour of the actor's life.

I forget which town we were in, but during one of those stops on the tour I decided that I wanted to go back to London to see Domini. We had a day off after a weekend performance of *Romeo and Juliet*, and since Tybalt dies in Act III, just before our intermission, I thought I might be able to skip the curtain call and get away early to catch a train for London. I did a trial run to see if it could be done: I brought my suitcase to the theatre, changed into my street clothes immediately after my death scene and took a taxi to the train station. But I found there wasn't quite enough time: I still needed another 10 minutes. As it happened, I felt that the pace of our production was, shall we say, leisurely, so I went to my fellow cast members and said: "Listen. It's terribly important that I get laid. We have to take 10 minutes off this show. If you can do that for me, I'll buy you all a beer."

On the appointed day, we came to the point at which Romeo kills Tybalt. I fell to the ground, Romeo fled with his friends, and Lady Capulet (played on the tour by Pamela Lane, the first wife of playwright John Osborne) came on to weep over my body. As she bent over me, keening and wailing, Pamela added to her exclamations of grief an uncanonical *sotto voce* line for my ears only: "Tybalt, my cousin! O my brother's child! O prince! O cousin! (Don't worry, you'll make your train, you crazy f___er.) O! the blood is spill'd of my dear kinsman . . . !"

I did make my train, with time to spare. In fact, my fellow actors told me later that by the time they got to the end of the play, they'd shaved a whole 20 minutes off the running time—which made me rather wonder just how slowly we'd been playing it before.

During that second summer at Regent's Park, I'd seen an RSC production at the West End's Aldwych Theatre that had opened my eyes to a whole new way of presenting Shakespeare: Peter Brook's legendary production of *A Midsummer Night's Dream*. When it had first opened in Stratford-upon-Avon on August 27, 1970, Brook's *Dream* had created an immediate sensation. It was a production, wrote Clive Barnes in *The New York Times*, "that is going to be talked about as long as there is a theatre, a production that, for good or ill, is going to exert a major influence on the contemporary stage." He was right about that: it is still seen as a turning point in the 20th century's approach to Shakespeare. It was also one of the hottest tickets in the theatre world at the time, and its London opening had been sold out for months ahead.

I'd been disappointed that I couldn't plan to go, especially since I happened to know the actress playing Hermia, Mary Rutherford (another Canadian), but quite aside from the lack of tickets, I had a *Dream* of my own to do that night. Then, however, on the very night of Brook's London opening, our performance was rained out.

We cancelled at 7:30, the same time that the RSC's *Dream* was scheduled to begin. I had no ticket, of course, but I decided to try my luck anyway. Perhaps a ticket holder might have failed to show up, in which case I might be able to squeeze in during a break in the performance. I hastily scrubbed my face, pulled on my clothes over my body makeup and ran off in the downpour to find a taxi.

I arrived at the Aldwych at 7:50, walked up to the box office in the now-deserted lobby and asked if there was any chance of a ticket. "Certainly," they said. As it turned out, the performance hadn't even started: they were holding the curtain for various dignitaries who had been delayed because of the rain. Perhaps I got one of those VIP tickets: in any case, I found myself seated right behind Peter Brook and Trevor Nunn, who (perhaps fortunately) did not seem to remember me from that opening-night party for *Oh! Calcutta!*

Watching the performance, I was struck by a thought: if I had chosen to accept my RSC offer a year and a half earlier, might I have had a chance to be in this astounding show? With its abstract white-box set, its ladders and trapezes, its stilt-walkers and acrobats, it was like no Shakespearean production I'd ever seen before. Dispensing with all the semi-naturalistic conventions of staging that had been with us since the Victorians, it overturned the whole idea of a "classic" as something that demanded a certain traditional mode of representation. Yet even though the style of Brook's production was completely contemporary, at the same time it was very respectful of the text, and, as Clifford remarked, it was beautifully spoken. It made a profound impression on me.

Afterwards, I went backstage to see Mary, who invited me to the opening-night party. I got the impression from her that rehearsing the production had not been a particularly happy experience. "I'm sorry to hear that," I told her. "But, you know, the result is absolutely fabulous." At the party she introduced me to Peter Brook, rendering me almost speechless with awe.

"So," he said to me: "you're an actor. What are you doing at the moment?"

"Well," I replied, sheepishly, "I'm playing Puck in Regent's Park." Having just seen this stunning, epoch-making production of his, the work we were doing at Regent's Park seemed to me to be mired in the traditions of another century. But Brook's reply was wonderfully generous and reminded me that the magic of the theatre depends neither on sophistication nor on radical innovation.

"Do you know," he said, "the very first production of the *Dream* I ever saw was in Regent's Park, and that's when I first fell in love with it."

Still, Brook's production had awakened in me the desire to tackle Shakespeare in more adventurous ways than were offered at Regent's Park. I didn't know if I'd be any good at it, but I wanted to try my hand at more experimental drama, something for which I felt the journey of *Oh! Calcutta!* had prepared me. I was very conscious, at that age, of the theatre's role in society: it was a way of helping people cope with life, rather as religion was. Therefore, it was vital to explore, to experiment with new forms, to find new ways of communicating with people. So when my tour with the New Shakespeare Company was over, I hitched my wagon to the star of a man whose stature as a guru of the avant-garde was arguably on a par with Peter Brook's: Charles Marowitz.

Born in America in 1934, Marowitz had first come to England in the 1950s to study at the London Academy of Music and Dramatic Art. In 1963, at the RSC, he and Brook had gathered together an experimental ensemble of 12 younger actors, including Glenda Jackson, to explore in practice the theories of the early 20th-century French playwright and director Antonin Artaud. The group's work had resulted, initially, in a collection of short pieces presented under the Artaudian title "Theatre of Cruelty" and, later, in Brook's celebrated 1964 production of Peter Weiss's play *The Persecution and Assassination of Jean-Paul Marat as Performed by the Inmates of the Asylum of Charenton under the Direction of the Marquis de Sade*, more familiarly (and more conveniently) known as *Marat/Sade.*

Marowitz despised the received wisdom, beloved of bardolators, that Shakespearean text was something sacrosanct: a kind of holy repository of eternal and universal truths that needed to be guarded assiduously by academics and approached by artists and audiences only with the utmost reverence. Instead of "keeping the classics alive," an approach that sounded to him suspiciously like keeping a terminally ill patient going on life support, he held that what theatre artists should be doing was giving the classics a good violent shake every so often, to see what new insights and new dramatic possibilities might fall out. Accordingly, in 1966, he'd created what became known as *The Marowitz Hamlet*, a radically cut and rearranged 80-minute version of Shakespeare's play that threw the narrative out the window in favour of a non-linear "collage" of themes and ideas. Traditionalists had been outraged at his impertinence; unrepentant, he'd followed it up with a similar treatment of *Macbeth*.

Then, in 1968, in partnership with former actress Thelma Holt, he'd started his own fringe theatre company in a small venue on the Tottenham Court Road called The Open Space, a name chosen in tribute, I assume, to Brook's influential book *The Empty Space*. With Thelma as his producer, he was now auditioning for people to work there on further Shakespearean collages and other projects.

Charles Marowitz: turning classics into collage

On a Friday in early January 1972, I phoned Thelma, who made an appointment to see me at 3 o'clock the following Tuesday. "By the way," she added, "don't tell Charles you're Canadian. He doesn't think North Americans can do Shakespeare."

"What do you mean?" I said. "He's a New York Jew, for heaven's sake."

I could hear the shrug in her voice. "He just doesn't believe they can."

In fact, I'd auditioned for Charles Marowitz once before, on my first visit to England in 1968. By a curious coincidence, the play with which he launched The Open Space that year was none other than *Fortune and Men's Eyes*, so naturally, having workshopped it at the

Stratford Festival back in 1965, I'd gone out for it. I hadn't been accepted; I'd been beaten out by yet another transplanted Canadian, Louis Negin (the brother of Mark Negin, as it happened, the designer of my Puckish little loincloth). Charles did not, however, seem to remember me when I met him this time, and I'd been in England long enough now that my accent was more than passable, so I dutifully pretended to be English. To explain away any stray treacherous vowels, I invented a whole "backstory" for myself: I'd been born in the north of England, but my family had moved to Canada when I was still quite young, and now I'd come back to my roots. I don't think I fooled him for a minute.

My preliminary meeting with Thelma on Tuesday lasted an hour and a half, in the course of which I learned that if I were hired my pay would be £16 a week. I was told to come back on Saturday for a full weekend of audition by improvisation. There would be 30 actors at the audition, from which 12 would be chosen.

Malcolm Storry: Enough improv to last a lifetime

Over the course of that weekend, I got to know two of the other actors who were auditioning along with me. Both came from Yorkshire: one was Petronella Ford, a delightful eccentric who looked like Marlene Dietrich and had an astoundingly high IQ; the other was Malcolm Storry, who went on to become a stalwart of the RSC and a frequent supporting actor in TV drama. I liked both of them very much, and my friendship with Malcolm has lasted to this day. I was delighted to hear that he'd landed the role of Gandalf in the British production of the musical-theatre version of *The Lord of the Rings* that premièred in Toronto in the spring of 2006.

At the end of the day on Saturday, the names of those who would be called back on Sunday were read out. After all those hours of gruelling improvisation, this had a surprisingly emotional effect: like listening to Henry V read out the names of the dead after the battle of Agincourt. Malcolm, Petronella and I were among those asked to come back next day for more of the same, after which all three of us were picked to join the company of 12.

There ensued six more months of improvisation—enough to last me a lifetime. I don't think I was alone in feeling surfeited: about 15 years later, on a visit to England, I was reminiscing with Malcolm when he said to me, "You know, Richard, I can't improvise at all now."

Charles took improv very seriously, was very articulate and rigorous about it and was very good at structuring it. He might instruct us, for example, to form a circle with one of us in the middle. Someone else then had to go up to that person and say something that would initiate a dramatic situation: for example, "Stick 'em up: I want your money." Then, while the first actor was resisting the second, a third actor would be told to go in and say something incongruous—"Sir Edmund, what are you doing here in the club this morning? I heard your wife had died"—that would force the other two to modulate into a whole new situation without breaking the flow. And so on, till the whole group was involved. We got to be fabulously adept at this, and used our skills in a lunchtime improv show called *Ham-omlet*, based on the theme of death, to which, perhaps predictably, audiences came in droves of two or three at a sitting—some of them, I think, expecting a brunch.

We also mounted a lunchtime production of a one-act play by Howard Brenton, *How Beautiful with Badges*, in which I played Jesus. As a former devout Catholic who had in his boyhood contemplated becoming a priest, I found the scene I had to play—a macabre spoof of the Crucifixion—daring, to say the least. I had to come on carrying my cross, set it up and then mime nailing both of my own feet to it. Then I had to nail one of my hands in place, only to realize that there was now, of course, no way of driving in the final nail. So after a couple of futile attempts to bang it in with my head, I had to pull all the nails out again and walk off. The laugh, if there was one to be had, should have come at the point where my predicament dawned on me; but nothing I tried—neither simple freeze, nor slow burn, nor double take—got any reaction. One day, I resorted to exclaiming "Jesus!" which did get a bit of a laugh. The playwright, believe it or not, was deeply offended.

Meanwhile, in the evenings, I was playing Laertes in a revival of *The Marowitz Hamlet*. We later took it to the Edinburgh Festival, where, despite its notoriety, hardly anybody came to see it, not even after Charles, in a desperate effort to generate publicity, rented a horse-drawn hearse and had us drive it down Princes Street, with Hamlet's coffin in the back. One thing I shall always remember about that production was Hamlet's death, which was very slow: he sort of melted, like an ice cube, while all of us around him held our breaths. The effect was amazing, and I subsequently stole it for one of my own productions.

The rest of our time was devoted to developing a new creation called *An Othello*. Like *The Marowitz Hamlet* and *A Macbeth* before it, *An Othello* used fragments of Shakespeare's text to form a non-narrative collage; this time, however, Charles had also contributed dialogue of his own. In composing this material, he'd been inspired by a passage written by Malcolm X, in which the celebrated black activist had articulated the distinction between the slavery-era "House Negro," who, by embracing his comparatively well-treated position in a white household, helped perpetuate his own subservience, and the "Field Negro," whose constant mistreatment bred a more revolutionary spirit. In Charles's version, Othello (played by Rudolph Walker) corresponded to the complacent House Negro, while Iago (also played by a black actor, Anton Phillips) corresponded to the resentful Field Negro, whose radicalism would ultimately subvert not only Othello's domestic peace but also Shakespeare's play. In this interpretation, Iago's motive for destroying Othello, ambiguous in Shakespeare, became crystal-clear: if Iago was a Black Panther, Othello was an Uncle Tom.

An Othello thus made race and culture the central issues of the play. Desdemona's father, Brabantio, was memorably portrayed by actor Edward Phillips as a caricature of a New York Jew, complete with "oy vay" accent. ("We're so low down the social ladder," Charles told me, "the only people we can pick on are the blacks.") This deliberately stereotypical interpretation—"Vould you like your daughter to marry vun? Some joke. My daughter *did* marry vun, and I can tell you, I vouldn't like my daughter to marry vun"—was outrageous, of course, but also, because it was such an unexpected take on Shakespeare's character, wildly funny. Edward, by the way, had worked with Charles before. "He's a really interesting director," he warned me once, "but he's liable to say things like 'Don't subvert the subtext with tertiary movements.'"

I played Lodovico in the show, and Malcolm played the Duke of Venice, while public interest was further stirred by the fact that Desdemona was played by Judy Geeson, who'd starred opposite Sidney Poitier in the 1967 film *To Sir, with Love,* had appeared topless in the 1969 film *Three Into Two Won't Go* and had also featured in a popular soap opera, *The Newcomers,* on British television. I thought she was a fine actress and a wonderful person.

The London première of *An Othello* was scheduled for June 8, 1972, at The Open Space. Before that, though, on May 26 and 27, we were to give two performances of it at the International May Festival in Wiesbaden, Germany, which had actually commissioned the piece. While The Open Space seated about 150 people, the Schauspielhaus in Wiesbaden seated about 2,000 and had a huge stage with a steep rake. So not only did we have to build two different sets for these two very different venues, we also had to be prepared to adjust the scale of our performances accordingly.

With Judy Geeson backstage at The Open Space

On the day of our first performance in Wiesbaden, Charles (possibly underestimating the sophistication of the average European theatregoer) had warned us that most of the audience wouldn't understand English, never mind black American slang, so we shouldn't expect much response. We were startled, therefore, when our first scene, a wordless, imagistic vignette of only a few seconds' duration in which Othello was shown being yanked in all directions by means of ropes attached to his limbs, was greeted with vigorous applause, as was each and every one of the ensuing scenes. We were completely flummoxed by this seeming rapture on the part of our audience until someone explained that it was simply the custom in Germany to applaud at every blackout between scenes.

Back at The Open Space, the day after *An Othello* opened there to generally laudatory (if not entirely convinced) reviews, Charles began rehearsals for a new play by Sam Shepard, *Tooth of Crime*. I'd read the script, basically the fictionalized story of an Elvis Presley type and a Mick Jagger type, and thought it was sensational. Shepard, then 28 years old and resembling a Botticelli angel with long blond hair, had written the music for it himself. I was surprised when Charles, who at one point had shocked me by telling me that my work as an actor was very camp, offered me one of the leading roles. I could not, however, in all conscience accept it, because, camp or not, there was one important area in which I knew I could not meet the demands of the script. "This is a brilliant work," I told him, "and if I do it, I will wreck it, because I can't sing."

I did, however, hang around and watch many of the rehearsals, as I'd become very attached to my colleagues in this company. I was startled when, at one point in the rehearsal period, Charles gave a lecture to the company in which he said, "I know that Sam has told you that he has written a naturalistic play here. But I'm telling you that Sam is wrong."

Call me old-fashioned, but given that Sam Shepard was actually around to hear this, it struck me as an extraordinary thing for Charles to say, like Konstantin Stanislavsky telling Chekhov he didn't understand his own plays. Still, I thought his production of *Tooth of Crime*, very stark and abstract with no set, was quite brilliant. Not long afterwards, if my memory serves me correctly, another production of the same play was done somewhere in a naturalistic manner, and it failed horribly.

I believe Charles offered me that role in *Tooth of Crime* because he knew I was thinking of going back to Canada, and he wanted to keep me with the company. "Don't go," he said to me when I told him what was in my mind. "If you do, you'll never come back to England. There's more money in North America."

He was right, of course, but there were two compelling reasons for me to return to Canada. One, for which there seemed to be no remedy to hand, was the fact that my visa enabling me to work in the United Kingdom would shortly run out. I'd made enquiries of the relevant authorities about staying on, and the responses had not been encouraging. What, I'd asked, if Domini and I got married? Would not that entitle me to stay in Britain? No, came the reply. At that time, it was the male partner in a marriage whose nationality determined the couple's residency status. If Domini and I wanted to be together, even if we got married, she would have to come with me to Canada; it didn't work the other way round.

My other reason for wanting to return was the news from home of my mother's failing health.

It was with great sadness that I bade farewell to England, and to my friends and colleagues at The Open Space. In the course of that year, we'd shared an extraordinary artistic experience, we'd learned much from Charles (certainly I had), and we'd had lots of fun. Twelve secular apostles, with Charles as our caustic, iconoclastic and endlessly inventive Messiah, we'd improvised together, rehearsed together, performed together and even lived together. Since we weren't being paid very much, we all slept in one large communal room, with a tiny separate room off it that we had to book when any of us had romantic intentions. It's possible to live like that when you're young and eager for experience, both in art and in life.

And England as a whole had been, for me, a life-changing experience. I had seen and worked in an incredible amount of theatre of all kinds, from the most traditional to the most cutting-edge, had explored a vast range of repertoire and had absorbed a vast range of influences. I had performed in the open air, in regional theatres and in the West End. I had more than faced down the shyness that had held me back as an actor, and in doing so I had been part of a historic moment in British theatre. I had worked with many of the country's finest artists. I had made many friends. And I had fallen in love.

Whatever lay ahead of me, I was far better equipped to deal with it than I had been when I made my Shakespearean debut at the age of 19. Indeed, without wanting to get too fanciful about a passing coincidence, I can't help noting the faint parallel between this turning point in my life and the one that Hamlet arrives at in the last act of his play.

When he is first charged with the mission of avenging his father's murder, Hamlet is famously ineffectual, finding all kinds of reasons not to fulfil his vow. But then Claudius tries to get rid of him by sending him off to England—not, in this case, to seek stardom, but to be summarily put to death. Hamlet escapes, though, and when he returns, he's a changed man: confident, unhesitant, ready at last to take decisive action, whatever it might cost him. "If it be not now," he says, "yet it will come: the readiness is all." So it seemed appropriate that I too should look forward to returning home from England a new man, imbued with a keen and steady resolve, ready for anything.

I didn't exactly go out in a blaze of avant-garde glory, though: my last engagement in London was not with The Open Space but in a West End play called *The Dirtiest Show in Town,* in which I'd been hired as an understudy and had then replaced the leading man. It was a cleverer and more worthwhile piece than its title suggests—although it did involve nudity and sexual content, it also had some serious things to say, mostly about air pollution and the Vietnam War—but I can't say it represented any significant step forward for me as an actor.

I didn't know it yet, but that next step would be waiting for me back in Canada.

CHAPTER SEVEN

A Most Triumphant Lady

Antony and Cleopatra, Act II, scene 2

In February of 1970, while I was still on my tour of Wales, a brand new theatre opened its doors in Toronto: the St. Lawrence Centre for the Arts. It was operated by the Toronto Arts Foundation (later renamed Toronto Arts Productions), an association of theatre companies that had been formed in 1966 by cultural icon Mavor Moore and that had later absorbed what was left of Theatre Toronto. Leon Major, co-founder of the Neptune Theatre in Halifax, had been appointed general director of the foundation and theatre director of its new facility.

During my last summer in London, in 1972, Leon dispatched Kurt Reis (who'd directed me in the Crest Theatre's Hour Company and in my *Romeo and Juliet* excerpts on TV) to England to scout out talent for the St. Lawrence Centre's 1972-73 season. That season was to include *Twelfth Night*, directed by Leon, and Euripides's *Electra*, directed by Kurt. Domini and I were living at the time in a palatial, high-ceilinged flat in Hampstead, tastefully furnished with *objets* from an antique stall that Domini ran for a while to supplement her earnings from the stage. When I heard that Kurt was in town, I invited him to stay with us.

The St. Lawrence Centre's Leon Major

While he was there, Domini and I had one of our more spectacular rows. Kurt was so impressed with our histrionics that he offered both of us roles in *Twelfth Night*: Domini would be Viola, and I (an afterthought on Kurt's part, I suspect) would be Orsino. The offer to Domini was provisional on Leon's consent, which she obtained after paying a flying visit to Canada to audition for him. In addition, Kurt offered me Orestes in *Electra* and gave both of us roles in the season's opening production, which he was also directing: a dramatization of Franz Kafka's *The Trial*.

Since my application for an extension of my work visa had been denied, the timing of this seemed too good to pass up. Accordingly, we wound up our affairs in England and flew to Toronto together in the fall. A spooky thing happened: above the fireplace of our Hampstead flat we had an enormous antique gilt mirror. As we were leaving the flat for the last time, it fell off the wall and shattered.

After a rocky start to the season in November with *The Trial, Twelfth Night* opened on December 12 to some grudgingly positive notices. ("It really seems kind of strange to be praising the St. Lawrence Centre for a change," mused one reviewer, Don Rubin.) Besides Domini and me, the cast included Robert Benson as Malvolio, Ron Bishop as Sir Toby Belch, Jennifer Phipps as Maria, Vivian Reis as Olivia and the Australian actor Gary Files, later of the TV soap opera *Neighbours*, as Feste.

Domini—whom I, already feeling the stirrings of the directorial impulse within me, had been coaching in the role at home in our apartment between rehearsals—hated her own performance as Viola, though to this day I think she was just about the best Viola I have ever seen (and not just because she was so young and beautiful).

As homecomings go, this one seemed to be off to a reasonably good start. And then, just a few days before *Twelfth Night* ended its run, my mother died at the age of 53.

The death of a parent, no matter what your relationship with that person has been, is one of the most profoundly significant passages in anyone's life. Why this should be is not entirely clear to me; in the case of a mother, perhaps it may have something to do with unconscious pre-birth memories of umbilical connection. Or it may simply be because when your parents go, you can't help being conscious that you're next up on the Grim Reaper's list. In any case, I wept from the bottom of my soul.

I don't really know what she died of; the doctors seemed unable to say. She'd had a brush with stomach cancer when I was still quite little (I remember how everyone around her used to whisper the word *cancer*, like Big Daddy's family in *Cat on a Hot Tin Roof*, as if to say it aloud would intensify its effects), but I don't think that was the immediate cause. She'd gone into a deep coma before the end, and I'd visited her in hospital. "Get better," I'd murmured into her ear, having been told that the hearing is often the last sense to desert a comatose person.

In order to attend my mother's funeral, I would have to miss the last two performances of *Twelfth Night*. We had no understudies, but by an extraordinary stroke of luck an actor friend of mine, Patrick Christopher, had recently played Orsino somewhere else, and he agreed, at a day's notice, to step into the part. Another spooky thing: the night before I flew to Montreal for the funeral, I borrowed an alarm clock from Patrick, so I wouldn't miss my flight. After I'd set it, Domini and I stayed up late into the night. When we checked the clock some time later, we found that its hands were going backwards.

My mother in happier days, as I like to remember her

Afterwards, Domini joined me in Montreal, and together we emptied out my mother's subsidized apartment. She'd been on welfare when she died, and there wasn't much to move. One thing, though, I knew we'd find in abundance. "All over this apartment," I told Domini, "there will be pills that she has hidden." So we looked in all my mother's bags and pockets, in the backs of all her drawers and under the mattress. By the time we'd finished, we'd half-filled a brown grocery bag with pills—most of them white, with a handful that were bright red.

"I want you to witness this," I told Domini, as I emptied the bag into the toilet bowl. The water gradually took on a pinkish tinge, as if from blood, as the red pills started to dissolve. "If I ever start to take pills—if that tendency is in my genes—I want you to remind me of this moment." With that, I flushed the toilet. To this day, I have a dread of pills. In the last few years I have had to take medication for various ailments, and it has taken all my willpower to force it down.

As a memento of the beautiful, spirited, sparkling woman my mother once was, I kept her jewellery. One item among it was a good-luck charm of a kind that many Italian women wear. Shaped like a little red pepper, it's called a *cornu*: a "devil's horn." I kept it until 1988, when I directed *The Taming of the Shrew* for the Stratford Festival, a production that incorporated elements drawn from my childhood memories, such as my mother's methodical smashing of plates that night when my father was late coming home and she threatened him with the knife. As an opening-night gift, I gave my mother's *cornu* to Goldie Semple, who played Katherina, the Shrew. There is a tradition in the theatre of handing on things of significance from one production to another, so the next time the Festival did *The Taming of the Shrew*, in 1997, Goldie presented the *cornu* to Lucy Peacock, who was then playing the role. Lucy, in turn, gave it to Seana McKenna, who played Katherina in 2003. I hope it may go on being handed down from actress to actress, generation to generation, for as long as the play continues to be performed at Stratford.

Rehearsals for *Electra*, my next commitment at the St. Lawrence Centre, weren't scheduled to begin for another two weeks, so after the funeral, Domini and I went on holiday to Jamaica, where a cousin of mine, Robert Mallamo, was stationed as an engineer. He and his wife, Manon, had a little girl, Valerie, one of the most beautiful children I'd ever seen, and when we arrived at their house, she came down the steps carrying a familiar-looking doll. It turned out that my mother had made this for Valerie as part of her therapy during one of her stints in a mental institution. I don't know if she intended some oblique form of atonement, or if she simply couldn't think of any other way to design such an object, but the doll was very like Pom-Pom, my beloved childhood companion that she had made me consign to the flames.

Later, back in Toronto, Domini made me an even closer replica of Pom-Pom. I'd described it to her, in detail, and shown her a picture of it, and she worked on it in secret, when I was out at rehearsals for *Electra*. It was her way of trying to help me overcome the pain of what she knew was a very deep scar. I have this doll still: it has eyes in the shape of crosses, and it looks truly demented.

We had to cut short our visit to Jamaica when I was called back a week early to participate in preliminary chorus work on *Electra*. Domini was furious with Kurt and the St. Lawrence Centre management for that, and I thought it was rather insensitive myself. I'd had only a week to grieve, and now suddenly I had to gather myself up and focus on a play. I would feel the same sense of injustice at the Stratford Festival a few years later, in 1976, when the Festival wouldn't release me from a technical rehearsal of *The Tempest*—even though it was a day of setting lighting cues, for which my presence wasn't essential—to attend my brother's wedding. Mark was, quite rightly, very upset and never let me forget it, even though I tried to laugh him out of it by saying, "Since I didn't come to your wedding, you don't have to come to my funeral." Those two experiences made me realize something that can be all too easy for artists to forget: that life is more important than theatre. Accordingly, in my tenure as artistic director, I always made every effort to release artists for family funerals and weddings. As Tanya Moiseiwitsch, the Stratford Festival's founding designer, used to say, "It's only a play."

Sometimes, though, a play can also be an exorcism. There could hardly have been a more cruelly ironic piece for me to work on while grieving for my mother's death than *Electra*. Part of a series of ancient Greek tragedies chronicling the fateful misdeeds of the house of Atreus, it concerns the growing realization on the part of Electra and her brother, Orestes, that their mother, Clytemnestra, has been guilty of the murder of their father, Agamemnon. In the climactic moment of the play, Orestes takes revenge by killing Clytemnestra. To be playing this matricide, opposite the eminent Québécoise actress Monique Mercure as Electra, sounded harrowing resonances for me, to say the least.

I put my whole heart and soul into playing Orestes. In fact, I wasn't acting at all; rather, I was using my performances as therapy, reliving the whole sorry story of my parents' marriage, dredging up every painful detail. I had wanted to learn to *be* on stage rather than just to *act*, and that was certainly what I was doing now. And what did it get me? Some of the most dreadful reviews of my career.

There was a lesson there, too. What Michael Langham had said to me contained a great truth, but there is more to that truth than first meets the eye. "Being" in acting does not just mean being yourself; rather, it means *being somebody else*. You have to find the elements of the performance within yourself, it is true, but at the same time, you have to use those elements to give the character his or her due. In a classical piece, especially, that character has a certain size and meaning, delineated by the language of the verse, that you have to inform. It is not enough to dredge up your own emotions, however deep they may be, and then self-indulgently wallow in them. You have to use those emotions not as bathwater but as rocket fuel, to fill and propel something larger than yourself.

"Acting is being" is not only a caution against trying to "assume" a character, like putting on a suit of clothes; it also implies using your emotional and intellectual energies to expand yourself into

As Orestes in *Electra*, with Monique Mercure in the title role, at the St. Lawrence Centre in 1972

both a character and a highly charged mode of speaking. In a verse play, especially, that requires rigorous technique: a careful steering between the rhetorical Scylla of bombastic posturing and the mumbling Charybdis of naturalism. Attempt to speak Shakespearean verse too naturalistically, and no matter how intensely you may "feel" it, the poetic power will drain out of the verse, and the play will become footling. Acting requires a carefully judged balance between authenticity and artifice. Or, as Bill Hutt once put it to me, "The most important quality in an actor is truth. And the sooner you learn to fake that the better."

Anyway, while no one can be subjective about his own performances, it's conceivable that in *Electra* I let myself be so swamped by the play's pertinence to my own experience that I failed to transmute that experience into anything that was pertinent to the play. If so, it wasn't too long before I pulled myself together.

In the spring of 1973, after the St. Lawrence Centre season closed, Domini found work at the Shaw Festival in Niagara-on-the-Lake, playing Margaret Knox in *Fanny's First Play*, while I was invited to return to the Stratford Festival, where Jean Gascon was now sole artistic director, the collaboration between him and John Hirsch that had been put in place in 1967 having fallen apart after two years. Apart from this, and the adoption of the Third Stage on Lakeside Drive (now the Tom Patterson Theatre) as a venue for workshops, the Festival didn't seem to have changed much in the half-dozen years I'd been away, and this part of my homecoming turned out to be something of an anticlimax.

I'd been cast as Lucentio (a secondary but still reasonably attractive role) in Jean's production of *The Taming of the Shrew*, but my other parts in the season were essentially walk-ons: Montano in *Othello*, directed by David William, and three roles—First Servant, Third Knight and the Fisherman—in *Pericles*, which Jean also directed. It was good to be back on that wonderful stage again, of course, but after all my experiences in England I couldn't help feeling that, in terms of my career, I'd now taken a retrograde step. It was almost as if the fates were telling me so when, in *Pericles*, I threw my back out while wielding the very heavy sword that I had to fight with, and ended up having to spend three weeks of the season immobile in my bed while my parts were played by Raymond O'Neill.

The only other memory that has stayed with me from that season is of *Othello*, in which the title role was played by the eminent Israeli actor Nachum Buchman. He was a very nice man and tried very hard in the part, but unfortunately his heavily accented English just wasn't quite up to it. He'd learned his lines phonetically, and they didn't always come out exactly right. Act V, scene 2 of the play, in which Othello strangles Desdemona (played by Martha Henry), begins with Othello entering the marital bedchamber with the words "It is the cause, it is the cause, my soul; / Let me not name it to you, you chaste stars, / It is the cause." An incongruously bucolic note was introduced into some of the performances when Mr. Buchman emerged from the shadows and declared, "It is the cows, it is the cows. . . ."

I also recall that on opening night in that same scene, as Othello advanced upon Desdemona with murderous intent, an audience member who had perhaps imbibed too freely at dinner beforehand began to sing, "If a body meet a body, coming through the rye. . . ."

The season over, I returned to the St. Lawrence Centre, where Domini and I appeared together again in Arthur Wing Pinero's *Trelawny of the "Wells"*. Beautifully directed by Leon and with Domini in the lead, this was a great success. Although I had only a smaller role, as Tom Wrench, one review said I gave "the best performance of the show," accompanying this praise with a large photograph of me in the luxuriant mutton-chop side-whiskers I wore for the role. I also appeared in two other St. Lawrence Centre productions that year: a Canadian historical drama by Michael Cook called *Colour the Flesh the Colour of Dust* and Bertolt Brecht's *The Good Woman of Setzuan*. Again, I seemed to have a flair for never being out of work.

As Tom Wrench, with Domini in the title role, in *Trelawny of the "Wells"* (St. Lawrence Centre, 1972)

I decided not to seek employment at Stratford for the following season, because something else of greater interest to me at the time had come up. While we'd been working on *Electra* the year before, Monique Mercure had mentioned to me that Michel Tremblay had written a new play that she thought I would be very good in. Its name, she said, was *Hosanna*.

Michel Tremblay had practically reinvented Quebec theatre with his 1968 smash hit *Les Belles-Soeurs*, a comedy about 15 working-class women whose lives are affected by a sudden windfall. Written in *joual*, the socially disdained dialect I'd grown up with in Montreal, that play had established Tremblay as the pre-eminent theatrical voice of the new Quebec—more secular, more progressive and more self-assertive—that had emerged from the Quiet Revolution of the 1960s, a Quebec very different from the one in which my father had felt it necessary to send me to an English school to ensure me a future.

Hosanna, a two-hander, was also written in *joual*, and its subject matter, delving into Montreal's gay and transvestite subculture, was even more controversial. It depicts the events of one night in the relationship between Claude Lemieux, a former farm boy turned hairdresser and drag queen who has adopted the female persona of Hosanna, and his boyfriend, the gone-to-seed biker Raymond Bolduc, who goes by the name Cuirette. All his life—or rather *her* life, to give the character her proper due—Hosanna has been obsessed by her desire to emulate the on-screen glamour of Elizabeth Taylor, particularly as seen in the role of Cleopatra in the 1963 movie epic of that title. When the owner of the drag club that she frequents announces a Halloween party with "famous women of history" as its theme, Hosanna sees her chance to fulfil her fantasy. She spends two months creating her Cleopatra costume, designing her makeup and dreaming of the fabulous impression she will make. Then, on the night of the party, she makes her grand entrance, only to discover that she has been the victim of a cruel practical joke: every other patron of the club, knowing of her obsession, has also dressed as Cleopatra, many of them outdoing her in glamour. To make matters even worse, she realizes that Cuirette has been in on the joke. The play takes place during the hours immediately after Hosanna has fled the scene of her humiliation.

Tremblay, a staunch separatist, had made a point of refusing to allow English-language productions of his plays in Quebec itself, but translations had successfully been presented in Toronto. The St. Lawrence Centre, for instance, had produced *Les Belles-Soeurs* in English in April 1973, after I'd left the company to go back to Stratford. It was just a month after that, on May 10, that *Hosanna* premièred in French at the Théâtre de Quat'Sous in Montreal, with Jean Archambault in the title role and Gilles Renaud as Cuirette. I didn't see it, but then I learned that the Tarragon Theatre in Toronto was going to present the play in English the following year, directed by the Tarragon's founder and artistic director, Bill Glassco. (Born in Quebec City, Bill had an affinity for French-Canadian culture: it was he who'd mounted, in 1972, the first English-language production of any of Tremblay's plays: *Forever Yours, Marie-Lou.*)

I obtained a copy of the English script of *Hosanna,* translated by John Van Burek and Bill himself, and, after reading it, resolved that nothing was going to stop me from playing the title role.

I went to see Michel Tremblay to discuss the play; then, that summer, when Bill visited Stratford, I buttonholed him and asked him if I could read for it. I followed up with a letter but received no reply. Clearly Bill didn't think I was right for the part. Over the next eight months, I bombarded him with letters, telegrams and phone calls demanding an audition. Even though he'd already come very close to offering the part to someone else, I eventually wore him down to the point where he agreed to see me.

Why did I want *Hosanna* so badly? In the first place, of course, it was a great role: perhaps the best I have ever played, outside of Shakespeare. And although I had no personal interest in cross-dressing, I'd always felt that, as an actor, I was very good at exploring the feminine side of my psyche: something that, as any Jungian will tell you, is there within every male. When it comes to sex and gender, human beings are more complex creatures than our traditional social roles allow. (There's an interesting line in *Antony and Cleopatra* where Cleopatra talks about feminizing Antony as an element of heterosexual eroticism: "Ere the ninth hour, I drunk him to his bed; / Then put my tires and mantles on him, whilst / I wore his sword Philippan.") But there was also, and perhaps most importantly, a cultural motive at work, something that had been nagging away within me for some time and that had been intensified by my experiences in Britain.

Although for many of its audiences the central and most shocking aspect of *Hosanna* was the fact that its two characters were gay lovers, this wasn't a play about the "issue" of homosexuality. As Tremblay himself insisted, the underlying theme was largely political. Hosanna's transvestism (or rather the character's multi-layered adoption of personae: Claude as Hosanna, Hosanna as Elizabeth Taylor, Elizabeth Taylor as Cleopatra) was an edgy metaphor for Quebec itself, a society that, by aping American culture, was trying to dress up as something it was not. During the course of the play, in what Tremblay referred to in interviews as a kind of "emotional striptease," Hosanna gradually takes off her Hollywood Cleopatra makeup and her costume, going from full drag to, in the last few moments of the final scene, total nudity.

With that nudity comes self-awareness and self-acceptance. "Look, Raymond," says Claude, having removed the last vestige of Hosanna, "I'm a man . . . I'm a man, Raymond." At the end of the play, Claude embraces not just Raymond but also his own true identity—just as, in Tremblay's view, Quebec needed to do in order to move ahead as a self-confident society.

One did not, of course, have to be Québécois to respond to *Hosanna*, any more than one had to be gay or a transvestite. Though the political metaphor is undeniable, the play also operates on a completely personal level. "What makes it work is its heart," Tremblay had told me. In its broadest terms, it's about shedding your outer skin and learning to live without your illusions, a universal theme that has informed drama from Sophocles to Tennessee Williams. But given my own particular circumstances, it had an irresistible resonance. After spending five years as a *faux* Englishman in Britain, I knew only too well what it felt like to be masquerading as something you're not.

Acting is, to some extent, a form of relating to a community, and the community I'd been born into was French-speaking Quebec. Spiritually, I was Québécois; in many ways, I still am. The way I speak and act—my intonations, my vocal rhythms, the way I use my hands—is part of my Latin temperament, and it was not always perfectly suited to English theatre. All those British-born directors I'd worked with had kept trying to rein in my emotional excesses. "Richard, that's too much," they'd say. "Not in my family, it's not," I'd retort. "We do that sort of thing all the time."

My acting style was thus in many ways better suited to the more vibrant energies of Quebec theatre, but that was a body of work from which I was now cut off by language. My early life had been a linguistic mish-mash: I had grown up speaking *joual* with Alfred and Eva, Italian with the Tondinos and English with my father. Getting into Loyola High School, a Jesuit, Irish, English-speaking school, had undeniably given me huge advantages, but those advantages had come at a price. As a result of my education, English had become the only language in which I now felt comfortable. I was a walking example of the kind of thing that

René Lévesque's Parti Québécois government would later try to eradicate with Bill 101: an anglicized Quebecker.

Not only did I feel a kind of guilt about having forsaken my French roots, I also realized that, had I not taken the route I did, had I gone to a French school and embraced French as my primary language, there might have been less of a disconnection between my particular talent and the English-based culture in which I was attempting to use it. Though I hadn't done at all badly in England, I hadn't, after all, managed to fulfil my brief dream of becoming a star there. Now the suspicion had begun to creep up on me that, had I done things differently, I might have stood a chance of becoming a star in Quebec.

Tremblay's play, with its mouthy, temperamental, vividly self-dramatizing title character, bridged that gap between my abilities and my opportunities. It was the perfect match, thematically, emotionally and linguistically, for what Domini later came to call me: a *Québécois manqué*.

I finally got my chance to read for *Hosanna* in February 1974. Kaftans were popular at the time, and Domini had one that I could actually fit into, so I wore that to the audition. I had been practising reading aloud from the script in my thickest Québécois accent. Domini, knowing next to nothing about Canada at that early point in her residence here, had listened dutifully but couldn't really figure out at the time why this play meant so much to me.

When I went into the audition, I said to Bill, "I'd like to read this with a French-Canadian accent." He replied, "Absolutely not."

Reluctantly, I read in my normal English-Canadian voice, which, to my ears, made Hosanna sound like nothing more than a cliché homosexual from Greenwich Village. Something about my reading must have struck Bill, however, because he then said, "Okay, why don't you try it with the French accent?" It was one of Bill's greatest attributes as a director that he wasn't afraid to change his mind.

As soon as I used the accent, the text started to soar, like music—which it is, particularly in the second act. Its speeches are like arias and duets. Bill had me do it again with the English accent, and then again with the French. It was quite clear to both of us how much more alive the English text became when I brought it back to its

French roots. Also, the character became much more exotic, and exoticism was a quality that Bill wanted for the role. At last, he said, "I need three days to think about this, because I do actually have somebody else in mind." At the end of those three days, he again had the courage to change his mind and offered me the role.

My determination couldn't have paid off more highly, for Hosanna was the break-through role that made my name in Canada. And although, as I had predicted, it was perfectly suited to my talents, I could never have done it without all those exercises in *Oh! Calcutta!* I don't just mean the brief bit of nudity at the end. If I hadn't done *Oh! Calcutta!*, I couldn't have become as connected with myself as an actor, emotionally and spiritually, as I needed to be in order to play not just Hosanna but also other roles in my future, including my second Hamlet in 1976.

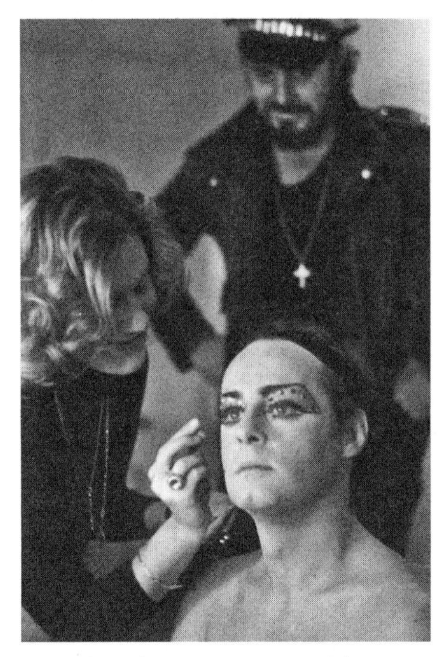

Penny Ritco makes me up as Hosanna while Richard Donat looks on.

Premièring at the Tarragon Theatre on May 15, 1974, *Hosanna* generated immense public interest, partly because after the FLQ crisis of October 1970, English Canada had suddenly become a lot more anxious to understand Quebec than it had been in previous decades, and partly because the subject matter of the piece violently shattered whatever preconceptions Ontario audiences might still have had about theatre in *la belle province*. Anyone who came expecting some picturesque rural drama about peasants in *sabots* was in for a shock.

Cuirette was played by Richard Donat, a wonderfully sensitive actor whom I hadn't known very well before, though I'd acted at Stratford with his brother Peter. (Their uncle was the film star Robert Donat.) Critical reaction to both of us, and to the play, was ecstatic. The phrase "tour de force" appeared in review after review. "The play, the production, these actors make theatre going a privilege," wrote Urjo Kareda in the *Toronto Star*, adding, "Richard Monette's Hosanna is . . . fabulous." George Anthony, of the *Toronto Sun*, said, "Monette's Hosanna is a profound experience . . . his electricity makes it all magic," while Herbie Whittaker, in *The Globe and Mail*, called it "a man-sized job of acting."

The praise that meant the most to me, though, came from my friends and colleagues. When William Hutt came to see the show, he came backstage afterwards, looked me straight in the eye and said, "Richard, this is one of the few star performances by a Canadian—perhaps the *only* one—that I have ever seen." The word *star* was not used lightly in those days, and to hear it from someone of Bill's stature was a compliment indeed. (John Hirsch, however, who was working at the CBC at the time, did *not* like *Hosanna*, which he found melodramatic.)

Domini was amazed by my transformation in the role. She saw the show several times and said that each time she found me literally unrecognizable, except for the hurt and the vulnerability: that side of the character she could see in me. The physical component of that transformation, of course, was achieved in large part by makeup, which took me two hours to apply before every performance (not counting the time I had to spend at home shaving my chest). I used as my model a colour photograph of Elizabeth Taylor as Cleopatra in the film, and our stage manager, Penelope Ritco, helped me apply the finishing touches to my eyes. I also wore high heels, which completely altered my walk, and long false nails, which caused my hands to give a performance all their own. Although I'd mimed having long nails in rehearsal, this hadn't prepared me for the awkward reality of having to pick up such objects as lipsticks or packs of cigarettes while wearing them. "My God," I thought: "How do women *do* this?" (As for the heels, they may have been partly responsible for the comment made by Robin Phillips, then about to become the Stratford Festival's next artistic director, when he came backstage after the show: "You have wonderful woman's legs, but you don't have good male legs.")

My crowning glory was a stunning headpiece that had been borrowed from the Stratford Festival: the same one, in fact, that Zoe

Caldwell had worn in our 1967 production of *Antony and Cleopatra.* As for the rest of my outfit, *Hosanna*'s designer, John Ferguson, had originally conceived an elaborate dress that made me look like the Fairy Godmother in *Cinderella*. Then, one night during rehearsals, John, Bill, Richard and I had gone to a gay club frequented by transvestites to get a sense of what the world we were trying to depict might really be like. I, for one, had never been to such a place before, and we were awed by what we found. All the young men's dresses were cut as tight as possible, with open backs that plunged to the cracks of their buttocks, and they looked fantastic. Based on that experience, John had completely redesigned my costume to make it sexier.

On another occasion, during a visit to Montreal to meet Tremblay, Richard and I had visited another gay establishment, supposedly the one on which the club in the play had been modelled. It turned out to be quite a rough place, full of biker types just like Cuirette, but not nearly so amiable. Richard, who is perfectly straight, seemed a little uneasy surrounded by these tall, burly leathermen, so I tried to reassure him: "Oh, don't worry: these people are all just role-playing. They're probably all middle-class opera lovers. It's quite harmless; nothing will happen." At which point a beer bottle flew past our heads, precipitating our hasty departure.

Hosanna is an acidly witty character, for whom Tremblay had written some brilliantly funny lines. As we proceeded through the first week of the run, I found more and more of the humour in those lines and started to get more and more laughs. I couldn't have been more pleased with myself. And then Bill Glassco came to see the show again and told me afterwards, "Richard, you're getting too many laughs."

It may be imagined how hard I fought him on this. "What do you mean?" I said. "It's the whole crux of the character. It's her mouth that gets her into all this trouble." But he kept insisting that I was making the character too funny. Eventually, I said, "All right, next performance I'll cut back on the laughs. You come and see it, and I will prove you wrong."

At the very beginning of the run, the audiences had given us standing ovations. But toward the end of that first week, although they'd been laughing much more, they were no longer standing. That night, when I followed Bill's instructions and played down the humour, the performance was electric, and at the end the whole audience rose to its feet. So I bowed to his greater wisdom for the remainder of the run.

During that run, I gave an interview to Urjo Kareda for the *Star* in which I mentioned the lengths to which I had gone to get the part. The resulting article prompted Bill's wife, Jane Glassco, with whom he'd co-founded the Tarragon, to send me a droll tongue-in-cheek rebuke.

In the title role of *Hosanna*, with Richard Donat as Cuirette, in the 1974 Tarragon Theatre production

"OK, Monette," she wrote. "You've had it. Boy, have you had it. Where did you get that mouth from? Thanks to your words to Urjo on how you got the *Hosanna* part—*because you badgered Bill for eight months*—Bill has run away. Do you *know* what a line like that *says* to every unemployed actor/ess or would-be actor/ess in the vicinity of the *Star* circulation? Uh-huh. The phone is ringing, letters arriving, people at the door—so Bill has disappeared and may *never* come back. . . . He's gone. Vanished. So I'm suing you as co-respondent in our divorce. OK?

"You owe me a million and a man.

"Big mouth!

"Love, Jane."

Exposing Bill to the importunities of starving artists remains, by the way, the only ground on which I might be accused of intervention in the Glasscos' marriage. For many years after *Hosanna,* the rumour went around that Bill and I had become embroiled in a homosexual affair. Like so many of the other fascinating stories I've heard about my sex life over the years, this was entirely untrue.

Hosanna played at the Tarragon for six weeks, closing at the end of June. During the run, my friends and colleagues at the Tarragon helped me celebrate my 30th birthday by laying on a party for me, at which they all turned up in drag. From *Hosanna* I went directly back to the St. Lawrence Centre, where Theatre Plus, a new company founded the year before, was presenting a summer season. It included a production of Lillian Hellman's *The Little Foxes,* directed by Kurt, in which I played Leo Hubbard. Joseph Shaw was in it too, as was Frances Hyland, whom I'd held in the greatest esteem ever since we'd acted together in my first season at Stratford. I'd gone to a talk she gave once in Stratford, in which she said something that has always stayed with me: "Acting is the best way I know of exploring the human condition."

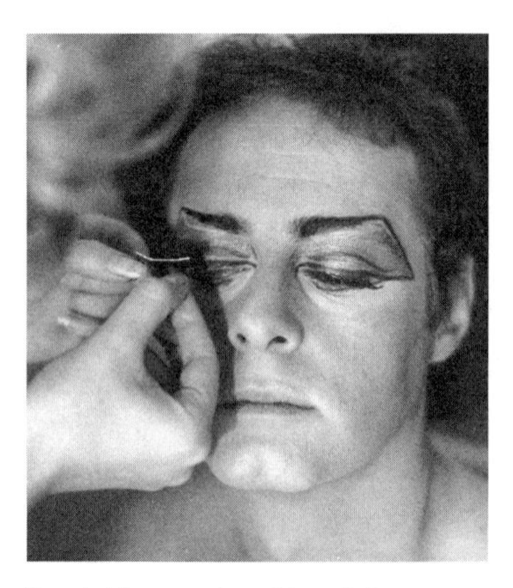

Penny helping me apply my false eyelashes

Meanwhile, the American producer Norman Kean—who, coincidentally, had produced *Oh! Calcutta!* in New York—had been negotiating with the Tarragon about bringing *Hosanna* to Broadway. As an out-of-town tryout, we reopened on September 11 at the now-defunct Global Village Theatre on St. Nicholas Street in Toronto, where we played for three weeks, again to capacity audiences, then in October we transferred to the 600-seat Bijou Theatre on West 45th Street, New York.

Demolished in 1982 to make way for a hotel, the Bijou was sandwiched between the Morosco Theatre, where Colleen Dewhurst and Jason Robards were playing in Eugene O'Neill's *A Moon for the Misbegotten,* and the Plymouth Theatre, where the Broadway production of *Equus,* starring Anthony Hopkins, began previews on the same day we opened, October 14, 1974. When we arrived at the Bijou, production photographs for *Hosanna,* showing me in my full cross-dressing glory, had already been posted up. We actually received a complaint about these from the management of the Plymouth, which apparently found them sleazy—this despite the fact that *Equus* contains a nude scene (performed, coincidentally, by Peter Firth and my old friend Roberta Maxwell).

Cards, notes and telegrams from well-wishers poured in. Leon Major and others at the St. Lawrence Centre offered a variation on the traditional actors' good-luck wish of "Break a leg": their telegram read, "Break a bra and God bless." Another message, "From Hamlet the prince to Hosanna the queen. One giant step for Richard Monette," came from Marigold Charlesworth and Jean Roberts, my old co-directors at the Crest.

We opened to reviews that could best be described as mixed. Martin Gottfried, in the *New York Post,* was one of the most enthusiastic, describing the play as "truly moving" and "ultimately noble," and my playing of the title role as "magnificent, calling upon technique, trickery and bravura performance." *The New Yorker* was non-committal, dwelling on the seedy sadness of the characters: "One thinks forebodingly as the lights go down, Another day, another dolor." John Simon, in *New York* magazine, said I played Hosanna "faultlessly," except for my "slightly errant French-Canadian accent." (Bizarrely, he wasn't the only critic to accuse me of struggling with my native mode of speech.) "Mr. Monette," he went on, "accomplishes the near-impossible feat of making extravagant flamboyance as absorbing and warming as a cozy fire in the grate"—which I *think* was a compliment. On the negative side, Douglas Watt in the *Daily News* called the play "essentially a rather silly little anecdote filling the evening with invective and little more. There are times," he continued, "when the U.S.-Canadian border seems wider than the Atlantic Ocean."

The review that would seal our fate, though, was the one by Clive Barnes in *The New York Times.* It wasn't a pan, by any means. It was something much worse: a mild endorsement of a play that was, he said, "far from being without interest." (Now *there's* a billboard quote if ever I heard one.) He praised my performance, sort of—"He is never cheap. He never for a moment descends into easy female impersonations"—and allowed that Tremblay's writing revealed "real wit and insight." But his closing line was the kiss of death: "This play is not exactly Hosanna in the highest, but it is Hosanna on a perfectly respectable middle ground."

The result, New York being essentially a one-paper town, was that, to repeat an old refrain, our show did not do as well there as we had hoped. We managed to hang on for 24 performances, and closed on November 3, barely a month after we'd had our first preview. To be fair, it wasn't just this lukewarm *Times* review that hurt us: we'd probably been hoist with our own petard by over-promoting the political sub-text of the play, which many of the reviewers had dutifully remarked on. In our efforts not to be overlooked as just another "gay play" in New York, we had perhaps inadvertently persuaded our potential audiences that *Hosanna* was no *more* than a tract about the self-deluded state of Quebec society, hardly a subject calculated to inflame the imagination of the average New Yorker.

Before we closed, our producer, Norman Kean, had asked if I'd consider taking a cut in salary. He'd bid on the movie rights to Tremblay's plays, and apparently one of the conditions of the deal was that *Hosanna* run for at least a month on Broadway. I replied that he was already getting half my salary, as I'd invested financially in the production. (Several years later, in 1988, Kean came to a bizarre end when he fatally stabbed his wife and then jumped to his death from the roof of his Manhattan apartment.)

Still, even if we hadn't taken New York by storm, we'd certainly enjoyed a *succès d'estime*: *Hosanna* was nominated for the 1975 Drama Desk Award for outstanding new foreign play, and I received the nomination for outstanding actor in a play. (Both awards, as it happened, went to *Equus*.) Meanwhile, I'd heard that Michael Bawtree, who knew me from Stratford, was looking for someone to play Jack Absolute in Sheridan's *The Rivals* for the Roundabout Theatre Company. I auditioned for him, and afterwards he said, "That was very good, but our leading lady is extremely tall." I stand five feet, 10 inches: not exactly short, but. . . . So I sent Michael a telegram, reminding him that the great 19th-century actor Edmund Kean was only five foot two, and got the part. (Clive Barnes called my performance "sterling"; *The New Yorker* called me "admirable"; Douglas Watt, in the *Daily News*, said I was "very respectable, though lightweight"; and Martin Gottlieb, in the *Post*, didn't mention me at all.)

Toward the end of *Hosanna*'s run in New York, I went with Richard and his girlfriend, Maggie, to see David Bowie at Radio City Music Hall. Approaching Times Square as we walked back to our hotel, we were stopped dead in our tracks by the sight of a huge billboard on which workmen had not quite finished pasting an ad for our show. There, looming on the New York skyline, were our two names, "Richard Monette" and "Richard Donat," along with half of the play's title. This was an eerie experience. Two thoughts came to me in quick succession. First: "Wow. That's the first and probably last time I'll see my name on a Broadway billboard." And then: "They'll never finish pasting it up, because we're closing."

I don't think they ever did, but at least this time they'd spelled my name right.

Hosanna's crowning glory was the same headdress Zoe Caldwell wore in *Antony and Cleopatra*.

I wasn't quite done with *Hosanna*, though. I think it was Bill Glassco who suggested a couple of years later that we revive it. The idea was to open the show at the Vancouver East Cultural Centre in November 1976, move it in December to the National Arts Centre in Ottawa and then bring it home to the Tarragon at the start of the new year. Unfortunately, it turned out that the Tarragon wasn't available for the final leg of this tour, which led me to take a wild leap into a role I'd never anticipated.

At the time, Domini and I had just bought a house in Stratford together, the house on Douglas Street where I still live. We were no longer a romantic item by that point, but we were still friends. We shared the mortgage, and because the house was a duplex, we could each rent out our own portion of it whenever we were working out of town. We'd cashed in our life insurance policies to make this investment, and I'd been counting on the income from *Hosanna* to keep up my payments. So when I learned that the Toronto portion of the proposed tour was in jeopardy, I went to Penny Ritco, our stage manager, and asked, "Have you ever produced a play before?" She said she hadn't. "Nor have I," I said. "But we're going to do so now."

And so, after we'd been to Vancouver and Ottawa, Penny and I produced *Hosanna* for Toronto Workshop Productions at their theatre on Alexander Street (now the home of Buddies in Bad Times), where it was again a tremendous hit, making back all the money I needed. It was while we were performing in Vancouver, incidentally, that René Lévesque's separatist Parti Québécois came to power in the Quebec provincial election of November 15, 1976, a historic event that lent a whole new resonance to the political element of our play.

In the heat of performance and, occasionally, of rehearsal, you can sometimes get so absorbed in the imaginary world you are creating that you can forget for a moment that it isn't real. An example of this occurred during rehearsals for this revival of *Hosanna*. Richard Donat was again co-starring with me, and we were recreating bits of business that we had performed for real many times before. At one point in the play, my character had to answer a telephone call. I would pick up the phone, and Richard would then grab it out of my hand. In performance, of course, we'd done this with a real telephone, but in rehearsal for the revival, we were simply miming its presence. In one of those rehearsals, I'd just picked up the imaginary phone and Richard had just mimed snatching it away from me when Bill said, "Let's do that again." At which I found myself quite unthinkingly retrieving the imaginary telephone from Richard, replacing the imaginary receiver and laying the whole imaginary apparatus carefully on top of the (real) table. When I'd done, we both gaped at each other in amazement.

Hosanna did eventually return to the Tarragon Theatre, but not then, and not with me in the title role. Ten years later, in 1987, I directed the play there with Geordie Johnson as Hosanna and

Dennis O'Connor as Cuirette. It remains, in my view, a beautiful, heartfelt and deeply moving drama, one of Michel Tremblay's finest achievements.

Certainly it seemed to have an extraordinary effect on its audiences, both in Toronto and in New York. It pushed certain people over some kind of edge—even, apparently, changed their lives. One woman in Toronto, who later married someone quite famous, came to almost every performance and sat in the front row. She wrote out the entire text of the play, backwards, in longhand and sent it to me along with a white feather. I have no idea what she meant by that. In New York, another woman accosted me outside the theatre to tell me, "All my life I have been actively fighting against homosexuality, and you've changed my mind." I didn't have the heart to tell her that that was hardly our intention. And I can hardly forget the man who, at the end of the play, when Hosanna stands naked in front of Cuirette, completely lost his composure and started yelling: "You stupid crazy f___er, put on your clothes! Put on your clothes!"

Having had that brief backstage meeting with Elizabeth Taylor 10 years earlier, I always imagined a little bit of a psychic connection to her when I was performing *Hosanna*. I always wondered if she might come and see the show in New York, where there was a faint chance she would have heard about it. But she didn't, as far as I know. (And I doubt very much that she could have sneaked unobtrusively into the back row of the Bijou without our hearing about it.)

My New York friend Aviva Slesin and I saw Taylor on stage once, playing Regina in the 1981 revival of *The Little Foxes* at the Martin Beck Theatre. It was an extraordinary experience. Taylor made her entrance from the top of the set down a flight of stairs. She was encrusted with jewels and had a décolletage that Dolly Parton would have envied. As she came down those stairs, bobbing away, the audience was buzzing. I could hear people around me whispering to each other. Were those the real diamonds that Richard Burton gave her? Had she had breast implants?

She came to the bottom of the staircase, went to the liquor cabinet, poured two glasses of bourbon, walked around the sofa, gave one of the glasses to the other actor on stage and then, as I recall, walked all the way *back* to the liquor cabinet and put seltzer in her own drink.

All this before the scene had even begun. In fact, they almost needn't have bothered with the dialogue, because the audience was already going berserk.

I don't remember how the rest of her performance was, and it wouldn't really matter if I did. This wasn't acting as we normally know it; it was a star lighting up a stage with her incredible charisma. It was utterly riveting and worth every penny of the admission price.

For many years after *Hosanna*, whenever I found a postcard on my travels that had an image of Elizabeth Taylor on it, I would send it to Bill Glassco. He kept them all, and sent them all back to me shortly before he died. At his memorial service, Richard and I gave a reading from the last few moments of the play. Because *Hosanna* talks about the real live elephants in Taylor's film *Cleopatra*, our designer, John Ferguson, had provided a necklace with little elephants on it for me to wear in our production. I'd kept that necklace all those years, and I wore it for our reading at Bill's farewell.

There were quite a number of gay people in the Montreal apartment building where my French-Canadian grandfather, Alfred, was the janitor, and I remember my grandmother Eva saying to me one day, "If all these *fifis*"—the French equivalent of "fairies"—"don't like women, why do they act like them?"

I'm not sure if my grandmother expected me, at the age of 10, to be able to answer that from my own experience, but in any case I personally *did* like women, and always had, which I thought was one reason why I had found it so easy to act like one in *Hosanna*. As a young man (obviously, given *Oh! Calcutta!*), I was a great champion of the sexual revolution, which seemed, at the time anyway, to hold out great promise of emancipation for women. I belonged to the first generation of men whose female peers had access to the Pill, and this fact made a huge impression on me. Although the women in my family, particularly my mother, had their share of wilfulness and ego, they weren't liberated in the sense that the younger professional women who were my friends—women like Domini, Aviva, Diana Leblanc and Roberta Maxwell—now were. I could see that women—and men too, for that matter—were in a huge historic moment of transition, not just because of reliable contraception but because of the changing tenor of the times, and the ones I knew and cared about were having to deal on a daily basis with the choices that this entailed. I felt immense compassion for them.

Whatever my *fifi*-scorning grandmother thought or didn't think about my own sexual proclivities, I do believe my mother must have suspected that there was something unduly effeminate about me when I was a child. Perhaps that was why she made me burn my doll. In any case, when I was about 10 years old and she decided it was time to give me a birds-and-the-bees talk, she started to discuss homosexuality. "If you're a fairy," she said, "you can never have babies."

She meant, of course, that procreation was impossible within a same-sex relationship, at least without recourse to surrogates and turkey basters. But I took her to mean it in a physiological sense: that gay men were unable to produce sperm. So when, at the age of 13, I experienced my first nocturnal emission, I thought I was saved. I *couldn't* be gay, because there was the sticky proof. As I continued through puberty and early adulthood, other evidence seemed to contradict this, but it still took me till the mid-1970s to fully accept the fact that, on the whole, I'd rather be in Philadelphia. So to speak.

I had, of course, had my relationships with women. The one to whom I'd lost my virginity when I was 19 had said, "You'll always remember me, because I was the first," and she'd been right. I'd had sex with no one for a year and a half after she'd gone, because I'd been so madly in love with her. At the same time, though, I had always found the male physique fascinating in a way that, when I was a child, of course, I couldn't begin to understand. When I was about eight or nine, I used to indulge, with a group of other boys of the same age, in a form of "playing around" that I later realized was clearly sexual. Even at the time, I realized that, whatever it was, it wasn't something the Catholic Church would be likely to approve of. I shall never forget the guilt I felt when, after one such session, I went home to eat, and my mother served me Kraft Dinner and Orange Crush: my favourite meal. Here I had been indulging what must surely be some kind of shameful sin, only to be rewarded by my unwitting mother.

Later, when I was 18, and understood the "danger" I was in, I resisted the advances of another boy while we were on a school trip, even though I felt an undeniable attraction to him. Then along came that first unforgettable female love, and for many years after that I was able to go on convincing myself that I was, if not completely "straight," at least functionally bisexual. If I wasn't perhaps a terribly good lover with women, I thought that was perhaps just because I didn't understand women's bodies. I understood men's bodies, because I had one, but women's were more of a mystery.

My love affair with Domini had seemed to hold out hope of marriage and, perhaps, children, but after it came to an end, some time after *Hosanna*, I had to acknowledge that this probably wasn't

The young lovers again, sometime in the early 1970s, before I finally realized that my destiny lay elsewhere

ever going to be in the cards. It was I who brought the affair to an end, but if I hadn't, she would have done. At first, she didn't want anything further to do with me, but I persisted in keeping in touch, sending her notes and letters, even Valentine cards. By the time we found ourselves working together again, at the Stratford Festival in 1976, we were both with other partners and we were able to segue comfortably into the quasi-familial friendship that we still enjoy.

I have, in fact, remained friends with almost all my former lovers, because I loved them as people. When you fall in love with somebody, you don't fall *out* of love with them—at least I don't. Even when someone hurt me dreadfully, as often happened, I still didn't want to drop them. I have a gift for falling in love—perhaps because of the loneliness of my childhood, and my sense of having been abandoned as my parents succumbed to their demons—and a gift for fidelity. I haven't had many relationships, but the ones I have had have been profound. With each person I fell in love with, it was total commitment. I have always been faithful to a fault: faithful in the sense of monogamy to whomever I was with at the time, and faithful to their memory afterward. This is not willpower; it's just something in my nature.

It is ironic, given this capacity and yearning for love, that I should have been the only artistic director in the Stratford Festival's history who did not have a partner during his tenure. This fact added enormously to the stress of the job, which is already by its nature isolating. I hadn't realized, when I went into it, just how completely alone I would be, or for how long. I have many dear friends, of course, but not that one special soul mate. My consolation has been that quasi-religious one of serving something larger than myself: in my case, that fickle mistress, the theatre. But it would have been nice to have someone to come home to at the end of the day.

Even today, when the love that once dared not speak its name can't seem to shut up about it, homosexuals are still largely outsiders in mainstream society. That is one reason why I have always had a soft spot for the outsider, and also one reason why I have so loved the work of Tennessee Williams, to my mind the greatest of 20th-century playwrights. I *admire* the work of Arthur Miller, tremendously. But that work is very Talmudic, in a very stern tradition of morality. Whereas Williams, being from the South, being homosexual, having had that troubled sister of his, has more poetry in his writing, more of the reverberations of an aching heart. He is insightful into his characters: the wounded, as he calls them. He doesn't censure them. And I share his love for the wounded.

Williams speaks to the heart, as Michel Tremblay's *Hosanna* does, and the heart is wiser than the mind. To quote Blaise Pascal, *"Le cœur a ses raisons que la raison ne connaît point"*: the heart has its reasons that reason does not know. I consider speaking to the heart to be the most important of all the qualities that the theatre has to offer us, and that is why I programmed so many of

Williams's plays during my tenure. I also made a point of trying to bring out the humour in them, for Williams himself believed his plays were often funny. I'd learned somewhere, for instance, that he thought Blanche's iconic line, "I have always depended on the kindness of strangers," as she is dragged off to the lunatic asylum, was simply hilarious.

Tennessee Williams was one of the people I would most like to have met. Once, in New York, I saw a man crossing the street in a white suit and a white hat, walking along jauntily with a cane. It looked just like him. I'm *sure* it was him. It was one of three unconfirmed "sightings" of famous people that I have had in my life, the first being that time after *Henry V* when Michael Langham brought a man who may have been Tyrone Guthrie backstage, the second being during my National Theatre audition in England, when I spotted a man in the aisle of the auditorium who I was sure was Laurence Olivier.

I should have just gone up to that white-suited man in New York and said, "Excuse me: are you Tennessee Williams?" But I didn't. I was still shy back then.

It *must* have been him.

CHAPTER EIGHT

Choice and Rarest Parts

King Lear, Act I, scene 4

While doing *Hosanna* in Toronto, I'd made no secret of the fact that I was keen to work with the man who'd been named to succeed Jean Gascon as artistic director of the Stratford Festival: Robin Phillips. It had been a controversial appointment. Phillips had been recruited from England, enraging those in the Canadian theatre community who felt that we could—and should—find people within our own ranks to lead our major cultural institutions. Jean Gascon, after all, was Canadian, so why revert now to the old colonial model? It wasn't as if there were no option: many people—among them Bill Glassco and Leon Major—saw an obvious successor in John Hirsch, who, though European by birth, had lived in Canada since 1947 and had already shared the Festival's leadership with Gascon in the first two seasons of Gascon's tenure. Another strong candidate—and one who'd been actively pursuing the job—was William Hutt.

While I thought it unfortunate that another Canadian hadn't, as far as I knew, been groomed for the position during Jean's tenure, I didn't believe artistic opportunities should be circumscribed by nationality. I'd worked with British directors in Canada before, and with an American director, Charles Marowitz, in Britain, and I'd come away from those experiences believing that what mattered was people's talent, not which country had issued their passports. And Robin Phillips certainly had talent. I'd seen the evidence myself when I was in England, where I'd been impressed by his productions of *The Two Gentlemen of Verona* and Edward Albee's *Tiny Alice* for the Royal Shakespeare Company. I'd also seen his production, for Northcott Theatre, Exeter, of Ronald Miller's *Heloise and Abelard*, which later went to Broadway. Indeed, I'd admired his work so much that I'd written to him asking (unsuccessfully) for an audition. I thought him an excellent choice for the Festival: not only a very good director but also young and energetic. He looked like someone from whom I could continue to learn. And so he turned out to be, though the process was not always easy.

My performance in *Hosanna* had established me as an actor of some importance in Canada, so when Robin first sounded me out about roles I might be interested in at Stratford, I jocularly affected the air of a grand diva: "Oh, you know, the usual: Hamlet, Romeo, Hal." Later, while I was doing *Hosanna* in New York, he followed up with a phone call. I told him I'd love to return to the Festival, though

I couldn't resist adding: "But, of course, you know I'm a big star now. A very big star." I heard nothing further on the subject until I received another phone call, this time from William Hutt, who was now working as an associate with the new artistic director.

"Robin says you're not interested in coming back," Bill said accusingly. "He says you told him you're too big a star."

"Bill," I said, aghast, "we're closing in a week. How could he possibly have taken what I said seriously? Of *course* I want to come back."

This was my first tiny indication of the difference in our styles and personalities that would bedevil my relationship with Robin Phillips. Over the next few years, my opinion of his talent would be amply confirmed, and I would be immensely indebted to him for all the opportunities he gave me. But I would find no evidence of a sense of humour, at least not one that coincided with mine. No doubt he found me as hard to read as I found him, and my vision of myself as a "young Turk," coupled with my tendency to mouth off from time to time, may well have irritated him. But from my point of view, he was a total enigma: a brilliant, bewildering puzzle.

With him as artistic director, the next six years of my career would be perhaps the most varied and richly creative that I have ever known as an actor. During them I would become what I had dreamed of being ever since that first awe-inspiring encounter with *As You Like It* and *Othello* in 1959: a leading Shakespearean player at the Stratford Festival of Canada. I'd been at least partly joking when I'd proposed to Robin the roles of Hamlet, Romeo and Prince Hal. In the years of his tenure, I would play all three.

My first leading role for Robin Phillips, and for the Festival, wasn't actually Shakespearean: it was Algernon Moncrieff in *The Importance of Being Earnest*, which he directed in 1975, the first year of his tenure. In addition, I had two supporting roles: Lucio in *Measure for Measure*, with Martha Henry as Isabella and Brian Bedford (whom Robin had brought to Stratford for the first time that year) as Angelo; and Sparger in *Kennedy's Children*, which Robin had asked Bill Glassco to direct—partly, I'm sure, to defuse the criticisms of his appointment.

Kennedy's Children, incidentally, featured in its cast a wonderful young actress named Brenda Donohue, who died tragically early of cancer. Not only did she have talent, beauty and kindness, but there was a quality in her work that I knew was lacking from mine. One day I asked Bill Glassco what it was. "Brenda always goes for the jugular of a part," he told me. "She doesn't censor. But *you* tend to censor."

Kennedy's Children and *Earnest* both opened late in the season, so when rehearsals for the season started in the spring my efforts were focused entirely on *Measure for Measure*, which Robin directed brilliantly. Lucio isn't a large role, but it can be a tremendously effective one, and Robin rehearsed me in it morning, noon and night. We tried out every conceivable approach. I did it with accents. I did it singing. I did it dancing. I did it chewing gum. There was nothing I didn't do. But even while he was giving me all this attention, there was an odd dynamic between Robin and me. Every day, I would arrive in the rehearsal room—on time—with a cheerful "Good morning, Robin." Yet for some reason he would never return my greeting.

As Lucio in *Measure for Measure* (Stratford, 1975)

Eventually, I concluded that he just didn't like being addressed first thing in the morning. Perhaps he wasn't a morning person. So I decided that henceforth I would just show up and say nothing. The first day I tried that, he quite pointedly said to me, "Good *morning*, Richard." The incident was trivial, yet it was typical of my every encounter with this man: I never seemed to be able to find the right way to connect with him on an ordinary day-to-day level.

I consider Oscar Wilde's *The Importance of Being Earnest* to be the greatest comedy, outside of Shakespeare, in the English language. Not only is it written in dialogue of the most perfect symmetry, but it takes all the conventions of classical comedy, from parallel love affairs to assumed identities to long-lost brothers, and synthesizes them brilliantly, even as it sends them up. And it has a serious theme: hypocrisy, the same theme, in fact, that Wilde explored more overtly in his melodramas *A Woman of No Importance* and *An Ideal Husband*. The play itself is a deceiver: a moral satire posing as a frivolous comedy of manners.

I was joining a stellar cast. Nicholas Pennell, who'd first come to the Festival in 1972 and with whom I'd been good friends since we appeared together in *The Taming of the Shrew* and *Pericles*, was playing Jack Worthing. Others included Pat Galloway as Gwendolen; Marti Maraden, in her second Festival season, as Cecily; Tom Kneebone as Canon Chasuble; Meg Hogarth as Miss Prism; and, in the iconic role of Lady Bracknell, a cross-dressing William Hutt.

Our first meeting—it wasn't exactly a rehearsal—was held at Robin's home. (I arrived late because I'd ordered a dozen green carnations from a local florist, and they hadn't been ready in time. The green carnation, a symbol of gay culture in Paris in the 1890s, had been adopted by Wilde as his trademark, and I thought it would be fun to present them to our director.) An interesting exercise then ensued. Urjo Kareda, formerly the drama critic of the *Toronto Star*, had been hired as the Festival's literary manager and he'd brought to the meeting a sheaf of quotations. Half of these, he told us, were from Oscar Wilde and half from Anton Chekhov, and he asked us to guess which was which. In every case, the ones we thought were Wilde were really Chekhov and vice versa. The point of this was to prepare us for our director's approach to *Earnest*, which was not going to concentrate on the most obvious aspect of the play: its comedy. Instead, Robin wanted us to play it as if it were Chekhov.

This wasn't as bizarre as it might sound. There is, for example, a moment near the end of the first act when Algernon and Jack are sitting around at loose ends, smoking cigarettes and saying to each other: "Well, what shall we do?" "Nothing." "It is awfully hard work doing nothing." You can play the scene as repartee and get an easy laugh. Or you can explore the subtext and catch a glimpse of a spiritual and emotional void in the lives of these smart young men-about-town, a void that they play their games of intrigue to avoid having to confront. Played in a certain way, this could indeed evoke Chekhov—if not Pinter or even Beckett. Robin had Nicholas and me plumb the implications of that smoking scene to the fullest and brought in the rest of the cast to watch us do it.

The result, as I recall, was that we were distressingly unfunny on opening night, though things warmed up considerably as we went along. One thing that was hilarious from the start, though, was the remarkable performance at the play's centre. It had been a stroke of genius to cast Bill Hutt as Lady Bracknell, and Bill gave a masterfully contained performance with never a hint of the pantomime dame.

Everyone, of course, associates the role with Edith Evans in the famous 1952 film, using the full force of her voice and physical presence and swooping down multi-syllabically on the famous line "A handbag?" Bill did just the opposite. He kept his voice and movements tiny, and when informed that the suitor for his daughter's hand had been abandoned as a baby in a handbag, he responded with little jerking movements of his head, like a bird finding something unexpected in its field of vision. His gaze would then fall upon his own tiny purse, which he would examine in wonderment before clasping it protectively to his bosom and musing faintly, "A handbag?" Audiences went wild.

As for me, I'd told Robin on a couple of occasions that I saw Algernon as a lounge lizard, but he didn't seem to be familiar with the expression. "What do you *mean* by that?" he said, blankly. "Well, you know: a lounge lizard," I repeated helplessly, at a loss for a synonym for that certain kind of indolent but smartly-turned-out male who might be found propping up the bar in hotel lounges and private clubs. However, he did have me wear a moustache, which suited the kind of character I had in mind. He didn't think much of my English accent, though, even after my five years in England, and in the end he had me play Algernon as an American. Americans, he told me, were very fashionable in English high society when the play was written.

The critics didn't care for me much (though the American actor Eli Wallach and his wife, Anne Jackson, came to see the show and thought I was fabulous, maybe because of my accent), but I loved every minute of playing the part. I was particularly proud of my "buttonhole" scene with Marti Maraden in Act II. We managed to make it very sexy, with lots of double meanings, and I strove for the same effect when I directed the play myself in 2000.

The first scene between Jack and Algernon in *The Importance of Being Earnest* hinges on Jack's cigarette case, which Jack has left behind at Algernon's flat on a previous visit. As an opening-night present, Nicholas gave me a cigarette case, inside which was a tiny book: a 1918 edition of Oscar Wilde's poem *The Ballad of Reading Gaol*, first published in 1898 after Wilde's release from two years' imprisonment at hard labour for the offence of "gross indecency." Wilde's name appears nowhere in the book: the author is identified only by his prison number, "C. 33": block C, third floor, room three. I still have the book; the cigarette case I kept until 2000, when I had it inscribed and gave it to Graham Abbey, who played Algernon in my production. I hope it, too, like my mother's *cornu*, will pass to someone else when the time is right, as a symbol of continuity: the handing on of theatrical lore and tradition from one generation of artists to the next.

William Hutt as Lady Bracknell in the 1975 Festival production of *The Importance of Being Earnest*

Robin's Chekhovian *Earnest* became such a hit that we restaged it the next year, 1976, for the proscenium-arch Avon Theatre, with Eric Donkin taking over as Canon Chasuble and my old friend Amelia Hall as Miss Prism. It was revived there again in 1979, with Domini Blythe as Gwendolen. I wasn't in any of these revivals (my role was taken over by Barry MacGregor), and it wasn't until I saw the show from the outside that I realized how successful Robin's approach had been. By putting a lid on the play's more farcical elements, he'd brought the subtext bubbling to the surface and made it the real action of the piece, which was quite fascinating. Still, I couldn't help noting the irony of the fact that Chekhov always insisted his plays were comedies and that it was Stanislavsky's direction that had made them seem so mournful.

At some point during our first season together, Robin asked me what I thought about playing Hamlet again. He was going to direct the play (jointly, with William Hutt) at the Avon Theatre in 1976, along with *The Tempest,* in addition to reviving his *Measure for Measure* at the Festival Theatre. I was thrilled at the prospect—rare in any acting career—of getting a second chance to tackle this Everest of roles. I heard nothing more about it, though, for quite some time, until my friend Patrick Christopher, who'd stepped in for me in the St. Lawrence Centre *Twelfth Night* when my mother died, told me that he'd heard a rumour that Nicholas Pennell was going to play Hamlet at Stratford.

Eventually I summoned up the courage to confront Robin in his office. "I know this is foolish," I said, "but it's gnawing at me. I've heard that Nicholas is playing Hamlet, and I thought *I* was playing Hamlet." There was a long pause, then Robin replied, "You're *both* playing it." Nick and I were going to alternate in the role, he explained, within the same production.

Nicholas Pennell (left) and I alternated as Hamlet in the 1976 Stratford Festival production.

I didn't know if this was something he'd intended all along or if he'd just invented it on the spur of the moment, but, whatever the case, I was perturbed. Acting is a very territorial pursuit, and to cast two people as Hamlet in the same production would mean that neither could feel that the role was entirely his. Besides, such an arrangement could only invite comparisons: one of us would surely be deemed to be better than the other. Not only would the critics be polarized, but so, more importantly, would the company. As indeed, to some extent, it was. All this was complicated by the fact that Nick was my friend—and also, I had to admit, because he, like Robin, was English and I was not. That old idea that Shakespeare came more naturally to English-trained actors was a hard one to kick.

In retrospect, Hamlet being such a complex character (combining, as Ophelia observes, the qualities of courtier, soldier, scholar and prince), it was probably a much better idea than I thought at the time. Indeed, as artistic director myself, I had a short-lived plan to program *six* different studies of the role—two of them female—at the Studio Theatre in 2006. Each of the actors I had in mind would bring certain qualities to the role without bending anything in the text. The role draws different things out of different people, and I thought of this idea as a gift to these individuals, all of whom would benefit as actors by examining themselves in the context of that play.

Graham Abbey, I thought, would be a good choice to explore the soldierly Hamlet, while Michael Therriault could capture the younger, more sensitive side. David Snelgrove would be ideal for the princely Hamlet, while Jonathan Goad would push the envelope of the character's "antic disposition." Lucy Peacock would be the romantic Hamlet, while Seana McKenna would be Hamlet the intellectual. I would direct three of these productions (those with Lucy, David and Michael), while Stephen Ouimette, who by then had played the role himself, would direct the rest. In the end, the plan fell through when all the actors but David and Lucy dropped out. It would have been an interesting experiment, though, and may well have been exactly the sort of thing that Robin had in mind.

He had another surprise in store for me. I had expected to be cast in *The Tempest* as Ferdinand, the romantic lead. Instead, he asked me to play Caliban, the "savage and deformed slave" who rebels against Prospero, a role I would never have imagined myself playing. I wondered what on earth he was thinking—and what, if anything, I was to conclude from the fact that Nicholas was cast as Prospero's servant Ariel, the "tricksy spirit" who, as the embodiment of the master magician's imagination, represents the diametric opposite of the brutish Caliban, "this thing of darkness." Again, I was worried about us being played off against each other, as I feared we would be in our Hamlets. We actors are insecure creatures, who expend a lot of energy parsing the possible meanings of the roles we have been offered.

In fact, Caliban turned out to be a tremendous acting challenge for me and something of a triumph. At an early rehearsal, when we were all sitting round in a semicircle, Robin said to me: "One of your problems in this role is that you speak too well." He then produced two ping-pong balls and made me put one in each cheek—uncomfortable, to say the least. He then asked me to attempt one of Caliban's speeches: "This island's mine, by Sycorax my mother, / Which thou tak'st from me." Naturally, it was all but impossible for me to articulate the words. At first, the effect was comical, and everyone was laughing. But by the end of the speech they had been silenced, partly by the realization of how difficult language is for Caliban, who has been taught it by Prospero, and partly by the tears that were now flowing down my face. (They weren't caused by emotion or even pain; the distension of my cheeks somehow seemed to affect my tear ducts.)

Bill Hutt, who was playing Prospero, was mesmerized. He'd never encountered something so exceptional in a rehearsal. But as we all came to learn, it was typical of how Robin worked. He seldom discussed plays in thematic terms, but on practical acting points he used oblique methods that could have revelatory results. In my case, he could simply have said: "You're speaking too clearly. I want you to make it sound like it's more of an effort," which would have caused me to put on some kind of slurred, distorted voice. Instead, he gave me the actual physical *feeling* of inarticulacy, so that instead of trying to speak poorly, I would be struggling—as Caliban struggles—to speak as well as I possibly could.

As Caliban in *The Tempest* (Stratford Festival, 1976)

I couldn't do a whole performance, though, with ping-pong balls in my mouth. I did rehearse with them for a while, but it just hurt too much. So I tried having my dentist make me a special denture, but that too began to hurt after a while. Then I resorted to wads of Kleenex, but they stuck to my gums. In the end, I realized I needed no artificial aid: the point was to *remember* how the obstruction in my mouth had felt.

I drew on another memory too. While in New York with *Hosanna*, I'd been out walking one snowy day with a friend who lives there, Muffie Meyer. (Like my other New York friend, Aviva, Muffie makes documentaries: she won an Emmy Award for her 2002 film on the life of Benjamin Franklin.) As we walked along, chatting away, we saw a shapeless mass in front of us, which turned out to be a tarpaulin. When we came nearer, the tarpaulin was suddenly flung angrily aside by the homeless man who was under it, lying across a grate. We'd startled him, and he certainly startled us. I used that memory to create Caliban's physicality, particularly in the scene where Stephano and Trinculo encounter him hiding under his cloak.

"Do you think Hamlet is a man of action?" Robin asked Nicholas and me on the first day of rehearsals for the play in which we would take it in turns to dither over the avenging of our father's murder. It was a rare instance of him inviting theoretical discussion. Nick and I tentatively suggested that, yes, perhaps he is: although famously hesitant to kill Claudius, he does act decisively toward other people, usually with unfortunate results. This seemed to be the answer that was expected, and we proceeded to rehearse our two versions of the play.

Apart from our respective Gertrudes—Pat Bentley-Fisher played mine, while Pat Galloway played Nick's—the cast was identical in both versions. Nick and I were not, however, allowed to watch each other rehearse. Robin didn't want either of us influenced by what the other was doing, so he kept us apart. He got quite agitated once when, quite spontaneously, I tried out a bit of business. I forget what it was—I knocked over a chair or something—but it instantly aroused his suspicions.

"What are you doing? Why did you do that?"

"I don't know," I said. "I just improvised it." It turned out that Nick had done exactly the same thing earlier that morning, and Robin was convinced we had colluded.

On another occasion, we were using improvisation to help us create the milieu of Claudius's court. After Hamlet has killed Polonius, Claudius asks him where the body is. "You shall nose him as you go up the stairs into the lobby," retorts Hamlet cheekily. I'd always assumed that Hamlet's aim in this scene was to provoke Claudius to anger, so in this rehearsal, to get the maximum reaction out of the actor playing Claudius, Michael Liscinsky, I made funny faces and gestures, and generally tried to be as annoyingly comical as I could.

Robin seldom got visibly angry, but on this occasion, apparently thinking I was making fun either of Michael or of the production, he spoke quite sharply to me. However, as soon as he realized from the taken-aback look on my face that my intentions had been entirely honest, he softened his tone and gave me a truly insightful piece of direction. "You've just killed your girlfriend's father," he told me. "And although you're making all these jokes, they're jokes you *have* to make to try to suppress the pain. But the pain always rises through." This was exactly the observation I needed to help me find my way in that scene.

Robin was good at curbing my worst excesses as an actor. In the soliloquy "How all occasions do inform against me," I had been taking a pause before the last two lines: "O, from this time forth, / My thoughts be bloody or be nothing worth!" Here was the turning point of the play: the moment when Hamlet finally summons up his resolve. Such a moment, I figured, deserved a good long dramatic pause. The longer I held that pause, the more brilliant I thought I was being. *Hamlet* is already, of course, a very long play. Eventually, Robin said, "Richard, if you don't cut that pause, I'm doing a blackout on the line before it."

He also had to save me from myself during my death scene. Hamlet's last line, as he dies from being poisoned by the point of Laertes's rapier, is "The rest is silence." Poison can be a nasty way to die, so I worked hard on my death throes. Having gasped out "The rest is silence," I'd cough and gurgle and puke and bubble and squeak, until finally I expired. Brilliantly realistic, I thought, and terribly moving. After seeing me do this a few times in rehearsal, Robin finally said: "I have a note for you. When Shakespeare wrote, 'The rest is silence,' he *meant* it."

Nearly 20 years later, when I directed Stephen Ouimette as Hamlet in 1994, he too decided to go to town on his dying noises. So I told him my story and suggested that he rein it in, which he did. During the play's run, though, I went to see one of the matinées, only to find that Stephen had slipped back into his old ways. His final line was all but lost amid retching and spluttering, whereupon an elderly lady in the audience turned to her husband and asked, very loudly, "WHAT DID HE SAY?" Equally loudly, her husband replied, "HE SAID, 'THE REST IS SILENCE.' " At that, all those corpses strewn about the stage in the last scene of *Hamlet* started heaving with uncontrollable laughter. I don't think Stephen did it again.

In March 1976, before *Hamlet* and *The Tempest* opened at Stratford's Avon in June, we toured both productions, first to the Grand Theatre in Kingston, Ontario, then to the Place des Arts in Montreal. We also performed *Hamlet* at the National Arts Centre in Ottawa from the end of March to the middle of April. Any first performance is a stressful occasion, particularly with a play as difficult and complex as *Hamlet*. In the final days of rehearsal, we'd do a complete run-through of the play—and then do it *again*, in order to build up our stamina. By the time we came to our first performance in Kingston, we were all very tired.

Still, all went well until Act IV, scene 4, in which Hamlet meets a troop of soldiers belonging to Fortinbras, Prince of Norway. He asks their captain, "Good sir, whose powers are these?" The Captain replies, "They are of Norway, sir." Hamlet then asks, "How purposed, sir, I pray you?" and receives the answer "Against some part of Poland." On this occasion, the Captain, played by Don Hunkin, went completely blank, and I found myself conducting a dialogue with myself.

"Good sir, whose powers are these?"

Don gaped at me, panic-stricken.

"Are they . . . of Norway?" I prompted.

He nodded, gratefully.

"How purposed, sir, I pray you?"

Another helpless silence. Again I prompted: "Against some part of Poland?"

Eventually, the lines came back to him, and we finished the scene. Afterwards, Don came to my dressing room and apologized profusely. "Don't worry about it," I said. I was too tired even to care.

After that same performance, Robin knocked on my dressing-room door, poked in his head to announce, "Richard, you're too funny in this part," then shut the door again. I was dismayed by this, but I remembered Bill Glassco's comment during *Hosanna*, and so I tried to tone down the humour, even though I thought it was clearly there in the lines. Later, Robin ran through all my scenes with me and the rest of the cast. I was so deflated by that time, so sick at heart, that I just let go of everything and gave a reading that to me felt very flat. This must have resulted in the simplification that he wanted, because he seemed very pleased. At the end of the run, he wrote me a lovely note, saying what a wonderful performance I'd given.

Bill Hutt, who'd co-directed the production with him, paid me a compliment that I have never forgotten. He said I was a perfect Hamlet in that my feet never touched the ground, yet my head was never in the clouds. He meant, I think, that I'd caught the essence of Hamlet's indecisiveness, his sense of being caught between two worlds: "What should such fellows as I do crawling between heaven and earth?" as he says in the nunnery scene.

As Hamlet in 1976: the essence of indecisiveness

Eva, my French-Canadian grandmother, came to see me play Hamlet in Montreal. I believe it was the first play she'd ever seen in her life. "What did you think?" I asked her afterwards, to which her only response was, "I didn't like the way you treated your mother." This struck me as strange in view of that story she'd told me about her friends who'd got all dressed up to watch TV. Perhaps it was a testament to the power of live performance.

At that time, I was in a very stormy relationship with a young man, and the tour to Montreal coincided with a period when we had parted in anger. One day, during the second intermission of *Hamlet*, I telephoned him from the pay phone backstage and declared, "If you will have me back, I will leave *now*." Fortunately, he dissuaded me from so rash a course of action. Few things do more damage to a career in the theatre than walking out in the middle of a performance. But finding myself in such an emotional extremity did help me to understand certain behaviours in Shakespearean characters, such as Antony shamefully abandoning the battle of Actium to follow the fleeing Cleopatra. There are moments in life when we'll sacrifice anything for the sake of some goal that blinds us to all else. Fortunately, it doesn't happen too often.

The other memorable incident on that pre-season tour pertained to *The Tempest*, in which we used a smoke machine during the apparition of the goddesses Iris, Juno and Ceres. The machine was mounted under a little platform on which Pat Galloway, who was playing all three of these deities (I forget how she managed that), rose up from under the stage, enveloped in the smoke. At one performance in Kingston, the device caught fire. Bill Hutt, as Prospero, soldiered gamely on as the smoke got thicker and thicker and the fusillade of coughing spread from the front rows to the back, until finally the stage manager came out and stopped the show. Without missing a beat, Bill stepped forward and in his most magisterial voice started giving instructions to the audience on how to exit the building: "This side will stand, and go out that door. The people at the rear will go out the back. The people on this side will go out *that* door." It was an extraordinary moment when art and life seemed to interconnect: Bill was conducting the audience's exit, like Prospero orchestrating the spirits of the island.

The story has often been told that the firemen came in from the front of house while Bill was still standing there and asked him, "How do we get on the stage?" To which Bill is said to have replied, "You'll have to audition like everyone else." Alas, it's not a true story. But it's a good one, invented by Bill himself.

Talking of apocryphal theatre stories, there's an old one about a 19th-century actor playing Richard III. It takes various forms and is attributed to various illustrious names from the past, but in each case the point is that the actor concerned is heckled by someone in the audience (or in some versions, accosted backstage by the theatre manager) with the words, "Sir, you are drunk!" To which the tipsy thespian replies, "If you think *I'm* drunk, wait till you see the Duke of Buckingham!" It's a joke that appeals to actors because it plays upon two of their deep-seated fears. Being drunk on stage is one of several "worst-nightmare" scenarios; another is that of being heckled from the audience. I'd already had a near miss with the former when I was doing *Hay Fever* at the Crest; now, when we brought our *Hamlet* home to Stratford, I had a disturbing encounter with the latter.

It happened at a Saturday matinée, one of our few preview performances at the Avon Theatre. The house was packed with an audience that included actors Hume Cronyn and Carole Shelley. Carole, who'd been a member of the Festival company the year before, was in town to visit her friend Nicholas Pennell and to see our duelling Hamlets. All went smoothly until we came to "To be or not to be." I had just delivered the final lines of this most famous of all Shakespearean soliloquies when a man's voice rang out from the auditorium, "Richard, you are a bullshit actor."

I thought for a moment that I might be hallucinating. Hamlet is a part notorious for playing tricks with an actor's mind, and indeed when I'd performed it at the Crest I'd had one or two strange moments when I'd fancied I'd seen pages of the script floating in the air before my eyes. But it immediately became apparent, from the hubbub in the audience, that I wasn't imagining this. Someone had actually heckled me. "Oh, God," I thought for one wild moment, "is it Robin?"

Whoever it was, I had two choices. I could either walk off, wait till the person had been evicted, then start again from the beginning of the scene, or I could carry on and try to prove him wrong. I opted for the latter. Perhaps I wasn't Sir John Gielgud, but I'd been doing this long enough to know that I wasn't rubbish either. So I plunged on. My Ophelia, Marti Maraden, who'd witnessed my discomfiture while waiting in the wings to join me for the "Get thee to a nunnery" scene, came dashing on, white as a sheet, and we whipped through the scene in about 15 seconds, with me flinging her around like a Frisbee. Meanwhile, my nemesis was located and escorted out of the auditorium.

After the show, Carole went back to Nick's place and told him what had happened. Aghast, he phoned me immediately.

"Richard," he said, "this is appalling. I can't believe it. What on earth did you do?"

"Well," I told him mischievously, "I took a moment's pause, and then I said, 'If you think *I'm* a bullshit actor, wait till you see Nicholas Pennell play this part.' "

It turned out that my vocal critic on that day had been one Gary Reeves, a 29-year-old theatre director who worked with a small alternative company in Toronto called Creation 2. Afterwards, he sent me a three-page letter in which he elaborated on his attack. "I was compelled to speak to you," he began, "not morally, or intellectually, but physically. My body exploded with the words."

The gist of his argument appeared to be that he had come expecting "Shakespeare's Hamlet"—whatever that might be—and had instead been offered "Monette's Hamlet," which he found too emotional for his taste. "Your agony, your sound and fury, are vastly more powerful than any of William's words," he wrote. "You're only in each other's way. . . . Do you actually enjoy being a gladiator of the soul like this, all of you hacking away at each other up there on the stage in front of a bunch of strangers?" (Not a bad description of the art of acting, come to think of it.) What particularly seemed to have upset him were some interviews I'd given to the press, in which I'd said, "Hamlet is me," or something to that effect. Reeves saw this as self-indulgent on my part: using Shakespeare's play to "express myself."

The reality, of course, is that there can be no such thing on stage as "Shakespeare's Hamlet," because both the play and the role exist objectively only as words on a page: a set of instructions, if you like, for making an infinite variety of possible theatrical Hamlets. (Even the instructions vary, depending on which version of the text you use.) For a Hamlet to actually appear in the flesh, an actor has to create him by deciding *how* to speak the words, what thought processes might inform them and what actions should accompany them. Those choices will necessarily be shaped in part by the actor's own personality. Others might disagree with them, but it would be absurd to object to the making of choices *per se,* because there isn't any other way to do it. "It isn't your Hamlet," Reeves insisted in his letter, "or Pennell's or Chamberlain's or Burton's or Williamson's or Olivier's or Barrymore's. It's Shakespeare's Hamlet." But he was wrong. The only Hamlet you can have on a stage is some *actor's* Hamlet. You can't make a Hamlet without parading egos.

He concluded his letter on an ominous note: "May you always hear my voice each time you finish that speech, this year or next. Perhaps it will at least keep you on your toes." To that extent, anyway, he certainly got his wish. For the rest of my acting career, I could never again be quite sure that some jeering voice wouldn't come out of the darkness, calling into question my whole reason for being.

The official critics were more positive. The usually vitriolic Gina Mallet, who'd taken over Urjo Kareda's old job at the *Toronto Star*, described my Hamlet as "witty and romantic" and declared that Nick and I were "worthy contenders both," while Max Wyman of the *Vancouver Sun* praised the "freshness" and "naturalness" of our performances. Audiences, particularly younger ones, were extremely enthusiastic about the production, and so at the end of our Avon Theatre run we reblocked our two versions for the thrust stage and transferred them for four performances—two school matinées of each—to the larger Festival Theatre. My last performance was received ecstatically by a house packed with students. When I took my final bow, they were standing up and screaming, waving their programs in the air. I felt like a rock star.

In my triumph, I peeled off the gloves I'd worn for the duel scene at the end and flung them into the audience. Patrick Crean, the Festival's long-time fight director, liked the panache of that gesture so much that he presented me afterwards with a pair of gloves that had been given to him by Douglas Fairbanks, with whom he'd worked in the movies. I in turn gave them to another fight director, John Stead, when I directed *The Three Musketeers* in 2000.

Then, after the curtain call, I went storming backstage in search of Don Hunkin. I was furious with him because, in this last performance of a role that had meant so much to me, he'd had the gall to play a stupid prank: he'd pretended to forget his lines again in that very same scene in which he'd blanked out on me when we first opened eight months earlier. What kind of a dumb joke was that? I marched to his dressing room and flung open the door, ready to throttle him. "I'm sorry," he cried, as soon as he saw me with madness in my eye and murder in my heart. "I really dried. It wasn't a joke. I'm so sorry. I really did dry." And he really had.

It didn't matter, anyway. I was now on top of the world. I had successfully played Hamlet at the Stratford Festival of Canada. That meant I was now indisputably a leading Shakespearean actor, with all the adulation and glory pertaining thereto. To say nothing of incalculable wealth: at the age of 32, I could now scrape together enough money to buy my first stereo.

That same season, I reprised my role as Lucio in the revival of *Measure for Measure*. Douglas Rain took over from Brian Bedford as Angelo, while the minor role of Mistress Overdone, played the year before by Sheena Larkin, was assumed by Maggie Smith. Someone told me Maggie had come to Stratford that season partly because she'd been getting a rough ride from the critics in England. Also, her sons were quite young at the time and I believe she thought Canada would be a good place to further their education.

It is one of the glories of the repertory system that a tiny part such as Mistress Overdone can be given to a great actress and made into a star turn, and Maggie—who was also that year playing Millamant opposite Jeremy Brett's Mirabell in William Congreve's *The Way of the World* and Cleopatra opposite Keith Baxter's Antony—is not only a great actress but a *very* great comedienne. There were two places in *Measure for Measure* where we'd pass each other backstage. As I came off from playing one of my scenes, she'd be waiting to go on. Then, after she'd done her scene, we'd meet a second time as she came off and I went on again. One day we had what actors call a "slow house," and the audience didn't laugh at all in my first scene. As I came off, Maggie asked me, "How are they?"

Maggie Smith as Judith Bliss in *Hay Fever* at the Stratford Festival in 1977

"I don't think they're very smart," I replied. "I didn't get a single laugh." She went on and proceeded, in the course of a very short scene, to raise three huge laughs and win a round of applause on her exit. As she passed me backstage again, she remarked suavely, "Oh, I don't think they're so bad."

I acted with her again the following year, 1977, when she played Judith Bliss in *Hay Fever*, and I was cast as Sandy Tyrell. (Bill Hutt played David Bliss, and Domini Blythe, who'd joined the company for the first time the year before, played Sorel.) Maggie was brilliant in *Hay Fever*, and the houses were packed, but we had one audience during the run that was so unresponsive that it defeated even her. I was in the wings, waiting to go on, when she said to me, with a weary kind of sadness, "Why are these people *here*?" Knowing that, even if they weren't laughing much, they were still basking in the radiance of a star, I replied, "Maggie, they're here to see *you*."

She performed some extraordinary bits of business in that production. I remember her seeming to just *slide* down a staircase in her high heels in order to interrupt her stage husband's canoodling with visitor Myra Arundel, played by Pamela Hyatt. Elsewhere in the show, as she searched through a tray of sandwiches for the filling she wanted, she'd riffle the sandwiches as if they were a pack of playing cards. She also had a moment where she poured herself coffee from a pot while reading a newspaper. Without looking at it, she'd raise the pot to an incredible height and never once miss the cup. That kind of clowning ability is extremely rare. Beatrice Lillie had it. Lucille Ball had it. Carol Burnett has it. And Maggie Smith has it in spades.

Hay Fever again, with Domini Blythe as Sorel

Though she won her second Oscar while she was here, for *California Suite*, in 1979, she never neglected her craft as a stage actress. She would always, for instance, attend the pre-show warm-ups and the voice classes. She set the bar very high and wouldn't hesitate to let the rest of us know if we weren't measuring up. I remember her once telling a young actor who was giving too introverted a performance: "Dear, there's no point in looking at the floor. There's nothing there. Except," she added acidly, "the play." There was one member of the cast of *Hay Fever* who Maggie felt had a tendency to be slow on her cues. I'd be sitting beside Maggie on the couch in the scene where the characters play a party game, and I'd notice her rapidly tapping her foot in impatience. Eventually, at one performance she turned to me and interjected the last line from Bernard Shaw's *Saint Joan*: "How long, O Lord, how long?"

The only unfortunate legacy she left us was the matter of her hands. They were very expressive, and she had a way of waving them in the air. (One critic—I believe it was Pauline Kael—once called her "Our Lady of the Wrists.") By the time Maggie had been with us for a few seasons, it seemed that every actress at the Festival had adopted the habit of acting with her hands above her head.

Apart from being stage-struck by Maggie Smith, I had quite a crush on her, despite my now clear preference for my own team. She was 42 when we did *Hay Fever* and had a glorious body, which I found wildly attractive. But for some reason, although she was always perfectly friendly (and sent me a lovely note on a Festival postcard with a picture of me as Hamlet, praising my performance in the role), I always had the feeling she didn't like me. I was astonished to find this misapprehension was mutual when she sought me out at a party once and declared, "You don't like me, do you?" I could only stammer: "No, no. That's not true." It seemed my awe of her had come across as aversion. I never did find out what, if anything, she really thought of me.

Many years later, in 1990, I went to see her in *Lettice and Lovage*, which Peter Shaffer had written for her. By the time I saw it, she'd refined her performance to the point where she was actually *conducting* the audience's laughter. Her character had a cold in the third act, which allowed her to flourish a white handkerchief. She'd start a line of dialogue with her arm by her side, the handkerchief hanging from her hand. She'd gradually raise that arm as she neared the punch line, then, *on* the punch line, she'd flick the handkerchief. She'd keep her arm raised as the audience laughed, lowering it only when she'd decided it was time for them to stop. It was a brilliant display of technique.

I went backstage to congratulate her on her performance (for which she won a Tony Award). I'd put on quite a bit of weight by that time, and when she saw me she greeted me with some amazement: "Richard! There are two of you!"

Another star at Stratford during the Phillips era was Peter Ustinov, who played King Lear at the Avon Theatre in 1979 and then again in 1980. It was the only Shakespeare role he'd ever tried and the only one he ever wanted to. I adored him, and he was kind enough to praise my own performance as Edmund, one of the villains of the piece.

He was, of course, a great raconteur. Before every rehearsal, we'd all gather at his feet and listen to him. At the first rehearsal, Robin posed another uncharacteristically thematic question: "What do you think *Lear* is about?" Peter's response was to tell a story about General Franco. The Spanish dictator was on his deathbed, and a crowd had gathered outside the hospital to pay their respects. Franco heard the noise outside his window and asked his daughter what it was. "It's the Spanish people, Father," she replied. "They've come to say goodbye." "Oh?" said Franco. "Where are they going?" People like Lear, Peter was telling us, never imagine they will lose their power.

In another rehearsal, Robin told Peter, "Today I would like you to play the fifth act *singing* the role." I don't know what our director was aiming for, but the result was one of the most spectacular pieces of improvisation I have ever seen. Peter, who was a great opera buff, began the act singing the words in the style of Monteverdi. He then continued to parody the styles of great composers, in chronological sequence, ending up—in the scene in which Lear enters carrying the dead body of Cordelia in his arms—with the 12-tone modernism of Arnold Schönberg. "Howl, howl, hooowl, *how-ow-ow-el!*" he sang, dodecaphonically, then kneeled down to lay Cordelia reverently on the ground. Then, looking up at us, he concluded wryly, "And I've just split my pants."

Although he was a very good Lear, he did have difficulty sometimes with the lines. In Act V, scene 3, Lear and Cordelia are captured by Edmund, who orders that they be taken to prison. Lear has a long speech that begins:

> We two alone will sing like birds i' the cage;
> When thou dost ask me blessing, I'll kneel down
> And ask of thee forgiveness. So we'll live,
> And pray, and sing, and tell old tales, and laugh
> At gilded butterflies. . . .

and so on, at the end of which Edmund says, "Take them away." At one performance, Peter began, "We two alone will sing like birds i' the cage. . . ." and then he dried. "We'll sing . . ." he repeated, "and then we'll sing some more. Oh, we'll laugh. . . . We'll dance. . . . And then . . . we'll sing some more." Realizing what had happened, I tried to save him by coming in early with my line: "Take them away." He regarded me with mild curiosity, then waved me away with his hand—"Foof, foof, foof"—and began the whole speech over again, determined to say it all.

William Hutt (left) as the Fool and Peter Ustinov as Lear in *King Lear* (Stratford Festival, 1979-80)

In 1980, the second year he did his Lear, I made one of my first major forays into directing. Penny Ritco and I co-produced (and I directed) *Stevie*, Hugh Whitemore's three-person play about the poet and novelist Stevie Smith, for Young People's Theatre in Toronto. Roberta Maxwell played the title role, with Kate Reid as her aunt, while the one male character was played by Michael Fawkes. Both actresses won Dora Mavor Moore Awards for their performances. Just before we opened, at the beginning of November, Roberta got married. The ceremony took place on top of the CN Tower, with me as best man and Kate as matron of honour.

A few days later, Kate celebrated her 50th birthday. After a matinée of *Lear*, Peter drove into Toronto to attend her party, knowing that the press would be there and that his presence would bring us some welcome publicity. I was very impressed by his generosity.

Besides Sandy in *Hay Fever*, I'd been offered two Shakespearean roles for the 1977 season. One was Parolles in *All's Well That Ends Well*, directed, as it happened, by David Jones, who'd auditioned me for the RSC back in 1969. (He turned out to be a very talented director.) The other was a part I'd always wanted to play and the one that had been the catalyst for my departure from the Festival 10 years earlier: Romeo. It must have been in the summer of 1976, while I was still playing Hamlet, that Robin offered me this coveted role, and it was that fall, just after *Hamlet* closed, that my anxiety to ensure I would do it justice resulted in one of the most fascinating nights of my life: what my friend Joseph Shaw and I invariably refer to as "The Gielgud Evening."

In the fall of 1976, Sir John Gielgud, who'd been a memorable Romeo in his youth, was in Toronto playing opposite Sir Ralph Richardson in Harold Pinter's *No Man's Land* at the Royal Alexandra Theatre. At some point, I remarked to Joseph that it would be wonderful if I could talk to Gielgud about Romeo and perhaps pick up some pointers from him. Somewhat to my surprise, he replied, "Well, I might be able to arrange that."

Joseph had met Gielgud once through the Crest Theatre, and though he didn't expect the great man would remember him, he didn't feel embarrassed about making use of that faint connection. So he phoned the Park Plaza Hotel, where Gielgud was staying, and asked to be put through. In a few moments, he heard the famous voice, which Alec Guinness once memorably described as "a silver trumpet muffled in silk," on the other end of the line. "Yes?"

After introducing himself, Joseph came straight to the point: "A friend of mine is a rising young Canadian actor who has just played Hamlet and is about to play Romeo. He'd love to meet you. We wondered if we could offer you some supper one evening, with just three or four people." There was a brief pause, then Gielgud replied, "Tuesday suit you?"

We sprang into action. Joseph had a home in Toronto, but it wasn't quite the sort of place to which you could take Sir John Gielgud. So my friend Ben Solway agreed to let us use his apartment, near Upper

Canada College. Then there was the question of transportation. Joseph had a little Toyota Corolla, which again didn't seem entirely suitable for picking up knighted celebrities. So off he went to a car rental company and came back with one of those boat-like vehicles of the 1970s: a Ford Fairlane, I believe.

I was put in charge of the food. The menu, catered by Paul's, a firm in Forest Hill, included lobster thermidor. We also had two bottles of Dom Perignon, which Robert Macaulay, a former provincial cabinet minister who was a friend of Ben's and a fan of Gielgud's, had sent over in his chauffeur-driven car. I invited two more of my friends to join us at the supper: Roberta Maxwell and Frances Hyland.

On the appointed Tuesday, Joseph and I drove down to the Royal Alex in time for the final curtain and sent in our names. We were ushered into Gielgud's dressing room, where he received us cordially and offered us vermouth. Joseph made some remark to get the conversation going, whereupon the star began to chat away to him like an old friend. As he spoke, Gielgud divested himself of his dressing gown and stood before us in his briefs as his dresser wordlessly handed him shirt, tie, pants, socks and shoes. He donned them all without pausing in his conversation, then shouted to Ralph Richardson in the next dressing room, "Goodnight, Ralphie!"

Outside, he dismissed his limousine: "Don't wait for me: these gentlemen will see me home." With Gielgud in the front and me in the back, Joseph carefully drove the Fairlane up Avenue Road to Ben's apartment, where Roberta was waiting. Frances Hyland, much to our disappointment (and hers), had had to back out at the last minute, and Ben, thinking it best to leave us theatre people to it, had already declared his intention of turning in for the night. So it would just be the four of us. Joseph made the introductions, we took our seats at the table, and the Dom Perignon was produced. It was then supposed to be up to me to gradually steer the conversation round to the subject of *Romeo and Juliet*. But I was tongue-tied: completely speechless. Not just because I was in awe of the man, but because I couldn't get a word in edgeways and didn't want to interrupt him.

We enjoyed a fabulous meal, the champagne flowed, and the conversation sparkled, covering all sorts of subjects from the great 19th-century actress Eleonora Duse, whom Gielgud had seen perform late in her life ("I thought she was just a rather cross old lady prowling about the stage"), to pornographic cabarets in Paris and Cairo. He was obviously having a wonderful time: he never stopped to draw breath. Throughout it all, I stayed as mute as the Dormouse at the Mad Hatter's Tea Party.

Finally, at the end of the evening, after much wine, I ventured a question: I asked him who, in his opinion, had been the best Hamlet he'd ever seen. He replied, "John Barrymore." When I asked why, he gave a fascinating answer: Barrymore, he said, had achieved the greatest balance of the male and female sides of the character's psyche.

At about half past two in the morning, our guest announced, "I must go. I have a matinée tomorrow." As we drove back down Avenue Road to his hotel, with me again in the back seat, I finally blurted out the question that had been the whole *raison d'être* of this elaborately planned and expensive evening: "Now, Sir John, I wonder if you have any thoughts for me about playing Romeo."

In *Romeo and Juliet* at Stratford in 1977, with Marti Maraden as Juliet

In response to which, the great actor offered this memorable distillation of his experience: "Well, it's very difficult. You see, in the first act you get a crick in your neck from the balcony scene. And the second act's difficult because the f___ happens offstage."

Romeo and Juliet was directed by David William, with Marti Maraden as Juliet. Just as Robin Phillips inspires by his practical suggestions, so David inspires by his examinations of a play's themes. He talked to us about separation: how the lovers are separated first by their families, then by the killing of Tybalt, then finally by death. "Separation," he said, "is a kind of madness." His insights were sometimes cryptic, always fascinating and occasionally hurtful. "You know your problem?" I remember him once saying to an actor who he didn't think was up to snuff. "You've got a dusty soul."

I was given an unfortunate wig and a blowsy dark blue costume that made me look like a pregnant grape. I complained about it vociferously, so David gave me instead a costume that had originally been designed for Tybalt. My costume, though, was the least of my worries. A far greater problem was the fact that during our earliest rehearsals for *Romeo and Juliet* I was also commuting to Toronto every night to appear in the 1977 revival of *Hosanna* that I had undertaken for Toronto Workshop Productions in order to pay my mortgage. I had just enough energy—for a while—to rehearse in Stratford in the daytime, make the nearly two-hour drive to Toronto (in the middle of winter), perform *Hosanna* and come back the same night. Eventually, though, David had to take me aside and say, "This isn't working."

He happened to catch me at a moment when I had to agree with him. "I know," I said. "I've waited all my life to play Romeo, and now it's not working out." In tears, I bit the bullet: "I think you should replace me." I told him I'd just seen Brent Carver play Romeo beautifully in Edmonton. "Get him," I said. But David must have seen something in me that made him believe I could still get through this and pull it off. In any case, he didn't replace me; instead, he told me to skip rehearsals for the rest of the week, until *Hosanna* was over.

Despite this bold and generous leap of faith on David's part, I don't think Romeo was one of my successes. Perhaps there was an omen at our opening performance. In the final scene of the play, I had to carry the unconscious Juliet from her upstage tomb all the way down to the front of the stage and stand there, still holding her, as I delivered a 90-line speech—the same speech, in fact, that I'd spent so much time on with Eleanor Stuart. But at that very point in the opening performance, a great commotion broke out in the audience. I could tell something was going on, but I couldn't see what. So I pressed on. Afterwards, I learned that a bat had been swooping around in the auditorium, emboldened no doubt by the sepulchral darkness of the tomb scene. So after all that work with Miss Stuart, nobody had been listening to a word of what I had to say about the yoke of inauspicious stars.

It was during that production that I first met Cynthia Dale: she was then about 15 or 16 years old, and her older sister Jennifer was understudying Marti as Juliet. Cynthia came up to me in the

Avon Theatre's Chalmers Lounge after the show and said to me, quite innocently, "You have a great ass." I took that as a great compliment, coming as it did from someone with a dancer's eye for men in tights.

Otherwise, the critical reaction to *Romeo and Juliet* was so negative that I suffered a brief but total collapse of confidence. In truth, I was exhausted, having played a string of immensely demanding roles within the space of a year and a half, with very little break between them. In that final scene of *Romeo and Juliet*, in which I had to spend about 20 minutes dead on stage, I used to fall asleep. Sometimes I'd start to snore, and Marti would have to nudge me. She always had to make sure she died right beside me, so that she could continue to keep me conscious by surreptitious pokes and pinches. As is often the case, however, with critically reviled productions, the show was extremely popular with audiences.

Realizing that I needed time off, I applied for and received another Canada Council grant, which enabled me at the end of the season to go to Europe, where I recharged my batteries and, incidentally, did something I'd always dreamed of but had never been able to afford to do before: explore my roots in Italy and France.

The new year found me in Philadelphia, a city that is not only the cradle of American democracy but that also boasts the oldest gay club in the country. I enjoyed myself immensely in that city, while playing Dunois in a production of *Saint Joan* with Domini in the title role. Joan, of course, is a peasant girl who leads her army of resistance while dressed in male attire. Dunois has a page, a boy, who in this production was played (for reasons known only to the director, Douglas Seale) by a young woman named Marilynn Meyrick in bright red lipstick and tons of eyeliner. A friend of Domini's, the actor Brian Murray, came to see the show and remarked to her afterwards, "My God, when I saw that page, I thought your movement was spreading."

It was as well I took that break, because in the 1978 Stratford season, Robin directed me in one of the most gruelling projects I've ever undertaken: the one-man play *Judgement* by Barry Collins. Urjo Kareda had recommended the piece, which was based on an incident from the Second World War that had been recounted by George

Steiner in his book *The Death of Tragedy*. A group of captured Russian officers, imprisoned and abandoned by the Nazis in the cellar of a monastery, had turned to cannibalism in order to survive. By the time they were found, only two were left alive, both of them mad. *Judgement* purports to be the testimony of one of the two, Andrei Vukhov (assumed for the purposes of the play to still be sane), before he is shot by his disgusted comrades.

As written, the play ran for three hours. (When its author, Barry Collins, came to see the production, he told me that he'd sent the script to Peter O'Toole, who'd then summoned Collins to his home and announced his intention of reading the whole piece aloud. Collins confessed to me that he'd had actually fallen asleep during this recitation of his own work, awakening only toward the very end.)

As Dunois in *Saint Joan* at the Walnut Street Theatre in Philadelphia, with Domini Blythe in the title role

We cut the script down to an hour and three-quarters, without intermission, but it was still nightmarishly difficult to learn. My character was speaking in the present about things that had happened in the past. Within that past-tense narrative, though, there were references to a more distant past, as well as to a present and a future as seen from that perspective. Also, in the present moment in which my character was speaking, there was also a future. So the tenses alone were incredibly difficult to keep straight. Once in rehearsal, Robin noticed that my left knee was shaking.

"We know you're nervous in this trial," he said. "There's no need to have your knees knocking."

"I'm not acting," I replied; "I'm terrified."

I would learn 10 pages each week. We would rehearse those 10 pages, then run from the beginning everything I'd learned thus far. As an aid to memory, I would cut photographs out of newspapers and magazines and assign each of them to one of the people mentioned in the script—Blok, Rubin, Tretyakov, Lysenko and so on—to give myself something visual to connect with the names. As the burden of recall got greater and greater, my concentration could break at any time. During this, Robin heroically gave up smoking, because every time he lit a cigarette it would distract me, and I would dry. (This, of course, was in the days when smoking in a rehearsal room was not only legal but practically *de rigueur*.) Even so, I would still go blank from time to time. Once when that happened during a run-through, Robin prompted me from memory—which was startling enough to make me dry again.

As Andrei Vukhov in *Judgement* (Stratford, 1978)

Robin was a superb coach. Although the performance was mine, he shaped it and made many of the key choices. Only one move was allowed me in the entire hour and 45 minutes: to go to a table and pour myself a glass of water. I did this in rehearsal, and then Robin, in one of his flashes of inspiration, said, "Don't drink it." It was a brilliant choice, which created enormous dramatic tension. I could have done with the water, though.

On opening night, as Robin watched from the wings, as was his habit, I had to hobble back on to the stage to take my second curtain call. Some people thought I was begging for sympathy for the character (or for myself), but the simple truth was that after all that rigid standing I could no longer walk properly. Once, near the end of a performance, I suffered an involuntary spasm that made me jump up in the air. The audience must have thought I (or my character) was finally going insane.

In September, we gave nine performances of *Judgement* at the Vancouver East Cultural Centre. Afterwards, Robin wrote me a lovely note and sent me a dozen white roses, which I thought very generous of him. At the same time, there was also word of taking the show to New York next summer, so I turned down other work that winter in order to keep myself free for rehearsals. But the New York trip never materialized. I was bitterly disappointed about this: like so many actors (even ones with stereos), I was living from hand to mouth, and I'd been counting on that income.

I played three more Shakespearean leading roles during Robin's tenure: Berowne in *Love's Labour's Lost* and Prince Hal in the two parts of *Henry IV* in 1979—a huge season for me, since that was also the first year of Peter Ustinov's *Lear*—and, in 1980, Robin's last year as artistic director, Henry V. (Also in 1980 I played a small role in *Foxfire*, co-written by Hume Cronyn and Susan Cooper.) The two parts of *Henry IV* were directed by a protégé of Robin's, Peter Moss. Douglas Rain, who'd given a superb performance as Prince Hal back in 1965, when I'd had my wordless cameo as Lord Harcourt, played the title character. I still remembered every single intonation he'd given to the lines back then, when I'd been listening on the backstage Tannoy, and without that memory, my own performance as Hal would have been greatly diminished.

Douglas is a brilliant actor for whom I have the greatest respect, but our relationship during *Henry IV* took some odd turns. My 1978 season had consisted of *Judgement* and a role in another play, John Whiting's *The Devils* (a piece that I thought creaked even back then), plus my first directing assignment at the Festival: *Come and Go*, a short piece presented at the Third Stage under the umbrella title *Four Plays by Samuel Beckett*. So I hadn't done any Shakespeare for a year, and I felt a little out of practice.

One day, walking to the theatre for rehearsals, I passed Douglas's house. He was outside shovelling snow, and I stopped to talk to him.

"Douglas, I'm so pleased you're going to be playing my father. I haven't done Shakespeare for a while, so I hope you're going to help me out."

"No," he replied. "Do it on your own."

I was shocked: not by the reply, which was actually the best possible advice he could have given, but by what I perceived as the sharpness of its tone. Was he getting into character already, I wondered, to set up the antagonistic onstage relationship between father and son?

When we started rehearsals, I hung on to my script for quite a long time. Eventually, Douglas said to me: "When are you going to learn your lines? I've been looking at the top of your head during this entire rehearsal period." I replied by hurling my script into the auditorium and snapping back, "I know my lines."

"All right," said Peter Moss, "we've had the father-and-son fight; now let's do the father-and-son fight *scene*." So we proceeded to rehearse the first play's Act III, scene 2, in which Henry IV lectures his son. At one point, I turned away from Douglas, as if Hal were saying, "I don't have to put up with this." Douglas responded by racing across the stage, grabbing me by the shoulder and spinning

As Prince Hal in *Henry IV*, Parts 1 and 2, with Lewis Gordon as Falstaff (Stratford Festival, 1979)

me round. An entirely appropriate bit of business—but because of what had already taken place between us, I instinctively reared back my hand and made a fist. It was a moment of sheer electricity. So we kept it in.

These tensions came to a head at the opening-night party, when, in response to some remark of Douglas's that I interpreted as being critical of my performance, I completely lost my temper and responded with a fury out of all proportion. "Douglas," I snarled, "if you say one more word, I'm going to smash your head against the cement wall behind you and suck out your f___ing brains." So much for the shy newcomer who had quaked before him in my first year.

Still, I learned a lot from Douglas. He said something to me once that ranks high up in my list of memorable maxims about the theatre. It resonated with me because I'd been drawn to the social art of performing partly by the loneliness I had experienced as a child.

"Theatre," he said, "is made *by* lonely people *for* lonely people."

Love's Labour's Lost, the same year, was very popular but not very funny, as Shakespearean comedies go. Robin didn't *want* me to be funny as Berowne: again, he wanted to reveal the underside of the play rather than just going for the easy laugh. To me, however, going for the easy laugh seemed to be exactly what Berowne does: it's the keynote of his character and it's what gets him into trouble. Berowne's comic flaw, if you will, is his wit.

The production was set, as so many of Robin's productions were, in the Edwardian era. He explained once that he favoured that period because North Americans didn't have a cultural memory that predated photographs, as Europeans did. Still, I got awfully tired of plays in Edwardian dress. Beige Edwardian dress. Robin wasn't big on colour, as he wasn't big on humour. We went through a beige period, and then we went through a black period. Monochromatic design was part of his way of keeping a lid on things.

A strange thing happened during a tech dress: a rehearsal where we ran through the play with all the props and sound and lighting cues. At the end of what has hitherto been a romantic comedy, the tone of *Love's Labour's* suddenly becomes sombre when a messenger arrives announcing that the Princess of France's father has died. Thereupon, the women bid their farewells and impose a 12-month penance on the men who have been wooing them, at the end of which, if the men have remained true, they will be married. Presumably to plant in our minds some seeds of this sadness that blooms in the final scenes, Robin began our rehearsal by delivering a kind of elegy about the great English actress Dame Sybil Thorndike, who had died three years earlier. We then proceeded to run the play.

Domini was playing opposite me as Rosaline, the woman Berowne loves. Rosaline has the last major speech by a woman in the play, in which she remarks on Berowne's sometimes careless use of wit—"The world's large tongue / Proclaims you for a man replete with mocks"—and instructs him to spend his 12 months visiting "the speechless sick" in hospital, using that wit of his to cheer them up. When Domini came to this speech she suddenly underwent a complete meltdown. Choked with emotion, she couldn't speak at all. It was as if she'd been hit by a thunderbolt.

The other actors on stage froze, watching her out of the corner of their eyes, wondering what to do. I went over to her, held her by the arms and held her gaze, willing her to go on, until she was able to speak again.

She didn't explain it fully at the time, and I'd always assumed she'd just been overcome for some reason by the play's sad reminder of mortality, intensified, perhaps, by Robin's remarks beforehand. (She'd met Dame Sybil once, when the great actress visited her drama school.) But much later—when I was gathering the material for this book, to be exact—she explained that her tears had nothing to do with late great English actresses; rather, they had come because at that moment she had suddenly identified Berowne with me. She was seeing not Berowne on stage at that moment, but me: someone she loved (as a brother, now) and someone, she said, who used humour—"all the fierce endeavour of your wit"—to turn grief into laughter. The speech had seemed to her to capture my essence, and that was why it had moved her so much.

As Berowne in *Love's Labour's Lost*, with Domini Blythe as Rosaline (Stratford Festival, 1979)

Robin knew, obviously, that something had happened, but we never discussed it with him. "That was an extraordinary moment," he remarked afterwards, "but don't ever try to do it again. It's the sort of moment you can never repeat, so don't try. Just remember it as you act this scene during the season. There will always be a vestige of it there." And there always was.

Having played Prince Hal in 1979, I naturally wanted in 1980 to continue the same character's journey when he assumes the crown and becomes Henry V. By that time, however, something seemed to have gone sour between Robin and me. At any rate, I was hurt when Peter Moss came to my house and told me that I would be playing *Henry V* but that I'd be sharing the role with another actor, Kenneth Welsh. Shades of the duelling Hamlets. Salt was rubbed in the wound when Kenneth dropped out and *another* actor, Jack Wetherall, was asked to share the role with me. Was I being punished for something, I wondered? If so, what was the crime?

I don't know how well my Henry V was received. I'd stopped reading reviews the year before, when I had to open in leading roles in three productions in a row—*Love's Labour's Lost* and the two parts of *Henry IV*—with *King Lear* to come later in the season. If I were panned in the first of these, I thought, I'd be so depressed that I'd never get through the rest. So I didn't read the reviews that year and found it an easy habit to maintain. As for the audiences, most nights, I'd come out at the end to polite applause. But there was one performance when the entire audience stood and cheered. It had never happened before with that show, and it never happened again. I have no idea why. Whatever it was, I was glad it occurred when it did, because my friends Kate Reid and Roberta Maxwell just happened to be attending that particular performance. What an unpredictable thing the theatre is.

The years in which I worked with Robin Phillips were hectic, challenging, deeply rewarding and immensely important to my development as an artist. I learned a lot from him about the craft of acting, and I shall be forever indebted to him for giving me those leading Shakespearean roles—those enormous canvases, as I call them—for even despite my star turn as Hosanna, it is unlikely that I would have had the opportunity anywhere else to tackle them in such quick succession. Most roles in the theatre are tied to age, and Time hath, my lord, a wallet at his back. You can only hope to play Prince Hal, or Prince Hamlet, for so many years before you start to be a more likely contender for Falstaff or Polonius. In the space of six seasons, I'd been given a huge range of demanding roles, Shakespearean and others, to say nothing of my first opportunity, with *Come and Go*, to direct at the Festival.

I admired, too, much of what Robin did in his own art, even if it wasn't always to my taste. Before him, the work done at Stratford had been, by English-theatre standards anyway, very rhetorical: loud, fast and full of energy. He changed all that. Under him, there was a much deeper investigation of the text: we looked words up and explored nuances of meaning. And, despite the objections of some traditionally minded patrons, he allowed—and indeed required—those of us who were Canadian to use our own native pronunciation for playing Shakespeare.

Samuel Johnson once remarked that the poet John Milton "was a genius that could cut a Colossus from a rock, but could not carve heads upon cherry-stones." Both forms of art are legitimate, and both can express genius. Robin's genius, though, was not of the Miltonic kind. It was curious to me that Bill Glassco should have told me during *Kennedy's Children* that I tended to censor; from my point of view, that was more Robin's style than mine. In his productions you felt laced in (and not always just figuratively: in *King Lear*, for some reason, he made all the men wear corsets under their costumes).

Robin Phillips: a deeper investigation of the text

Some people found this restrained approach, which yielded valuable insights of its own, hard to work with. I didn't, particularly; but it wasn't, and isn't, my way. My approach as a director is more like Jean Gascon's or, as I was once flattered to be told by Tanya Moiseiwitsch, Tyrone Guthrie's. I like theatre to be theatrical, and I'm interested in the expansion of artists, not their restriction. There's a quotation from Pablo Picasso that I'm very fond of: "Good taste is the enemy of creativity."

I have suggested that Robin Phillips aimed to put a lid on the unrulier energies of the theatre. While intending no disrespect to that approach, I did everything I could, in the course of my own tenure as artistic director, to take it off again.

CHAPTER NINE

Raging Rocks and Shivering Shocks

A Midsummer Night's Dream, Act I, scene 2

No one was more shocked than I myself when, at the Stratford Festival's 1980 annual general meeting (an event attended by some 800 people, including members of the media), I called the president of the board of governors a pig.

The events that led up to my outburst, and those that followed it, are amply detailed in Martin Knelman's 1982 book, *A Stratford Tempest,* and I don't need to recount them at any great length here. Indeed, at the time, I wasn't privy to the whole sorry saga: I knew only that Robin Phillips's resignation as artistic director had triggered a succession crisis, as a result of which four of my fellow artists had been shabbily treated. My anger at that AGM sprang not from any firm grasp of the Byzantine manoeuvrings that had gone on behind the scenes but merely from a vague intuition that something was rotten in the state of Stratford.

To briefly set the scene: in the summer of 1978, Robin Phillips, exhausted and in poor health, had informed the board of governors that he intended to resign at the end of the 1980 season. Instead of immediately starting to look for a suitable successor, the board had responded by offering him a sabbatical in 1979 and promising to devise a new leadership model that would enable him to stay on past 1980 in some less all-consuming capacity.

The solution eventually proposed, after nearly two years of deliberating, was a two-tier, nine-person group directorate that would run the Festival under Robin's "guidance," thereby freeing him up to continue directing plays and attracting stars. I thought this was a recipe for disaster, and indeed, two weeks after it was announced, in August 1980, the directorate started to fall apart when Robin, apparently suspecting it was simply a ploy to lure him into going on as before, decided he wanted no part of it.

By mid-September, only four members of the original group remained on board: Pam Brighton, Martha Henry, Urjo Kareda and Peter Moss. It wasn't long before some wag dubbed them "The Gang of Four," in ironic (and, as it turned out, prophetic) reference to the four prominent members of the Chinese Communist Party who in 1976 had became scapegoats in the struggle for power after the death of Mao Tse-tung. That label stuck, and the Four were given the go-ahead to plan a 1981 season, *sans* Robin.

At a company meeting held in a Festival Theatre rehearsal hall on

September 18, before the official announcement went out, I asked if the Four had received contracts, a question that seemed to irritate everybody. Urjo told me that they had a "letter of intent."

In fact, unknown to the Four, a parallel negotiation was still going on with a view to bringing in a single artistic director. Some time after Robin had first handed in his resignation, overtures had been made to another English director with an international reputation: John Dexter. (He'd directed the Broadway production of *Equus*, which had been playing next door to us when we did *Hosanna* in New York.) Dexter had come away with the impression that a serious offer of the top job was being made, but had then become annoyed when no one followed through on the initial approach.

The Four—who pulled together a proposed 1981 season in heroically short order—were quite keen to have Dexter direct a production for them. Dexter, however, wasn't interested in anything less than the artistic directorship—and he was being encouraged to hold out for it by another British import, Peter Stevens, who'd recently been hired as the Festival's executive director. It was Stevens who persuaded the board that the Four's proposed season was economically unviable, and it was Stevens who then dangled before the board the prospect that it might not be too late for Dexter to come in after all and save the day. At a full board meeting early in November, those in attendance voted unanimously to rescind the Four's appointment and invite Dexter to be the new artistic director.

When this betrayal became public, the outraged Canadian Actors' Equity Association promptly instructed its members to boycott the Festival. Meanwhile, it was becoming clear to Lloyd Axworthy, the minister of employment and immigration, that the board hadn't conducted an extensive search for qualified Canadian candidates before offering the job to an Englishman, and at the end of November he announced that Dexter would not—for the moment, anyway—be granted a work permit.

The president of the Festival's board during all this was Robert Hicks, a corporate lawyer from Toronto. His final duty before handing over the reins to his successor, John Lawson, was to chair the Festival's annual general meeting on December 6, 1980.

The meeting was held, as it usually is, in the auditorium of the Festival Theatre, with Hicks and other members of the board's executive seated on the stage. It began at the appointed time of 11:30 in the morning but lasted far longer than any Festival AGM before or since, finally winding up, if I recall correctly, at about six in the evening. I was there from the start and, as a result, had nothing to eat all day. Low blood sugar may have contributed to my mutinous state of mind by the end of the afternoon.

After some routine business, an eloquently crafted formal statement by the disbanded—and now seriously disaffected—Gang of Four was read out by company member Greg Wanless. It was then responded to, at some length, by Hicks. Further comments were made by, among others, Douglas Campbell, Martha Henry and Robin himself. During a break in the proceedings, I was standing in the theatre lobby with Nicholas Pennell when we were approached by two journalists, one of whom, as I recall, was the late Mira Friedlander. Since they weren't entitled, as members of the media, to ask questions at this meeting, they wanted us to do it for them. Would we ask the board if it was withholding information?

I didn't feel comfortable doing this, and neither did Nick. So instead we asked Rod Beattie, who was that year's Equity deputy in the company (and who would later become well known to Festival patrons as the performer of the Wingfield series of one-man comedies) to pose the question.

When the meeting resumed, Rod spoke up: "I wonder if the board would tell the meeting whether there is any plan for a press conference after the meeting to make any statement to the press, or if there is any plan to release information to the press that has not been released to the corporation."

Hicks began to reply: "There is a board meeting that is being held now, as a result of which there may or may not be something addressed to the press. Now—"

In fact, there was nothing sinister about this: the new board always meets immediately upon its election at the AGM, and the "something" that would be announced, if all went well, was the creation of a search committee to find a new artistic director—which was what people were saying should have been done in the first place. But something about Hicks's reply got under my skin. It may have been the perceived equivocation of those words "may or may not." Or maybe it was irritation at the thought that no one would have deigned to mention any of this to us at all if Rod hadn't been requested to ask. Whatever it was, the rest of what Hicks was going to say is lost to history, for at that point I blew my stack. Leaping from my seat in the auditorium, I screamed out, "You *pig!*"

I am not by nature a confrontational person. I have been called "feisty" by friends and colleagues, but it is an adjective that perplexes me. In my own mind, I would go to great lengths to avoid a fight. Though I might have overcome the shyness that had kept me in my teens from crossing the street at intersections, I have never by any means seen myself as scrappy, punchy or otherwise aggressive. Indeed, Domini once told me how much of a coward she thought I was. But that afternoon, I'd grown tired of all the doublespeak we'd been hearing around the issue of the Festival's future leadership, and Robert Hicks had the misfortune to provide a momentary focus for my rage. Only two or three times in my life have I lost control of my anger in such a way, and it scared me more than anyone.

"You pig!" My moment of madness at the 1980 AGM

As the crowd gasped, Hicks tried to reassert control of the situation. "In fairness," he began, "you have elected—"

Again, I cut him off. "We have spent our *lives* in this theatre. We have given of our time, and we care about art. You talk to us about money all the time. You have no morals. I don't know how you can sleep. And I care deeply and passionately about this place, and you must address yourselves to your consciences, and to your hearts."

"I have no intention of presuming—" Hicks began, then broke off to ask, "What is your name, sir?" Another gasp: people were appalled that he didn't seem to recognize me as one of the Festival's leading players. This was in fact unfair to him: when you're on that stage, as Hicks was, with the light in your eyes, it's all but impossible to make out faces in the auditorium.

Two security guards were making their way toward me; however, I beat them to the exit, assisted by Leon Major, whom I hadn't noticed there before. Amid the uproar, Hicks tried to bring the meeting to a close, but before I left the auditorium, my old friend Amelia Hall managed to have the last word in a wonderfully articulate and impassioned piece of oratory that made my words seem like the disjointed ravings they probably were.

"Back before 1953," she declared, "when there were no arts councils and no corporations giving money to theatres, I happened to belong to a non-profit professional theatre, and I remember one day meeting on the street a businessman who was the president of our board of directors. He was also the lone figure who stood behind our bank debt. And he said to me, 'Well, Amelia, we dropped a thousand dollars on that production last week, but by God we can be proud of ourselves.'

"Theatre isn't a building. It isn't a foundation. It isn't proxies. It isn't balance sheets. It isn't power plays. Theatre is heart and spirit, and in 1953 when this theatre went up like a great rocket, it was heart and spirit that did it." She ended with a (slightly misquoted) line from the book of Proverbs: "Hold on to thy heart with all diligence, for out of it are the issues of life."

My explosion at that annual general meeting made me something of a national hero: a poster boy for cultural nationalism. The irony, of course, was that no such thing had been in my mind. I had no objection to Dexter *per se*, as I hadn't had to Robin Phillips (who'd been a huge success, after all, and had elevated the Festival in the eyes of the world). Had the board conducted a proper search in the first place and then at the end of it come up with John Dexter, I certainly wouldn't have had a problem with that, nor do I think there would have been such a crisis upon his appointment. (Nick, mind you, had apparently heard some stories. I remember him telling me, "John Dexter may be a wonderful director, but he will wreak havoc in this theatre.")

What bothered me was not Dexter's nationality but the murkiness that seemed to surround all the participants in this debacle. That and the fact that the Gang of Four had been dumped not for valid artistic reasons but because their proposed season had been arbitrarily deemed to be a money-loser. For me, this was an issue not of cultural nationalism but of keeping faith with one's fellow artists.

Shortly afterwards, Gina Mallet published an article in the *Toronto Star* claiming, incorrectly, that my outburst had been premeditated. Because a point of honour was involved, there being a world of difference between a deliberate strategy and an impassioned, spontaneous *cri de coeur,* I initiated a lawsuit. Suing people is always a costly and unpredictable business, though, and newspapers have deep pockets, so in the end I let it drop.

The incident did, however, cost me a friendship. As it happened, the evening before the AGM, I'd been visiting someone with whom I'd been close friends since we were both in our early 20s. (We'd also, briefly, been lovers.) When Mallet's article appeared, actor Peter Hutt, nephew of Bill Hutt, told me that it was this man who'd been her source.

When I confronted my friend about this—"Were you the one who spoke to Gina Mallet?"—he denied having done any such thing.

"Peter Hutt says you told him you did."

"No, I didn't."

"I will forgive you," I said, "if you admit this." Again he said no. I didn't believe him, though, and I never spoke to that person again from that day on.

I was worried on more than one count about what I had done. In the first place, of course, it looked as if I had just made a spectacularly career-ending move—certainly as far as the Stratford Festival was concerned. At the same time, I was also wondering if I had harmed not just myself but the Festival, perhaps irreparably so. One or two people had in fact come up to me in the street and asked me outright why I had chosen to bite the hand that fed me. And, finally, there was the worry that what I had done had simply been futile: a display of empty histrionics that would make no difference to anyone.

At the same time, I still felt it had been the right thing for me to do, given my position in the company at the time. (As Trevor Nunn is reported to have said to the actor Alan Howard once at the RSC, it's not enough to play leading roles; you also have to lead the company.) Some years later, at a time when my emotional life was in turmoil over an unfortunate relationship, I went to consult a psychiatrist, and at one point we discussed my lingering doubts about my actions at the AGM. "Who do you think loves Stratford the most?" he asked me. "You or the board?" I avowed that I did, to which he replied, "Well, now you have your answer."

One day after the Gang of Four had been dismissed but before a new artistic director had been found, I was working in my garden when I suddenly found myself thinking, for no particular reason, about Nicholas Pennell. In the distance, I heard a church bell ringing, and as it did so, my phone also began to ring. It was Nick, wanting to come over. When he arrived, he told me that he'd just been sounded out about becoming the Festival's next artistic director. He'd replied that he would consider it only if I would undertake to share the job with him.

In some ways, this was an intriguing idea. As leading lights of the company, Nick and I enjoyed a certain profile, and we already had good relationships with other Festival artists. Also, we were friends, and if Nick's Englishness were going to be any kind of problem, well, who better than the hero of the AGM to lend ethnic legitimacy to the appointment? Here would be an incredible opportunity for me to put my services where my big mouth had been.

My instincts, however, sensed a poisoned chalice for both of us. "Nicholas," I said, "I just don't think we'd have a chance." Given the atmosphere of hurt and distrust that now prevailed at the Festival, it seemed to me that it was going to take a real heavyweight to put the house back in order: someone with the credentials of a John Hirsch. And neither Nick nor I had that kind of experience. So I regretfully declined his proposal.

Afterwards, I phoned John Hirsch and pleaded with him to come. He'd already been approached by the search committee, and he did eventually agree to take the job. His other commitments prevented him from assuming its duties immediately, so he put in place a producer, Muriel Sherrin, who did a stellar job of assembling a 1981 season under extreme pressures of time and circumstance.

I didn't expect to be a part of that season. Indeed, I wondered if my new-found notoriety might compromise two other projects I already had lined up in Toronto: a voice-over advertising an exhibition on Vincent van Gogh and Cloisonism for the Art Gallery of Ontario and the title role in *Count Dracula*, a comic adaptation of Bram Stoker's novel that was to open at Young People's Theatre on New Year's Eve. Peter Moss was directing that production, and other members of the Festival company were acting in it, and I didn't want them to feel their careers might be tainted by association with me. I met with Peter and the rest of the cast and offered to withdraw, but they dismissed the idea at once. The AGO, too, stood by its decision to hire me.

After one matinée performance of *Count Dracula*, I was leaving the theatre when I was stopped by an elderly couple who introduced themselves as Otto and Evelyn Beyer, born in Germany and now residents of Kitchener, Ontario. They'd been coming to the Stratford Festival for many years, they told me, and had enjoyed my work there. News of my outburst at the AGM had finally prompted them to speak to me. They admired my courage and my integrity, they told me—whereupon they presented me with a cheque for $1,000. "You're going to need this for the lawsuit," smiled Otto.

Otto and Evelyn Beyer: like second parents to me

This charming and eccentric couple quickly became great friends. Otto, an architect, had been conscripted into the German army at the very end of the Second World War. When it was over, he and his brother had gone into construction, rebuilding their country's bombed cities. (Evelyn told me she'd once found a diamond amid the rubble of a ruined house.) Eventually, concerned about the Cold War, they'd left Germany, first for Tobago, then for Australia, before finally settling in Ontario, where Otto taught at the University of Waterloo. Besides being an architect, Otto was also, like my uncle Gentile, a painter, and he and Evelyn took me to art galleries in Montreal, Ottawa, New York and Washington, D.C. A gentleman of the old school, he always wore a tie, even when he painted. Evelyn was a voracious reader, averaging a book a day, and between the two of them the Beyers were not only extremely generous to me but practically gave me a second education.

Otto has since died, but I still have many of his paintings. Evelyn is now in a home, where I send her flowers and, of course, books. My friendship with them was one of the most remarkable and significant relationships of my life. For all too short a time, they were almost like second parents to me.

In April and May 1981, I played Max in Martin Sherman's play *Bent* at the Bathurst Street Theatre in Toronto. Brent Carver initially played Horst but then dropped out and was replaced on April 19 by Ralph Small. The play had been recommended to me by a friend who was also, I think, a friend of the playwright.

As Max in *Bent*, with Stewart Arnott (right) as Rudy, at the Bathurst Street Theatre in 1981

I was quite shocked at first by the script, in which Max, a gay man in the Dachau concentration camp, pretends to be straight and Jewish because the Nazis' treatment of Jews was far better than that accorded to homosexuals. Unsure whether I should venture into such politically sensitive territory, I sent the script to Urjo Kareda, who wrote me back saying, "This is a gay *Sound of Music.*" But there was something about the second act that struck me as being more like Samuel Beckett than Rodgers and Hammerstein, and I couldn't get it out of my mind. So I decided to take it on, especially after Ian McKellan played the same role to great acclaim in London, and Richard Gere followed suit in New York.

Another example of the bewildering ways in which members of the public sometimes seem to interpret theatre: one day I went into the coffee shop next door to the theatre, as I had done many times, and the woman who served me said, "I never knew you were Jewish." I guess she must have seen the play, but her remark made me wonder what on earth it had meant to her. I wonder if she thought I'd really died at Dachau, too, as Max does at the end. (And why didn't she say, "I never knew you were *gay*?")

After *Bent*, much to my surprise, I was invited to return to Stratford for the 1981 season after all. In retrospect, perhaps they couldn't *not* have asked me back, since that would have been seen as a pointed statement, and the new regime was still very shaky and vulnerable to public opinion. Or maybe they just wanted me back regardless. In any case, I was glad to be asked, not just for the sake of my career but because I wanted to be counted in. I wanted to be in the midst of this theatre that I loved, at this crucial juncture in its history, and to help heal whatever wounds I might have unintentionally aggravated.

My roles were Jack Absolute in *The Rivals* (the same part I'd played at the Roundabout in New York in 1974) and Harry Thunder in a 19th-century comedy called *Wild Oats*, which also included in its cast Nicholas Pennell and Barbara Chilcott, my Gertrude from the Crest *Hamlet*. Directed by Derek Goldby, a man of some eccentricity, *Wild Oats* later toured to the National Arts Centre in Ottawa, where Nicholas and I were intrigued to find on the wall huge photographs of ourselves as our respective Hamlets from 1976.

In *The Rivals*, directed by Brian Bedford, Lydia Languish was played—delightfully—by Mary Rutherford, that friend of mine who'd been Hermia in Peter Brook's *Dream* in London. Pat Galloway was Mrs. Malaprop, Colin Fox was Sir Lucius O'Trigger, and Nicholas was Faulkland. As for me, having done the play before, I knew where all the laughs were, and I thought it one of my finer performances.

Nick's role and mine were really the leads in the play, and I felt that the final curtain call should go to us, as a pair. However, the role of Sir Anthony Absolute was being played by an actor brought in from England—David Langton, best known as Richard Bellamy in the 1970s TV series *Upstairs, Downstairs*—and Brian had chosen to give the final bow to him.

No doubt there were good reasons for this: Langton was a senior actor, after all (although not with our company), and a TV star, of sorts. Maybe the curtain call was written into his contract. But to me it smacked of some sort of colonial old boys' network, and I resented it, especially since I was working like a dog in my role. So, at our first preview, in which I got so many laughs I felt like a stand-up comedian, I did something of which I am not particularly proud: I didn't go out on stage for my curtain call.

Brian was beside himself. "What's the matter with you?" he complained afterwards. "They were eating out of your hands."

"Oh, they don't want to see *me*," I replied with heavy sarcasm. "They want to see *him*." My fit of ego passed, and I took my curtain call at subsequent performances. But I still thought it was an injustice.

After the Stratford season closed, I took a short holiday, then, at the end of December, began rehearsing the role of Jerry (with Alan Scarfe as Robert and Barbara March as Emma) in Harold Pinter's *Betrayal* at the Saidye Bronfman Centre in Montreal. It was only the second time—the first being that 1976 tour of *Hamlet* and *The Tempest*—that I had acted in the city of my birth. *Betrayal* is a wonderful play, and I enjoyed doing it, though Domini said my English accent was appalling. What I primarily remember, though, is that I was so cold the whole time that I vowed I would never again visit Montreal in the winter.

In 1982, John Hirsch fully assumed his role as the Stratford Festival's new artistic director. I liked John and learned a lot from him, but I never really knew what he thought of me. I did notice, though, that my parts suddenly became smaller than they had been under Robin Phillips. That season, I was offered Dr. Caius (a good role, but not a lead) in Robert Beard's production of *The Merry Wives of Windsor*; Sebastian in John's own production of *The Tempest* (a smaller role than Caliban); and one of the lesser conspirators—I can't now remember which—in *Julius Caesar*, directed by Derek Goldby.

The reason I can't remember that role in *Julius Caesar* is that I didn't play it. Instead, I did something that no actor would normally do: I held out for a *smaller* part.

"No, no," I told the producer, John Hayes, who was issuing the offers, "I want to play Cinna the Poet."

"But Richard," said John, well aware that I was now used to leading roles, "Cinna the Poet is only seven lines. What we're offering is a lot more."

"I know," I replied. "But Cinna the Poet has been played by such great actors as William Hutt, and every time the play is produced, that's the part that steals all the reviews. I want to play Cinna the Poet." And I was right: I got better reviews for my seven-line Cinna than I'd had for many of my leading roles. (Even if I wasn't going to read them, I wanted to know they were there.)

I have described Derek Goldby as "eccentric." Others might use more colourful terms. I remember him saying to us at an early stage in rehearsals for Julius Caesar, in his strong regional English accent: "'Course, you knaow it's *daingerous*. Theatre's *daingerous*. Some of you will be 'urt. Thass theatre, innit?"

As Cinna the Poet in *Julius Caesar* (Stratford, 1982)

Mark Antony in that production was played by R. H. (Robert) Thomson, who also appeared that season (his only one at Stratford to date) as Slender in *The Merry Wives of Windsor* and Mortimer in Friedrich Schiller's *Mary Stuart*, which John was directing. Although he'd played a wonderful Mercutio once and would go on to play Hamlet at Toronto Free Theatre, Robert didn't seem to me to be entirely comfortable with classical drama: I gathered he somehow felt it wasn't truthful.

At one of the last rehearsals for *Mary Stuart*, John Hirsch expressed some concern about how Robert was playing the role.

"Well," explained Robert, "I just haven't found it yet."

"Vot do you mean, Robert?"

"Well, John, it's just not in my body."

"Robert, ven do you think it *vill* be in your body?"

"Well, I don't know, John. I don't know."

To which John replied: "Robert, Robert. Ve preview in two days. I admire your *sang-froid*. But quite frankly, *I'm shitting my pants!!*"

In a repertory season, in which each actor plays roles in more than one production, it can sometimes be difficult to remember which play you're doing on a given day. That season, Robert and I shared a dressing room with Richard Curnock, a wonderful character actor who always seemed to arrive at the theatre late and always seemed to be in a flap about something. His roles were Pistol in *Merry Wives*, Alonso in *The Tempest* and Decius Brutus and Volumnius in *Julius Caesar*.

Falstaff in *Merry Wives* was being played by Douglas Campbell, but Douglas wasn't in either of our other two productions; his other role that season was Major Petkoff in *Arms and the Man*. It so happened, though, that for some reason Douglas was hanging around backstage one day when we were getting ready to perform *Julius Caesar*, and Richard must have seen him as he arrived, late and flustered as usual, at the theatre. Anyway, Richard burst into our dressing room and started putting on his moustache, beard and wig for *The Merry Wives of Windsor*.

"Richard," I said, "we're not doing *Merry Wives* tonight. We're doing *Julius Caesar*."

"Oh, shut up," he said, thinking I was kidding him, and continued putting on his makeup. It was now quite close to the performance's starting time.

"Richard," I said, "look at me. Look how *I'm* dressed. Look how Robert is dressed."

Richard paused in his application of facial hair long enough to take in our appearances. He then became enraged, since it was quite clear to him that we'd dressed up as our *Julius Caesar* characters in order to play a practical joke on him. He marched out of the dressing room to demand of the stage manager, "What play are we doing tonight?" Having received the answer he didn't expect, he stormed back into the dressing room. "Well!" he exclaimed, ripping off his moustache and beard, "I have only one thing to say: they should *not* allow Douglas Campbell into this theatre when *we're* doing *Julius Caesar*."

John Hirsch came to Canada as a young orphan of the Holocaust, and the horror of his early years had left its mark. The story goes that when he had to choose a place to stay, he looked at a map of the

Martha Henry as Frosine and William Hutt as Harpagon in *The Miser* (1998).
Photo by Cylla von Tiedemann

Brian Bedford (foreground) as Sir Peter Teazle, with (from left) Donald Carrier as Charles Surface, Michelle Giroux as Lady Teazle and Steven Sutcliffe as Joseph Surface in *The School for Scandal*, which I directed in 1999. Photo by Michael Cooper

Brian Bedford as Bottom and Seana McKenna as Titania in *A Midsummer Night's Dream* (1999). Photo by Cylla von Tiedemann

Brian Bedford in the title role of *Tartuffe,* which I directed in 2000. Photo by Cylla von Tiedemann

Thom Marriott as Porthos, Andy Velásquez as Aramis, Benedict Campbell as Athos and Graham Abbey as D'Artagnan in *The Three Musketeers,* which I directed in 2000. Photo by Cylla von Tiedemann

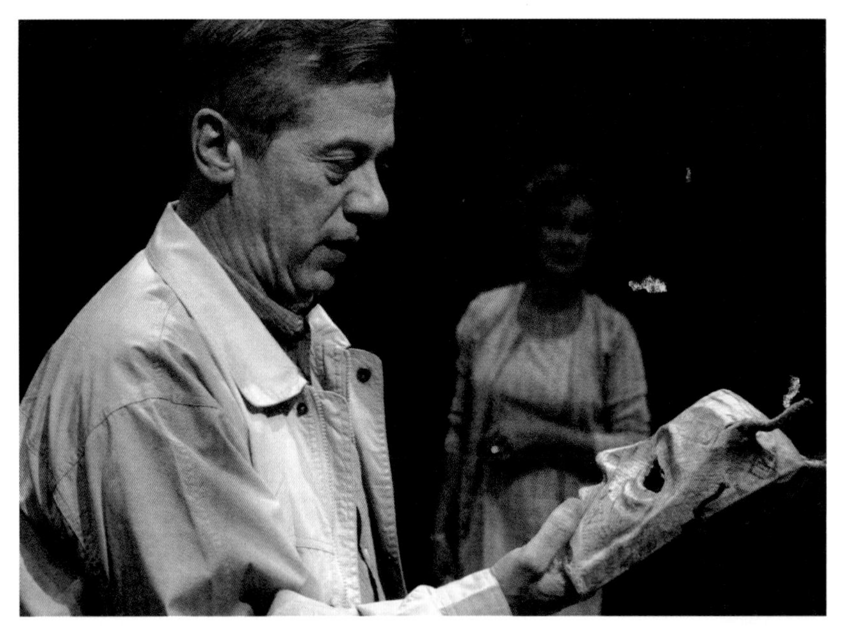

Stephen Ouimette as Gord and Chick Reid as Margery in *High-Gravel-Blind,* which I directed at the new Studio Theatre in 2002. Photo by Terry Manzo

Lucy Peacock as Helena and William Hutt as the King of France in *All's Well That Ends Well,* which I directed for the Festival's 50th season in 2002. Photo by V. Tony Hauser

Patricia Collins as Aunt Alicia, Jennifer Gould as Gigi and Domini Blythe as Mamita in *Gigi*, which I directed in 2003. Photo by Michael Cooper

Claire Jullien as Cressida and David Snelgrove as Troilus in *Troilus and Cressida*, part of my Greek season in 2003. Photo by Michael Cooper

Thom Allison (left) as the Duke of Suffolk and Walter Borden as Cardinal Wolsey in my 2004 production of *King Henry VIII (All Is True)*. Photo by Coopershoots/David Cooper/Michael Cooper

David Snelgrove as King Edward in my 2005 production of Christopher Marlowe's *Edward II*. Photo by David Hou

David Snelgrove as Brick and Cynthia Dale as Margaret in *Cat on a Hot Tin Roof*, which I directed in 2005. Photo by David Hou

William Hutt taking his curtain call after his final performance as Prospero in my 2005 production of *The Tempest*. Photo by Richard Bain

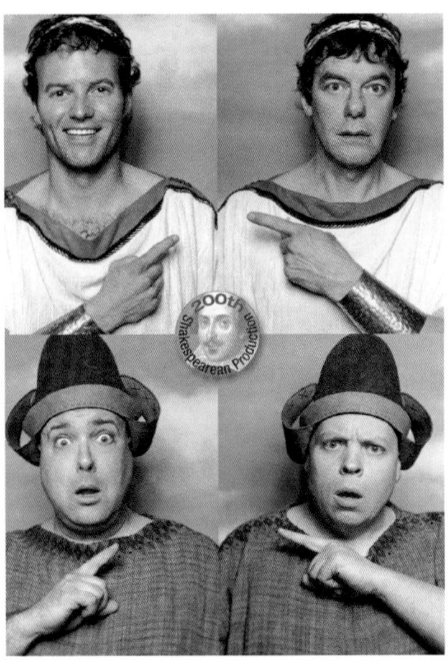

Clockwise, from top left: David Snelgrove as Antipholus of Syracuse, Tom McCamus as Antipholus of Ephesus, Steve Ross as Dromio of Ephesus and Bruce Dow as Dromio of Syracuse in *The Comedy of Errors* (2007). Photos by David Hou

Festival founder Tom Patterson and his wife, Pat, look on as I shake hands with Queen Elizabeth II at the dedication of the renewed Festival Theatre in 1997. Photo by BDS Studios

Me at mid-century: a photo taken during my 50th birthday party in 1994

Looking doctoral after receiving an honorary doctor of laws degree from the University of Western Ontario in 2005

With Christopher Plummer in 2003, after he received an honorary doctorate from the University of Toronto. Photo by Steve Frost, courtesy of the Office of the President, University of Toronto

With Antoni Cimolino, then executive director of the Stratford Festival, at the opening of the new Studio Theatre in 2002

"The pilot wants an *audition*?" (See pages 301–302)

With my executive assistant, Elke Bidner, at the opening night of the 2007 season. Photo by David Snelgrove.

With a promotional Punchinello in front of the renewed Festival Theatre in 1997

Rejoicing with Domini Blythe over our paid-off mortgage on the house I still live in

My brother, Mark, and his late wife, Christine

Christmas at my house, with (clockwise around the table, starting from my left hand) Ben Solway, Jean Beaudin, Pat Collins, William Hutt, Domini Blythe and Judy Lane, partner of my brother Mark, who took the photo

Another happy Christmas: me with Mark and Judy

Christmas with the Cimolinos: me, Sophia and Gabriel

country and pointed to Winnipeg, because it seemed to be the city furthest from anywhere else and thus the safest from invaders.

As a director, he was an intellectual—someone who makes artistic decisions in his head rather than his heart—but also a man of passion: a rare combination in my experience. He spoke his mind, sometimes hurtfully so (as he did that time when Kate Reid was having trouble with her props in *The Cherry Orchard*), but if he was sometimes impatient with actors it was because he had a powerfully articulate vision of each play he directed, and he was determined to see that vision realized. There was never anything general about his readings: they were very specific and very detailed. He became an artist because he had a lot to say, and he said it with great credibility. Even though this passionate intellectual could also be very funny (an even rarer combination), his productions were, as a rule, very dark. A notable exception was his 1982 production of *The Tempest*, a play that was obviously dear to his heart.

Although I was in it and can thus hardly be objective about it, I have since watched the CBC videotape of the production, and I still think it was wonderful. It had a stunning design by Desmond Heeley: the kind of gauzy, transparent gorgeousness that only Desmond can achieve. I still have some of the notes that John gave us when we were rehearsing it: in them, he urges us to strive above all else for the clarity of the words and of the thought. The production had that clarity, but it also had the sheer size that I believe is so essential to Shakespeare. It was operatic, even mythic, in its scale.

In rehearsal, John spoke to us about the fairy-tale aspect of the play, which he wanted us to make as real as we could. As Sebastian, I had the line "Now I will believe / That there are unicorns." In one note session after another, John would say to me: "Richard, I can't hear you on that line. I can't *hear* you." Every time we rehearsed that scene, I would say the line louder, and every time John would say he still couldn't hear me. Eventually, I turned to Nicholas Pennell, who was playing Stephano (brilliantly), and said, "Nicholas, I am now *screaming* this line. What does he mean?" And Nicholas replied, "He means he doesn't *believe* you."

John spoke to us, too, about what he called the "moral declension" in the piece. Among other things, this referred to the gradations of evil seen in my character, Sebastian, and in Antonio, played by

Colin Fox. Antonio embodies aggressive evil, John said, while Sebastian is only passively evil. As he spoke of this, I couldn't help thinking—though he made no reference to it—of the difference between those who actually ran the concentration camps and those who just stood by and let it happen. I had never before understood the point of an exchange between Antonio and Sebastian in Act II, scene 1, until John clarified it for me. "The ground indeed is tawny," says Antonio, surveying the island on which he and his companions have been shipwrecked. "With an eye of green in't," responds Sebastian. This too, is a "moral declension": a subtle indication of a crucial difference in how these two characters see the world.

In the same scene, Antonio and Sebastian mock Gonzalo with a string of Jacobean jokes that few modern audiences would be able to follow. Among them is an exchange in which Sebastian says, "I think he will carry this island home in his pocket, and give it his son for an apple," to which Antonio replies, "And sowing the kernels of it in the sea, bring forth more islands." Thinking that this obscure bit of byplay would just send the audience over the edge in what was already a linguistically and thematically difficult scene, I said to John, "Couldn't we just cut these lines? Nobody's going to understand them." Eventually, with the greatest reluctance, John agreed to let them go—for which I got my come-uppance later in the season when I went to hear the great critic Northrop Frye speak on the play in a lecture series presented by the Festival.

As Sebastian in *The Tempest* (Stratford, 1982), with Colin Fox (left) as Antonio

"If we find in Shakespeare a passage of dialogue which seems pure blither," Frye remarked at one point in his talk, "we should congratulate ourselves, because that is likely to be where some of the deepest and most central themes of the play are to be found." My heart sank as he went on to cite the very lines I had persuaded John to cut. Worse, Frye wound up his lecture by saying that those lines may well provide a metaphor for what we, as theatregoers, are supposed to do with the play: sow the seeds of Shakespeare's imagination in our own lives.

I consoled myself with the thought that what may be crucial to a play's meaning from a literary point of view isn't necessarily what's going to work in the theatre. But still. . . .

It was a wonderful production, that *Tempest,* and a seminal one. It certainly inspired me when I came to direct the play myself in 1999 and again in 2005, both times with William Hutt as Prospero. Both times, I told my cast that whatever merit I might bring to the production would be owed entirely to what I'd learned from John Hirsch.

It was during the next Stratford season, 1983, that my father died. His mother, my grandmother Eva, was still alive at the time and living in Vancouver. She flew to Montreal for the funeral, and afterwards we went to the home of one of our relatives. There, Eva kept saying, "*J'ai chaud, j'ai chaud*: I'm hot, I'm hot."

I suggested she take off her sweater, which she did. But she still kept complaining of the heat, though it wasn't that warm in the room. When I pressed her to explain the source of her discomfort, she said, "It's my breasts, my breasts."

"I don't understand," I said. "What's the matter with your breasts?"

"It's the money," she replied evasively, as if she were being forced to discuss something indelicate.

Eventually, the mystery was solved. In the old days, when Eva and Alfred had lived on their farm, no one used cheques, and credit cards were unheard of. So she still had, taped to her chest beneath her clothes, the wads of cash with which she'd flown from Vancouver: the money to pay for her son's funeral.

I acted in only one production that year: *The Country Wife,* directed by Richard Cottrell, a wonderful man who had a terrible stammer. One day, giving a direction, he said, "Will you fu-fu-fu-fu-fu-f___ing get on with it? Goodness!" he continued: "What a dreadful word to stammer on." I played Sparkish in that production, with Domini giving an amazing performance as Margery Pinchwife. Desmond Heeley designed it, and he gave me such a fabulous costume that I used to do a pirouette on my first entrance to show it off, for which I'd get a round of applause.

When the show was taped for television, I tripped and fell in the curtain call. Finding myself flat on the floor in something that was going to be broadcast, I tried to make it look like a deliberate bit of business by whipping off my wig and flinging it into the orchestra pit. In this I was all too successful: nobody in the cast would believe I hadn't fallen on purpose, even when I showed them the gash and the bruise on my leg.

My other contribution to the 1983 season was to direct Douglas Campbell in *Blake*, a one-man show that we'd workshopped the year before. Written by the Festival's then literary manager, Elliott Hayes (Urjo Kareda having left after the Gang of Four was dismissed), it was a portrait of the visionary artist and poet William Blake. Michael Langham came to see it and remarked, "This is the best acting Douglas has done in decades." And Douglas had *always* been a fine actor.

When John Hirsch was planning his 1984 season, he called me in and asked me, "Who do you think could play Romeo and Juliet?" I was astonished at the question—why would he seek *my* opinion?—but I replied instantly, "Colm Feore and Seana McKenna."

Colm had first joined the company in 1981, playing Clitandre in *The Misanthrope*, Tranio in *The Taming of the Shrew* and a couple of walk-ons in *Coriolanus* and *The Comedy of Errors*. He'd then made a major breakthrough as Claudio in Michael Langham's 1983 production of *Much Ado About Nothing* for the Young Company. Seana had come along the year after Colm, making her debut as Helena in the *Dream* and Diana in *All's Well That Ends Well*, and then in 1983 playing the key role of Mariane in John's production of *Tartuffe*. I don't think John was entirely convinced by my recommendation, but he went ahead and gave them the roles anyway, casting me as Mercutio.

The director of *Romeo and Juliet*, Peter Dews, was having some health problems, and I felt, rightly or wrongly, that the production was suffering as a result. Since I'd played Romeo and was still very familiar with the play as a whole, it seemed natural enough for me to offer a helping hand to some of my fellow cast members. And, of course, having recommended Colm and Seana to John, I had a vested interest in seeing them succeed.

I was sharing a dressing room with Colm that season, and we started discussing his role as Romeo. This led to my coaching him privately in my living room, just as Bill Hutt had done with me all those years ago when I'd been trying to figure out how to bear a standard. We'd go through each of his speeches, he would listen diligently to what I had to say, and then he'd write it all down. Gradually, the idea of my offering the pearls of my wisdom began to permeate through the rest of the cast, until even as experienced a performer as Patricia Connolly, who was playing Lady Capulet, was coming to me and asking, "What did you think tonight?" Her performance had been all a-twitter, with fluttering hands, and I regret to say I wasn't as tactful as I might have been: "I thought you were acting like a demented budgie."

The production was a great success, and I think—although I don't know for sure—that word went round about my behind-the-scenes role as unofficial acting coach. That role had, in fact, been a very dangerous one to play. Although I'd sincerely been trying to help, I could have done much harm by inadvertently interfering with the director's process. I'd been lucky enough to get away with it, however, and the considerable satisfaction that I derived from helping my fellow actors shape their performances doubtless planted a few more seeds of my future as a Festival director.

That season, Colm and I were also in *The Merchant of Venice*, in which I played Antonio and he played Salerio, one of a pair of confusingly named characters (the other being Solanio) that actors jokingly refer to as "the Salads." John Neville played Shylock, with Domini as Portia, and the production was a big hit. It was directed by Mark Lamos, who told me—unfairly, I thought, since I felt I was putting my heart and soul into it—that I was a "lazy" actor. But perhaps he was picking up on something else: my growing discomfort with the play itself, something I hadn't felt 16 years earlier when I'd played Lorenzo in Regent's Park.

"You're not going to do *that* play?" my friend Ben had said to me, incredulously, when I first mentioned my role as Antonio to him.

"Well," I'd said defensively, "it's part of the canon, and even if it *is* anti-Semitic, it should still be done."

I'd given a lot of thought, as I've said earlier in this book, to the implications of portraying evil on stage. Besides that elusive passage about artists inhabiting a separate moral universe, I'd read somewhere—and this had made a huge impression on me—the proposition that no truly great work, as opposed to mere hate literature, can genuinely espouse anti-Semitism or any other morally hateful viewpoint, even if it might at first glance seem to. A work that did so could not be truly great. Furthermore, even if such a thing *were* possible, then it would be our duty as artists to make the work available for scrutiny, so that this terrible flaw could become apparent.

In this case, I felt certain that the question didn't arise. I didn't—and don't—believe that *The Merchant of Venice* was meant to promote hatred: it has too much compassion, too much insight, for that. To me, it's both a lyrical fairy tale and an allegory about justice: the eye-for-an-eye retributive justice of the Old Testament versus the greater

As Antonio (right) in *The Merchant of Venice* (Stratford Festival, 1984), with Colm Feore as Salerio

emphasis on mercy found in the New. It's undeniably a thorny piece: technically it's a comedy, in the sense that all the lovers end up marrying, but at the same time, it's certainly not a comedy for Shylock. (Shakespeare realized, I think, that society had to have its critics: Shylock, Malvolio, Jaques, Falstaff. In his plays, the outsider is as important a part of the social fabric as the insiders: in a sense, they couldn't exist without each other.)

But though intellectually I didn't have a problem with *Merchant* when we began rehearsing it, I was unprepared for what it would actually feel like to stand centre stage at the end of the play, calling for Shylock's forced conversion to Christianity, to the cheers and applause of an audience of 2,000 people. I found this mortifying.

I thought it was my fault: that I wasn't, as an actor, communicating the complexities of the situation, even though I was playing the scene with as much compassion as I could muster, taking the point of view that Antonio sincerely wants to convert Shylock not as a punishment but in order to save his soul. The audience's simple glee in Shylock's fate was devastating to me, and I had tears in my eyes during the performances.

When Ben came to see it, he said afterwards, sadly: "You see? What did I tell you?"

"You're right," I acknowledged. "I will never do this play again." And I have never again acted in it, though I have programmed it during my tenure, usually because a leading actor wanted to play Shylock. I included it in the 2001 season, for instance, at the request of Al Waxman. I told him about my experience playing Antonio, and how I'd conceived a personal distaste for the play. He responded by insisting that I direct it myself. Tragically, Al died while undergoing surgery before the season started, and the role was taken over by Paul Soles, who played it with great natural empathy: a quality that can be neither learned nor simulated. Still, I found it a very difficult play to direct.

My other role in the 1984 season was that of Boyet in *Love's Labour's Lost*, a production that Michael Langham had directed with the Young Company at the Third Stage the year before and which he was now remounting at the Festival Theatre. It was wonderful getting to know Michael again after so many years, but his work on the production itself felt perfunctory to me, as if he were simply regurgitating what he'd done before. His directions to me were practical rather than revelatory: "Move there. No, no, not there: there. You need to be fatter. Your lips should be redder. Your cheeks have to be redder. Your nose has to be redder. Redder! Redder! Much redder!" Maybe he saw the character as an alcoholic; in any case, I don't really know if I did well in the part or not.

Although my most notable achievements as an actor thus far had been on stage rather than screen, I'd never completely abandoned the medium in which I'd made my professional debut. Since that leading role in *With My Head Tucked Underneath My Arm* back in

1963, I'd appeared in such other CBC TV dramas as *Mary of Scotland, The Reluctant Agent* and *Certain Practices*. I'd played Mozart in a film for CityTV, and in England I'd been on the BBC children's program *Jackanory*. (And let's not, of course, forget *Big Zapper*.) But my one real experience of mainstream Hollywood filmmaking remains a film that I worked on from February to May 1983, before that year's Festival season began: the science-fiction thriller *Iceman*.

Released in 1984, *Iceman* is a fantasy-cum-fable about a 40,000-year-old Neanderthal (played by John Lone) who is found frozen in a glacier and comes back to life when thawed out. The scientists involved, played by Timothy Hutton (who'd won an Academy Award in 1981 for his supporting role in *Ordinary People*) and Lindsay Crouse, then have to fight to protect their find from less sensitive colleagues who want to experiment on him. Directed by Fred Schepisi, an Australian, the film was produced by Canadian Norman Jewison, who'd been on the Stratford Festival's board of governors. I was one of three Canadians in the film's supporting cast, the other two being Amelia Hall and Philip Akin.

Also in the film were Danny Glover (now, of course, a huge celebrity) and David Strathairn, later nominated for an Academy Award for his role as broadcast journalist Edward R. Murrow in George Clooney's 2005 film *Good Night, and Good Luck*. The role of Maynard in the film was played by James Tolkan, who shared with me his technique for making himself laugh on stage (a much harder feat for most actors than crying on cue): "I imagine a pigeon on each audience member's head." I tried it once, but it didn't work for me.

I made good friends with Lindsay Crouse, whose father was Russel Crouse, one of the co-writers (along with Rodgers and Hammerstein) of the musical *The Sound of Music*. He'd named her—a bit self-servingly, I thought—after his writing partner, Howard Lindsay: her full name was Lindsay Ann Crouse, as in "Lindsay and Crouse." In 1985, she received an Oscar nomination for her role as Margaret Lomax in the film *Places in the Heart* and later had a supporting role as Maggie Walsh in a season of the cult TV series *Buffy the Vampire Slayer*.

Lindsay was married at the time to the playwright David Mamet, who accompanied her on the shoot. I used to hang around with him, and found that he had a wonderful sense of humour as well as a curious fascination with firearms. When we went shopping together, he always seemed to be looking for books and guns. He and I went to a movie together one day: Richard Attenborough's film *Gandhi*. It was nominated for that year's Academy Award for best original screenplay, which it subsequently won. David's own script for *The Verdict* was also nominated that year, though in a different category: best screenplay adapted from another medium. He was openly scathing about *Gandhi* when we went to see it. "Look at this," he complained loudly to the packed theatre: "there aren't any action

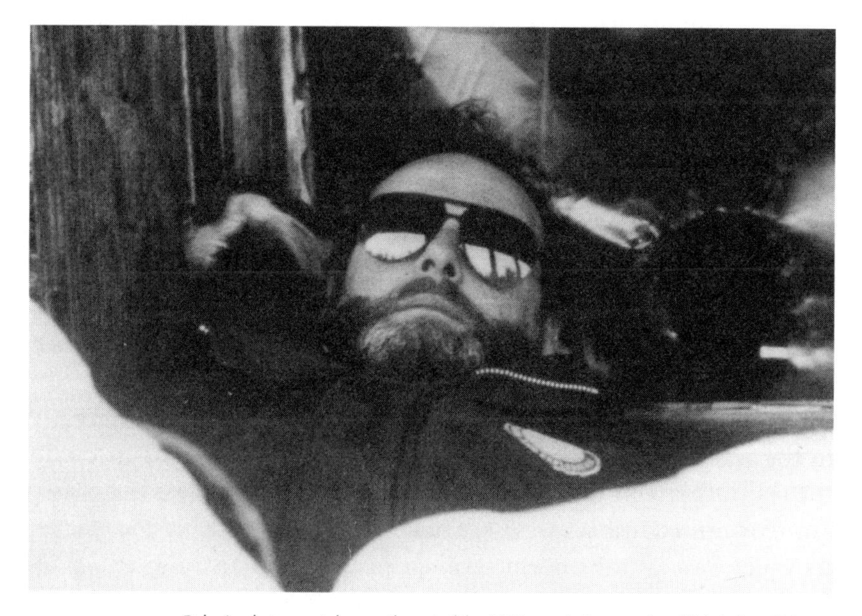

Relaxing between takes on the set of the 1984 movie *Iceman*, in which I played Hogan

shots. These are all production shots. There's no *story* here." David is a wonderful writer, and it has been one of my regrets that I was never able to program one of his plays during my tenure.

Iceman was the first film I'd been in that actually had a budget. Much of it was shot on location, first in Churchill, Manitoba, and then on a glacier in Stewart, B.C., to which we'd be flown every day by helicopter. (We'd be flown out again for lunch: I don't know where they found the food, but it was always fabulous.) Before we went out for the first time, we were warned that there was always the possibility of fog moving in. If that happened, we'd have to camp on the glacier overnight. I think it was Amelia Hall who raised the question, "So in that case, how would we eat?" Our costume designer, a beautiful and statuesque woman with long blonde hair who always dressed to the nines, had an amazing answer to that. "All the buttons on your costumes," she said, "are edible. You can make a small campfire, melt some snow into water, and eat your buttons."

There was a man on the set whose job it was to stick a pole into the ice every half hour or so to see if it was getting soft. If he determined that it was, we'd have to pick up all our gear and move somewhere else so we wouldn't fall into a crevasse. One day, this man complimented me on one of my Stratford Festival performances (I forget which one: it may have been Sebastian in *The Tempest*). I was a little surprised to find myself on a glacier with a Festival patron. "We're a long way from Stratford," I said to him. In fact, he'd never been to the Festival: he'd seen the production on TV. This confirmed my belief in the value of those CBC videotapes that were made in the 1960s and the 1980s. Although it's prohibitively expensive to broadcast Festival productions nowadays, I took every opportunity during my tenure as artistic director to get the Festival's work into *some* other medium, even if it was just audiotape, so that it could be shared with a much wider audience.

Because snow is so hard to film against, we'd shoot either early in the morning or late in the afternoon, when the sun was low in the sky. Otherwise everything would just come out as a white wash. I once ventured into a cave of ice that had formed itself on the glacier. Its walls were a translucent blue-green. It was the strangest feeling in the world. I felt as if I'd discovered Plato's Cave of Shadows.

I'm not fond of flying, so those helicopter trips to the glacier weren't much fun for me. Even worse, the film called for a scene in which the iceman fell from an airborne helicopter, while my character leaned out the door trying to catch him. This was long before the days of computer-generated special effects, so getting the shot meant actually going up in a helicopter and doing it. Norman had asked me to do my part in this scene myself, rather than having a stunt double stand in for me, and like a lunatic I'd agreed. My unease was made worse by the fact that there was no telling when I'd be called to do this: we had to wait till the weather was just right.

I was wandering around with David Mamet in downtown Stewart

(what little there was of it), when a member of the film crew rolled up in a truck and announced that they were ready to do the scene.

The plan was that I'd go up in the helicopter with two stuntmen, one of them wearing a helmet-mounted camera, the other costumed as the iceman with a concealed parachute. When we were high enough, the stuntmen would step out from the rear of the helicopter on my side and sidle along the landing skid, clinging to the fuselage, till they were outside my door. Then, as the one standing in for the iceman hung from the skid, the one with the camera would let himself fall backwards, filming up at his hairy-suited colleague, who'd then release his grip on the skid and fall as well. Meanwhile, I'd be seen in the shot leaning out the open door frantically grabbing at the iceman as he fell. Having got as much footage as they dared, the stuntmen would then open their parachutes.

"Does anyone have a Valium?" I said, only partly jokingly, as they strapped me in. I tried to put a brave face on it, but the truth was that I was absolutely terrified. With the helicopter door open, there would be absolutely nothing between me and the ice sheet far, far below. My life would depend entirely on a couple of pieces of nylon webbing tethering me—at my insistence—to my seat.

We went up. I was sitting in the front of the helicopter, beside the pilot; the two stuntmen were in the back, where I couldn't see them. We reached the necessary altitude and hovered as the stuntmen went out on the skid. The first one fell, as planned; then, as I leaned out and flailed my arms, the second followed suit. When their parachutes opened, I drew myself back into the cabin, pulled the door shut and breathed a shuddering sigh of relief. It was done. Thank God, it was done. Please, dear Lord, let them have got the footage okay.

At that moment, there came a frenzied banging on my door.

I jerked convulsively round in my seat to meet a terrifying sight: inches from me, on the other side of the window, was the wildly grimacing face of a *third* man, clinging to the outside of the craft. As I sat paralysed in horror, this apparition screamed something at me, then fell from the skid. "He's going awfully low," commented the pilot, grimly, as this mysterious interloper plummeted toward the glacier. "I don't know if he's going to make it." At the very last second, though, a parachute blossomed open and the stranger landed safely.

It had been, I discovered when we returned to base, an elaborate practical joke at my expense. Knowing of my dislike of flying, the stunt crew had smuggled this third member of their party aboard to liven up their day's work—and, in the process, give me a little taste of what it might feel like to experience cardiac arrest.

David Mamet (who hadn't been in on the joke) recounted this episode in "Observations of a Backstage Wife," one of the essays in his 1986 collection entitled *Writing in Restaurants.* He describes me regaling the company and crew with the story over a lobster dinner that night. As I always tend to do, I turned a stressful experience into an amusing anecdote. At the time, though, it had been the stuff of nightmare. I don't know how much, if anything, it had to do with the fact that, half a dozen years later, my fear of flying would morph into a full-blown phobia that would make it impossible for me, in all but the most urgent of circumstances and then only under the heaviest of sedation, to travel by air.

Shooting the helicopter stunt in *Iceman*

Since leading roles seemed not to be in the cards for me at Stratford at the moment, I looked elsewhere for work after the end of the Festival's 1984 season. After *Iceman,* I was in greater demand as a screen actor than before, and over the next few years I guest-starred on such TV series as *Adderly, Night Heat, Alfred Hitchcock Presents, Diamonds, Street Legal, The Twilight Zone, E.N.G.* and *Counterstrike.* I appeared, sort of, in a 1986 film called *Dancing in the Dark* (my face was never seen in any of the shots), and I had a cameo as an art critic in Patricia Rozema's *I've Heard the Mermaids Singing,* released in 1987.

I didn't forsake the stage completely, though. In March and April of 1985, I played Lloyd Dallas in a U.S. production of Michael Frayn's

Noises Off that rehearsed in New York and went to Fort Lauderdale and Palm Beach in Florida. Ever since the Crest Theatre *Hamlet*, I'd had occasional problems with my voice, and while we were doing *Noises Off*, I lost it completely. Eventually, I was sent back to New York, where I consulted a doctor who had been recommended to me by a friend of Roberta Maxwell's.

I was told that this man had once been Sigmund Freud's doctor, and indeed there was an enormous oil portrait of Freud in his office, located in an apartment building, with the waiting patients lined up in the hallway. I walked in to find the good doctor in his slippers, with his fly undone. He looked about 200 years old.

"Say 'Ah'," he said, peering down my throat. Then he barked, "Out, out, out."

"What do you mean?" I asked, wondering if he was ordering me to leave.

"This afternoon," he replied, "we cut out those polyps."

The prospect of surgery at this man's hands terrified me. "Couldn't we wait?" I asked, timidly.

"Are you a doctor?" he growled.

"No, I'm not a doctor."

"Am *I* a doctor?"

"Yes, you are a doctor."

"Out, out, out."

Whereupon I fled and cured myself by not speaking a word for two weeks.

In 1980, the same year the Festival's succession crisis had come to a head, Leon Major had resigned as general director of the St. Lawrence Centre, to be succeeded by Edward Gilbert. In 1983, the centre's resident theatre company, formerly Toronto Arts Productions, was renamed CentreStage, and two years later Bill Glassco took over from Gilbert as its artistic director. I appeared in two of the productions of Bill's first season: the Restoration comedy *Love for Love* by William Congreve and, later, Frank Wedekind's *Spring Awakening*, in which Len Doncheff would give me that memorable piece of advice about the theatre taking what it needs.

Directed by Derek Goldby and brilliantly designed by Michael Levine, *Spring Awakening* was a brave attempt to put on a very difficult play. Its subject is the awakening of sexuality in adolescents, a tricky theme to handle under any circumstances, and not entirely helped by the fact that the younger members of the cast, kids from a drama school, were going through exactly that metamorphosis in their real lives. The production was extremely good; the play, however, was just a little too "out there" for its audience's tastes. At almost every performance, despite signs in the lobby warning about nudity and mature themes, patrons would leave in their outraged hundreds; by the time I came on for my last entrance, I'd be lucky to find anyone left in the house.

Otherwise, this was not a vintage year in my career. *Love for Love,* directed by Bill himself, featured one of the best casts ever assembled in Canada, including Martha Burns, Brent Carver, Jim Mezon, Eric Peterson, Fiona Reid and Susan Wright. Despite this, it was possibly the greatest fiasco with which I have ever been associated.

Bill and John Ferguson (who had designed *Hosanna*) unveiled the design for *Love for Love* with great ceremony: "We have worked on this set for six months," they said, reverentially. The idea behind it was clever: it was made to look like an extension of the theatre that surrounded it. This was thematically appropriate, since the characters in Restoration comedy are essentially extensions of their own audiences: the fops, rakes and ladies of fashion who went to the playhouse to see and be seen. But practically, there was a fatal flaw. The action of the play was supposed to take place on the second floor of a house, and John had decided that access to this would be by means of a trap door.

Restoration comedy, like French farce, depends on maintaining a crackling pace. This is hard to achieve when every entrance and exit is made by means of stairs and a trap—particularly so for women wearing elaborate costumes with wide skirts. Whenever a character came on, the audience would see him or her gradually emerge: first the top of the head, then the shoulders, then the torso. By the time the feet made their appearance and the scene could continue, all comedic tension had been lost.

Between *Love for Love* and *Spring Awakening,* I returned to the Tarragon Theatre to play Seward in *Farther West,* by John Murrell. Duncan McIntosh directed it, with Geordie Johnson and Nora McLellan as the leads. Diana Leblanc was also in the cast, along with

Diego Matamoros and Paul Boretski. A great sense of camaraderie arose between my fellow actors and me: the sort that springs up when people band together against impossible odds. Those odds were posed, in this case, by the script, which I found grotesque to the point of hilarity. When I first read it, I thought it should have been the libretto for an opera, and when John Murrell arrived for the start of rehearsals, I said to him: "John, how nice to see you. Did you bring the music?"

Our set involved a lot of sand and a lot of water, which got mixed together to produce a kind of sludge. Nora had to appear nude in her first scene and later simulate an explicit sexual act with me. Her character was later killed by being shot in the crotch. I had a scene in which I had to fight drunkenly in the wet sludge with two hookers, one of them played by Mary Haney (one of my favourite actresses of all time) in a fat suit. We called it the "bloat-and-float" scene. There was also a scene in which Diana had to thrust my hand into a burning woodstove. The effect of this was achieved by having a big jar of guck (a mixture of makeup, Vaseline and K-Y Jelly) inside the suitably illuminated stove. I'd stick my fist in the jar while shrieking in my agony, so that it looked red and blistered when I withdrew it.

I'm sure all this lurid melodrama, in that tiny *boîte* of a theatre, made a huge impression on the very few who saw it. I remember Diana turning to me at one point during the run and remarking, "This is hell."

It was freezing cold in the Tarragon at that time, and the building was full of mice. You couldn't flush the toilet during a performance because the sound could be heard from the audience. We were actually relieved every time we had to cancel a performance, which we had to do more than once. On one occasion, it was when Nora fell ill during the run; on another, it was when Geordie broke his arm and had to be replaced; and in a third case it was because a fire had broken out in the theatre.

Robin Phillips had directed this same play out west with Martha Henry in the cast. Apparently it was an immaculately restrained production, dressed all in white. I wonder how he managed it.

I have several reasons for disliking *Macbeth*, arguably the funniest play Shakespeare ever wrote. In the first place, why spend three hours in the company of two of the most hideous characters ever created: the Thane of Fife and his wife? I have to agree with Kenneth Tynan, who once remarked that the problem with Macbeth is that he starts out a thug and ends up a cornered thug. Secondly, there's the problem of the witches. In my reading of the play, they have Macbeth's fate sewn up from the start. He has no free will, so where's the drama? And finally, I just find the Grand Guignol of the piece—like that of *Farther West*—too hilarious for words. Never mind such unsayable lines as Macduff's "O horror! horror! horror! Tongue nor heart / Cannot conceive nor name thee," how can you take seriously a play that begins with three bearded ladies and ends with the protagonist's head on a pike?

As Macbeth in Skylight Theatre's 1986 production of Shakespeare's funniest play

Given all this, it was ironic that I should find myself, in the summer of 1986, playing the title role in an outdoor production of the dreaded "Scottish play," directed by Lewis Baumander for Skylight Theatre, in Toronto's Earl Bales Park. I did it because nobody else had ever given me the chance to play Macbeth, and I thought perhaps the experience might change my mind. It didn't, but I will be forever grateful to Lewis for giving me the chance. (His wife, Louisa, who played Lady Macbeth, was very kind to me. I was concerned about a scene in which I had to kiss her: the AIDS epidemic was very much in everyone's minds at this time, and many actors were worried that the virus responsible might be spread through their saliva or even their tears. I'd had myself tested, but it took forever to get the results. I offered to fake the kiss, but Louisa pooh-poohed the suggestion.)

Our set designer had provided a centre entrance so narrow that only one person could use it at a time. This led onto an enormous array of ramps, all leading nowhere, so if you went to the top of one, the only thing you could do was come back down again, like a rolling marble. At the bottom of a ramp, you'd disappear from view.

It was a modern-dress production (post-nuclear-holocaust, I believe), and, the budget being minuscule, we were wearing costumes that we'd more or less brought from our own homes. I wore a leather coat—which, as it was about 300 degrees in the shade that summer, I'd don just before I had to go on—with jeans and boots. Within minutes, I'd be drenched with sweat. Still, I fared better than the three witches, whose costumes were made out of Glad bags stapled together. Whenever there was a gust of wind, they sounded like 3,000 pigeons taking wing.

There were three sound cues in the production: a bell ringing, an owl screeching and a baby crying. At one evening performance, the cues came in the wrong order. This incensed me: with only three sound effects in the whole show, how hard could it be to get them right? Losing control, I went storming off to eviscerate the sound person, who was sitting in a booth atop a nearby hillock. On my way, I accidentally stepped on something in the dark, resulting in the unscripted addition of a fourth sound effect: the loud yelp of an outraged dog.

I returned gratefully thereafter to CentreStage, where I played Luigi in Eduardo De Filippo's *Saturday, Sunday, Monday*—a very good production in which both Lally Cadeau and Butch Blake won Dora Mavor Moore Awards for their performances, and which inspired me to program the same playwright's *Filumena* in the 1997 Stratford Festival season.

A footnote about *Macbeth*: I've seen two productions in my life that managed to transcend my feelings about the play. One was Trevor Nunn's famous minimalist version for the RSC in the 1970s, with Judi Dench and Ian McKellan. The other was the 1962 Stratford Festival production with Christopher Plummer and Kate Reid. It got dreadful reviews, as I recall, but it was superb. Chris was thrilling in the role. When he came to the "dagger" scene—"Is this a dagger which I see before me?"—he made the most dramatic lunge I've ever seen. There was a long table on stage, and he flung himself upon it, sliding along its full length on his stomach, as he clutched at the illusory weapon before him.

Near the end of the play, when his enemies are closing in, Macbeth calls for his armour. His officer Seyton says, "'Tis not needed yet," to which Macbeth replies, "I'll put it on." Most actors would make that line a sharp rebuke to Seyton; Chris, though, said it with exaggerated weariness, like a long-suffering husband reluctantly undertaking a household chore. It was a brilliant choice to introduce a comic note at that moment of extreme tension, and it brought down the house. There are relatively few productions I wish I could go back in time and see again, but that was one.

The same year I played Macbeth, John Neville succeeded John Hirsch as the Stratford Festival's artistic director, and I was asked back for the following season, 1987, to play a part I'd always wanted: Benedick in *Much Ado About Nothing*, directed by Peter Moss. Frankly, I thought I was now, at nearly 43, a little old for the role, but I suspected they'd had some trouble casting it. I came to realize, though, that you can credibly go on playing this gift of a part until quite an advanced age: not only does Benedick have all the good lines, he also gets plenty of breaks and doesn't have to do any fighting.

My Beatrice, with whom I got along very well, was Tandy Cronyn, daughter of Hume Cronyn and Jessica Tandy, and I suggested to Jessica and Hume that they should consider playing Beatrice and Benedick some day. They never did, but when I directed the play myself in 1998, I followed through on my idea by casting Brian Bedford and Martha Henry as the warring couple, and I thought that middle age added a touching dimension to these characters' bickering obsession with each other.

Benedick is, in some ways, an extension of Berowne, the character with whom Domini had so memorably identified me in *Love's Labour's Lost*. Both characters use wit as a defence, so that they don't have to come into touch with their true feelings, and I think it's significant that many gay men are extremely witty, having plenty of pain to protect themselves against. Certainly I, as all my friends testify, have always used humour as a means of dealing with the many things in my life that have hurt me.

I loved playing Benedick. I had no idea that it was going to be, for the foreseeable future at any rate, my last Shakespearean role.

CHAPTER TEN

Surprised with an Uncouth Fear

Titus Andronicus, Act II, scene 3

It was while I was playing Cinna the Poet in Derek Goldby's 1982 *Julius Caesar* that I first experienced the symptoms: a sudden sensation of dizziness, accompanied by a ringing in my ears. Such dizzy spells would affect me from time to time over the next few years, for no apparent reason. They'd occur offstage as well as on and were on occasion quite severe. In 1986, for example, just before one of my soliloquies in *Macbeth* at Earl Bales Park, I had the sudden feeling that I was going to pass right out. In what I hoped would look like a planned move, I sank to the floor, from where I delivered the whole of my speech. None of this, however, prepared me for the life-changing incident that took place one night in January 1988.

CentreStage was mounting its final season at the St. Lawrence Centre before merging with Toronto Free Theatre later in the year to become the Canadian Stage Company. The season included George F. Walker's *Nothing Sacred,* adapted from Turgenev's *Fathers and Sons,* in which Bill Glassco had cast me as Pavel Krysanov. It was a good script, and we had a solid cast, including David Fox, Diane D'Aquila (later a leading member of the Stratford Festival company) and Michael Riley (who went on many years later to star in Walker's CBC courtroom drama series *This Is Wonderland*).

My only problem was with the set, a kind of rolling mountain of wooden slats. It won great acclaim when the production opened, but on first encountering it, I found it extremely difficult to walk on. I have a pet peeve about what I call "tyranny by design" in the theatre, so I complained to our designer, Mary Kerr. She replied, "I expect every actor to be a dancer," to which I retorted: "And *I* expect every designer to be an actor. Why don't *you* get up there?" (John Colicos, by the way, came to see the production, and he too remarked unfavourably on the set: not on account of its vertiginous properties but because the wood it was built of was exactly the same colour as the actors' faces. "I couldn't *find* any of you," he said to me afterwards.)

Still, I got used to it, more or less, and we rehearsed *Nothing Sacred* without incident. It was shaping up to be a very good production, and I was pleased with my own performance in it: I certainly had no reason on that count to feel apprehensive.

Near the end of the play, a duel is fought with pistols between my character, Pavel, and the nihilist Bazarov, who was being played by

Robert Bockstael. Pavel fires prematurely and misses, then insists, as a point of honour, that his opponent shoot too. Reluctantly, Bazarov fires and hits Pavel in the leg.

I'd been in enough plays involving firearms (including *Farther West* and Tom Walmsley's *Something Red* at the Tarragon in 1980) to know that gunplay on stage is like Russian roulette in reverse: sooner or later there's bound to come a fatal moment when the pistol just goes "Click." And, since saying "Bang!" is hardly a viable option, there's nothing the stranded actor can do about it. "Can we *please* have a backup gun?" I begged, but nobody paid any attention to me.

We came to the night of the first preview. The performance proceeded smoothly till we got to the duel scene, in which I was positioned at the very top of the mountain of slats, facing off against Robert's Bazarov. I took my shot at Robert, then, as scripted, urged him to reciprocate. "Shoot," I said, as Pavel. "You must shoot . . . and you must do it seriously." Robert raised his pistol and pulled the trigger.

Click.

As stage disasters go, this was far from the worst imaginable. I hadn't forgotten my lines. I hadn't fallen off the stage. I hadn't skipped whole pages of dialogue. The roof of the theatre hadn't caved in. All that had happened was that, as I'd predicted, a prop gun had failed to go off. Not, in the scheme of things, such a hideously big deal—and it wasn't even my fault. And yet, as I stood there transfixed, a monstrous serpent of dread slithered up from nowhere and coiled itself about my heart.

"Shoot!" I repeated helplessly, as my head began to swim.

Click. Some uncertain tittering from the audience. Was this part of the play? Was the gun supposed to go off or not? Click.

"Shoot! Shoot!! *SHOOOOOOT!!!*" I heard my panicked voice rise to a scream, as darkness came and went, and the stage below me tilted crazily. I gasped for breath, my lungs turning to stone.

Click.

Eventually, someone backstage had the wit to grab a piece of scrap lumber that fortunately happened to be lying around and bang it against a sewer pipe. At that, I clapped my hand to my leg, where I was supposed to be wounded, and rolled down the hill. I struggled through the mercifully few remaining moments of the scene, then, shivering uncontrollably, was helped off stage by my fellow actors. In the wings, my dresser threw a coat around me. As he did so, his face turned pale, for he'd observed a pulsing around my chest. It was my heart, pounding visibly even through my costume.

I had one more scene to go. Somehow, I got through it, my heart still racing, then I collapsed in a bewildered heap in my dressing room. What the hell had happened out there? Had I just had a heart attack? Was I about to die? It certainly felt like it.

Domini was in the audience, and although apparently I'd done nothing more than flinch when the gun failed to go off, she could see that all was not well. She'd already noticed, as early as the production of *The Country Wife* that we did together in 1983, that a new element of nervousness seemed to have entered into my stage performances. When she arrived backstage, I said to her: "I have to go to an emergency room. *Now.*" As it happened, she'd come to the theatre with a friend whose father was the head of a cardiac ward, and it was to his hospital that they drove me.

As Pavel Krysanov in *Nothing Sacred* at CentreStage in 1988, with Robert Bockstael (left) as Bazarov

The woman at reception started to take down my information. When I told her my name, she gasped in recognition. "Oh, Mr. *Monette!* I saw you play Hosanna. You're *such* a wonderful actor. Why, I was in Stratford just this past season. . . ." On any other occasion, I'd have been delighted to encounter so enthusiastic a fan. But since I was, after all, dying, I rather wished she'd get on with it.

Halfway through filling in the forms, she was replaced by another woman, who was French. *"Monsieur Monette?"* this new person exclaimed, on seeing my name. *"Le grand comedien?"* She, too, took this opportunity to express her undying admiration as my life ebbed away. Eventually, with Domini accompanying me, I was wheeled into an emergency room, where a swarm of interns in white coats hooked me up to a monitor. "Well, look who we have here," remarked one of them in surprise, "Richard Monette *and* Domini Blythe."

"You know, Domini," I said, "I'm wasting my time at CentreStage. I should be performing here in the cardiac ward, where all my fans are."

A doctor came in. She was Polish and looked like Juliette Binoche in *The Unbearable Lightness of Being*. After regarding the monitor, she declared: "There is nothing wrong with you. You have had an anxiety attack. I will give you pills." (Beta blockers, these would have been.) "These pills are taken by pianists to steady their hands. But," she added, "you will become, when you take these pianist pills, impotent."

This side effect, she said, could last for up to four hours. "That's all right," I replied. "I seldom do it when I'm on stage."

It wasn't my sex life, though, that was thrown a curve by this episode; it was my career. *Nothing Sacred* was scheduled to run for three weeks. I prayed that CentreStage wouldn't try to extend it. As it was, I was obsessively counting the days, hours and minutes till it would be over. By some miracle, I managed to stagger through the nightmare of those three weeks, but by the time the run at last came to its end, I had completely lost my nerve. It would be another 10 years before I could act on stage again.

It was a mystery to me why that gun failing to go off should have triggered, as it were, such an extreme response. Yes, it had put me in an awkward position—though not as awkward as that of my opponent in the duel, who was the one actually wielding the uncooperative weapon. But it wasn't as if I were a novice at this game. I should have been able by then to cope with things going wrong. And it was, after all, only a play. No lives had been at stake. So why had I been so paralysed with terror?

Bill Hutt was puzzled too. "It makes no sense," he said. "You're like me: you're at home on stage. For you, it's like being in your own living room." But sadly, that was no longer true.

Clearly the *Nothing Sacred* incident had been merely a catalyst. The bigger question remained: what was the underlying problem? Convinced that it must be physical, I went to heart specialists. They found nothing wrong. I went for brain scans and epilepsy tests.

All came back negative. Eventually, I was forced to confront the possibility that it was psychological, so I raised the question with the psychiatrist I'd been seeing: the one who'd asked me whether I or the board of governors loved Stratford the most.

I'd originally consulted this man (who was not only brilliant but quite famous in his field) to help me find the strength to end a destructive relationship with an alcoholic with whom I was living at the time. Like many people who seek therapy, I suppose I'd expected it to be like taking your car to a mechanic: he'd listen to the funny noise my psyche was making, say something like, "Oh, that's your subliminal crankshaft," and then fix it. But that isn't quite how it works. The psychiatrist is more of a guide and facilitator, while the onus of actually detecting and fixing the problem lies more with the patient.

"Aren't you going to say *anything*?" I'd say to my shrink, who'd be so quietly passive when I talked that I suspected him of falling asleep. "I can't believe the health care system is paying you to say *nothing*." In my attempts to get a response out of him, I'd become more and more extravagant and outrageous in my discourse. I guess I was instinctively trying to entertain him, and indeed I did sometimes have him in stitches.

Eventually, he did make some comment or other, in which he used the word *hysteric*. I was so surprised that I sprang out of my chair, ran out of his office into the waiting room and exclaimed dramatically to his secretary: "My *God!* He's *said* something—after *three years!* I can't *believe*," I continued (like Dogberry in *Much Ado About Nothing* indignantly repeating that he's an ass), "that I'm a hysteric." I went back in to find my shrink rolling about with laughter. "Was there a young man out there, waiting to come in?" he asked, between convulsions.

As a matter of fact, I had noticed someone in the room while I was making my scene. "Yes, there was."

"Well," he said, "that young man is terrified of his own shadow. I'm now going to have to deal with the panic you must have instilled in him."

My psychiatrist did make one or two other memorable remarks over the course of our professional relationship. "I could cure you," he once said—of what, he didn't specify—"but I'm afraid it would destroy your talent." He also remarked that I seemed quite a different person after I'd finished *Macbeth*, which surprised me.

"You say serious things," he told me on another occasion, "but you say them in such a way as to make people laugh, so they don't know how to take you." I've always used humour to avoid sounding too portentous or melancholy. But it's true that people seem to have a hard time knowing when I'm being serious and when I'm just being funny. I've never been able to change that: it's just my personality.

Another time, he asked, "Are you trying to make up for things in your childhood: to save your mother and father?" A good question, to which I do not have an answer.

The most useful thing he said to me, though, came in response to some question I'd asked him (I can't remember what). "Let me answer that with another question," he said: "are you good in bed?" To which I replied immediately, "It depends on who you ask." This was exactly the answer he'd wanted.

This little catechism impressed me deeply, and I subsequently used it many times during my tenure at Stratford to illustrate the futility of trying to make predictions or absolute judgements in artistic matters. "Do you think this play will sell tickets?" the board might ask me, or "Was this production good or bad?" In all cases, I'd reply: "Am I good in bed? It depends on who you ask." That answer used to irritate the hell out of the board. But really, it was the best one I could give.

My psychiatrist did help me find the strength to end my relationship with the alcoholic, and not, I think, at any significant cost to my talent. But we never did solve the mystery of my stage fright.

Ironically, as a result of this cataclysm, my performing career now took a much more lucrative turn. My remuneration as a Shakespearean actor had seldom stepped o'er the bounds of modesty. Now, however, the only performing avenues open to me were film, television and voice-over work, all of which paid extremely well.

As a voice-over artist, I was in particularly high demand. After years of cigarettes and alcohol, my voice had acquired a gravelly quality that sounded to me like somebody dying of emphysema, but everyone seemed to love it. I became, for instance, the Canadian voice of the Korean car company Hyundai (which, I quickly learned, is pronounced to rhyme with "Sunday"). I went to audition for this in a sound studio, where I could see, but not hear, about 25 Koreans talking to each other in the control booth. I read the script for the ad, whereupon the Koreans went into an excited huddle. Over the loudspeaker, the man directing the taping said to me, "Could you shave off one second?"

"Certainly," I said. I read it again, taking off a second, and again I saw the 25 Koreans in animated discussion.

"I know you're going to think this is odd," said the director eventually, "but could you now *put on* two seconds?" I did so, and got the contract.

For a classical actor, this was the easiest of easy money. There's only so much exploration of character and motive that you can put into such a line as "Drive a Hyundai," so I soon got to the point where I could complete my day's work in a couple of brief takes. On one occasion, the man who signed my contracts grumbled a bit: "It galls me that I'm paying you all this money for 10 minutes' work." I didn't hesitate in my reply: "I've done 25 years of poorly paid classical theatre to get this voice, and you're the lucky son of a bitch who's gonna pay for it."

I had no qualms about taking that position: to me, a good voice is by far the most valuable of an actor's assets. It's significant that in the 18th century people would talk about going to "hear" a play—not *see* but *hear*. I cannot listen to actors who have ugly voices, especially when delivering verse. Ugliness limits the resonance of the poetry, makes it pygmy-like, naturalistic, low to the ground. If you have an ugly voice as an actor, it behooves you to work on it. I asked Bill Hutt once how he'd acquired that wonderful voice of his, and he replied, "When I was 13, my voice changed, and it settled perfectly." He is one of the lucky few who receive vocal beauty by grace; the rest of us have to achieve it by works, as I'd done since my days with Eleanor Stuart.

I've been fond of telling young actors that if they can play Shakespeare they can do anything they want in film, television, radio or advertising voice-overs. My own situation after 1988 proved that. The reverse, however, is emphatically *not* true.

One of the more pernicious effects of the Method school of acting has been to enshrine the mumble as a legitimate means of delivering verse. That was one of the reasons why, in 1998, I established what is now the Birmingham Conservatory for Classical Theatre Training at the Stratford Festival of Canada: an in-house theatre school for professional actors. Existing theatre schools were preparing their students for contemporary drama, for film and for television, not for the classics, and when my colleagues and I auditioned young actors for the Festival company, we too often found them ill-equipped (even when immensely talented) to meet the demands of our repertoire.

It's an arduous process to change your voice, but it can be done. Some of the greatest actors and orators had huge vocal impediments to overcome. Henry Irving, for example, the first actor ever to be knighted, had a stammer. The best example I can think of in my tenure of an actor's determined attitude to vocal development is that of Michael Therriault, a graduate of our Conservatory who went on to play many leading roles on our stages and subsequently starred as Tommy Douglas in the CBC TV docudrama *Prairie Giant* and as Gollum in the stage musical *The Lord of the Rings*.

At Stratford in 1999, Michael played the spirit Ariel in *The Tempest*, a part for which, being small-boned and delicate, he is physically well suited. At one point in the play, though, Ariel appears in the guise of a harpy and speaks in a thunderous voice that the text describes as a "deep and dreadful organ-pipe." Michael's own voice is naturally quite light and high.

A year before he was to play this part, I spoke to him on the terrace outside the Festival's lunch room. "You're a brilliant actor, Michael," I told him, "and some day you should play Hamlet. But there's one thing you need to look to first. You're young, and you don't get your true voice till you're 30, but where your voice sits now will limit you in classical work. It would be good if you could lower it."

Being the artist that he is, he went to Janine Pearson, the Festival's head of voice, and asked her what he needed to do. One of the instructions she gave him was not to sing for an entire year. Michael, who first came to us as a musical-theatre performer in 1997, loved to sing and would do so every day. But he made that sacrifice, and by the end of the year he had greatly extended the low end of his range.

Though it seems far-fetched, I've occasionally wondered if my stage fright was some form of subconscious wish-fulfilment, a way of forcing myself out of acting in order to pursue more seriously another avenue that I had hitherto only dabbled in: directing. A curious incident had taken place during John Hirsch's tenure in the early 1980s that might support such an interpretation.

I'd gone one day to John's home, just up the street from mine, and asked him to let me direct something at the Festival. He'd dismissed the idea: "I don't think actors can direct. You should stick to acting." While we were arguing about it, I began to experience one of my dizzy spells. Was it a direct response to his refusal?

Whether it was or not, the episode reached an absurd conclusion. While the world was spinning before my eyes, John's phone rang, and he went off to answer it. As he left, I pitched forward onto his living-room floor, as I would later do in *Macbeth*. I could vaguely hear John's end of the phone conversation—it was a personal call, one that seemed to be upsetting him—but I felt too ill to get up. When he hung up the phone, apparently assuming I had left, he went into the kitchen and started to make borscht. I could hear him muttering to himself as he prepared his food, rehashing out loud whatever had been discussed on the phone. Eventually he returned to the living room.

"Oh. You're still here."

"Yes. Could you take me to the hospital?" And so ended my appeal to John Hirsch to be taken seriously as a director.

Working against the wish-fulfilment theory, though, is the fact that by the time I had the attack in *Nothing Sacred*, I was already working on what would prove to be my breakthrough assignment as a director.

It seemed remarkable that John Neville would entrust a full-scale Shakespearean production on the stage of the Festival Theatre to someone whose professional directing résumé at that point consisted only of the short Beckett piece *Come and Go*, the one-man show *Blake* and the three-person play *Stevie*, but I was thrilled (and not a little terrified) when he asked me to direct the 1988 season's production of *The Taming of the Shrew*.

I suspect John had been having difficult finding anyone to take it on. Like *The Merchant of Venice*, *The Taming of the Shrew* is a political minefield. Written in an era when women were viewed as the chattels of men, its storyline—an aggressively spirited woman, Katherina, is married off to Petruchio, a self-declared fortune-hunter who subjects her to a program of carefully calculated humiliation that turns her into a meek and obedient housewife—is frankly offensive to modern sensibilities, and so directors have to think very carefully about how they approach it. I knew from my own experience how sensitive the issues surrounding the play were: when I'd played Lucentio in the Festival's 1973 production, with Alan Scarfe as Petruchio and Pat Galloway as Katherina, the audience had booed Pat's final speech of submission.

A director of *Shrew* has limited options. You can try to evade the issue altogether by presenting the play in its own period, as a piece of social history: "That's just the way things were back then; nothing we need to worry about." There's a downside to this approach: it locks you into pumpkin pants and farthingales and thus makes the piece seem a tad fusty. Or you can decide to explore the full implications of Katherina's treatment by Petruchio and present it as a disturbing psychological drama about the bullying and brainwashing of women by men. Of course, then it ceases to be a comedy. Or you can suggest that Katherina and Petruchio are, consciously or subconsciously, in cahoots with each other, playing a willing (though brutal) game of domination and submission either for their own erotic gratification or as an ironic comment on the society they're living in. It's a nice idea, but a hard one to put across, being not entirely supported by the text.

Colm Feore as Petruchio and Goldie Semple as Katherina in *The Taming of the Shrew* (Stratford, 1988)

I didn't worry about any of the above: I just presented the play as a portrait of my own family.

Well, perhaps that's an exaggeration. But it's true that I drew my inspiration from the Italian part of my own background, and that many of the moments in it—I have already mentioned the throwing of plates—were derived from my own childhood. (Another bit of business that I introduced, Katherina's insouciant dismemberment of Bianca's teddy bear in front of its sobbing owner, owed more than a passing nod to the death of Pom-Pom.) For me, the dynamics between Katherina and her family and Katherina and Petruchio needed no disguising, apologizing for or explaining away: this was just the way people of certain temperaments behaved.

I set the play in the period of my own late childhood and early teens: the 1950s. It could be no later, because the setting had to predate the Pill. As I've mentioned, I was very conscious of the immense changes wrought in women's lives by that innovation, and I felt the story would make little sense if it took place post-women's-lib. John Neville had asked Jeannette Lambermont, who'd worked with him on his 1987 production of *Othello*, to assist me, and together we did months of preparation, subjecting every single line of the text to the closest scrutiny. (This was my big chance: I was determined to get it right.) Since I was spending so much time at that point doing voice-over work in Toronto, I'd bought a house there, in addition to my home in Stratford, and Jeannette and I would sit in its basement watching videos of Italian movies from the '50s and '60s.

As written, *Shrew* is a play within a play, though the device that sets this up, the "Induction" scene at the beginning featuring the tinker Christopher Sly, is often cut in production. Robert Beard, who'd directed me in the 1982 *Merry Wives*, suggested that I do the play within the context of a movie shoot. I didn't pursue that idea, but it did get me thinking about the Italian cinema, especially the films of Federico Fellini. Using two VCRs, Jeannette and I painstakingly assembled a montage of clips from the films we watched and showed it to our actors. I wanted the visual aspects of the production to suggest those films, hence the Vespa motor scooter on which I had Petruchio arrive on stage after his wedding.

I also wanted that Fellini-esque dream-like feel, so I kept in some of the Induction scene, making the play proper become Sly's dream after he passes out in a drunken stupor. Colm Feore, who was playing Petruchio, would also play Sly, while our Katherina, Goldie Semple, would also appear in the Induction as the hostess of the tavern, thus reinforcing the dream idea.

I'd spent many hours with the designer, Debra Hanson, before rehearsals began, discussing how the production should look.

I wanted every costume, for example, to tell some story about its owner: something that I don't think I've ever been able to achieve so completely in any production since. We had one wish, though, in which it looked as if we were going to be thwarted. We had planned to build a little car that would come on stage bearing some of the leading characters. I had good reasons for wanting this large prop: every production has to find its rhythm, its pattern of stillness and movement, of quietly intimate moments versus big splashy ones, and I needed something at this particular moment—something congruent with the world I'd envisioned for the play—that would make this entrance a high point.

Colm Feore as Petruchio and Goldie Semple as Katherina in *The Taming of the Shrew* (Stratford, 1988)

But there were budgetary concerns, and at a design meeting attended by John Neville various design elements were cut, among them the car. Debra was in tears by the end of the meeting, and I was left racking my brains for how else to achieve the effect I had wanted. I was still pondering the problem when we began rehearsals.

But then I *think*—and this is pure conjecture on my part—that someone went to John once rehearsals were under way and reported that the production was shaping up to be a big hit. Whatever the reason, suddenly we were given permission to build the car after all. That incident made me realize how important it is for a leading institution such as the Stratford Festival to *always* have the resources to allow its artists to make the choices they deem necessary.

The show was perfectly cast, something for which I cannot take the credit. Casting in a repertory company is usually a matter of compromise between the director's preferences and the availability of artists. When different productions are running simultaneously in three venues, an actor can appear only in those that don't play against each other in the schedule, which limits your choices drastically. In this case, though, I got not only what I needed but far more than I might have dared to expect. Besides Colm and Goldie, the cast included Henry Czerny as Lucentio, Keith Dinicol as Grumio, Kate Hennig (whom Jeannette and I had auditioned backstage in my dressing room while I was doing *Nothing Sacred*) as the Widow, Kim Horsman as Bianca, William Needles as the Pedant, Brian Tree as Gremio, Scott Wentworth as Tranio and Geraint Wyn Davies as Hortensio. They and all the others—including a little girl, Jennifer Stewart, who grew up to feature in the musical *Hairspray* in Toronto—were ideally suited to their roles.

Even with all this talent at my disposal, the rehearsal period was by no means smooth. This was, after all, my first time directing a large cast, and I didn't always know the best way to handle my fellow artists' egos or how best to communicate my wishes to them. I resorted to coy wheedling with one sulking actor: "If you cheer up, I'll buy you an ice cream."

Although I'd been determined not to modernize any of the dialogue, I did interpolate certain things, such as Petruchio's prayer, written in Italian for us by cast member Juan Chioran. I also had the song "Sigh no more, ladies," from *Much Ado About Nothing*, translated into Italian and performed crooner-style by Scott Wentworth in the wedding scene.

That song, along with other music in the show, was composed by Louis Applebaum, the Festival's first director of music and the composer of its famous fanfares. Lou's preferred musical style was quite formal, so when I'd turned up at his house with 20 cassette tapes of music from the 1950s as examples of the kind of thing I wanted, I'd wondered how he might react. I needn't have worried: he responded eagerly to the challenge, and his *faux* '50s music was a highlight of the show.

Normally, original music is composed for Festival productions. For one particular scene in *Shrew*, however, when Lucentio woos Bianca, I wanted some song that the audience would recognize: one of the era's signature tunes, if you will. It was Don Lewis (better known to audiences by his stage name, Lewis Gordon) who suggested the 1957 Johnny Mathis hit "Chances Are." We secured the rights to play a short passage from it—for a substantial fee, of course. "Congratulations, Richard," Lou said to me: "this is the first time in the history of the Festival that we've ever had to pay musical royalties." Still, it was worth every penny. Unfortunately, we weren't able to extend those rights to the video of the production, for which we ended up having to compose something of our own after all.

We also tried out many sight gags, not all of my devising and not all of which made it to opening night. Colm, who'd initially balked at the Vespa ("What's this for: the bowling league?"), thought nothing of imparting a new meaning to one of Petruchio's lines—"What dogs are these!"— by pulling out a long string of wieners. He also wanted at one point to refer back to the idea of the play being Christopher Sly's dream by producing, as Petruchio, a red handkerchief that he used as Sly. I put my foot down on that one. "Colm, no," I admonished him. "This is a rag herring."

One of our more delightful moments of miscommunication involved William Needles, a member of the Festival's original company in 1953 and beloved by everyone as one of the theatre world's true gentlemen. In his role as the Pedant, Bill one day tried out some physical mannerisms: speaking with a stammer and tugging at his clothes, as if he were trying to pluck his thoughts out of them. I thought this was hilarious. But at the next rehearsal—when he also happened to be trying out a hat—he didn't do any of it.

"Bill," I said, "could you do it the way you did it the other day?" He looked at me blankly. So I tried to imitate what he'd done: I affected a stammer and pulled at my clothes as if I had an infestation of fleas. After I'd finished my demonstration, Bill said, in sincere puzzlement, "So you don't want me to wear the hat?"

The first dress rehearsal of a production is an important occasion, and I was concerned that I hadn't quite succeeded in getting the cast into the frame of mind they needed to take this next big step forward. Fortunately, John Neville happened to drop into the auditorium as we were about to start the run. John always dressed well, but on this occasion he was looking particularly smart: he must have had an important meeting that day. I asked him if he wouldn't mind just sitting there for 10 minutes or so, while I gave notes to the cast.

"Sure," he said. I didn't actually *have* any significant notes to give, but I summoned the whole cast on stage and made a few improvised remarks. What I really wanted was for them to see the artistic director sitting there, in all his immaculate sartorial glory. My ploy worked: though John left when the lights went down, the cast, not knowing if he was still there or not, gave an electric performance.

The *Shrew* was stage-managed by Nora Polley, who can "call a show" (that is, oversee a performance) the way a great violinist can play a Stradivarius. She has a great sense of rhythm and a keen interest in the text. For opening night, in an allusion to the Vespa, which had a carousel-style horse's head mounted on the handlebars, she made me a little pin in the shape of a horse. I've worn that pin to almost every Festival opening since. When the play was a comedy, I'd wear it on my lapel; when a tragedy, I'd wear it *behind* my lapel.

Opening nights can be strange beasts. Jeannette and I had worked on this production almost every day for a year, and the opening performance could not have been better. Colm was fast as lightning and completely in control. The others in the cast, too, were at their absolute best. Nevertheless, as I recall, the entire first act was greeted with precisely one laugh: on the business with the teddy bear. At the intermission, I said to Jeannette, "These actors are on *fire*; I don't understand why the audience isn't responding." By the second half, though, the crowd seemed to have warmed up considerably, and the evening ended as a great success.

Another of those mysterious what-makes-it-funny equations: Brian Tree, as Gremio, had an exit line in the second half: "My cake is dough; but I'll in among the rest, / Out of hope of all, but my share of the feast." In the previews, he never got a laugh on that line or a round of applause as he left. So I proposed that he cut the last part of it: "Just say, 'My cake is dough,' Brian, and leave." He was reluctant at first to try this, but when he eventually did, he brought down the house and got his well-deserved exit round.

The theatre gods, it seemed, were smiling on me. *The Taming of the Shrew* became to my nascent career as a director what *Hosanna* had been to my now-defunct career as a stage actor. The reviews—I'm told—were ecstatic. One journalist, Sid Adilman of the *Toronto Star*, said to me, "Your reputation will live for 10 years on this." A conservative estimate, as it turned out: nearly 20 years later, the production is still remembered as one of the Festival's greatest all-time hits.

A year later, in 1989, when John Neville ended his tenure as artistic director, I spoke at the celebration held in his honour. "You know, John," I said, in my most modest tone, "I thank you for establishing me as a director. But I want you to know that you've deprived the world of a wonderful actor."

Susan Wright: a great actress and a beloved friend

In the winter of 1988, Young People's Theatre asked me to direct *Count Dracula*, the same show I'd played the lead in seven years earlier. In the title role, Geordie Johnson gave a performance that was darker, sexier and not as comic as mine, ably supported by a cast that included Stewart Arnott, Peter Donaldson, Graham Harley (who'd been in *Macbeth* with me), Don Lewis, Lucy Peacock (recommended to me by Peter Moss) and Susan Wright.

I'd first met Susan on one of my tours to Vancouver: either *Hosanna* or *Judgement*. Whichever it was, she was there too, playing Maggie in *Cat on a Hot Tin Roof*. She gave a wonderful performance in that role, as she did in everything she appeared in. I admired her instantly as an actress and came to love her dearly as a friend and confidante.

Despite the strength of the cast, the *Dracula* rehearsals weren't going well. I was finding it difficult to get some of my actors to hit the right tone. The play was, after all, a spoof—in fact, it was really a farce—and I had devised all kinds of broadly comic business. But I could tell that not everyone was convinced, or even understood what I was driving at. In particular, Don Lewis (a wonderful actor and a dear friend, but sometimes a tad literal-minded) seemed to be acting in quite a different production: something serious and realistic, full of Gothic foreboding. (He was a big fan of 1940s film noir, which may have had something to do with it.)

I didn't think anybody was deliberately being difficult; they just didn't share my vision of the play. But I needed to find some way to *make* them share it—or at least do what I wanted them to do. Some assertion of directorial authority was required, but I didn't want to hurt anyone's feelings in the process. So I asked Susan to help me out.

"Susan," I said to her, "you're wonderful in this, and you're doing everything right. But things aren't going well, because the cast as a whole isn't doing what the text demands, or what I want. So at the next note session, can I pretend to give you a hard time?"

She generously agreed to play the role of sacrificial victim *pour encourager les autres*. When next I gave notes, I invented things to criticize in her performance and just let her have it. In one of her entrances, for example, she came down a staircase. She had been making the entrance brilliantly, but I affected to find fault with it and made her do it over and over again till I deemed it was "right." Our routine had the desired effect: nobody else wanted to be put on the spot like that, so they quickly got on side and made the show a great success.

I worked again with Geordie Johnson and Lucy Peacock the following season at Stratford, when the Festival presented a drastically cut version of *The Comedy of Errors* as one half of a double bill. (The other half, *Titus Andronicus*, was given to Jeannette. We seemed to have become established in people's minds as a directorial double act.) I'd never thought much of *Comedy*, one of Shakespeare's early plays, and I wasn't exactly thrilled when I was asked to direct it. When I started studying it, however, I realized what an extraordinary accomplishment this play really is. One thing I have learned over the years is that one must always be humble when approaching Shakespeare.

The Comedy of Errors is based on *Menaechmi*, by the Roman dramatist Plautus, with a bit of another Plautine comedy, *Amphitruo*, added to the mix. I was intrigued to find that Shakespeare had apparently written *Comedy* before *Menaechmi* had been translated into English;

ergo, he must have read it in the original Latin. Years later, I visited the ancient city of Ephesus, where *Comedy* takes place, and was even further intrigued to find how well Shakespeare's vision of the place concurred with the geographical and historical reality.

Because the action of the play, with its two sets of identical twins constantly being mistaken for (and by) each other, is so absurdly irrational, I set it in the 18th century: the Age of Enlightenment. Nothing funnier, I figured, than Reason being thrown out the window in the very era that worshipped it. Noticing that there are frequent references in the text to the time of day, I decided to place a huge clock atop the onstage balcony. Its hands would move in synch with the action, and it would strike the hours. I was very proud of this innovation and thought myself very clever for having thought of it.

Halfway through rehearsals, I read somewhere that when the great Russian director Fyodor Komissarzhevsky had directed *The Comedy of Errors*, he too had had a giant clock on stage. I was deflated. Everything that *could* be done to Shakespeare, it seemed, *had* been done. What insights were left to discover? But then I perked up: if as great a director as Komissarzhevsky had come up with the same idea, then at least that proved it was legitimate.

I don't consider myself musical, though the Festival's current director of music, Berthold Carrière (to whom I'm sure I must be distantly related on my great-grandfather's side), would disagree. I do listen to a lot of music, though, and I have a strong sense of the rhythm of a production and of its musical needs. For *The Comedy of Errors*, I told Bert, we needed something that would be fun in an unexpected way. "Maybe Bach," I said.

"Bach?" Bert echoed, evidently wondering where the fun was in that.

"Yes, but Bach as the Swingle Singers would sing it."

That was exactly what Bert composed for me, and to this day our Conservatory participants are shown the archival videotape of *The Comedy of Errors* as an example of how much fun can be had with incidental music.

That season too, at the Avon Theatre, I directed the late 17th-century comedy *The Relapse*, by Sir John Vanbrugh. The key role of Lord Foppington was played by Brian Bedford. Brian is, of course, a brilliant actor, and we are great friends, but he can be, let us say, strong-willed. As a result, we have long waged a "merry war" of wits, like Beatrice and Benedick (though *not,* just to set the record straight, with any of that relationship's romantic component). We have the kind of friendship in which we can happily say the most cutting things to each other, and I place as much value on that as I do on Brian's immense talent. Our contests of will are usually brief, and he usually wins.

Lord Foppington is a gentleman obsessed with the finery of his wardrobe. Indeed, there's a scene in which he dresses—or rather, *is* dressed—on stage. Inspired, perhaps, by my memory of Sir John Gielgud and his dresser backstage at the Royal Alex, I had made this a comic highlight of the production. The scene involved a host of minor characters who clustered around Brian and assembled Foppington's costume for him, starting with his shoes and working their way up to his wig. (The wigmaker was played by a young actor who'd made his debut with the company the year before: Antoni Cimolino. He used an Italian accent and made the role into a hilarious cameo.) All this had been painstakingly choreographed, and hours of rehearsal had been devoted to it. Lou Applebaum had even written music for it.

From left: Brian Bedford as Lord Foppington, Tim MacDonald as La Verole and David Lloyd-Evans as Cupidon in *The Relapse* (Stratford, 1989)

Only two previews were scheduled, with one last rehearsal between them. On the morning of that last rehearsal, Brian phoned me to announce that he didn't want to do the dressing-up business. From the audience's reaction at the first preview the night before, he didn't think it was working.

"But we've spent months on this," I protested, exaggerating just a little.

"No, no: we have to cut it."

When Brian makes up his mind about something, he is as firm

as Lady Bracknell, so there was nothing for it but for me to break the news when the company assembled for the start of rehearsal. Or rather, *allow* the news to be broken. "Ladies and gentlemen, *Brian* has something to tell you," I announced maliciously, thereby neatly passing the buck back to its startled originator.

The production was a hit anyway, but I still think Brian was wrong. Some years later, when he wanted to not only direct Noël Coward's *Present Laughter* but also play the principal role in it, I took great delight in warning him, "But Brian, you must realize that your leading man is undirectable."

One of my favourite gags in *The Relapse* involved (be still, my convulsing heart) a gun. Paul Boretski, who'd acted with me in *Farther West*, played a country bumpkin, carrying a blunderbuss. At the end of one scene, as he left the stage, he'd fire it up into the air. At the start of the scene immediately following, a fake dead duck would fall from the flies onto the stage. This always got a laugh. But it was nothing compared to the laugh we got when a large black dog, owned by former company member William Malmo, was loosed from the wings, came on stage, grabbed the duck in its mouth and trotted back off with it. It was, though I say so myself, one of the funniest things I have ever seen in the theatre.

Kay Tremblay, who played Mrs. Calico in *The Relapse*, told me that the very same routine used to be popular in circuses. I hadn't known that; as with the clock in *Comedy*, I thought I'd just invented it.

Later that year, Jeannette and I were asked to establish a young company at the Citadel Theatre in Edmonton. I was to direct *Julius Caesar*; Jeannette was to do *The Miracle Worker* and a children's play by Dennis Foon. It was not a happy experience. The Citadel was between artistic directors at the time, its staff seemed burned out, and both time and money were short. Someone had put in place some bizarre rules: I seem to recall some offensive nonsense about our company not being allowed to ride in the same elevators as the main company.

I had a cast of only 15 for *Julius Caesar*, which I eventually ended up presenting on a bare stage. I set it in a modern-day banana republic, for no other reason than that it would be cheap to costume. There were some good things in the production, but not enough to prevent me from panicking. Under the stress, I took to drinking at lunchtime, which did nothing to help. Jeannette, bless her, took on the responsibility of organizing everything for me, even though she had her own shows to direct. (Her *Miracle Worker* was very good, with a wonderful performance by Shannon Lawson.)

Robin Phillips was at the Citadel at that point too, directing plays with the main company. (He later became the theatre's director general.) I don't think I saw him once the entire time I was in the building.

At the end of the 1989 season, David William succeeded John Neville as Stratford's artistic director. He offered me two productions to direct in 1990: *As You Like It* and—what, *again?—Julius Caesar*.

When I approach Shakespeare, I begin by trying to figure out not the author's intentions (which no one can ever know) but simply what the text means to *me*. One of the things *As You Like It* seemed to me to be about was nature. So I asked myself, "What does nature mean to me, as a Canadian?"

We have very distinct seasons in Canada—even if one of them, spring, is often so short you can miss it if you sleep in on the wrong morning. And *As You Like It* is full of references to the seasons, especially in its songs: "Under the greenwood tree," "Blow, blow, thou winter wind," "It was a lover and his lass . . . in the spring time." I decided, therefore, that my production should cover the entire journey of our seasons here in Canada. Specifically, I set it in Quebec, the year before the battle of the Plains of Abraham, though this was not in any sense intended as a political statement. I simply thought it an evocative moment in our country's history.

The design, by Debra Hanson, was stunning. The stage was dominated by a huge spreading maple tree, whose leaves turned to a glorious red as the season changed. I had planned to include another iconic image of the approach of a Canadian winter: the passage overhead of a flock of Canada geese. We were going to use fake geese on wires, and several of these were actually built. (The Festival's artisans are justly renowned: they can make anything.) But someone decided that the challenge of making them fly was too great, and we had to fall back on a sound effect alone.

I have always believed that anything can be made to work if only the will to do so is there. However, there are always, in any organization, forces of inertia that resist the more imaginative impulses of artists and artisans. The mysterious "they"—as in "They say it can't be done"—have caused me some of the greatest disappointments of my career as a director and an artistic director.

Those hand-made geese are still scattered about the Festival Theatre building, including one in the stage management office. People have hung on to them as little symbolic reminders of the magic that might have been.

For the many songs in *As You Like It*, I asked Bert Carrière to create arrangements of the traditional tunes he and I had grown up with as French-Canadian kids, and he did wonders with them. And thanks to serendipity in the scheduling, I had at my disposal in the supporting roles members of the Festival's musical-theatre company—to say nothing of two onstage musicians—who could perform them beautifully. I'm very fond of musical performers, who, unlike some actors, must master very specific skills in order to survive. My colleagues have many times heard me say: "Hire a singer—they can sing. Hire a dancer—they can dance. Hire an actor—pot luck!"

David William as Jaques and Lucy Peacock as Rosalind in *As You Like It* (Stratford, 1990)

The downside, of course, is that musical theatre performers aren't necessarily ideal for Shakespeare, and I have to admit that my *As You Like It* wasn't in all cases the most perfectly cast show I've ever worked on. Still, there were some outstanding people in the leads. Ron Sarosiak was a wonderful Orlando: he, like Shannon Lawson, who played Phebe, had been in my young company at the Citadel. William Dunlop gave a great performance as Touchstone. And—this was a coup indeed—I got David William to play Jaques.

When I'd asked him if he would, he'd insisted on going through an audition. As I'd anticipated, he was exactly right for the role, and he played it beautifully. For one scene, in which Jaques was sitting with Orlando by a stream, I suggested that David take off his shoes and socks. "The public find it very endearing to see the artistic director's toes," I told him. "They never think you have any."

But the performance that gave the production its heart, and made it so much of a gift to me, was that of Lucy Peacock as Rosalind. Lucy had been great fun to work with in *Count Dracula* and *The Comedy of Errors*, but neither of those productions had prepared me for what she would do with the longest female role in Shakespeare. I can think of no other actress who has so completely caught the character's vulnerability and the pain of her love for Orlando. To this day, hers is the best Rosalind I have ever seen: better even, in my opinion, than the justly celebrated one that Maggie Smith gave us in 1977.

A great Shakespearean performance: Lucy Peacock as Rosalind in *As You Like It* (Stratford, 1990)

This superb performance was achieved seemingly effortlessly. Technically, Lucy is an incredibly proficient actress, and she immediately absorbed the most complicated instructions I gave her. She was also utterly gracious throughout the rehearsal process, never once questioning a direction or complaining about any of her fellow actors (though in one case, she had good cause to do so). And she was also possessed of a natural beauty, enhanced during the run of the show when she became pregnant with her first child, Harry (who, coincidentally, would grow up to play Prince Edward in the production of *Edward II* that I directed in 2005).

At one rehearsal, as I sat in the auditorium watching Lucy on stage, I wept, overcome by my awareness of the ephemeral nature of theatre and of human life itself. I could not bear the thought that this beautiful, vibrant young woman would one day grow old, and that the magic of the performance she was giving could live only in this moment, here and now. "Our revels now are ended," says Prospero in Act IV of *The Tempest*:

> These our actors,
> As I foretold you, were all spirits and
> Are melted into air, into thin air.

Although, like all Festival productions, that 1990 *As You Like It* is preserved on a single-camera archival video, I very much regret that it was not professionally taped for broadcast. As a result, we are left with only a faint and distant electronic echo of one of the greatest Shakespearean performances I have ever seen.

At one dress rehearsal for *As You Like It*, I had Ron Hastings, who was playing the shepherd Corin, come on with a live pig. I got the idea partly from a comedy film that Maggie Smith had been in a few years before, called *A Private Function*, in which pigs invade a home. Also, I'd kept a pet pig for a few years at my French-Canadian grandparents' farm.

Ron came on stage, carrying the pig, whom we dubbed Petunia, in his arms. I don't know exactly what I'd expected the animal to do when it found itself in such unfamiliar surroundings (though we'd provided it with a diaper to accommodate the most predictable contingency), but its reactions were hysterical in both senses of the word. It squealed. Its eyes bulged. Its ears stood straight up. Its reactions, taking me completely by surprise, were freakishly comic—vivid to the point of being unearthly—and I laughed until, quite literally, I cried. We had to stop the rehearsal because I was beyond rational thought. Outside of that dog in *The Relapse* fetching the duck, I'd never seen anything so funny.

It was a thrilling moment of true pandemonium in the theatre, and my only concern was that the rest of the production would never recover from it. There were, however, other people in the building with different ideas. Perhaps they were allergic to pigs, or perhaps they thought it was cruel. (We did in fact describe to the owner of the pig how it had reacted, and he'd reassured us: "Oh, the pig's fine.

She's not terrified, just excited.") In any case, I was told I couldn't have a live pig.

Having sacrificed this great comedic moment, I called the company together and addressed them thus:

"I am tired of thinking that pigs have wings. Just as I was sorry to tell you that the geese had to be cut because 'they' wouldn't make them work, so now, even more sorrowfully, I have to tell you that Petunia Pig, for whom I had great aspirations as an actress, has now also been cut. On account of the humanitarian reasons that 'they' gave, Petunia is now going to Mr. Schneider's to be made into sausages. So, to whoever is responsible, thank you for your compassion."

Julius Caesar was what we call a late opener, meaning that it opened in the middle of the season, when other productions were already up and running. Late openers are notoriously hard on the artists, because of the difficulty in scheduling sufficient rehearsal time. You often end up rehearsing late at night on a Sunday, when everyone is tired. Fortunately, I had a fabulous cast, including Brian Bedford, Colm Feore, Marti Maraden, Nicholas Pennell, Goldie Semple and Scott Wentworth, and not only had I been in the play myself twice before, but of course I'd just directed it that past winter at the Citadel. Still, it's a difficult play to stage, and I felt we only just pulled it off. Because of that experience, I made a point as artistic director of building in longer rehearsal time for late openers. (Likewise, because of *The Relapse*, I would insist on more preview performances before shows opened.)

David William begged me *not* to set *Julius Caesar* in a banana republic this time. Caesar, he argued, was a great historical figure of mythic proportions, and to depict him as some tinpot dictator could only be reductive. On this, he and I were in complete accord: my choice at the Citadel had been dictated purely by necessity. There's no question that presenting Shakespeare in modern dress can remove the barriers of historicism and allow interesting parallels to be explored, and that those who argue this isn't "true" to Shakespeare's intentions are deluding themselves. We don't *know* what Shakespeare's "intentions" were, because (unlike, say, George Bernard Shaw) he didn't tell us. We can see for ourselves, however, that anachronism is not only rife within his work but almost a central principle of it, and it's clear from both the historical record and the plays themselves that even his English histories and Roman plays were originally presented in what was, for him, modern dress.

At the same time, our own era's dress isn't always the best choice. It tends to reduce the stakes of the play, its language and the size of the emotions. When you costume an actor as an emperor or a monarch in some era when that implied a certain sartorial grandeur, that actor will instinctively rise, vocally and physically, to match up to the ermine and the jewels. But if the same actor is costumed in army fatigues, or a business suit, or jeans and a T-shirt, his or her performance will tend to be pitched much lower. This can be effective in comedy, which, as Shaw argued, is rooted in realism, but less so in tragedy. I don't think, for example, that it works to have the witches in *Macbeth* portrayed as cleaning ladies. And so, knowing I had a cast that could rise to the level required, I set *Julius Caesar* in period.

Colm Feore as Cassius, Nicholas Pennell as Caesar, Scott Wentworth as Mark Antony and Brian Bedford as Brutus in *Julius Caesar* (Stratford, 1990)

Well, sort of. My designer was one of those who rejoice in a single name—Ultz—and his design was very high-concept and post-modern, with neon lights installed around the balcony to indicate flashes of lightning. I always suspected he wanted to direct the play, and in effect he did, because his design imposed such strictures that I had little choice but to go along with him.

Ultz had done a lot of research on the play. It was Julius Caesar, he told me, who had invented the heel on footwear, an innovation that enabled his sandal-clad soldiers to march more efficiently. As an analogy for this, he had the soldiers in my production wearing modern sneakers. Caesar had also, apparently, invented the T-shirt.

So the warring factions in the play wore yellow and red T-shirts to distinguish them, thus enraging patrons with more "traditional" tastes. Ultz had also investigated the toga—how it was cut and how it was worn—and had come to the conclusion that nobody in the world really knew. The togas he came up with looked much like everyone's vision of a toga, except that they were made of paper. I'd heard of paper tigers, but paper togas. . . ?

In fact, there was a good reason for this choice of material. In Act III, scene 1 of *Julius Caesar* the title character is killed on stage by multiple stab wounds. "And let us bathe our hands in Caesar's blood / Up to the elbows," says Brutus afterwards, "and besmear our swords." To achieve the effect suggested by those lines, you need to splash around a fair amount of some liquid concocted to look like blood, which normally means a lot of post-performance washing, rinsing and spinning. So instead we had *disposable* togas.

One might suppose that in the more than 50 years of its existence, the Stratford Festival would long since have hit on the ideal formula for stage blood and would keep it safely locked away somewhere, like the recipe for Coca-Cola or Colonel Sanders's secret blend of spices. But *no-o-o-o-o*. Nobody seems to have the formula; we seem to have to reinvent the stuff every time. I must have had half a dozen meetings with our then director of production, Paul Shaw, solely about the colour of the blood that Ultz wanted. At the last of these, I said, "Paul, I have a solution." Whereupon I held out my wrists and yelled, "TAKE MINE! TAKE MINE!!"

Ultz, of course, had a very specific vision of how he wanted the blood to look. On opening night, he and I were out smoking in the lobby (you could do that back then) while the patrons were taking their seats. Becoming aware of a commotion over by Aisle 6, we went to investigate. It turned out that an elderly lady had fallen on the steps on her way down to her seat and had cut her head. A gurney was brought, the lady's head was bandaged, and she was wheeled out of the auditorium. As she passed us on the gurney, Ultz pointed to the bloodstain already seeping through her bandage and discreetly murmured to me: "You see that? *That's* the colour I wanted."

He even had an idea about the music. "It should be played by a string quartet," he told me. When I relayed that to Bert, who was composing the show, Bert just looked at me, agog. But I told him to go ahead with it anyway—and Ultz turned out to be right. Bert, who is a truly brilliant composer, wrote some of his most beautiful music for that show. I would cry every time Scott Wentworth, as Mark Antony, did his speech over Caesar's body, in no small part because of the underscoring.

If that *Julius Caesar* was another example of tyranny by design, the results were undeniably impressive. Although I directed the actors, it was Ultz whose vision informed the production, and I give him full credit for making it interesting, original and vivid. He did go on to direct, in fact, eventually becoming an associate director of London's Theatre Royal Stratford East.

I was grateful, though, to be back with Debra Hanson that fall, when we collaborated on a production of *Saint Joan* at Theatre Plus in Toronto, with Seana McKenna in the title role. I wanted to do it in period—*real* period, with no sneakers sneaking in—and we had a budget of about three cents. Fortunately, Debra had access to the vast collection of costumes in the Festival's warehouse.

I had a great cast: in addition to Seana, it included Richard Binsley as the Dauphin, Al Kozlik as de Stogumber, Tom McCamus as the Inquisitor, Jim Mezon as Warwick and Chick Reid as the Duchess de la Tremouille. Duncan McIntosh, the artistic director of Theatre Plus, was very helpful and supportive. But it proved to be a more difficult show than I had anticipated, partly because I was exhausted and partly because I find it hard to make Shaw, that most cerebral of playwrights, come alive.

Because Joan is so different from anyone else in the play, I asked Seana to play her with a French-Canadian accent. (I've always referred to Seana as Canada's Meryl Streep, not just in terms of looks and abilities but also because of her extraordinary facility with accents.) She tried this in rehearsal, but I could tell her heart wasn't in it, so eventually I had her abandon it.

She reminded me of this years later at Stratford, when I directed her as Katherine of Aragon in *King Henry VIII* in 2004. On that occasion, I again wanted to emphasize the notion that, as a Spaniard in England, Katherine is an outsider. "Perhaps," I said to Seana, "you should give us a little bit of an accent."

"Oh, you always say that," she replied. "You wanted me to do a

French accent when we did *Saint Joan.*" I didn't in fact feel strongly about the accent in *Henry VIII;* I'd just thought that Seana might find something valuable in the idea. So I let the matter drop. Then, at a rehearsal some time later, I suddenly noticed that I could barely understand what she was saying, because she'd adopted a heavy Castilian accent.

"All right," I conceded, suspecting that this was her way of proving to me that it wouldn't work. "The language is hard enough, we don't need the accent." So she dropped it. But then, at the second preview, it began to creep back. At the third preview, it was stronger.

"Seana," I said, "you're doing a Spanish accent."

"Am I?" she replied, winsomely.

By the time we opened, she was playing the role with a flawless and perfectly comprehensible accent. When my friend Aviva Slesin, who didn't know Seana, came from New York to see the show, she asked me afterwards, "Why did you cast a foreign actress as Katherine?"

Seana was wonderful in *Henry VIII,* as she had been in *Saint Joan,* for which she won a Dora Mavor Moore Award.

As, indeed, did I.

Seana McKenna as Katherine in *King Henry VIII (All Is True)* at the Stratford Festival in 2004

Brian Bedford had won a Tony Award for playing Arnolphe in Molière's *The School for Wives* in New York in 1971, so it was a little intimidating for me to have to direct him in the same role at Stratford 20 years later. In the play, Arnolphe plans to marry his young ward, Agnès (played by Ann Baggley), whom he has brought up as a virtual prisoner, to keep her from knowledge of the world and away from potential rivals for her hand. The production was designed, brilliantly, by Desmond Heeley, who had created for Agnès a beautiful yellow dress.

The set incorporated a house façade with an upper window. At the end of the play, I wanted a little symbolic touch in which a yellow canary would fly out of this window to freedom. But "they" seemed to feel it couldn't be done.

"What's the big deal?" I asked. "All I want is for a little toy bird to come flying out the window and over the audience's heads."

Eventually, someone told me that the problem was that Desmond didn't want the canary. I went to Desmond, for whom I have the greatest respect, and asked him why. "Oh, no, no," he said. "The canary's fine with me. It's Brian Bedford who doesn't want it."

I went to Brian. "No, *I* don't mind about the canary at all," he told me. So I went to the theatre's technical director. "I have spoken to the designer," I said. "I have spoken to the leading actor. Neither of them objects to the canary. Get me the canary."

Late one night, I was in the stage manager's office at the Avon Theatre discussing this with my assistant director, Micheline Chevrier, and the stage manager, Catherine Russell, when a member of the technical staff happened to walk by. Overhearing what I was ranting about, he observed, in the most sepulchral of tones, "You won't get the canary, you know, because *they* don't *want* you to have the canary." With that, he melted away into the shadows like an apparition.

This time, however, "they," whoever they were, did not prevail. I got my canary, and it gave us, as I had predicted, a wonderful moment on which to end the show. The first time we tried it out, Brian Bedford happened to be there. As soon as he saw it, a gleam of inspiration came into his eyes. "I've got a wonderful idea," he said to me: "*I* will release the canary."

Now, the whole point of the play is that Arnolphe does everything in his power to *prevent* Agnès from flying the coop. Far be it from me to suggest that maybe Brian didn't want the last moment in the show going to a prop bird instead of to him, but it certainly seemed to me to be completely out of character for Arnolphe to release the canary.

Besides, to do so, Brian would have to climb up the stairs to the very top of the set, and I knew he'd been having back problems. "Oh, no problem; I can do that," he assured me when I raised this objection. With amazing alacrity for one in so much pain, he fairly sprinted up those steps. So there was, once again, nothing for it but to let him have his way. And it must be said that, wrong as I thought it was in terms of the character, from the point of view of pure theatricality, the moment was undeniably effective.

From the point of view of the canary, it may have been a different matter. As brilliant an actor as Brian is, handling props isn't one of his fortes. His grip on this fake bird was so tight that it would get crushed and had to be rebuilt several times during the run. John Hirsch would have had a fit.

Besides Brian and Ann, the cast of *The School for Wives* included, among others, Douglas Chamberlain, Colm Feore, Don Lewis, Albert Millaire and Anne Wright, Susan's sister. Fine performers all, yet Micheline, my French assistant—who knew her Molière—wasn't happy with how things were going. "This is terrible," she said. "Terrible."

The School for Wives (Stratford, 1991): Brian Bedford (left) as Arnolphe, Ann Baggley as Agnès and Colm Feore as Horace

Just before our first preview, I took her out to lunch. "Micheline," I said, "don't worry. The talent in this production is extraordinary, and it will be marvellous."

"How can you know that?" she protested.

"Because I have worked with these actors before, and I know they're all barracudas. None of them wants to fail. It'll all turn out right in the end."

There is always a mysterious energy at a first preview. As an actor, you're flying by the seat of your pants, and you don't know how the audience will react. And if they do react positively, then that has the same kind of a slingshot effect that a gravitational field has on a space probe: the whole production is suddenly energized and accelerated.

At that first preview of *The School for Wives*, with a full house, the actors were electric. It was as if they had been shot out of a cannon. It was a fantastic performance.

"How did you know they would do that?" asked Micheline afterwards, amazed.

"I just knew," I replied, "because I know *them*."

Because first previews have such an inordinate amount of nervous energy, Brian sounded a note of caution: "We may never do that again." But in fact they kept it up for the rest of the run.

I directed three other productions in 1991. They were *Much Ado About Nothing* at Stratford (a production of which I seem to have few memories of note), with Goldie Semple and Colm Feore as Beatrice and Benedick; Willy Russell's one-woman comedy *Shirley Valentine*, performed by my friend Susan Wright, at the Grand Theatre, London; and, for the Canadian Opera Company, my first attempt at opera: Beethoven's *Fidelio*.

The COC had had big hits with *Bluebeard's Castle*, directed by Robert Lepage, and with *Salome*, directed by Atom Egoyan, so there was something of a trend of engaging directors from outside the opera world. It was Brian Dickie, who'd succeeded Lotfi Mansouri as the company's general director in 1989, who invited me to take on *Fidelio*. At first, I turned him down flat. Although I like opera very much and have seen a lot of it, I'd never directed one and wasn't comfortable with the idea. But he persisted, and eventually I agreed to meet with him and the conductor, Mario Bernardi. At that meeting, I learned that *Fidelio* would be sung in its original German.

"Do you know German?" Mario Bernardi asked me.

"Maestro," I said—I always called him Maestro—"I know nothing of German, but I know a lot more about German than I do about opera."

His eyes widening, Maestro Bernardi told me that he'd once conducted a Mozart opera under a famous theatre director, and it hadn't been a good experience.

"Who was that?" I asked him.

"Gielgud," he said.

Ah well, I thought, that explained his concern. Once, while attempting to direct an opera, Sir John had famously said, "Stop, stop, stop all that dreadful music so I can think." Promising to be more sensitive than that to the singers' needs, I gamely agreed to take it on. Equally gamely, Maestro Bernardi accepted me as a director. He mentioned that his wife had seen *Hosanna*, so perhaps she'd put in a good word for me.

Staging an opera is significantly different from directing a play. Opera singers maintain a "repertoire"—a number of roles that they know by heart—and fly about the world performing them. They arrive, get fitted for their costumes, learn their blocking (which in opera is usually minimal) and do their stuff. In opera, not much time is spent investigating such vitally important theatrical matters as motivation and subtext: the director's job is essentially to tell the singers where to stand.

But I wasn't familiar with all this, so I was alarmed to find that we had precisely nine days in which to rehearse—and this was a new production, not one that was being revived or imported from somewhere else. Nine days, I thought, wasn't much time to stage an opera from scratch. I know God made the world in six, but. . . .

Fortunately, I'd done a great deal of preparatory work. I'd listened to many recordings and read many books, and I had it all figured out. *Fidelio* seemed to me as much an oratorio as an opera, and I decided to base my production on the Catholic mass. I thought myself pretty well prepared. I didn't realize how nervous I was until the morning of the first rehearsal, when I went to the bathroom to shave and was promptly sick to my stomach.

I was introduced to my assistant, Marilyn Powell, who knew all about opera. I don't know what I would have done without her. "How exactly do we go about this?" I asked her.

She pointed to the score. "You see these bits where it's white? Well, that's where you direct. Just think of it as the opposite of putting music into a film."

Because of financial constraints, the design of the production was modern: vaguely suggestive of Romania under the Ceausescu regime. The whole thing took place on a landscape of grey rocks. It was an odd design but effective.

Meanwhile, Brian Macdonald, who'd made a name for himself at Stratford in the 1980s with his brilliantly reinvented productions of Gilbert and Sullivan operettas, was also at the COC that year, directing *La Traviata*. Our set, with its fake rocks, was at one end of the rehearsal hall in the Joey and Toby Tannenbaum Opera Centre; his, which included some fake trees, was at the other.

Some birds had found their way into the hall. They'd plucked some of the plastic leaves off the *Traviata* trees, flown across to our set at the other side of the hall and built their nests in our rocks. A rather sweet case of life not so much imitating art as putting it to good use.

Fidelio concerns the efforts of a Spanish noblewoman, Leonore, to find and free her husband, Florestan, who is being held in a dungeon as a political prisoner. To achieve this, Leonore disguises herself as a youth, Fidelio. Leonore was sung by the Swedish soprano Helena Döse, who asked me earnestly at our first meeting, "How much vill ze audience boo on opening night?"

"What?" I said. "They're not going to boo at all."

"No? In Sveden zey boo all ze time."

"Not here," I said. "We're a very polite country. We don't do that." ("Much," I might have added, under my breath.)

Helena was delightful, and very patient with my inexperience of her world. In rehearsal, when we came to the scene in which Leonore and Florestan are reunited, I told her: "When you meet your husband after not seeing him for so many years, you should do two things. One is that you should look at him. The other is that you should embrace."

She replied: "You do not understand. You see, if I sing *to* him, ze audience von't hear ze notes properly. And if I *hold* him, he vill be deaf."

I saw what she meant, having already had an awe-inspiring demonstration of the sheer power of the operatic voice. At the beginning of the second act, Florestan—played in our production by American tenor Mark Baker, a born-again Christian who looked like a trucker, and whom I found to be a wonderful person—has a huge and famous aria in which he imagines he sees Leonore in his prison cell. The first time I heard Mark sing this was in the rehearsal hall, accompanied just by the piano.

I'd been told that opera singers seldom use their full voices in rehearsal: often they just "mark" the song, to save their vocal cords for the performance. But in the rehearsal hall that day, Mark sang the entire aria with full commitment and full voice. As I sat there listening, my whole skeletal structure vibrated from this incredible sound. Only once before had I felt anything like it: when the bell rang while I was on top of the Campanile in Venice.

By the time Mark was finished, I'd almost regained my faith. With tears in my eyes, not knowing how to respond, I turned to Maestro Bernardi. His eyes, too, were wet with tears. "It makes you believe in God, doesn't it?" he said, echoing my thoughts exactly.

At the end of the opera, Florestan and the other prisoners are freed, as they sing some of the most beautiful (and difficult) music in the world. To represent this moment of liberation, our designer had created two mammoth cubes on stage that rose into the air, revealing the prisoners, with shaved heads, huddled beneath. It was a stunning moment, eerily reminiscent of the Holocaust. Unfortunately, once they were inside the cubes, the chorus could neither hear the music nor see the conductor, so getting them to start singing on cue was a problem. Nor could the chorus be heard from out front until the cubes had started to rise.

Maestro Bernardi laid down his baton and turned to me. "We can't hear each other. What are you going to do?"

In a panic, I turned to the designer and said, "What are *you* going to do?" The rehearsal came to a halt as we thrashed it out. Eventually, we incorporated some wire mesh into the sides of the cubes that enabled the sound to pass back and forth. But it was a hair-raising moment.

I don't know how I got away with directing that very difficult opera. Perhaps if I'd been given something more in the *verismo* style (a Puccini, perhaps, or a Bizet), I might have brought more of my dramaturgical skills to it. Still, I went to every performance of *Fidelio* save one, and I was moved every time. The power of the music, perhaps. But I can't have been that bad, because I was asked to revive the production for 1998 (which I did, though it wasn't as happy an experience).

I've never tried another opera, though I have now directed several musicals, beginning with *Camelot* in 1997. As I said to Maestro Bernardi at the time, "Beethoven wrote only one opera. And I am going to *direct* only one."

After *Fidelio*, I directed Susan Wright in *Shirley Valentine* at the Grand Theatre in London, Ontario. Susan was, of course, wonderful in the role, and the production was a delight. There was a huge bond between us: we both liked to drink too much, and she was one of the few people in whom I felt I could completely confide. During rehearsals, she, Nora Polley (who was stage-managing the show) and I would travel back and forth from Stratford together. On one of those trips, the question arose of why I always had a little doll in my productions, so I told Susan and Nora the story of Pom-Pom. Later, as a Christmas present, I gave Susan a garden ornament in the shape of a doll.

The plan was that Susan would reprise her role for me when I remounted the production at the Tom Patterson Theatre in Stratford the following year. (She was also going to play Mistress Overdone in *Measure for Measure*, Denise in Michel Tremblay's *Bonjour,*

Susan Wright in my 1991 production of *Shirley Valentine* at the Grand Theatre in London, Ontario

là, bonjour and some roles in an adaptation by Elliott Hayes of Robertson Davies's novel *World of Wonders*.) But then something unthinkable happened.

At the end of 1991, Susan was renting a house in Stratford from one of her best friends, Brent Carver. Her parents came to visit for Christmas, and stayed with her there. On the night of Sunday, December 29, the house caught fire, and Susan and both her parents died in the blaze.

Like most people in the theatre world, I was shattered by this news; yet, strangely, I found myself at first unable to cry. Once, not long afterwards, I was driving back from Don Lewis's place in the country, and as I was coming into the city, one of Susan's favourite songs, "Midnight Train to Georgia," came on the radio. I pulled over into the parking lot of a convenience store and listened, willing myself to break down and sob. I wanted to, badly. Yet still the tears would not come. The shock had been just too great.

It didn't happen till her memorial service, at which Brent sang "When the Red, Red Robin Comes Bob-Bob-Bobbin' Along" *a capella*, and I read from *Shirley Valentine*. I don't know how either of us got through it. At the end, though, when I was sitting backstage, the dam finally burst, and I howled with grief in a way I had not done since my mother's funeral.

I still think of Susan at least once a week. One of the things that haunts me about her death is how many years it takes to mature a talent, and how frail a thing that talent is. Like Brenda Donohue, like Kate Reid, Susan Wright had a unique and irreplaceable gift. Melted into air, into thin air.

At the end of *Shirley Valentine*, the character gives up her life in England and leaves a note for her family: "Gone to Greece." After the final performance in London, Nora Polley had given me the note as a memento, and ever since the fire I have kept it in my office, framed with Susan's picture.

CHAPTER ELEVEN

Love Wrought These Miracles

The Taming of the Shrew, Act V, scene 1

No sooner is an artistic director of the Stratford Festival appointed than thoughts turn to the question of a successor. It takes at least a year, and preferably two, to conduct a search for suitable candidates, interview them and arrive at a decision. The person chosen then needs to spend a year as a "designate," learning the ropes and planning a first season, before beginning his tenure. (Or hers, though until the announcement in 2006 that Marti Maraden would be one of my three successors, along with Don Shipley and Des McAnuff, all the Festival's artistic directors had been male.) So the process ideally needs to start three years in advance.

David William presented his first season in 1990 and would be leaving at the end of 1993. Thus it was in 1991 that the board of governors had to start looking around for his replacement. Muriel Sherrin, whom John Hirsch had installed as producer at the beginning of his tenure, was on the search committee, and I suspect (on no evidence whatsoever, merely my intuition) that it was she who recommended me as a candidate. It was David himself, however, who first broached the subject with me.

"Would you be willing," he asked, "to have your name included on a list of candidates?"

This was an honour for which I had not looked. "I don't want to do your job, David," I replied. "It's too much like homework. I went into the theatre so I could play."

I truly did not want such a crushing responsibility. I'd been around the Festival long enough to see for myself how beleaguered, bothered and bewildered past artistic directors had become. It was no wonder to me that most of them had served for no more than five or six seasons. Michael Langham's record of 12 seasons was an extreme anomaly, and in any case that had been in the days when the Festival was a much smaller and more manageable organization. If I were to take on this burden, my life, such as it was, would be eaten up by it. And I wasn't at all sure I *could* do it, anyway. I'd never run anything, apart from my short-lived stint with the Citadel's young company, and that hadn't exactly been a stellar success.

"Oh, just put in your name," David urged. "You can always withdraw."

The fact that he'd asked me in the first place suggested that the committee was having trouble coming up with a list of candidates.

I thought it might be helpful to them to at least foster the illusion that there were plenty of people interested in the job. "Okay, fine," I said: "put me on the list."

Even if the job itself didn't appeal, I still couldn't help daydreaming about the seasons I'd devise *if* I were crazy enough to take it on. I revelled in visions of Susan (who was still with us when David first spoke to me) as a key member of my company. I savoured in my mind her Cleopatra, her Beatrice; I envisaged her in any number of other Shakespearean roles. When she died, many of my dreams died with her.

Those pleasing fantasies then suddenly had to give way to the real and immediate question of what to do about the 1992 remount of *Shirley Valentine*. After consulting with Susan's sister, Janet, David William proposed that she take over the role. At the time, I thought this a grotesque idea; however, as so often with David's decisions, it proved to be very wise. Not only was Janet superb in the role, but the process provided much-needed therapy for her, for Nora and for me. We spent every rehearsal for this light-hearted comedy crying our eyes out.

Susan's sister Janet Wright in *Shirley Valentine* at Stratford in 1992

In addition to *Shirley Valentine*, David had asked me to direct *Romeo and Juliet* that season. Megan Follows, the star of the CBC drama series *Road to Avonlea*, was to play Juliet, with Colm Feore as Mercutio, but we still lacked a Romeo. So we auditioned people in the company, and one who came forward was the young actor who'd played the wigmaker in my production of *The Relapse*: Antoni Cimolino.

For his audition, I asked him to prepare what is perhaps Romeo's most difficult scene: the one in Friar Laurence's cell in which he learns of his banishment for killing Tybalt. "Banished?" cries Romeo. "O friar, the damnèd use that word in hell; howling attends it."

He then goes on to throw what amounts to a fit of hysteria. You always know a good Romeo if he can execute that scene. It requires the actor to summon up an overwhelming amount of emotion, something that's extremely hard to do in an audition.

I decided to try something: instead of having Antoni deliver Shakespeare's words, I asked him to give us the gist of the speech in Italian, which I knew was actually his first language. He did this on the spot, and the result was stunning. Afterwards, I conferred with David, who agreed that we should give Antoni this chance.

Driving home later with a friend, I spotted Antoni at the wheel of another car. Since he was currently between engagements as an actor, he was working at his other job: delivering pizzas. I followed his car, and when he got out, I hailed him: "Antoni, before you deliver that pizza, I just want you to know that you're playing Romeo next year."

Antoni Cimolino as Romeo in the Stratford Festival's 1992 production of *Romeo and Juliet*

Being able to offer such a gift to a young actor struggling to make ends meet was one of the most fulfilling moments of my entire career.

A peculiar thing happened to me during rehearsals for *Romeo and Juliet*. We were having some trouble or other with that very same "banishment" scene with which Antoni had auditioned. Eventually, I got up on my feet to demonstrate what I wanted him to do.

"No, no, it's like this," I said, and began to speak the lines: "Banished? O friar, the damnèd use that word in hell; howling attends it"—whereupon I suddenly burst into tears.

What on earth. . . ? Red-faced with embarrassment, I took a moment to compose myself and started the speech again. Once more, my throat choked up, tears started in my eyes, and I was unable to continue. A third time—the same result.

"I'm terribly sorry," I said to my colleagues in the room. "I don't know *what* this is about, but I can't seem to stop myself. This isn't helping anybody; let's move on to something else."

When the rehearsal was over, I went home and began cooking meatballs for dinner. As I moodily pushed them around the pan, I puzzled over what had happened that afternoon. Was it some kind of emotional recall from when I myself had played Romeo back in 1977? It was true that I'd cried real tears at that very same point in the play, but then that had been part of a performance: a very different situation from just demonstrating something in a rehearsal hall.

I shifted the pan of sizzling meatballs off the stove and found myself staring at the electric element, which was glowing red hot. Suddenly, as if in a moment of *satori*, that flash of enlightenment in Zen Buddhism, three images crowded simultaneously into my mind. One, vividly retained from my Catholic childhood, was of the fires of hell. Another was of Susan dying amid the flames of that house fire just a few months earlier. The other, its pain preposterously keen after the passage of more than 40 years, was of my childhood doll withering to ash in the incinerator's heat.

As fresh torrents of tears poured down my face, I understood at last what had lain behind my bizarre breakdown in that afternoon's rehearsal: a chain reaction of griefs, ancient and modern, unleashed by Romeo's words about the damned howling in hell.

I was the first to be called for an interview for the artistic director's job. Muriel was there, as was Tom O'Neill, then president of the board of governors. Since I had nothing at stake, I spoke freely. I made it clear that my interest was purely hypothetical. I offered no grand vision for the future, because I didn't have one. "There's nothing wrong with Stratford," I told the interviewers. "What we're doing here is right. All it needs is a paint job." I even explained to them why I wasn't right for the position. "One of the qualities I believe an artistic director should have is an interest in power. Even though some will abuse power, an interest in it is an essential quality in a leader. And power does not interest me, certainly not for its own sake."

In the spring of 1992, after all the other candidates had been interviewed, the committee asked to see me again. I gathered it was not uncommon in this kind of search for the first person who'd been interviewed to be seen a second time, for the sake of fair comparison, so I went to the interview just as a matter of form.

Nonetheless, I then started to get cold feet. What if the board *did* take my candidacy seriously? I had better advise them, I thought, that I really wasn't in the running. So I sat down and composed a letter.

"Dear Tom O'Neill:

"After much thought I have decided to withdraw my name from the list of applicants for the Stratford Festival's artistic directorship.

"I wish to express much gratitude for your interest and my thanks for a pleasant initial interview.

"If I can be of any assistance in the selection process, I would be most willing to help."

That same night I was in a downtown bar—Bentley's, as it is now, though I think at that point it was still called The Jester's Arms—when I was joined by Janice Price, who just a couple of months earlier had been appointed as the Festival's director of communications. Although I didn't know it at the time, Muriel Sherrin had just told Janice that she should start preparing to make an announcement. So in her conversation with me, Janice started testing the waters to see how I might react.

"You know, Richard," she said, "I think you have a very good chance of getting this job."

"What?"

"Well, I think they're going to decide very soon."

"Janice, two hours ago I sent the president of the board a letter withdrawing my name."

Her eyes widened. "Really?"

"Yes, really."

Was it pure coincidence that the following morning Tom O'Neill knocked at my front door? "Could we have a chat?" he asked.

"Certainly," I said, inviting him in.

He came straight to the point. "What would you say *if* we offered you the artistic directorship?"

"Tom, what would you say *if* I told you that on Monday morning you'll be getting a letter from me saying that I'm withdrawing my name from this race?"

A momentary pause, then: "Do you have a beer?"

By the time we'd finished our beer and our conversation, we'd agreed that Tom would disregard my letter and make me a formal offer of the job.

In deciding to accept it, I reasoned that the search committee must be truly desperate. They'd scoured Canada. They'd interviewed in England and in the States. Everyone suitable must have turned them down. Though Tom denied it, I was sure they'd arrived at the bottom of the barrel, and I was the only apple left.

And I had to admit I did have two great qualifications for the job. One was my extensive experience with the Festival, dating back to 1965. The other, far more important, was my love for the place, which I had in abundance. Now abideth faith, hope, love, these three; and the greatest of these is love. Faith you need on every opening night. Hope you constantly need in the theatre. But love was the determining factor. I could not have done this job for any other theatre, because I would not have had for it the love that I have for the Stratford Festival.

I took heart from the fact that the offer was for a term of only three years. "Okay," I thought: "three years of this, and then if it doesn't work out I can go back to my voice-overs, and they can find someone else." Little did I realize how long the road ahead of me was going to be.

My appointment as artistic director was announced in Toronto on June 15, 1992, four days before my 48th birthday. After the customary designate year, my tenure would begin when David's ended on October 31, 1993.

As I mentioned at the beginning of this story, my brother Mark surprised me by flying in from Los Angeles to attend the press conference. That night we shared a bedroom, as we had done as kids. For some time after putting the lights out, we lay in the dark, talking.

I had, of course, some grave apprehensions about the role I had taken on, not the least of them being the prospect of my first meeting with the full board of governors. I knew that when that moment came, there would inevitably be an elephant in the room—or rather, a pig. How could any board be expected to overlook the fact that 12 years earlier I had compared their president to that very quadruped?

"Mark, what am I going to say to them? This thing is going to hang over me like the sword of Damocles."

My brother was in no doubt about the best course of action: confront the issue immediately and defuse it with humour. "Thank them for hiring you," he told me, "and then say, 'I know I once called the president of the board a pig—but now here I am at the trough.' "

I followed his advice, won a huge laugh from the assembled governors and never worried about it again. (Tom O'Neill told me later that he'd paved the way for me by impressing on his board colleagues that the events of 1980 did nothing to disprove my love of the Festival. "I love my wife," he'd told them, "but we do shout at each other from time to time.")

The news of my appointment generated a tremendous amount of goodwill among the Canadian theatre community. Not only was I Canadian through and through, but I was in many ways a child of Stratford. And I had proven myself not only as a classical actor but, in such plays as *Hosanna*, *Something Red* and *Farther West*, a notable exponent of home-grown drama as well. As Diana Leblanc recently put it, the general reaction at the time was one of "Wow, what a brilliant idea."

I received a postcard of congratulation from Joy Coghill, author of the play *Song of This Place* and the founder of Holiday Theatre, Canada's first children's theatre company. The picture on the front showed a buffalo in a snowstorm, plodding doggedly along the tundra, its head bowed against the wind. Joy knew what it could be like to run a theatre company.

I've kept that postcard, which proved to be prophetic.

I'd known that taking the job would mean a drop in my income. Being artistic director of the Stratford Festival was a prestigious position, but it didn't pay nearly as well as voice-over work. Still, I'd been prepared to make that sacrifice for the sake of the theatre I loved. I had no idea when I accepted the offer that I was about to find myself facing bankruptcy.

Because my life had become so hectic, as I ran back and forth between Toronto and Stratford, I'd been finding it harder and harder to keep on top of my financial affairs. As it happened, one of my acquaintances was an accountant who'd decided to leave the large firm he worked for and strike out on his own. He asked if he could take me on as a client, and since I liked him and needed someone to take charge of my finances, I agreed. I even brought him other clients, including Nicholas Pennell.

My new financial wizard suggested that, since I was away so much, I grant him power of attorney, enabling him to pay my mortgage and file my income tax returns. Needless to say, agreeing to this request proved to be the worst mistake of my life.

This man took every penny I had, and then some. Everything went: the money from the films I'd made, from the voice-over work, from the sale of my house in Toronto. The mortgage on my Stratford house, which my so-called accountant had assured me had been paid off, was still outstanding. Worst of all, he had falsified my income tax returns. As a result, not only was I broke, but I now found myself owing the government $53,000.

He was never caught, as far as I know. I believe he fled the country. Perhaps my grandmother, with her money taped to her chest, had the right idea after all.

In addition to having to pay my back taxes, I needed to carry out some renovations to my house in Stratford. The artistic director needs to be able to entertain donors, board members, visiting artists and other VIPs; it doesn't do to bring such people into a dilapidated fixer-upper. The renovation was going to cost a great deal of money, which of course I no longer had, and people warned me that I'd never be able to pay it back, on top of my debt to the government. But I set out to live on $100 a week, while every remaining penny went either into the house or to Revenue Canada. It took me more than half my tenure, but I did at last get back on my financial feet.

Paying my debts has always been very important to me. When I was younger, I often had to borrow from friends. Ben Solway, for example, lent me money to cover my tuition the year I went to York University. He would also, whenever I asked, give me a couple of bucks here and there for bus fare or other sundries. When I got my first job at Stratford, I went to settle up with him. To his astonishment, I presented him with the tuition money plus payment of all those other little "loans," which I had carefully documented: "On January 15: $2. On January 21: 50 cents," and so on. Ben was astonished at such obsessive scrupulousness, but to me it was a point of honour. (And yet somehow I managed to forget all about this episode until about eight years ago, when Ben reminded me of it. "Ben," I said in amazement, "how *wonderful* I am.")

When I arrived to commence my designate year, I was given a tiny office in the Festival Theatre, across from the orchestra loft. Little more than a closet, it now holds the refrigerator for the lunch room. There was barely room in it for a desk and a telephone; my secretary, Sean Trofin, had to sit outside on a chair in the hallway. Nora Polley made a sign for me: "Artistic Director Designate," which I still have. It is my intention to hang it on the refrigerator when I leave.

There is no formal program of training in how to be an artistic director. You just learn on your feet, as you go. So I was fortunate in my designate year to have David William as my model and mentor.

David and I went back a long way—to that *Twelfth Night* in 1966—and I felt closer to him than to any of his predecessors. Himself a brilliant actor (his astounding performance as Richard II can be seen in the 1960 BBC series *An Age of Kings*, produced and directed by Peter Dews), he is also, like John Hirsch, a man of daunting intellect. On the first day of rehearsals one year, he told the company, "If I meet you in the hall tomorrow and I ask you, 'What's a dactyl?' I expect you to know what a dactyl is." (For the benefit of any of my readers who may have temporarily forgotten, a dactyl in poetry is a metrical foot consisting of a stressed syllable followed by two unstressed ones, as in "CAN-a-da.")

At the same time, again like John, he would use emotion to get results. An actor told me once that his only objective in a certain rehearsal had been to hide behind everyone else so David wouldn't scream at him. But David never meant to be hurtful. As he explained to me, "You can fly off the handle in the rehearsal room, but then you completely forget about it." Of course, it might be easier for *him* to forget about it than for the terrified object of his anger.

David made me attend many board meetings in my designate year. It became apparent that some board members were just as nervous about me as I'd been about them. In one early meeting with the executive, I suddenly stood up after an hour to go out and smoke. Every head in the room swivelled in my direction, and I could see the alarm in their eyes. Was I walking out?

"It's all right," I said, "I'm just going out to have a cigarette, because all your heads look like filter tips to me." Some past artistic directors, I was later told, had always gone to board meetings with resignation letters in their pockets, just in case they felt the urge to quit.

It was during my designate year that I stumbled upon the person who would become my right-hand man. I had one show to direct, *Antony and Cleopatra*, with Leon Pownall and Goldie Semple in the title roles. There was only a small part in it for Antoni Cimolino, and he wanted to do something more. So Nora Polley suggested to him, "Why don't you ask Richard if you can be his assistant director?"

He came to me with this proposal, and because I felt sorry that I had no better acting role to offer him, I agreed, not supposing for a moment that he would be remotely useful to me. Although he'd been a good Romeo, I'd argued quite vehemently with him at one point over the meaning of a line, and I'd come away thinking, "This young man just doesn't understand this stuff." I'd soon discover how wrong I was.

Between responsibilities in Stratford, I was in Toronto directing a piece called *Power Play*, written by a good friend of mine, Martin Hunter. While I was working on that project, Antoni, on his own initiative, arrived in the city and announced that he wanted to start preparatory work with me on the text of *Antony and Cleopatra*. Though taken aback by this show of eagerness, I naturally agreed, and we sat down together in Martin's house with our copies of the play.

I was completely unprepared for Antoni's grasp of the text, which—to my dismay—turned out to be far better than mine. He was so insightful that, after several sessions, I found myself wondering if he was using some other, non-actorly part of his brain.

I misjudged him on another count, too. One afternoon while we were still engaged in this preparatory work, we went out for lunch. As we passed a men's clothing store on Bloor Street, Antoni glanced in the window and remarked, "That's a wonderful tie."

"Go in and buy it," I said.

"Oh, no," he replied. "My wife handles all the finances. She'd murder me."

Aha, I thought. Another actor who can't manage money. This kid may be smart about Shakespeare, but he has no head for figures.

I persisted in this error for about three years until even I had to acknowledge what rapidly became apparent as Antoni took on more and more responsibility: that he is a genius with numbers. Early in my tenure, he became my artistic associate. He then rose to become general manager, then executive director. He is now the Festival's general director, with ultimate responsibility for all its operations, including, after my departure, its artistic ones. Seldom have the words "and the rest is history" seemed so appropriate.

Besides learning the ropes and directing *Antony and Cleopatra*, my immediate priority in 1993 was to put together my playbill for the following season, my first as artistic director. I had a plan: since I'd worked with (and learned from) every artistic director the Festival had ever had, except for Tyrone Guthrie, I wanted to symbolically honour my predecessors by inviting all the surviving ones to participate in my first season.

I invited Michael Langham to direct *Husbands and Cuckolds*, a double bill of two one-act comedies by Molière: *The Imaginary Cuckold* and *The School for Husbands*. I asked David William to play Malvolio in *Twelfth Night* at the Festival Theatre, and Robin Phillips to direct *Cyrano de Bergerac* and *Othello* at the Avon. I can't now remember what I asked John Neville to do, but I didn't get far in my plans before circumstances forced him to drop out.

I also wanted to make a symbolic gesture of reconciliation to erase the lingering wounds of the 1980 crisis. Martha Henry, for instance, had naturally been wounded by the ignominious disbanding of the Gang of Four and had refused to work at Stratford ever since. I wanted to "hold the olive in my hand," as Viola says in *Twelfth Night*.

I had a play in mind for Martha to direct at the Tom Patterson Theatre: Eugene O'Neill's *Long Day's Journey Into Night*. It's an autobiographical piece, its characters—the actor James Tyrone, his drug-addicted wife, Mary, and their sons, Edmund and Jamie—based on O'Neill's own family. I thought the part of Tyrone would be perfect for William Hutt, who was now back at the Festival after a four-year absence. Bill and Martha were friends, and I thought if anything could bring her back, it would be this.

At the time, Martha was artistic director of the Grand Theatre in London, where I'd done my first *Shirley Valentine*. To my delight, she didn't turn me down out of hand. She said she'd try to make room for it in her schedule, so I sent her the script. Then, when she'd read it, she phoned me right back.

"I don't want to *direct* this play," she said; "I want to play Mary Tyrone." Martha had always assumed that the character of Mary was much older than she was. On reading the script carefully, however, she'd realized that she was, at that time, exactly Mary's age. This was beyond my wildest hopes: Bill Hutt *and* Martha Henry together on a Stratford stage in the first year of my tenure. "Who do you want to direct it?" I asked, and she replied, "Diana Leblanc." So that was settled.

One of the productions that had been planned by the Gang of Four back in 1980 was *Hamlet*, with Stephen Ouimette in the title role. Of course, that plan had fallen through when the Four were dismissed. Knowing how important the chance to play that role is to an actor, I asked Stephen to play it in a production that I would direct, and he accepted.

Martha Henry as Mary Tyrone and William Hutt as James Tyrone in *Long Day's Journey Into Night* (Stratford Festival, 1994)

Eventually, my season fell into place. It would open with *Twelfth Night*, which I would direct. Lucy Peacock would play Viola, with Alison Sealy-Smith as Olivia, Brian Bedford as the clown Feste, Yanna MacIntosh as Maria and Stephen as Sir Andrew Aguecheek. The season would also include *The Pirates of Penzance*, directed by Brian Macdonald, and *The Comedy of Errors*, directed by Richard Rose, who would also direct a new Canadian play, *In the Ring*, by Jean Marc Dalpé. Marti Maraden would direct another new piece, an adaptation by Canadian poet and playwright James Reaney of Lewis Carroll's *Alice Through the Looking Glass*.

Commissioned by David William and workshopped by Marti in my designate year, *Alice* seemed to me to be the kind of repertoire that the Festival desperately needed more of: something that would appeal to younger audiences. I had to beg the board to let me program it: laden with props, costumes and special effects, it would be expensive to produce, and there were fears it wouldn't sell. I was convinced that, on the contrary, there was a barely tapped market out there for family-oriented repertoire on our stages, and that we needed to start cultivating it. The children of today, I reasoned, were the theatregoers of tomorrow, and we had to get them interested in us.

As insurance, we had a star in the lead: 14-year-old Sarah Polley, who played Sara Stanley in the TV series *Road to Avonlea*. (By coincidence, Sarah's mother, Diane Polley, had played a lady-in-waiting in my first *Hamlet*.) And if that weren't enough to draw the people in, we were also offering the public the unique opportunity to see Douglas Rain as both the Walrus and Humpty Dumpty.

My idea of incorporating past artistic directors into my first season brought me some unexpected headaches. During September and October 1993, long before the season started, negotiations with Robin Phillips concerning *Cyrano de Bergerac* and *Othello* fell apart in a flurry of faxes to and from the Citadel Theatre in Edmonton, where Robin was still director general. Once again, he and I somehow failed in those exchanges to find each other's wavelengths, just as we had from the very beginning of our relationship. Whatever the rights and wrongs of this sorry affair, it left me feeling completely estranged from Robin, a feeling that, regrettably, persists to this day.

The direction of *Othello* was taken over by Brian Bedford, who had originally been going to play Iago in the production, and Iago was assigned instead to Scott Wentworth. After searching all over the country, as well as England and Los Angeles, for someone to play the title role, Brian settled on Ron O'Neal, the star of a 1972 action movie called *Super Fly*. Mr. O'Neal didn't arrive in Stratford until about three days after the first read-through, by which time we had all become very nervous.

As for *Cyrano de Bergerac*, I'd asked Derek Goldby, who'd directed an acclaimed production of the same play at the Shaw Festival some years earlier, to step into the breach. We disagreed over one of his ideas for the production, which was to bring a live horse onto the stage.

As should be clear from my misadventure with Petunia Pig, no one is more open-minded than I when it comes to allowing livestock its chance at stardom. Unfortunately, though, we'd determined that the Festival stage wasn't built to support the weight of even a moderately sized horse, so I had to veto the idea. While the appearance of a real horse, nostrils flaring and hooves stamping, would have unquestionably been a stunning *coup de théâtre*, we didn't want it causing an *écroulement du théâtre* as well.

The title role in *Cyrano*, by the way, was played by Colm Feore, who that year also played the Pirate King in *The Pirates of Penzance*. He'd been a leading player at the Festival for many years and was now anxious to explore other avenues. "I don't want to just stay here and become one of those actors who have lost all their ambition and all their interest," he said. I was deeply grateful to him for staying on for my first year, but I entirely understood that he had to move on.

"You will return, won't you?" I pleaded.

"Yes," he said, "some day I will." And he kept that promise, returning first in 2002 to play Henry Higgins in *My Fair Lady* and then again in 2006 to play *Coriolanus*, Don Juan (in both English and French) and Fagin in *Oliver!*

Colm Feore in the title role of *Cyrano de Bergerac* (Stratford Festival, 1994)

David William did play Malvolio in my *Twelfth Night* and gave exactly the performance I'd hoped for: vivid and unsentimental. Unfortunately, however, his presence in the company the very year after he'd ceased to be artistic director created some discomfort among his fellow actors. This was no fault of his: I should have realized there'd be a problem with conflicting loyalties among some of the people who'd worked with him in his former role and who now had to contend with me.

Even Michael Langham's fine contribution as director of the Molière double bill came with an unanticipated side effect. "Richard," Michael said, when he arrived in Stratford to begin rehearsals, "you've got to take care of yourself. It's a very hard job, and death is no excuse." Never, as it turned out, was a truer word spoken.

Michael's intention from the beginning had been to remount the two Molière comedies in New York after their run in Stratford. I knew that Brian Bedford, who was playing Sganarelle in both plays, wasn't entirely happy with some of his fellow actors in the Stratford cast (which, sadly, included my friend Roberta Maxwell, who I thought was wonderful in the piece), but I was startled when Brian came into my office to show me—out of respect for my new position—a letter he was going to send to Michael, requesting extensive changes for the New York production. Those changes included including the replacement of many of the actors, Roberta among them.

My hair stood on end. "He's never going to send this," I thought to myself. "And if he does, Michael will never agree to it." But Brian did send it (though I didn't know that for sure until later), and Michael acceded to every one of his requests.

When Roberta found out that I had known of this letter, she was upset that I hadn't warned her. Perhaps I should have done, but since the Stratford Festival wasn't involved in the transfer of the production to New York, I didn't really feel that what Brian and Michael might decide between them was any of my business. Besides, there was always the possibility that none of the proposals in Brian's letter would come to pass, and I would have ended up making Roberta unhappy for nothing. As it was, though, the incident did serious harm to our friendship.

I had thought, when my tenure began, that I was going into the job with my eyes wide open. I knew that the Festival wasn't in good financial shape. There had been heavy losses in the preceding seasons. I did not, and do not, attribute this to anything David William had done but rather to a number of circumstances that he had the misfortune to encounter all at once during the course of his tenure: a major recession, cutbacks in government funding and in arts education programs in schools, the introduction of the Goods and Services Tax and the increased competition from mega-musicals in Toronto.

What did come as a surprise to me was how much money the Festival owed. I hadn't known about the roof repairs that hadn't been paid for or the health benefits that hadn't yet been paid to the unions. The first year of my tenure seemed to be marked by one revelation of economic difficulty after another.

Nor had I quite anticipated the pressure I would come under from people who had economic interests outside the theatre. I knew, of course, that Tom Patterson had founded the Festival in the first place for good business reasons rather than artistic ones. And having lived in Stratford for many years, I was aware, too, of the extent to which the city now depended on the Festival for its survival. But I hadn't foreseen how much of a burden this would place on me. Every artistic decision I made affected the fortunes of a whole community of people who ran shops, restaurants and bed-and-breakfast establishments. My job was to create art, not save the city; at the same time, I couldn't ignore the public-service component of that job. The reality was that the livelihoods of people besides artists depended on what I chose to put on our stages. Nor were those people about to *let* me ignore it.

The downtown merchants had been quick to express their dissatisfaction with the original line-up of productions at the Avon Theatre: *Cyrano, Othello* and *Alice*. Those titles wouldn't sell, they told me. I wrote back to one of them saying that *Alice Through the Looking Glass* would surely hold a strong appeal for children. I received the answer, "Yes, but children don't buy things in the stores." They were even less happy when I had to move *Cyrano* to the Festival Theatre with nothing to replace it, leaving only two shows at the Avon—one of them, *Alice*, a late opener.

This was a low, low time for me. It was made even worse by the fact that, on top of everything else, I had a falling out with Aviva that lasted for quite some time. As we headed into 1994, I wondered if I had made a terrible mistake by taking on this job. The theatre was in financial straits, my own finances were in ruins, and I seemed to be inadvertently alienating friends and colleagues at an alarming rate. But the survivor in me eventually reared its head. As my psychiatrist had said, "Who loves Stratford the most?" It was that thought that sustained me.

Something else I hadn't anticipated was the number of speeches I was now expected to make. It was a good thing I'd had all that public-speaking experience in high school, because now it seemed I'd be forever flapping my lips.

One of my first major appearances in that regard was at the annual conference of the Shakespeare Theatre Association of America, held in January 1994 at the Alabama Shakespeare Festival. I went there with Janice Price. We flew from Toronto to Nashville, which I found bad enough, but then to get from Nashville to Alabama we had to board one of those planes so tiny that the passengers have to be carefully arranged to balance it. We bounced about in the sky like a ping-pong ball in a washing machine.

I had recently given up smoking, but the moment we landed I went straight into the terminal building, bought a pack of cigarettes and chain-smoked my way through it. Janice took a photograph of me getting off the plane with my face frozen in a grimace of terror. She had it printed on a mug for me, with the caption "The pilot wants an *audition*?"

The circumstances in which I had to speak were quite informal, and the audience mostly comprised people who worked in the theatre, so there wasn't much pressure. But I was in a panic nonetheless. "What am I going to *say* to them?" I kept asking Janice. "What am I going to *say*?"

It was her task to introduce me. "Make this the longest introduction of anybody you have ever given," I hissed at her, "because I have not a thought in my head. Not one."

She did indeed spin out her remarks heroically: it was the longest introduction I have ever heard. But still I had not the faintest idea of what to say. As I started to rise apprehensively to my feet, Janice whispered in my ear, reminding me of something I'd said to her once. "Just start out by telling them what you told me: that being the artistic director of the Stratford Festival of Canada is like being a paramedic. You're constantly dealing with what seem like matters of life and death."

So I began with that, and then suddenly I couldn't shut up. I blathered away, with no idea where any of it was coming from, and people apparently thought me very funny. Toward the end, I mused, "What does an artistic director do after he's no longer an artistic director?" And a woman in the audience replied, "Well, *you* should get your own TV comedy series."

I was put to shame, though, by the keynote speaker at that conference, the actor Hal Holbrook. Without a note in his hand, he delivered one of the most inspiring speeches about the theatre that I have ever heard. He spoke with such passion, such conviction, that I could *feel* what he was saying. I thought to myself, "I've got to learn how to do this."

I don't know if I ever did match him, but I certainly tried. If nothing else, the sheer number of speeches I have given in the course of my tenure must have earned me a little corner in that part of heaven reserved for advocates of the arts. And my lip-flapping brought me a direct benefit too: my years of facing audiences in this new capacity gradually cured my stage fright. In 1997, after a nearly 10-year absence from the stage, I was again able to play a leading role in a Stratford Festival production: as Domenico Soriano in Antoni's production of *Filumena*. (My fear of flying, though, took a little longer to abate.)

At the closing dinner of the conference, I sat next to Winton M. Blount, the entrepreneur and former U.S. postmaster general who had donated $22 million to build the Alabama Shakespeare Festival's state-of-the-art theatre complex. His son was the architect who'd designed it. "He had an unlimited budget," Mr. Blount told me, "and he far exceeded it." He was quite a character, with a great sense of humour. "My friends," he liked to say, "spend your money before you die, so you can see what it'll buy you."

He sent me two books that he had written, and a copy of the prayer supposedly composed by Sir Francis Drake before setting off from Portsmouth harbour to sail round the world. I have used it as a source of inspiration throughout my tenure.

> Disturb us, Lord, when
> We are too pleased with ourselves,
> When our dreams have come true
> Because we dreamed too little,
> When we arrived safely
> Because we sailed too close to the shore.
>
> Disturb us, Lord, when
> With the abundance of things we possess
> We have lost our thirst
> For the waters of life;
> Having fallen in love with life,
> We have ceased to dream of eternity
> And in our efforts to build a new earth,
> We have allowed our vision

Of the new Heaven to dim.
Disturb us, Lord, to dare more boldly,
To venture on wilder seas
Where storms will show your mastery;
Where losing sight of land,
We shall find the stars.

We ask you to push back
The horizons of our hopes;
And to push us into the future
In strength, courage, hope, and love.

This we ask in the name of our Captain,
Who is Jesus Christ.

When my debut season opened, its prospects did not at first look good. The Cassandras of the downtown marketplace were proving to be right: *Othello* was not selling well, and advance sales for the late-opening *Alice Through the Looking Glass* were far from encouraging.

We did have one certified hit: *Long Day's Journey Into Night*. It got a glowing review from *The New York Times* and started selling out. Of course, it was at the Tom Patterson Theatre, which holds just under 500 people, so it wasn't going to be a huge revenue generator. Still, this was an unexpected bonus for a play that many people expected to be a box-office failure. (Among them was Robert Fairfield, the architect who'd designed the Festival Theatre. He'd written to advise me that in his opinion *Long Day's Journey* was the most disastrous choice of programming of the decade.)

The production was subsequently made into a feature film by Rhombus Media. Bill Hutt, Martha Henry, Peter Donaldson and Martha Burns all won Genie Awards for their roles in the film, and I'm sure the fifth member of the cast, Tom McCamus (a wonderful actor and a wonderful person), would have won one too, if he hadn't been in direct competition with Bill in the category of best actor in a leading role.

I was deeply despondent, though, about the dismal advance sales for *Alice Through the Looking Glass*, the show I had begged for. It seemed that my judgement in this case had been disastrously wrong. With two box-office failures at the Avon, the season was headed for another substantial deficit, and we could not afford another in 1995. Planning for that season had to begin now, so what could I do to stop the hemorrhage? The only solution I could think of was not to open the Tom Patterson Theatre that year.

I went to the Festival's general manager at the time, Gary Thomas, and said: "We have to do something drastic to make the budget for next year work. We have to close the Tom Patterson."

"We can't do that," said Gary. "The town won't like it."

"The town doesn't like it whatever we do," I replied. "It's a lose-lose situation."

Eventually, Gary agreed. So now, after all the blood, sweat and tears, I was going to go down in history as the artistic director who shut down the Tom Patterson Theatre.

A production for families:
Sarah Polley as Alice in *Alice Through the Looking Glass* (Stratford Festival, 1994)

Then *Alice* opened.

Whether it was the reviews, which were enthusiastic, or positive word of mouth, or just that, for some reason, people with children waited till the last minute to book tickets, *Alice* suddenly took off and went through the roof. It saved the season, and dramatically so. From a deficit of $1.3 million the year before, we ended 1994 with a surplus of $800,000: a turnaround of more than $2 million.

I went back to Gary. "I know it's really late in the day to be saying this, but with an $800,000 surplus, I really don't think we can close the Tom Patterson Theatre after all. The optics would not be good."

I had a plan: I would go to the casts and directors of *Long Day's Journey* and *The Comedy of Errors*, which had also done well at the Tom Patterson, and beg them to keep the theatre open by reviving their productions in 1995. It would cost very little to do that, since the costumes and props had already been built, and the casts wouldn't need much rehearsal. I would also add in a small-cast play by Timothy Findley: *The Stillborn Lover*. With that programming in place, the season at the Tom Patterson could be self-sustaining.

Gary hadn't been in favour of closing the theatre in the first place, but now that he'd committed to the idea, he wasn't keen to throw it out again. Making that kind of major shift in direction at an institution the size of the Stratford Festival is like trying to turn around an ocean-going liner in a bathtub. But to his eternal credit, he once again let me have my way.

William Hutt said to me later, "Richard, I don't know if this threat about closing the Tom Patterson Theatre was a reality or if it was a ruse. But it was brilliant." In fact, it was no ruse, and it was only the success of a little girl climbing through her mirror into the Looking-Glass World, brilliantly realized by director Marti Maraden, that saved it from being carried out.

I'd done it. I'd pulled off a successful first season—though at considerable personal cost. And yet I was nagged by a voice inside me that said I should have done better. We shouldn't have come so close to disaster: *every* show in the season should have been sold out. Why couldn't I have had a triumph on every front?

The answer to that, I would come to realize, lay in something that had been said to me by our late literary manager, Elliott Hayes. Elliott was the son of John Hayes, who'd been the Festival's producer before Colleen Blake, and when I was in my designate year, his career as a playwright was just taking off. He wanted to leave the Festival and follow his star. I begged him to stay, just for my first year. I came to wish I hadn't, because at the end of February 1994, Elliott was killed in a car accident by a drunk driver. A life with so much promise, a young man in mid-flight (in the words of Julia Foster, the new president of the board), snuffed out in a senseless accident.

What Elliott had said to me—and these words would come back to me season after season—was this: "People always say that the Festival's first year, in 1953, was a miracle. What they don't realize is that *every* year is a miracle."

CHAPTER TWELVE

Some Odd Quirks and Remnants of Wit

Much Ado About Nothing, Act II, scene 3

When I first embarked upon this memoir, my intention was to chronicle the years of my tenure in as much detail as I have the years that led up to it. However, as I mentioned in my preface, I eventually decided against that course.

One reason is that to do full justice to those 14 years would require a book in itself, and I have already perhaps presumed too much on the reader's patience. (An old theatrical maxim that every author, like every performing artist, does well to remember is "Leave them wanting more.") Another is that I am still, at the time of writing, *living* this particular chapter of my story. In the 1800 preface to his *Lyrical Ballads*, William Wordsworth remarked that poetry takes its origin from emotion recollected in tranquillity. The same may be true of autobiography. The incidents of my tenure, the triumphs and sorrows, struggles and surprises, dreams fulfilled and disappointed, are in many cases still too fresh in my mind for me to approach them from the same detached (or at least semi-detached) perspective that I have brought to bear on those that preceded them. Perhaps at some point in the years following my departure from this position on October 31, 2007, I shall find the tranquillity that will enable me to continue my story in a sequel.

There is yet another and perhaps more germane reason for my reticence. In many ways, that portion of the story that deals with my years in office ceases to be entirely *my* story; rather, it merges with the story of the Stratford Festival itself. Proud as I am of the major achievements of my tenure—the multi-million-dollar renewals of the Festival and Avon theatres, the founding of the Birmingham Conservatory, the launching of the For All Time endowment campaign, the creation of the Studio Theatre, the establishment of a formal program of new play development, the performance of the entire Shakespearean canon on our stages, the 14 consecutive seasons of box-office surpluses—they have been largely institutional in nature and thus seem to me to lie outside the scope of what has hitherto been a personal (and highly subjective) account of my life as an artist. My initial fear that becoming the Festival's artistic director would swallow up my life has proven amply justified: during the years of my tenure my life has *been* the Festival, and to discourse adequately on those years would entail a noticeable shift of focus and tone, from that of the memoirist to that of the theatre historian.

Some aspects of my time as artistic director have already been touched on in two previous books: Robert Cushman's *Fifty Seasons at Stratford* and my friend Martin Hunter's *Romancing the Bard: Stratford at Fifty*. I recommend them both to the reader who wishes to glean some sense of how the Festival fared under my leadership. Meanwhile, in lieu of a year-by-year chronicle of initiatives undertaken, artists engaged, plays directed, meetings attended, colleagues quarrelled with and speeches given, I offer in this final chapter a small selection of self-contained but tenuously connected memories and musings drawn from that past dozen or so years of my life and career.

On vision and vulgarity

Near the end of my first season in 1994, board president Julia Foster invited me to her country place in Georgian Bay to sound me out about extending my contract. We went there, astonishingly, in a helicopter, which she and her husband had rented. It was a foggy day, and it seemed to me that the pilot was visibly nervous. Given my history with helicopters, I felt as much at ease as a French aristocrat in a tumbrel. I pretended, as I usually do in such life-and-death situations, that I was in a film. Later, after we'd arrived and she'd had a swim (and I a cigarette or two), Julia asked me what my vision was for the Festival. "To keep the doors open," I replied.

Julia Foster, board president in 1993 and 1994

The same question has been asked of me many times since, and I have always given more or less the same answer. I have been derided for offering no more eloquent or elaborate articulation of my role; to me, however, that simple answer seems to be the first and most fundamental responsibility of my job. It is the artistic director's equivalent of the principle commonly (though mistakenly) believed to preface the Hippocratic oath: "First, do no harm."

Plays on a shelf are literature; only plays on a stage are theatre. And a play on a stage without an audience is not a performance; it is only a rehearsal. To keep the doors open, therefore, and to persuade people to pass through them in the greatest possible numbers, is the first and most sacred duty of any artistic director. All else flows from that. If I had done nothing else in my tenure to be proud of, I would be proud of the fact that I have been a "people's director" who did everything I could to make audiences feel as much at home in the theatres of the Stratford Festival as I do myself.

Critics have disdained this philosophy. One called for my resignation in the pages of *The Globe and Mail* at a time when more people were coming to the Stratford Festival than ever before. Even Urjo Kareda, one of the members of the Gang of Four on whose behalf I made such a spectacle of myself at that 1980 AGM, came to rebuke me for my populist ways 20 years later, in an article in the July 2000 issue of *Toronto Life* magazine. I was deeply hurt by that article, coming as it did from someone who had once been a friend and colleague, and who was himself (at the Tarragon Theatre) an artistic director. Entitled "Sold Out," it spoke of the "vulgarity" of the Festival's "house style" under my leadership and dismissed the organization's current state (achieved at no small cost to my personal life and, indeed, to my health) as a "tragedy."

So be it. My tastes are my own, and I can no more falsify them to suit other people's aesthetics than could, say, Michael Langham or Robin Phillips. If vulgarity is my style, well, perhaps I have that in common with Shakespeare, whose *Hamlet* was described by Voltaire as "a coarse and barbarous piece of work, which would not be tolerated by the basest rabble in France or Italy. One would imagine it to be the work of a drunken savage." (Voltaire, by the way, wrote many plays of his own, most of them in the best possible taste. You don't see many of them performed today.)

In an essay on the state of Canadian theatre contributed to the 1951 Report of the Royal Commission on National Development in the Arts, Letters and Sciences, better known as the Massey Report, the great Canadian novelist, scholar and critic Robertson Davies remarked that "the theatre is a vigorous, living and, in a certain sense, a coarse art; it is vulgar in the true sense of the word," by which he meant that it appealed to the *vulgus*, or common people. I am of a mind with him on that, and I can think of no higher accomplishment for a classical company than to be vulgar in the true sense of the word. Does attracting audiences in substantial numbers to the works of Shakespeare, Molière, Marlowe, Marivaux, Ibsen, Sartre or Williams violate the principle "Do no harm"? I think not, especially when you consider the alternative.

Anyone who attempts to lead an artistic organization sooner or later encounters criticism and opposition—from the press, from governments, from other artists, from one's own board—and it would be easy to fall prey to disappointment and cynicism. Corny as it will no doubt sound, what has sustained me through all my own battles has been the same thing that convinced me to take the job in the first place: my love of this great theatre. And what in turn sustains that love is the enthusiastic appreciation of our audiences. That appreciation—not just of so-called crowd-pleasing fare but also of the greatest and most challenging works in the dramatic repertoire—is the only vindication that counts.

On the importance of being innovative

In fact, I did have plans for the Festival, even if they couldn't be neatly summed up in a one-sentence "vision statement." To paraphrase Bottom's words in *A Midsummer Night's Dream,* I have had several "most rare visions" during my tenure: a multitude of dreams that have resulted in the innovations briefly mentioned above.

Early on, though, I discovered the difficulty of bringing change to a large organization that had become a little set in its ways. There were some around me who had their own ideas, ossified over many years, of how the Festival should be run. "That's not the way we do things at Stratford" was their mantra. And since Stratford Festival artistic directors would come and go every few years, they figured they could simply wait me out: "Three years and he'll be gone."

At that meeting in Georgian Bay, I told Julia Foster that, if I were to stay on, things at the Festival would have to change. I was worried, however, that I didn't have a sufficiently confrontational or manipulative personality to effect that change. "I'm not in any sense a political person," I told her.

"No," she replied. "But you *are* strategic."

My strategic thinking may be easily summed up: every year, I tried to introduce something new. This may have been something big, such as the renovation of a venue or the establishment of the

Birmingham Conservatory, or something relatively small, such as new ancillary programming or the transfer of one of our productions to another theatre, but it seemed to me to be vitally important to be always moving ahead in some way or another. As one of our board presidents, George Taylor, once memorably remarked to Antoni Cimolino, "Nobody is going to thank you for something you *didn't* do."

One of the earliest and most visible major innovations of my tenure, completed in time for the opening of the 1997 season, was the $15.6-million renewal of the Festival Theatre. The need to address the building's shortcomings had been apparent long before I was in a position to do anything about them. Once, during David William's tenure, I saw plans for a renovation laid out in someone's

Construction work on the Festival Theatre during the Act III renewal project of 1996-97

office, and I asked David what they were. "Oh, never mind about *that*," he said, assuming, with good reason at the time, that their fulfilment would lie far in the future. But early in my own tenure, our fortunes changed sufficiently to bring the dream within reach, and so we decided to seize the moment.

The original plan called only for improvements to the front-of-house facilities; it was I who pushed for a remodelling of the auditorium as well. In particular, I wanted to bring in the side walls, reducing the arc of the amphitheatre-style seating from 220 degrees to 180, and also to increase the space between rows, in order to give patrons more leg room. Together, these two changes would reduce the number of seats in the theatre from nearly 2,200 to 1,820. There was much contention about this. There were those who thought it would betray the original intentions of Tyrone Guthrie and his designer, Tanya Moiseiwitsch. Though the archival record is frustratingly unclear on this question, I was assured by Tanya herself, and by Douglas Campbell, a member of the first company in 1953, that the seating arc enclosed by the original tent accommodated about 1,500 patrons arranged in a 180-degree semicircle; thus the configuration I proposed was actually *nearer* to Guthrie's original concept.

Nonetheless, even with Tanya's and Douglas's support, and that of Desmond Heeley, who had been designing for the stage of the Festival Theatre since the permanent building opened its doors in 1957, there was reason for me to be apprehensive. As Antoni Cimolino put it, "You *would* shrink the theatre just at a time when we're finally filling it." As it turned out, however, it was the right thing to do. I shall never forget the day we went into the renewed theatre for our first onstage rehearsal of the 1997 season's musical, Lerner and Loewe's *Camelot*. It was a great moment, because the shape of the auditorium had changed, and even though there were no seats in place yet, it was clear to all of us that it was going to *work*.

Not everyone agreed with my choice of *Camelot*—the first musical I'd ever directed and one I'd always wanted to do—as the opening production of our 1997 season. Many thought it inappropriate to reopen our largest venue with anything other than a Shakespeare play. But I felt strongly that *Camelot* was the right choice. How better to celebrate the fulfilment of a renewal project that had been dubbed "Act III: Entrance to a New Era" than with a show that is about a vision, a new life, the future, the quest for the Holy Grail? The symbolism was perfect.

On the importance of exactitude

On June 28, a few weeks after the 1997 season had begun, Queen Elizabeth II arrived by helicopter to officially open the renewed Festival Theatre. I shall never forget the inverse hailstorm of spectators' hats, suddenly sucked up into the air by the draft from the machine's rotors, nor the pride I felt at seeing the royal standard flying from the flagpole atop the theatre's roof.

This royal visit was, however, a production in itself. For weeks beforehand, we were instructed in the finer points of royal protocol. There was great concern over the entertainment that we had proposed for Her Majesty: a brief excerpt from that season's production of *The Taming of the Shrew*. The production had been set in the Wild West, and at one point in the scene that was to be presented for Her Majesty's pleasure, Stephen Ouimette, as Grumio, had to discharge three shots from a stage revolver. There were snipers from the royal entourage positioned up in the theatre's ceiling, and they warned Stephen not to fire any *more* than three shots. If he did, they would return real fire. I have no reason to suppose they were joking.

On continuing to direct

As my predecessors had done, I continued to direct productions myself during my tenure. Cynics claimed that I did so in order to earn myself more money. This is untrue: directing productions was considered part of my job, and I received no extra fees for doing it. In fact, the primary reason was that, amidst all the non-artistic work of running the theatre that I was now required to do, I needed the creative outlet. I discovered, somewhat to my surprise, that I could change hats quite quickly, leaving aside my administrative concerns as soon as I walked into a rehearsal room and focusing entirely on the work at hand.

There were other reasons too. I wanted to maintain some continuity in the acting company, and by directing at least two productions a season I would be in a better position to offer roles to actors whom I wanted to stay with us. Besides, the artistic director can easily become invisible to the company. It's important to keep alive your relationship with the actors, and the best way to do that is by directing. (To say nothing of the fact that I often found myself having to take on a production at the last minute, after someone else had dropped out.)

There were some board members, though, who didn't think I should direct at all. "Well, what *am* I going to do?" I'd ask them. "Paperwork?" They'd reply, "Oh, just be an artistic energy." But I didn't understand what that meant. It sounded far too Sixties to me.

When I look back on the productions I directed during my tenure, I find that, almost without exception, I have liked them all. This may reveal egotism on my part, or blindness. But it is true nonetheless. Interestingly, the productions of which I have been proudest are often the very ones the critics have most loathed. *Camelot* was one example. Another was *The Miser*, which I directed in 1998 and which we took, along with my production of *Much Ado About Nothing* that same year, to City Center in New York.

I have always had a vision, sometimes obvious, sometimes more oblique, for each of my productions. In the case of *The Miser*, I had paid a visit to the Comédie-Française in Paris, where I saw the chair in which Molière had suffered a fatal seizure during his performance in the title role of *Le Malade imaginaire*. My concept for *The Miser* sprang from that chair. Harpagon, the miser, is totally alone in the world, with the exception of his money, which has become his best friend. It's a psychosis: he is desperate to accumulate and preserve money, but he doesn't want to *do* anything with it, not even for his own pleasure or comfort. So I imagined a stark, minimalist set: a white room with nothing in it but this isolated man and his chair. It was almost like a padded cell. Or like an indoor tennis court, which was perfect for Molière, since tennis courts were where his plays were originally performed.

In the production, I sought to tap into the grotesqueness that runs under all of Molière's comedies. Molière wanted to be a tragedian, but his true gift proved to be for comedy. Nonetheless, his comedy is very different from that of Shakespeare: there is something very dark at the heart of all his plays. Thanks to the splendid cast, led by Bill Hutt, and the fine work of my designer, Mérédith Caron, the production turned out to be everything I had hoped it would be. I loved it, in fact.

It was not, however, to the taste of the critics, either in Toronto or New York. "Monette massacres Molière's *Miser*," announced the headline over *The Globe and Mail*'s review on August 14 that year, prompting a letter of protest from novelist and playwright Timothy Findley. In his letter, Tiff (as he was known to his friends) pointed out that my production drew on the traditions of vaudeville and burlesque, which Molière himself had co-opted in writing his plays. But of course one couldn't expect the critics to know that.

If I sound bitter about that production's reception, well, I was, and still am. I couldn't understand why something of which I was so proud had so uniformly failed to connect with the critics—though the audiences seemed to be having no trouble. It was one of the most profoundly demoralizing experiences of my entire tenure.

On the tactical use of suits and salty language

To succeed, even the most well-conceived strategy has to be supported by effective tactics. Among the tactics I used in my tenure were clothing and curses.

As a schoolboy, I had always worn crisp, clean white shirts, courtesy of my father's involvement in the dry-cleaning trade. Later, my wardrobe consisted almost entirely of jeans and T-shirts, because as an actor you never know when you're going to be required to roll about on the floor of a rehearsal hall. Besides, when your job involves dressing up in costume, the last thing you want to put on afterwards is a suit and tie—though I did have a couple of those in which to audition. When I became artistic director, though, I made a conscious effort to change my image.

The job didn't come with an official dress code: John Hirsch had always worn sweatpants, which he would pull up over his head at the first sign of trouble, and David William had worn sandals and what seemed to me to be the same suit jacket for his entire tenure. But since I had come up though the ranks of the Festival company, I knew that I needed to distinguish myself from my former role as one of the boys. I took my lead from John Neville, who always dressed to the nines in suit, white shirt and bow ties and thereby commanded a certain respect.

I began putting a lot of thought into my clothes, something I had never done before. I would always wear a jacket and tie, to show that I took our enterprise seriously and was prepared every day to represent its interests at the highest level. (There was also another, more practical reason for the jacket. Its pockets provided accommodation for all the accoutrements of the director's trade: pen, notepad, glasses, cigarettes *et al.*) And I would be careful not to wear the *same* jacket and tie in the course of a week: I wanted the actors to see me in something different every day, so that they in turn would subconsciously try to bring something fresh to each day's rehearsal. I have no idea if this worked, but that was the rationale.

On the first day of rehearsals, I would almost always wear something red, since red is a "leadership" colour. When the Festival celebrated its 50th season in 2002, I made gold that year's thematic colour. I had a huge range of gold-coloured ties that I wore every day, and I made presents of gold ties, shawls or cufflinks to members of the company and staff.

Meanwhile, in counterpoint to this ostentatious (but never, I hope, vulgar) display of nattiness, I cultivated a certain persona, one that relied heavily on histrionics and salty language.

As a boy, and even a teenager, I was very proper and rarely used bad language. As a director and an artistic director, though, I became notorious for my free use of Anglo-Saxon expletives. I did this deliberately, even though it made some people uncomfortable, as a tool to shock and get attention. Rightly or wrongly, I suspected that nobody ever listened to a word I said, and this was my way of getting through. To my knowledge, no past artistic directors had done this. They might have been direct, they might have been forceful, they might have been wildly critical, but they hadn't used that sort of language. But I remembered the galvanizing effect of what one theatre director—not an artistic director—had said to his cast on an opening night: "I want you to go out there and play it like a good tight anal f___." Difficult as it might be to put such an exhortation into practice, that sort of shock tactic had worked for him; I didn't see why it couldn't work for me.

Even when the salinity level of my language was less elevated, I'd try to communicate in ways that were visceral rather than intellectual. In this, I emulated John Hirsch and David William, though perhaps rather more outrageously. David's acid remark to an actor about having a dusty soul was mild compared to what I once said to a male member of my young company at the Citadel: "You are so dull that while you were acting, I had 12 sexual fantasies, and not one of them was about you."

In 1999, while directing *A Midsummer Night's Dream* at Stratford, I was having great trouble with the entrance of the fairies for "Ill met by moonlight." They would sort of saunter on, whereas I wanted a great burst of energy. "Will you please *move*?" I said. "You're young actors: among the few things you have to offer are speed and sweat, so get on with it!"

We tried it three times, and each time the entrance got slower and slower. "All right," I said at last, getting to my feet. "If you're going to be that slow, I'm going to take off all my clothes," whereupon I started to remove my shirt. There was a chorus of squeals—of alarm and dismay, I hardly need add—and I got the result I wanted.

The designer of that same production, Teresa Przybylski, gave me a most rare vision of Hellenistic Greece: blue fairies, and the mechanicals all dressed in straw. It was all very dark, and I didn't want to do a dark *Dream*. Tyranny by design.

I said to her, "You know, this play is a sexual fantasy. It's a midsummer night's *wet* dream; that's what it's *about*. There is nothing remotely erotic or funny about these costumes."

"Well, you know," she said, "I am Polish. We Poles have suffered."

"That may be," I retorted, "but don't Poles have *sex* sometimes?"

Some people were shocked by such vulgarities on my part; others were amused. But few could ignore them.

On generosity and green-light people

When my mother died in 1972, I had no money, and neither did my father. So to pay for her funeral, I applied to the Tyrone Guthrie Award Committee, which each year awards grants from various funds that have been donated for the express purpose of enabling Festival artists to fulfil their personal dreams. Jean Chalmers, a celebrated patron of the arts and the mother of Joan Chalmers, to whom this book is dedicated, had established an award for which I qualified. I applied for and—not surprisingly—received it.

But then my mother's side of the family, all those uncles and aunts, pooled their resources and came up with enough to cover the funeral expenses. They refused my offer to repay them with the Guthrie Award, and so in the end I used it to go on my first trip to Europe. And that trip was an enormous benefit to me, both personally and as an artist.

Many years later, during my tenure as artistic director, Joan Chalmers joined the Festival's board of governors. One day, I went to her country house near Stratford and told her this story. "After all these years of keeping it to myself," I said, "I want to tell you how much your family's generosity and support for the theatre has meant to me personally. The expression 'cold as charity' has never been more wrong." Joan was so touched that she burst into tears.

No strategic or tactical efforts on my part would have advanced my plans for the Festival one inch without the generosity of philanthropists, or without the remarkable complement of what I call "green-light" people with whom I have been blessed throughout my tenure: people who, unlike their "red-light" counterparts, are eager to move things ahead. Janice Price, who went on to occupy a number of leadership positions in the arts world in both Canada and the United States, was one of the colleagues without whom my tenure could never have unfolded as it did; Antoni Cimolino is another.

So, too, have been the members of the Festival's board of governors and its presidents (now called "chairs") during my tenure: Julia Foster, Michael Meighen, George Taylor, Sandra Pitblado, Don Woodley, Tom Orr and Kelly Meighen. Serving on an arts board does not, in many people's minds, confer the same degree of prestige as serving on the board of a hospital, yet it is no less vital to a society's health and wellbeing. I am particularly grateful, therefore, that all those skilled, dedicated and generous individuals should have chosen to direct their altruism toward the arts.

It has been most gratifying (and astonishing) to me to discover the depth of people's passion for classical theatre. For all its recent box-office successes, the Stratford Festival could not have survived, far less grown, without the financial backing of arts lovers who have nothing to gain from their investment but the knowledge that they have strengthened and enriched the cultural life of this country. From the many thousands who support the Festival through annual membership donations to such rare philanthropists as Raphael and Jane Bernstein, Bruce and Betty Birmingham, David Green and Mary Winton Green, Michael and Kelly Meighen, Robert and Marion Murray, and Sandra and Jim Pitblado, all of whom have made astounding contributions toward the major innovations of my tenure, there has been ample evidence over the past 14 seasons that I am by no means alone in my love of the Festival.

So to all the above, and indeed to all the green-light people of the world, I owe my undying appreciation. Nothing is easier than saying no, and nothing is harder—or more fulfilling—than saying yes.

On seeing the world

In the fall of 2000, at the insistence of our then board chair, Sandra Pitblado, I took several months' sabbatical in Europe to recharge my batteries. I was appalled by the idea at first, for two reasons. First, what would happen to the Festival in my absence? And second, I had never before in my life experienced such an extended period of not working. What would happen to me? Would I lose my mind?

Knowing of my dread of flying, a friend bought me a ticket for the QE2, so that I could cross the Atlantic at sea level. My cabin on the ship was made up every day by the same Irish maid.

"I know ye," she said one day, in her thick Hibernian accent. "What do ye do?"

"I run a Shakespeare Festival in Canada," I told her. She absorbed this information thoughtfully.

The next day, she announced triumphantly: "I know who y'are! Ye're that Mountie, aren't ye?"

I immediately telephoned my executive assistant, Elke Bidner, and told her to contact Paul Gross, who had played the role of Mountie Benton Fraser in the TV series *Due South* and who was that season playing Hamlet in our Festival Theatre. "You are to tell Paul," I said gleefully, "that I have been mistaken for him by my Irish maid." Such an error was indeed flattering, for Paul is not only 15 years younger than I but also a major heartthrob.

The sabbatical turned out to be a brilliant idea on Sandra's part. Not only did it restore my energies, it also it yielded specific programming ideas. My decision to present *My Fair Lady* in 2002, for example, was inspired by the visit I paid to Covent Garden. *My Fair Lady* has always been one of my favourite shows, ever since I saw it in New York in my teens with my school friend Ed Sullivan, and it is also one of the few musicals in which I thought I might be able to perform. Having returned to the stage in *Filumena* in 1997, I thought it would be safe to cast myself (subject to the approval of musical director Berthold Carrière and choreographer Donna Feore) as one of three Henry Higginses who would appear during the season, the others being Colm Feore and Geraint Wyn Davies. It was a great disappointment to me when my voice gave out after just one preview, and I had to withdraw from the production.

More substantially, my sabbatical gave me the idea for my Greek season in 2003, which was presented under the thematic title "Tales Told and Retold." I had been desperate to go to Greece ever since high school, where I had I read the entire body of ancient Greek dramatic literature, and my visit there (along with my trip to Turkey, where the site of ancient Troy is believed to be) was the centrepiece of my sabbatical. I had always thought I would go to Greece with a lover, but in fact I found that I didn't need one, because when you're in Greece, that amazing country *is* your lover.

I went to the ancient amphitheatre at Epidaurus, which seats, I believe, 20,000 people. There is a centre spot on the stage where the acoustics are said to be perfect. Since there was hardly anyone else there—a group of four and one young man on his own—I decided to put this to the test. So I stood in that "sweet spot" and delivered Henry V's famous speech "Once more unto the breach, dear friends," every line of which, rather to my surprise, I remembered. The acoustics

Me delivering "Once more unto the breach," from *Henry V*, in the ancient amphitheatre at Epidaurus

were indeed all they were renowned to be, and when I was finished, the solitary young man came up to me and asked, in English, if I was an actor.

"I used to be," I told him. Then, noticing something about his accent I couldn't quite place, I asked him where he was from.

To my astonishment, he replied, "Rimouski, Quebec."

The ability to travel, to visit in person the great theatres of the world and the places associated with the great events of history and myth, provides vital nourishment for the imagination of artists. I am grateful for the opportunities afforded me in this regard by the generosity of others, and that is one reason why, in this, the last year of my tenure, a travel fund in my name has been established within the Festival's endowment foundation, to enable other artists to benefit in the future as I have done in the past.

On providing for the future

On another occasion during my sabbatical, I took a boat ride across the Hellespont, during which our guide told the story of the great 16th-century Turkish architect Koca Mi'mar Sinan Aga, better known simply as Sinan. The Michelangelo of the east, Sinan built palaces and mosques. One of his structures, so the story goes, was a monumental arch, with a keystone at its top. Many years after Sinan's death, the keystone fell out, and no one could figure out how to put it back. One day, while a workman was inspecting the hole in the arch, a bottle fell out. Inside it was a note, written by Sinan himself. "I suspect," said the note, "that someday this keystone will fall. You may have many modern ways of putting it back in place"—which, in fact, they didn't—"but here is how *I* did it." So they followed his instructions and replaced the keystone.

That story sounded a chord with me, for it articulates the philosophy behind the Birmingham Conservatory for Classical Theatre Training, which I founded in 1998. It is of great importance that we pass on, from generation to generation, our hard-won skills as classical artists, for when those skills are lost, they are immensely hard to reinvent.

Our Sinan, the first principal of our Conservatory, was Michael Mawson, who died while I was away on my sabbatical. I was in a hotel room overlooking the Bay of Naples when I received the phone call telling me the news. My room had a refrigerator with beer in it. I never drink beer, but Michael always did. So after I hung up the phone, I opened a beer and saluted him with it across the bay, as church bells rang in the distance.

On a historic half-century

In 2002, the Stratford Festival celebrated its 50th season. Many people mistakenly referred to this event as an "anniversary," which is nonsense. If the Festival had such a thing as a 50th anniversary, it fell on July 13, 2003, exactly 50 years since the very first opening night in 1953. But we celebrate instead by seasons: our first season was in 1953, our second in 1954 and so on till our 50th in 2002.

Whatever people wanted to call it, we all felt under tremendous pressure to get that season right. I am particularly proud of two things we did that year. We completed the renewal of the Avon Theatre (a project on a par with the Festival Theatre renewal five years earlier), and, in the process, we created what had long been dreamed of at the Festival: a fourth performing space, which we called the Studio Theatre, located within the Avon Theatre building, where the set-painting shop used to be. This was of particular symbolic importance to me. At the beginning of my tenure, I had feared I would have to close the Tom Patterson Theatre. Now, instead, I had opened a wholly new theatre, where new repertoire and new approaches to production could find an ideal home.

Tom Patterson, founder of the Stratford Festival

The renewed Avon Theatre opened with Martha Henry's production of *Richard III*, the same play with which the Festival itself had begun in 1953. We hoped to have the opening attended by Tom Patterson, the Festival's founder, but he was by then quite ill, and we realized we would have to play things by ear. At the last moment, Tom was driven here in an ambulance from his nursing home in Toronto, with a nurse in attendance, and just before the performance began, Antoni Cimolino brought him out onto the stage in a wheelchair as I announced, "Ladies and gentlemen, the founder of the Stratford Festival of Canada, Mr. Tom Patterson." I was so choked with emotion that I fumbled his name.

The audience gasped. The mere fact that Tom was there, on this historic occasion, helping celebrate this huge milestone for the Festival he had created, brought everyone instantly to their feet. The thunderous ovation, the cries of "Bravo!", seemed unlikely ever to stop. Eventually, I presented him with a bouquet of roses, and he was wheeled off into the wings to watch the opening soliloquy. Afterwards, I wrote him a note of thanks, which I concluded in my usual jocular style: "Don't let that standing ovation go to your head."

On beauty and bestiality

In 1982, while we were rehearsing *The Tempest*, John Hirsch brought in a man named Vivian Rakoff, a psychiatrist who taught at the University of Toronto, to speak to the cast. I shall never forget that talk, which offered a brilliant insight into how art works and what it does for us, and I have tried throughout my tenure to expound and enlarge upon that insight in many of my own speeches.

The events depicted in a play or an opera, Dr. Rakoff said (and I am necessarily paraphrasing his remarks), are often unbearably painful. What makes it possible for us to journey into them, and indeed enjoy their depiction, is the beauty of the language or the music. The beauty of the form buffers us against the pain of the content and allows us to delve safely into areas of human experience that could well destroy us in real life. By doing so, we can undergo what the ancient Greeks called catharsis. Looked at objectively, the events depicted in such a play as *King Lear*, for example, are elemental, unredeeming, vile and dehumanizing. But embodied in Shakespeare's verse, they become transformative: we emerge from our encounter with them with our sense of humanity enlarged rather than diminished.

To which let me add a thought of my own: the admiration of beauty alone, divorced from any examination of human behaviour, is *not* transformative. Beauty itself is a purely abstract quality: it has no bearing on morality. I am reminded of a day sometime in the early 1990s when my friend Aviva and I went to see the Frick Collection on East 70th Street in New York. In a corner of the museum was a glass case containing some fine examples of German porcelain. We were admiring this, when suddenly Aviva started to cry. It was a deep crying: tears welled up in her and started rolling down her face, but she made no sound. I asked her what was wrong.

"I'm not crying because I'm hurting personally," she said. "I'm crying because I don't understand how a people like the Germans could make something so beautiful, yet also destroy families." I told that story to the cast when I directed *King Lear* in 1996.

On August 21, 1983, the year after he'd spoken to the *Tempest* company, Dr. Rakoff made a public appearance in the Festival's lecture series. In that lecture, of which I have the printed text, he spoke of art as a form of what psychoanalysts call a "transitional space": a safe place "in which one may have transitional experiences poised between the real and the unreal." A play, in other words, is a means by which you can safely explore the most potent aspects of human experience, such as sex (the ultimate theme of comedy) and death (the ultimate theme of tragedy).

Dr. Rakoff also spoke about metaphor as a way of structuring experience, of giving it shape. In the "safe place" of a theatre, "we make metaphors of our experience and by giving experience rules and by contemplating it carefully, we seem to get a measure of understanding and control." The reason a society makes art, he went on to say, "is because until that happens it hasn't affirmed or understood its own existence." This reminds me of what my uncle Gentile, the painter, said to me when I was young: "You *have* to paint nature, because nature doesn't know itself."

In other words (and here I express an opinion that I have tried to articulate in various ways as an arts advocate during my tenure), that desire for enlargement through metaphor is why we bother with art at all. In fact, I believe it's more than a desire: it's a basic human need. The arts are the vitamins, if you like, in our spiritual diet, without which we will die. We overlook this fact when we become snobbish about the word *art*, refusing to allow it to encompass "lower" forms of metaphor-making: popular music as well as opera, a sitcom as well as a classical comedy. Shakespeare, of course, is much richer in vitamins than Spiderman. But when it comes to the sheer *need* for even the most lowly and trite form of metaphor and meaning, everybody, in the words of the Bruce Springsteen song, has a hungry heart.

If we look around us, we see safe places and metaphors everywhere: on TV screens, on iPods, in Cineplexes, on paperback stands at the airport. Such popular art forms exist because, regardless of quality, people want them and need them. Even the cliché scenario of a household on welfare, where the kids need new shoes and the rent is overdue, but there's a big TV in the living room, could be seen as evidence not just of the improvidence of the undeserving poor but also of the overwhelming human hunger for the imagery, rhythm, form and structure of drama—even if it's only the rudimentary drama of the football field, the game show or the wrestling ring.

We can afford to let the popular arts look after themselves in the marketplace. The more vitamin-rich classics, on the other hand, are too essential to our health to risk losing them, so it is imperative that we lend them public support. In either case, though, the arts are not a "frill" that a society can easily do without: on the contrary, they're one of the things that make us human. Those who insist that there are always more pressing needs than the arts to spend our money on should be reminded of King Lear's words:

> O reason not the need! Our basest beggars
> Are in the poorest thing superfluous:
> Allow not nature more than nature needs,
> Man's life is cheap as beast's.

On poor health and paranoia

It is a commonplace of popular wisdom that the leaders of large artistic institutions eventually become paranoid to one degree or another, so why should I have been any exception? As far as I'm aware, however, only once in my tenure did conspiracy theory prompt me to a course of action that might raise a few eyebrows.

In my earlier years at Stratford, a fellow actor had warned me cryptically, "Every word that is said in this rehearsal hall can be heard elsewhere." In those days too, it was often observed among the company, only half-jokingly, that you only had to talk about a certain person in a dressing room for that person to show up in the flesh shortly afterwards.

And then, one day during my tenure, there came an interesting moment when the phone rang only minutes after some colleagues and I had been discussing a particular title that might be included on the next season's playbill. The caller was an actress wanting to talk about that very play. A remarkable coincidence? Jungian synchronicity? Or . . . ?

I think it may have been in response to that incident that Elke Bidner, my executive assistant, reminded me of the old rumour that used to circulate that some parts of the building, including the artistic director's office, were bugged. Preposterous as the idea was,

I have to confess that I began wondering if maybe, just maybe, there might be something in it after all.

I went so far as to have Elke find me a specialist in electronic surveillance. We brought him secretly into the building and had him do a sweep for bugs. Needless to say, he found none, though we did have one intriguing moment when he detected a mysterious hum, which turned out to emanate from a headset accidentally left on by a stage manager. From such chance circumstances whole mythologies can arise.

Given my stage-fright experience, perhaps I had more solid grounds for another worry that afflicted me later in my tenure. Exacerbated, no doubt, by the stresses of the job, my health has declined in the past few years. (I have calculated that, in one two-year period, Elke took me to see 23 different doctors.) A year or so ago, for example, in addition to surgery for a chronic back problem, I underwent brachytherapy (the insertion of radioactive pellets) for prostate cancer.

As I contemplated the prospect of this procedure, not knowing what its outcome would be, an alarming thought struck me. Sexuality, I suddenly realized, lies at the root of my work as an artist. (In fact, this may well be true of all artists, but it had never occurred to me before.) So what if this treatment rendered me impotent? What would happen to my work?

Again, my fears proved groundless (on both counts), but they gave me much food for reflection on the mysterious quasi-sexual nature of artistic potency and the will to create.

On making magic

Robertson Davies's comment about the theatre being a "coarse art" may perhaps contain a faint echo of Prospero's speech in Act V, scene 1, of *The Tempest*, in which he renounces his magical arts:

> I have bedimm'd
> The noontide sun, call'd forth the mutinous winds,
> And 'twixt the green sea and the azur'd vault
> Set roaring war: to the dread-rattling thunder
> Have I given fire and rifted Jove's stout oak
> With his own bolt: the strong-bas'd promontory
> Have I made shake; and by the spurs pluck'd up

> The pine and cedar: graves at my command
> Have wak'd their sleepers, op'd, and let them forth
> By my so potent art. But this rough magic
> I here abjure. . . .

The Tempest is not exactly the last play Shakespeare ever wrote: he collaborated with other playwrights on such later works as *The Two Noble Kinsmen* and *King Henry VIII*. But it is, as far as we know, the last play he felt compelled to write on his own before going off to semi-retirement in Stratford-upon-Avon. It is tempting, therefore, to see in the passage quoted above not only the resolve of a character on stage to give up making things happen against the course of nature, but also a sly meta-theatrical allusion by Shakespeare to his imminent abandonment of his own "potent art."

The art of the theatre is indeed a kind of "rough magic," an unpredictable and potentially explosive mixture of the studied and the spontaneous. It is created in the here and now, by living people walking a kind of tightrope of the imagination. It is rough because, unlike a painting, a sculpture or a book, a piece of theatre cannot be laboured on with infinite pains over months or years, corrected and refined in every detail until it is deemed "finished": at best, it can only be given a few weeks of instruction in the rehearsal room and then sent out into the world, with all its imperfections on its head, to fare as best it can. The living work of art that is spawned in this way is born anew with every performance and can exist only in the moment, by the mutual consent of artists and audience. Sometimes the magic will hold and keep 2,000 people in its thrall; sometimes the spell will break, and the magic will dissipate amid coughs, fidgets and the rustle of programs.

I have practised this rough magic, in many different forms and with varying degrees of success, all my adult life. I have done so, in part, because it was the only way I knew of making my living but also because it was, to borrow Frances Hyland's words, the best way I knew of exploring the human condition. I might even go so far as to borrow the words of Domini Blythe, who was asked, when she auditioned for theatre school as a young woman, why she wanted to be an actress. "Because if I can't act," she replied, quite calmly and sincerely, "I will die."

On dying

My tenure has seen the passing of many of the Stratford Festival's pioneers: Tom Patterson, our founder; Tanya Moiseiwitsch, the designer of our thrust stage; Sir Alec Guinness, who in 1953, as Richard III, spoke the first words on our stage: "Now is the winter of our discontent / Made glorious summer by this son of York"; Irene Worth, the first actress to speak on that same stage; Louis Applebaum, our first director of music; Robertson Davies, who championed and chronicled the Festival in its early years and remained a staunch supporter all his life; Dama Bell, in whose home the founding committee held so many of its meetings, and who was one of the Festival's most tireless promoters; Timothy Findley, a member of the inaugural company and later one of this country's most celebrated authors; and many others.

Nicholas Pennell as Faulkland, with me as Jack Absolute, in *The Rivals* (Stratford, 1981)

The old guard has largely left us, and I don't know if we shall look on their like again. Nowadays, to paraphrase Tennessee Williams, the world is lit by lightning–the lightning of the electronic media–and few younger actors can afford to commit themselves so largely to classical theatre. I am glad to have had my career when I did: it has encompassed the end of a golden era.

On February 22, 1995, my friend and colleague Nicholas Pennell died of lymphatic cancer at the tragically early age of 56. He was to have appeared in the 1995 season as Duncan in *Macbeth*, Sir Jasper Fidget in *The Country Wife* and the Emperor Joseph II in *Amadeus*. Two days before his death, he wrote a letter to be read aloud to the company when they assembled for the first day of rehearsals. Here is part of what he wrote:

"My dearest company, stage management and crew: I wanted to write something to you on the occasion of your first day, from one who, for the first time in 24 years, cannot be there. Each year the miracle renews: we band of artists are released into the adventure again; to renew the act of faith in the recreation of the spirit of imagination. For it is that unique gift that is ours (our joy and our sorrow too): to delve into the stuff of our lives, and dig up with absolute fidelity and accuracy our happiness, our ecstasy, our pain, our misery, our laughter, our ironies, our intimacies passionate and unidentifiable—hot or icy cold; all unguarded and uncensored, free and truthful—and, through the medium of the text, allow the audience to receive the transubstantiation of our truth into their truth, their reality.

"To hold, as 'twere, the mirror up to nature.

"For that is what we *must* do as artists: demonstrate the shared wholeness of the human condition to our audiences; in order that together we may arrive where we started from and know the place for the first time."

One of the last things Nicholas said to me, apropos of our appearances over the years in the plays of Shakespeare, was this: "Well, Richard, at least we got to say those words."

On the power of words

"Why should calamity be full of words?" asks the Duchess of York in *Richard III*.

"Let them have scope!" replies Queen Elizabeth. "Though what they will impart help nothing else, yet do they ease the heart."

In the times we live in, we may need that heart-easing power of words more than ever. There are words in *The Merchant of Venice*—"The quality of mercy is not strain'd"—that are (or used to be) familiar to every schoolchild. Yet when Lucy Peacock, as Portia, spoke those words at a matinée performance on September 12, 2001, the atmosphere in the Festival Theatre suddenly became electric. It was as if the audience was hearing them for the first time. In the wake of the previous day's calamity, the meaning of that speech—must cycles of injury and retribution always be the human way, or can we find enough of the divine in us to forgive?—was brought home to everyone in that auditorium as never before.

And in some way, for the people there that day, it helped.

AFTERWORD: AND NOW FAREWELL

The Tempest, Act III, scene 1

This memoir was compiled to mark the conclusion of my tenure as artistic director of the Stratford Festival of Canada, so in that sense it may be seen, like Prospero's speech of renunciation, as a kind of valedictory performance: Monette's farewell to his art. That is a conclusion to which it would be premature to jump: like Shakespeare, I have every intention of being coaxed out of my retirement as often as possible. This ancillary world of board reports, AGMs, contract negotiations, press conferences and strategic planning meetings I here abjure, and heartily so. But not so the rough magic itself, for though I have done almost everything I wanted to do in the theatre over the course of my career, I cannot imagine I shall ever lose that need to explore, through the medium of art, the eternal and unanswerable mysteries of human experience.

Just as Ariel, the spirit of Prospero's imagination, is released by him at the end of *The Tempest,* so I look forward to being released, in the words of that last letter from Nicholas Pennell, into the adventure again. (Future artistic directors take note: I may have a Falstaff in me yet.) In the meantime, I hope I have to some extent fulfilled the promise I made in the preface to this book: that I would shed some light on my own personal mystery. I set out to reveal, to anyone who might be interested, something of who I am, what I have done with my life, and how these things came about.

All this I have, to the best of my ability, truly delivered. The rest, for now, is silence.

PROFESSIONAL ACTING ROLES

THEATRE

1964		
Hamlet	*Hamlet*	Crest Theatre, Toronto
Molière	*Impromptu*	Loeb Drama Center, Harvard
Player	*U.S.A.*	Loeb Drama Center, Harvard
Third Gentleman	*The Winter's Tale*	Loeb Drama Center, Harvard
Gardener/Mowbray	*Richard II*	Loeb Drama Center, Harvard
Berowne	*Love's Labour's Lost*	Loeb Drama Center, Harvard
1965		
Arnie Schofield	*They're All Afraid*	Shoestring Theatre
John	*Roommate*	Shoestring Theatre
Lord Harcourt	*Henry IV, Part 1*	Stratford Festival
Lord Harcourt	*Falstaff (Henry IV, Part 2)*	Stratford Festival
Dardanius	*Julius Caesar*	Stratford Festival
1966		
Simon Bliss	*Hay Fever*	Crest Theatre, Toronto
Montjoy	*Henry V*	Stratford Festival
Fiend/Soldier	*Henry VI*	Stratford Festival
Sebastian	*Twelfth Night*	Stratford Festival
1967		
Messenger	*Richard III*	Stratford Festival
Peter Simple	*The Merry Wives of Windsor*	Stratford Festival
Eros	*Antony and Cleopatra*	Stratford Festival
1968		
Denis Quévillon	*The Drummer Boy*	Theatre Toronto
Kenny	*Little Murders*	Theatre Toronto
Peter Dorland	*Soldiers*	Theatre Toronto
Detective Gentle	*A Festival of Carol's*	Theatre Toronto
Peter Dorland	*Soldiers*	Billy Rose Theatre, New York

1969		
Prince Edward	*Edward II*	Theatre Toronto
Godfrey Knellar	*In Good King Charles's Golden Days*	Theatre Toronto
Silvio	*The Servant of Two Masters*	Theatre Toronto
Lorenzo	*The Merchant of Venice*	New Shakespeare Company, Regent's Park, London
Panthino	*The Two Gentlemen of Verona*	New Shakespeare Company, Regent's Park, London
Montjoy	*Henry V*	Lyric Hammersmith Company, Bath
Fabrizio	*Mistress of the Inn*	Welsh Theatre Company (tour)
Tegeus-Chromis	*A Phoenix Too Frequent*	Welsh Theatre Company (tour)
Ensemble	*Return Journey*	Welsh Theatre Company (tour)
1970		
Boy	*Purgatory*	Welsh Theatre Company (tour)
Solange	*The Maids*	Welsh Theatre Company (tour)
The Devil	*Don Juan in Hell*	Welsh Theatre Company (tour)
Principal	*Oh! Calcutta!*	The Round House, London (later at the Royalty Theatre)
1971		
Tybalt	*Romeo and Juliet*	New Shakespeare Company, Regent's Park, London
Puck	*A Midsummer Night's Dream*	New Shakespeare Company, Regent's Park, London
1972		
Jesus	*How Beautiful with Badges*	The Open Space, London
Laertes	*The Marowitz Hamlet*	The Open Space, London
Lodovico	*An Othello*	The Open Space, London (also Wiesbaden, Germany)
Cyril	*The Dirtiest Show in Town*	Duchess Theatre, London
Player	*The Trial*	St. Lawrence Centre, Toronto
Orsino	*Twelfth Night*	St. Lawrence Centre, Toronto
Orestes	*Electra*	St. Lawrence Centre, Toronto
1973		
Lucentio	*The Taming of the Shrew*	Stratford Festival
Montano	*Othello*	Stratford Festival

Servant/Knight/ Fisherman	*Pericles*	Stratford Festival
Tom Wrench	*Trelawny of the "Wells"*	St. Lawrence Centre, Toronto
Soldier	*Colour the Flesh the Colour of Dust*	St. Lawrence Centre, Toronto
Third God	*The Good Woman of Setzuan*	St. Lawrence Centre, Toronto
1974		
Hosanna	*Hosanna*	Tarragon Theatre, Toronto
Hosanna	*Hosanna*	Global Village Theatre, Toronto
Hosanna	*Hosanna*	Bijou Theatre, New York
Jack Absolute	*The Rivals*	Roundabout Theatre, New York
1975		
Lucio	*Measure for Measure*	Stratford Festival
Sparger	*Kennedy's Children*	Stratford Festival
Algernon Moncrieff	*The Importance of Being Earnest*	Stratford Festival
1976		
Hamlet	*Hamlet*	Stratford Festival (also pre-season tour)
Caliban	*The Tempest*	Stratford Festival (also pre-season tour)
Lucio	*Measure for Measure*	Stratford Festival
Hosanna	*Hosanna*	Vancouver East Cultural Centre
Hosanna	*Hosanna*	National Arts Centre, Ottawa
1977		
Hosanna	*Hosanna*	Toronto Workshop Productions
Romeo	*Romeo and Juliet*	Stratford Festival
Parolles	*All's Well That Ends Well*	Stratford Festival
Sandy Tyrell	*Hay Fever*	Stratford Festival
Dunois	*Saint Joan*	Walnut Street Theatre, Philadelphia
1978		
Sewerman	*The Devils*	Stratford Festival

Andrei Vukhov	*Judgement*	Stratford Festival (also Vancouver East Cultural Centre)
1979		
Berowne	*Love's Labour's Lost*	Stratford Festival
Prince Hal	*Henry IV, Part 1*	Stratford Festival
Prince Hal	*Henry IV, Part 2*	Stratford Festival
Edmund	*King Lear*	Stratford Festival
1980		
Alex	*Something Red*	Tarragon Theatre, Toronto
King Henry V	*Henry V*	Stratford Festival
Prinz Carpenter	*Foxfire*	Stratford Festival
Edmund	*King Lear*	Stratford Festival
1981		
Dracula	*Count Dracula*	Bathurst Street Theatre, Toronto
Max	*Bent*	Bathurst Street Theatre, Toronto
Jack Absolute	*The Rivals*	Stratford Festival
Harry Thunder	*Wild Oats*	Stratford Festival (also National Arts Centre, Ottawa)
1982		
Jerry	*Betrayal*	Saidye Bronfman Centre, Montreal
Cinna the Poet	*Julius Caesar*	Stratford Festival
Doctor Caius	*The Merry Wives of Windsor*	Stratford Festival
Sebastian	*The Tempest*	Stratford Festival
1983		
Prologue/Sparkish	*The Country Wife*	Stratford Festival
1984		
Mercutio	*Romeo and Juliet*	Stratford Festival
Boyet	*Love's Labour's Lost*	Stratford Festival
Antonio	*The Merchant of Venice*	Stratford Festival
1985		
Lloyd Dallas	*Noises Off*	Zev Bufman Theatre Partnership (U.S. tour)
Scandal	*Love for Love*	CentreStage, Toronto

Seward	*Farther West*	Tarragon Theatre, Toronto
Masked Man/ Fastcrawler	*Spring Awakening*	CentreStage, Toronto
1986		
Macbeth	*Macbeth*	Skylight Theatre, Toronto
Luigi	*Saturday, Sunday, Monday*	CentreStage, Toronto
1987		
Benedick	*Much Ado About Nothing*	Stratford Festival
1988		
Pavel Krysanov	*Nothing Sacred*	CentreStage, Toronto
1997		
Domenico Soriano	*Filumena*	Stratford Festival
2000		
Reader	*The Trials of Oscar Wilde*	Stratford Festival
2001		
Reader	*The Creative Critic*	Stratford Festival
Reader	*Mr. Trueman and Mr. Lovewit*	Stratford Festival
2002		
Henry Higgins	*My Fair Lady*	Stratford Festival
2003		
Eryximachus	*Plato's Symposium*	Stratford Festival
2007		
Reader	*His Greatness*	Stratford Festival

FILM, TELEVISION AND RADIO

(Years refer to original broadcast date or cinematic release)

1963		
Evariste Galois	*With My Head Tucked Underneath My Arm*	CBC TV
Vladimir Rostov	*First Love*	CBC TV
1965		
Lead	*Two Half-Hour Documentaries*	National Film Board

1966		
Darnley	*Mary of Scotland*	CBC TV
Davis	*The Reluctant Agent*	CBC TV
Montjoy	*Henry V*	Stratford Festival/CTV
1968		
Principal	*Jackanory (five episodes)*	BBC TV
1973		
Rock Hard	*Big Zapper*	Delta Film Company
1975		
Neil	*Peep Show: The Lie Chair*	CBC TV
1976		
Bruce La Rousse	*Find the Lady*	Quadrant Films
1979		
Lead	*For the Record: Certain Practices*	CBC TV/PBS
1981		
Lead	*A Far Cry From Home*	CBC TV/PBS
Ed Jordan	*The Littlest Hobo: Suspect*	CTV
Wolfgang Mozart	*Titans*	CityTV
1983		
Sebastian	*The Tempest*	Stratford Festival/CBC TV
1984		
Sparkish	*The Country Wife*	Stratford Festival/Global TV
Hogan	*Iceman*	Universal Pictures
1985		
Jack Benson	*Mania: The Intruder*	Bullies Productions Inc.
1986		
Patrick Henley	*Popeye Doyle*	20th Century-Fox TV
Doctor	*Dancing in the Dark*	Dancing Productions
Frank Kendall	*Adderly: Rich Kid*	V.H. Productions
Joe Grant	*The High Price of Passion*	Taft Entertainment Corp.
1987		
Rolly McGuire	*Night Heat: Masquerade*	Alliance Entertainment

Brian	*Alfred Hitchcock Presents: Deathmate*	Townsend Film Productions Inc.
Benedick	*Much Ado About Nothing*	CBC TV
Joseph Dominic	*Night Heat: And Baby Makes Grief*	Alliance Entertainment
Guest star	*Diamonds: Good Hands*	Alliance Entertainment
Clive	*I've Heard the Mermaids Singing*	VOS/Telefilm Productions
Robert Bley	*Higher Education*	Higher Education Film Productions
Father Cooper	*Hello, Mary Lou: Prom Night II*	Higher Education Film Productions
Merrick	*T. and T.*	Nelvana Limited
1988		
Spooner	*Diamonds: Life Is a Lot Like Hockey*	Alliance Entertainment
Brock	*Street Legal: Mondo Condo*	CBC TV
1989		
Dr. Wilson	*The Twilight Zone: Father and Son Game*	Atlantis Films Limited
1990		
Greg Bradsky	*Conspiracy of Silence*	CBC TV
Ascot	*E.N.G.*	Alliance Entertainment
1991		
Norm	*Counterstrike: Going Home*	Alliance Entertainment
1992		
Dr. Lemmon	*The Good Fight*	Hearst Entertainment Productions
1994		
Dr. Lloyd	*And Then There Was One*	Freyda Rothstein Productions
1995		
Eric Shockley	*Harrison Bergeron*	Atlantis Films Limited
Reader	*Rogues and Vagabonds*	Glenn Gould Studio, CBC Radio
1995		
Hosanna	*Hosanna*	Glenn Gould Studio, CBC Radio

1996		
William Shakespeare	*The Dark Lady of the Sonnets*	Glenn Gould Studio, CBC Radio
1997		
Sal	*While My Pretty One Sleeps*	Grosso-Jacobsen Entertainment
1998		
Domenico Soriano	*Filumena*	Glenn Gould Studio, CBC Radio
2006		
Narrator	*Strauss, Hofmannsthal and Molière*	Glenn Gould Studio, CBC Radio

PRODUCTIONS DIRECTED

1978		
Come and Go	Samuel Beckett	Stratford Festival
1983		
Blake	Elliott Hayes	Stratford Festival
Stevie	Hugh Whitemore	Young People's Theatre, Toronto
1987		
Hosanna	Michel Tremblay	Tarragon Theatre, Toronto
1988		
Count Dracula	Ted Tiller	Young People's Theatre, Toronto
The Taming of the Shrew	William Shakespeare	Stratford Festival
1989		
Julius Caesar	William Shakespeare	Citadel Theatre, Edmonton
The Relapse	Sir John Vanbrugh	Stratford Festival
The Comedy of Errors	William Shakespeare	Stratford Festival
1990		
Saint Joan	George Bernard Shaw	Theatre Plus, Toronto
As You Like It	William Shakespeare	Stratford Festival
Julius Caesar	William Shakespeare	Stratford Festival

1991		
Shirley Valentine	Willy Russell	Grand Theatre, London
Fidelio	Ludwig van Beethoven	Canadian Opera Company
Much Ado About Nothing	William Shakespeare	Stratford Festival
The School for Wives	Molière	Stratford Festival
1992		
Romeo and Juliet	William Shakespeare	Stratford Festival
Shirley Valentine	Willy Russell	Stratford Festival
Power Play	Martin Hunter	Tarragon Theatre, Toronto
1993		
Antony and Cleopatra	William Shakespeare	Stratford Festival
1994		
Twelfth Night	William Shakespeare	Stratford Festival
Hamlet	William Shakespeare	Stratford Festival
1995		
Blake	Elliott Hayes	Glenn Gould Studio, CBC Radio
The Merry Wives of Windsor	William Shakespeare	Stratford Festival
Amadeus	Peter Shaffer	Stratford Festival
1996		
King Lear	William Shakespeare	Stratford Festival
The Little Foxes	Lillian Hellman	Stratford Festival
Amadeus	Peter Shaffer	Stratford Festival
A Fitting Confusion	Georges Feydeau	Citadel Theatre, Edmonton/ Stratford Festival
Diary of a Madman	Nikolai Gogol	Glenn Gould Studio, CBC Radio
1997		
Camelot	Lerner & Loewe	Stratford Festival
1998		
The Miser	Molière	Stratford Festival/ City Center, New York

Much Ado About Nothing	William Shakespeare	Stratford Festival/ City Center, New York
Fidelio	Ludwig van Beethoven	Canadian Opera Company
The Tempest	William Shakespeare	Glenn Gould Studio, CBC Radio
1999		
The School for Scandal	Richard Brinsley Sheridan	Stratford Festival
A Midsummer Night's Dream	William Shakespeare	Stratford Festival
The Tempest	William Shakespeare	Stratford Festival
2000		
Tartuffe	Molière	Stratford Festival
De Profundis	Oscar Wilde/ Merlin Holland	Stratford Festival
The Importance of Being Earnest	Oscar Wilde	Stratford Festival
The Three Musketeers	Alexandre Dumas/ Peter Raby	Stratford Festival
Twelfth Night	William Shakespeare	Glenn Gould Studio, CBC Radio
2001		
Inherit the Wind	Lawrence & Lee	Stratford Festival
The Merchant of Venice	William Shakespeare	Stratford Festival
2002		
All's Well That Ends Well	William Shakespeare	Stratford Festival
My Fair Lady	Lerner & Loewe	Stratford Festival
High-Gravel-Blind	Paul Dunn	Stratford Festival
2003		
Troilus and Cressida	William Shakespeare	Stratford Festival
Gigi	Lerner & Loewe	Stratford Festival
2004		
King Henry VIII (All Is True)	William Shakespeare	Stratford Festival
The Triumph of Love	Marivaux	Stratford Festival

2005		
The Tempest	William Shakespeare	Stratford Festival
Cat on a Hot Tin Roof	Tennessee Williams	Stratford Festival
Edward II	Christopher Marlowe	Stratford Festival
2006		
Henry IV, Part 1	William Shakespeare	Stratford Festival
2007		
The Comedy of Errors	William Shakespeare	Stratford Festival
An Ideal Husband	Oscar Wilde	Stratford Festival

HONOURS AND AWARDS

1967	Tyrone Guthrie Award, Stratford Festival
1968	Canada Council Grant
1977	Canada Council Grant Queen's Silver Jubilee Medal
1981	Canada Council Grant
1984	Derek F. Mitchell Artistic Director's Award, Stratford Festival
1991	Dora Mavor Moore Award for Outstanding Direction (for *Saint Joan* at Theatre Plus)
1994	Eugene O'Neill Medallion
1995	Honorary Doctorate of Humanities, University of Windsor
1998	Order of Canada (Member)
2002	Queen's Golden Jubilee Medal
2003	Honorary Doctorate of Laws, Concordia University
2005	Honorary Doctorate of Laws, University of Western Ontario
2006	Herbert Whittaker/Toronto Drama Bench Award for Outstanding Contribution to Canadian Theatre, Canadian Theatre Critics Association
2007	Named Paul Harris Fellow, Rotary International Bronze sidewalk star, City of Stratford Key to the City of Stratford
2008	Circular drive in Stratford's Upper Queen's Park posthumously renamed Richard Monette Way

ACKNOWLEDGEMENTS

My heartfelt thanks go to the many people who assisted in the preparation and publication of *This Rough Magic*. Foremost among them, of course, is David Prosser, the Stratford Festival's director of literary services, who spent countless hours interviewing me in the summer and fall of 2006, and many subsequent months shaping my recollections into a narrative far more coherent than anything I could have achieved on my own.

The contributions of two other Davids must not be overlooked. In the 1970s, actor and writer David Francis helped me compile an account of my experiences in *Oh! Calcutta!* His hand is much in evidence in Chapters Four and Five, which draw heavily on that unpublished manuscript. That same decade, director and producer David Gardner interviewed me at length for another book that we never wrote. The still-extant transcripts of those interviews have been an invaluable resource.

At one point, it was intended that my own reminiscences in these pages would be supplemented by those of friends and colleagues. I thank not only those who were interviewed while this idea was still in mind—Brian Bedford, Domini Blythe, Berthold Carrière, Cynthia Dale, David Francis, Martha Henry, Martin Hunter, William Hutt, Jeannette Lambermont, Diana Leblanc, Janine Pearson, Christopher Plummer, Joseph Shaw and Ben Solway—but also the many others who I know would have been no less eager to participate.

Without the vision and enthusiasm of Antoni Cimolino, the Festival's general director, and Anita Gaffney, its senior director of marketing and audience development, this project could never have been undertaken, let alone completed. My warmest thanks to them, as well as to Erin Wilson for her beautiful design of the book; to editor Nicole Langlois; to Festival archivist and researcher Jane Edmonds for her tireless work in sourcing and clearing photographs; to archives assistant Ellen Charendoff for scanning the images; to Lee Myers, Richard Rooney and William Whitehead, who read early drafts and offered valuable suggestions; to Leanne Perreault, the Festival's director of communication and patron experience; to Rachel Smith-Spencer, its director of advancement; and to graphic design and print production manager Andy Foster.

Special thanks to Sheldon and Patty Russell, proprietors of the Keystone Alley Café, where many of the interviews on which this book is based took place. Their hospitality, and that of their staff, has been very much appreciated.

There are many fellow artists, colleagues, friends and supporters who do not figure in these pages but who have nonetheless been very important to me during my tenure as artistic director. It would be cumbersome to name them all here, and unfair to name only a few, but I hope they know who they are and that none of them will feel left out. My deepest gratitude to all.

Finally, I wish to pay three very special tributes. The first is to my family, especially my brother, Mark, who has been such a source of strength for me through all the vicissitudes of my life and career. To him and to all my relatives—including my aunts Lorraine Ritchings and Antonia Tondino, my cousins Tony Mallamo and Robert Mallamo, and Robert's wife, Manon, all of whom supplied me with family documents and photographs—my deep and abiding love.

The second is to my godchildren, Sophia and Gabriel Cimolino, whose delightful innocence has been a welcome antidote to the cynicism I have too often encountered during my tenure.

And the third is to my friend and mentor William Hutt, whom I thank not only for his eloquent words in this book's foreword but also for the unfailing encouragement and support he has lent me—to say nothing of all the magic he has wrought on our stages—throughout the 35 seasons in which I have been privileged to call the Stratford Festival of Canada my home.

– Richard Monette

On September 9, 2008, Richard Monette died of a pulmonary embolus at the age of 64. I know he was proud of this memoir; I wish he could have been here to see this second printing, with its correction of the one or two glaring errors we discovered in the original. I can imagine him holding aloft a fresh copy and proclaiming, in his most richly sardonic tones, "*This* time we got my brother's birth date right!"

In addition to those whom Richard named in his acknowledgement above, my thanks are due to Rosalind Malcolm for her meticulous proofreading of my early drafts and to my wife, Barbara Dunn-Prosser, for her love and support during the writing of this book, and in all things else. And, of course, to Richard himself, not only for his kindness and generosity to me over the years, but also for entrusting me with the story, too soon ended, of his remarkable life.

– David Prosser

PHOTOGRAPHY AND IMAGE CREDITS

Pages v & xi: Richard Monette collection. Pages 1 & 7: Photo by Roy, Montreal. Page 3: Monette family collection. Page 4: Photo by Richard Monette. Page 9: Photo by Bernstein Studio, Montreal. Pages 10–16: Monette family collection. Page 19: Photo by Robert C. Ragsdale. Page 22: Photo by Judy Lane (Richard Monette collection). Page 23: Monette family collection. Page 24: Photo by Donald McKague (Stratford Festival Archives). Page 26: Photo by Terry Manzo (Stratford Festival Archives). Page 29: Photo used by permission of St. Michael's College, Winooski, Vermont. Page 31: Photo by Keith Clark (Richard Monette collection). Page 32: Photo used by permission of David and Dorothy Gardner. Page 33: Photo by Peter Smith (Stratford Festival Archives). Page 34: Photo by Len Dobbin, used by permission of Loyola College. Page 36: Photo used by permission of Aviva Slesin. Pages 40 & 43: Photos by Robert C. Ragsdale for the Crest Theatre, used by permission of The Canadian Stage Company. Page 44: Photo by Elisabeth Feryn (Stratford Festival Archives). Page 47: Richard Monette collection. Page 49: Photo by Douglas Spillane (Stratford Festival Archives). Pages 51 & 54: Photos by Peter Smith (Stratford Festival Archives). Page 55: Stratford Festival Archives. Page 57: Sketch used by permission of Desmond Heeley (Stratford Festival Archives – Dama and Alf Bell collection). Page 58: Photo by Robert C. Ragsdale (Stratford Festival Archives). Page 60: Photo by Peter Smith (Stratford Festival Archives). Page 62: Photo by Inge Morath (Stratford Festival Archives). Page 63: Photo by Peter Smith (Stratford Festival Archives). Page 67: Photo by Patrick Christopher (Richard Monette collection). Page 69: Photo by Peter Smith (Stratford Festival Archives). Page 70: Photo by Robert C. Ragsdale for Theatre Toronto, used by permission of The Canadian Stage Company. Page 72: Photo by Ida Kar, used by permission of the National Portrait Gallery, London, England. Page 74: Photo used by permission of the estate of John Colicos (Stratford Festival Archives). Page 75: Photo by Robert C. Ragsdale (Stratford Festival Archives). Page 76: Photo by Robert C. Ragsdale for Theatre Toronto, used by permission of The Canadian Stage Company. Page 81: Photo by Ludvik Dittrich for Theatre Toronto, used by permission of The Canadian Stage Company. Page 82: Photo courtesy of Richard Digby Day. Page 84: Photo by John Timbers, used by permission of the New Shakespeare Company, Regent's Park, England. Page 87: Richard Monette collection. Page 88: Photo courtesy of the Royal Shakespeare Theatre, Shakespeare Birthplace Trust. Pages 90 & 93: Welsh Theatre Company photos used by permission of Richard Digby Day. Pages 97–101: Photos by Michael Childers. Page 102: Photo by Al Parker Ltd. Pages 105–112: Photos by Michael Childers. Page 117: Photo by Chris J. Arthur – Trans World Eye). Page 119: Sketch used by permission of Allan Jones (Domini Blythe collection). Page 122: Photo by Chris J. Arthur – Trans World Eye. Page 125: Cartoon used by permission of the Birmingham Evening Mail. Page 129: Richard Monette collection. Page 133: Photo used by permission of Barratt's Photo Press Limited. Page 134: Photo by Aviva Slesin (Richard Monette collection). Page 137: New Shakespeare Company photo used by permission of Richard Digby Day. Page 138: Photo used by permission of Linda Marlowe. Page 143: Photo used by permission of Charles Marowitz. Page 144: Photo by Richard Monette. Pages 147 & 151: Richard Monette collection. Page 152: Stratford Festival Archives. Page 154: Monette family collection. Pages 157 & 159: St. Lawrence Centre photos used by permission of The Canadian Stage Company. Page 164: Photo by Kenn Duncan. Page 167: Photo by Robert A. Barnett, used by permission of the Tarragon Theatre. Page 168: Photo by Kenn Duncan. Page 171: Photo by Robert A. Barnett, used by permission of the Tarragon Theatre. Page 176: Photo by Aviva Slesin (Richard Monette collection). Page 179: Photo by Raymond O'Neill (Richard Monette collection). Pages 182–204: Photos by Robert C. Ragsdale (Stratford Festival Archives). Page 207: Photo used by permission of the Walnut Street Theatre, Philadelphia. Pages 208 & 210: Photos by Robert C. Ragsdale (Stratford Festival Archives). Page 212: Photo by Zoe Dominic (Stratford Festival Archives). Page 214: Photo by V. Tony Hauser (Stratford Festival Archives). Page 215: Photo by Carolyn A. McKeone (Richard Monette collection). Page 219: Photo by Tibor Kolley/ The Globe and Mail, used by permission of The Globe and Mail. Page 223: Photo by Richard Monette. Page 224: Photo by Nir Bareket, used by permission of the Bathurst Street Theatre. Pages 227 & 230: Photos by Robert C. Ragsdale (Stratford Festival Archives). Page 234: Photo by David Cooper (Stratford Festival Archives). Pages 237 & 240: Richard Monette collection. Page 244: Photo used by permission of Skylight Theatre/L. W. Conolly Theatre Archives, University of Guelph Library. Page 247: Richard Monette collection. Page 250: Photo by Nir Bareket for CentreStage, used by permission of The Canadian Stage Company. Pages 257 & 259: Photos by Michael Cooper (Stratford Festival Archives). Page 263: Photo by Robert C. Ragsdale (Stratford Festival Archives). Page 266: Photo by Robert C. Ragsdale (Stratford Festival Archives). Pages 269 & 270: Photos by David Cooper (Stratford Festival Archives). Page 273: Photo by Coopershoots/David Cooper/Michael Cooper (Stratford Festival Archives). Page 276: Photo by Coopershoots/Michael Cooper (Stratford Festival Archives). Page 278: Photo by Tom Skudra (Stratford Festival Archives). Page 283: Photo by Robert C. Ragsdale, used by permission of The Grand Theatre, London. Page 285: Photo by Jane Edmonds (Stratford Festival Archives). Page 287: Photo by Elisabeth Feryn (Stratford Festival Archives). Page 288: Photo by David Cooper (Stratford Festival Archives). Pages 297–305: Photos by Cylla von Tiedemann (Stratford Festival Archives). Page 307: Photo by V. Tony Hauser (Stratford Festival Archives). Page 309: Photo by Terry Manzo (Stratford Festival Archives). Page 312: Photo by Gwen Carleton (Stratford Festival Archives). Page 321: Photo by Martin Hunter (Richard Monette collection). Page 323: Photo by Mathew McCarthy (Stratford Festival Archives). Page 329: Photo by Robert C. Ragsdale (Stratford Festival Archives). Page 331: Photo by David Hou (Stratford Festival Archives).

Every effort has been made to contact photographers whose images have been used in this book. Please report any errors or omissions to Ellen Charendoff, archives coordinator, Stratford Shakespeare Festival, P.O. Box 520, Stratford, Ontario, N5A 6V2, Canada. E-mail echarendoff@stratfordshakespearefestival.com or call 519-271-0055, ext. 4310.

INDEX